Praise for

THE RIGHT

"A superb work of scholarship and a delight to read. Conservatives will relish the anecdotes, the explanations of half-remembered books; liberals will learn something about their adversaries... invaluable clarity."

—Barton Swaim, *Wall Street Journal*,
Best Politics Books of 2022

"Superb...[Continetti] brings an insider's nuance and a historian's dispassion to the ambitious task of writing the American right's biography, and he adds a journalist's knack for deft portraiture and telling details." —Jonathan Rauch, *New York Times*

"Mr. Continetti captures beautifully the ad hoc, rearguard nature of American conservatism." —*Wall Street Journal*

"*The Right* is readable and relatable, well-written and engaging. The author's command of facts is impressive." —*The Guardian*

"[A] sturdy account of the many divisions within modern conservatism...Rational, well thought out, and impeccably argued—of interest to all students of politics." —*Kirkus*, starred

"Matthew Continetti's *The Right* is a rich and detailed survey from the 1920s to now." —*Financial Times*

"Thoroughly researched." —*The Economist*

"Continetti's experiences have given him a valuable perspective on his subject...His description of life in the conservative machine has the feel of an eyewitness account." —*The New Republic*

"Matthew Continetti applies what scholars of all persuasions should do with American conservatism, treating it as a complex, contradictory movement, often at war between its populists and its intellectual elite wings.... Continetti is skilled in going places and making conclusions other rightists don't." —*The Federalist*

"An authoritative account of the complex interplay between conservative ideas, politics, and policy over the past century.... Continetti is particularly well-positioned to tackle the topic."
—*The Public Discourse*

"A compelling analysis." —*City Journal*

"A much more nuanced and satisfying portrait of the American right than is offered by most other journalists and historians."
—*Reason*

"Continetti's perspective is that of a consummate insider.... He is, as a result, better attuned than most to the role of elites in the conservative ecosystem, as well as to the limits of their power."
—*Unherd*

"Continetti's book is an excellent primer for understanding key aspects of the last century of American politics, and many of the author's recommendations are very shrewd. He covers a tremendous amount of ground with lucidity and panache."
—*American Purpose*

"Important.... Superior to any previous volume on this critical subject." —*Quillette*

"Well-researched, lucidly presented, and evenhanded."
—*Commentary*

"Matthew Continetti has written a superb history of the conservative movement."
—*World Magazine*

"[Continetti] skillfully leads us through the pulsing, fractious, improbable story of American conservatism all the way to today's fractured Republican party."
                                                                                    —*Mosaic*

"With *The Right*, Matthew Continetti has written a fine, comprehensive, and readable narrative of the rip-roaring history of American conservatism with its amazing repertory company of statesmen, philosophers, and eccentrics. It's a remarkable achievement and a great read."
                                                    —*Claremont Review of Books*

"A worthy analysis."
                                                                    —*Publishers Weekly*

"Matthew Continetti has earned his luminous reputation as the foremost contemporary chronicler of American conservatism's path to today's problematic condition. He traces conservatism's rich intellectual pedigree, from the founders' classical liberalism through twentieth-century conservatives' responses to the challenges of progressivism. The result is a thinking person's map for the road ahead."
                                                    —George F. Will, author of
                                                        The Conservative Sensibility

"Matthew Continetti has written an instant classic, sure to become the essential one-volume history of modern American conservatism. Balanced and subtle, it offers an engaging combination of intellectual and political history that makes sense of the immensely complicated story of the Right."
                                        —Yuval Levin, author of *A Time to Build*

"Deft and authoritative, Matthew Continetti illuminates conservatism's present through its long and often tumultuous past. *The Right* isn't just an engaging history and incisive analysis of the intra-conservative debate, but an essential contribution to it."
                                —Rich Lowry, editor in chief of *National Review*

"An immensely useful contribution."
                            —Jonah Goldberg, editor in chief of *The Dispatch*

THE RIGHT

THE
RIGHT

THE HUNDRED-YEAR WAR FOR
AMERICAN CONSERVATISM

MATTHEW CONTINETTI

BASIC BOOKS
NEW YORK

Portions of this work have been adapted from the author's articles in the following publications:
Chapter 8: *National Review,* "'The Conservative Sensibility' Is George Will's Definitive Declaration," July 8, 2019.
Chapter 9: *Washington Free Beacon,* "Crisis of the Conservative Intellectual," October 21, 2016; *Commentary,* "Learning from Commentary," November 2020.
Chapter 11: *Washington Free Beacon,* "The Era of Limbaugh," February 7, 2020.
Chapter 13: *Washington Free Beacon,* "Revenge of the Radical Middle," July 24, 2015; "The Party Divides," December 11, 2015; "2016: The Trump Election," December 15, 2015; "Donald Trump and Conservative Dogma," September 13, 2016; "The Politics of Dissociation," September 30, 2016.
Chapter 14: *Washington Free Beacon,* "Making Sense of the New American Right," May 31, 2019; *New York Times,* "Is Trump Really All That Holds the GOP Together?" December 22, 2020; *National Review Online,* "Trump Must Pay," January 6, 2021.
Conclusion: *Washington Free Beacon,* "What Do Republican Voters Want?" November 15, 2019.

Basic Books
Hachette Book Group
1290 Avenue of the Americas, New York, NY 10104
www.basicbooks.com

Printed in the United States of America

First Trade Paperback Edition: May 2023

Published by Basic Books, an imprint of Perseus Books, LLC, a subsidiary of Hachette Book Group, Inc. The Basic Books name and logo is a trademark of the Hachette Book Group.

The Hachette Speakers Bureau provides a wide range of authors for speaking events. To find out more, go to hachettespeakersbureau.com or email HachetteSpeakers@hbgusa.com.

The publisher is not responsible for websites (or their content) that are not owned by the publisher.

Print book interior design by Trish Wilkinson.

Library of Congress Cataloging-in-Publication Data

Names: Continetti, Matthew, author.
Title: The right : the hundred year war for American conservatism / Matthew Continetti.
Description: First edition. | New York : Basic Books, 2022. | Includes bibliographical references and index.
Identifiers: LCCN 2021043103 | ISBN 9781541600508 (hardcover) | ISBN 9781541600522 (ebook)
Subjects: LCSH: Republican Party (U.S. : 1854–)—History. | Conservatism—United States—History—20th century. | Conservatism—United States—History—21st century. | United States—Politics and government.
Classification: LCC JC573.2.U6 C6537 2022 | DDC 324.2734—dc23/eng/20211203
LC record available at https://lccn.loc.gov/2021043103

ISBNs: 9781541600508 (hardcover), 9781541600522 (ebook), 9781541600515 (paperback)

LSC-C

Printing 1, 2023

To Anne

What is conservatism? Is it not adherence to the old and tried, against the new and untried? We stick to, contend for, the identical old policy on the point in controversy which was adopted by "our fathers who framed the Government under which we live"; while you with one accord reject, and scout, and spit upon that old policy, and insist upon substituting something new. True, you disagree among yourselves as to what the substitute shall be. You are divided on new propositions and plans, but you are unanimous in rejecting and denouncing the old policy of the fathers.

—ABRAHAM LINCOLN, FEBRUARY 27, 1860

CONTENTS

INTRODUCTION

1150 Seventeenth Street

O N JULY 7, 2003, THREE MONTHS INTO THE SECOND IRAQ
War, I showed up at 1150 Seventeenth Street NW in Washington, DC. I had just turned twenty-two. It was my first day as
an editorial assistant at the *Weekly Standard*.

At the time, 1150 Seventeenth Street was more than an office building. It was an intellectual hub—the frontal cortex of the
American Right. The magazine where I was about to begin work
was the most influential in the city. Copies of the *Standard* arrived
at the White House each week. A photograph hanging from a wall
in the magazine's office showed President George W. Bush reading
an issue. The *Standard*'s editors appeared regularly on the most important source of information for Republicans and conservatives:
the Fox News Channel. But the *Standard* also had mainstream
credibility. One of its senior editors, David Brooks, was a fixture
on PBS and NPR. He was about to join the *New York Times*.

From 1150 Seventeenth Street emanated the ideas that shaped
the Republican White House and Congress and then the world. On
the same floor as the *Standard* was the Project for a New American

1

Century (PNAC). It was a small think tank cofounded by the magazine's editor that since its inception in 1997 had advocated for a defense buildup, containment of China, and regime change in Iraq. The top floors of the building housed the Right's premier think tank: the American Enterprise Institute (AEI). Taxes had been cut, welfare reformed, social programs redesigned, and governments toppled because of the intellection that took place within the walls of 1150 Seventeenth Street.

That morning I was walking into not just a building but an intellectual and political movement. A few years earlier, as an undergraduate at Columbia University, I had stumbled upon American conservatism and the theoretical works that undergird its thought. In the months before and after the terrorist attacks of September 11, 2001, I had read (and only somewhat understood) Russell Kirk's *The Conservative Mind*, Leo Strauss's *Natural Right and History*, Richard Weaver's *Ideas Have Consequences*, and Milton Friedman's *Capitalism and Freedom*. I picked up copies of William F. Buckley Jr.'s *National Review*, Seth Lipsky's *New York Sun*, Norman Podhoretz's *Commentary*, and the *Weekly Standard*. In 2004, when John Micklethwait and Adrian Wooldridge wrote *The Right Nation: Conservative Power in America*, I felt a thrill of recognition when these two British editors of the *Economist* identified 1150 Seventeenth Street as the center of a *rive droit*, a "right bank," a hub of conservative activity that included the Ethics and Public Policy Center, a small think tank next door; the offices of the *Public Interest* one block away; and the DC branch of the Hoover Institution and its publication, *Policy Review*, up Connecticut Avenue.[1]

The *rive droit* is gone now. The building at 1150 Seventeenth Street was demolished in 2016. AEI moved to a renovated mansion near Dupont Circle. Neither PNAC nor the *Standard* exists any longer. The George W. Bush administration is a distant memory. The twin projects of 1150 Seventeenth Street—the expansion of democracy abroad and a recommitment to traditional moral values at home—ran aground.

The intellectual community housed within 1150 Seventeenth Street dispersed. Many of the writers, wonks, and scholars who worked there found themselves in a strained relationship with the American Right. The center of gravity of American conservatism drifted toward Capitol Hill, where the Heritage Foundation, the Kirby Center of Hillsdale College, and the Claremont Institute's Center for the American Way of Life hosted scholars and speakers friendly to the administration of former president Donald Trump. The Right became more populist than it was in 2003. To define oneself as a conservative in the 2020s was to reject the ideas and practices of the "establishment" that 1150 Seventeenth Street had come to represent.

I have spent the last decade thinking about this change. In April 2011 I went to Portsmouth, New Hampshire, to follow Donald Trump as he visited the home of the first presidential primary. I watched as he spent a few hours in local diners. He extended the Trump brand, increased his leverage in salary negotiations with his employer, NBC, elevated himself as a celebrity opponent of President Barack Obama, and became the unquestioned leader of the conspiratorial birther movement, which claimed falsely that Obama had not been born inside the United States. It was obvious that Trump was not playing for the validation of established media outlets. Even then, his audience comprised voters who had been forgotten or ignored or dismissed as nuts. Readers of the *National Enquirer*, his adviser Roger Stone once said, were "the Trump constituency."[2]

It was a constituency that 2012 Republican nominee Mitt Romney must have thought he needed to win. Shortly before that year's Nevada GOP caucuses, Romney and his wife appeared in Las Vegas alongside Trump and accepted the billionaire's endorsement. "He's a warm, smart, tough cookie and that's what this country needs," Trump told CNN at the time. Romney won the caucuses but lost the general election. The Right told itself that Romney had failed because he lacked the requisite populist sensibility, fighting spirit, and antagonism toward the powers that be. He was more *Fortune* than *National Enquirer*.[3]

The week before the 2012 election, I had appeared on a panel sponsored by the American University College Republicans. My copanelist was Matthew Boyle of the national populist website Breitbart.com. I presented my case that the race was close but that independents could still carry Romney to the White House. Boyle shook his head. Romney was a loser, he told the small audience. Romney was going down, and an antiestablishment figure such as Senator Rand Paul of Kentucky would take over the GOP and win in 2016. I laughed Boyle off. I would not make the same mistake again.

As Obama began his second term, I began to research the history of the American Right. How, I wondered, had the conservative movement failed to motivate the white voters without college degrees who had comprised Richard Nixon's "silent majority," the "Reagan Democrats," and the "Republican Revolution" of 1994? What explained the gulf between my colleagues in Washington, DC, and conservatives beyond the Beltway? How had matters long thought settled—the importance of markets, the benefits of free trade, the blessings of immigration, the necessity of war—become so hotly contested?

The answers to such questions took me beyond the politics of Barack Obama and George W. Bush. They led to a broader and more extensive study of conservative intellectual and political history. In time, I began teaching the history of American conservatism to college students. One day in the summer of 2017, as that day's class ended, I asked the students what had surprised them about the course materials. One young man looked at me and said, "I'm surprised that any of this exists."

That is why I wrote this book. It tells the story of the American conservative movement through the experiences of its participants. It explains how the work of conservative intellectuals has interacted with, influenced, and been influenced by institutions, policies, politics, world events, and politicians. Unlike George H. Nash's *The Conservative Intellectual Movement in America Since 1945* or Patrick Allitt's *The Conservatives*, this book is not strictly an intellectual history. Nor is it a work of political sociology that traces the influence of corporations or lobbying or big donors or dark money in the rise of the American Right. All those things have a role in both conservatism and liberalism, but they do not drive ideas.[4]

My focus is on the writers who set in motion the interplay of ideas and institutions, of ideology and politics. My narrative is less about the details and development of intellectual arguments than about the ways in which those arguments responded and related to events. My study centers on the authors who planted the seeds of activism and political statesmanship. And my interest lies primarily with Americans or émigrés to America. Worthy British and European thinkers such as José Ortega y Gasset, Joseph Schumpeter, Michael Oakeshott, Wilhelm Röpke, and Michel Houellebecq do not factor in the discussion.

My intention is to describe how the varieties of American conservatism differed from another, how big those differences were, why the disagreements began, and what their effect was on American politics. My framework is the endless competition and occasional collaboration between populism and elitism. Is the American Right the party of insiders or outsiders? Is the Right the elites—the men and women in charge of America's political, economic, social, and cultural institutions—or is it the people? And is the Right even able to answer such a question?

In its quest to change America, the Right has toggled between an elite-driven strategy in both content and constituencies and a populist strategy that meets normal people where they are and is driven by their ambitions, anxieties, and animosities. A successful political movement must incorporate both elites and the people. Only intermittently, however, has the American Right been able to achieve such a synthesis. That is why its victories have been so tenuous—and why its coalition has been so fragile.

YEARS SPENT READING THE BACK ISSUES OF OLD MAGAZINES, acquiring books long out of print, rummaging through Internet archives, and conversing with my peers, mentors, and friends in the conservative movement and Republican Party left me dissatisfied with the stories that both conservatives and liberals tell themselves about the American Right. Conservatives, for example, like to say that their movement began in the wilderness. Then William F. Buckley Jr., the founder of *National Review*, came along. He led the American Right to political relevance by winning the 1964 Republican nomination for Arizona senator Barry Goldwater.

Goldwater lost that year, and by a considerable margin, but the ashes of his candidacy were fertile soil for Ronald Reagan, who brought conservatives to power in 1980. Since the heights of Reagan's presidency, conservatives say, the movement has endured setbacks and diversions. But the Right still shapes American democracy through the intellectual institutions and media platforms that give it a voice in public debate and an influence in politics that was unimaginable when the movement began. Conservatives admit that Donald Trump's June 2015 descent on the escalator in Trump Tower caused friction within the Right. But they also believe he recalibrated the Right along populist and nationalist lines and attracted new constituencies to the movement.

The liberal version of the story is not that different. It also begins slightly after World War II. It also begins with conservatives in exile. But the Left tends to ascribe the rise of the Right not to failures of liberal governance but to a racist backlash against civil rights that has grown only worse with time. While the story

that conservatives tell themselves highlights institutions and politicians, left-wingers play up grassroots organizations, big-league
financial donors, and psychological motivations. For the Left, the
story of American conservatism is the story of American populist reaction. It is a long-running, berserk refusal to submit to the
ministrations of liberal rule. For the Left, Trump is not a deviation
from American conservatism. He is its end point.

Both stories contain elements of truth. But neither one captures
the American Right in its full complexity. The conservative narrative is too neat. The edges of the movement have been smoothed
over. Its blemishes have been covered up or ignored. The Left's
narrative, however, overcorrects for the Right's mistakes. It ends
up pathologizing conservatism. It reduces a vast and complex
movement to nothing more than the ongoing expression of base
prejudices such as sexism, racism, homophobia, transphobia, and
Islamophobia. This diagnosis might explain the behavior of some
of the men and women who have associated with the conservative
movement and voted for Republican candidates. But it does not
explain the whole.

Another problem with the conservative and liberal stories is
Ronald Reagan. He is too large a presence in each. This is not sur-
prising: the rise of Reagan began not long after the conclusion of
World War II, and because both the Right and the Left start their
tales around 1945, each has a habit of focusing on the life story and
political trajectory of the fortieth president.

Reagan also holds totemic significance for both conservatives
and liberals. For conservatives, he is the protagonist in a hero's
journey. He began by weeding Communists out of the Screen Actors Guild and ended up defeating the Evil Empire. For liberals,
Reagan is either a befuddled clown or a charming adversary. He
either accidentally or slyly manipulated white America into en-
acting a pro-corporate agenda of tax cuts, reductions in welfare
spending, and hostility to labor.

Unlike most other histories of the American Right, however, this book is not just about Ronald Reagan. In these pages, he is one character among many. The reason is that Reagan's charisma and clarity were something of an exception. His unique political talent led almost every faction of American conservatism to think that he was on its side. To this day, every conservative wants to claim him. The truth is messier. Reagan's presidency was not the inevitable outcome of the conservative movement. His triumph in 1980 was contingent, unplanned, and unpredictable. It was not until he left office that he acquired mythic status.

Reagan was one alternative among many. There is not one American Right; there are several. Yes, American conservatives are firm believers in the US Constitution. Yes, they oppose state intervention in the structures that lie between the individual and government, such as family, church, neighborhood, voluntary association, and the marketplace. Yes, they resist the totalitarian Communist regimes of the former USSR and the People's Republic of China.

Go further, however, and differences emerge. Fault lines appear. Conservative writers and thinkers disagree more than they agree. They comprise a movement defined by a lively debate over first principles. They look for deviation and betrayal. And sometimes they form a circular firing squad.

Nor is the Right synonymous with the Republican Party. In the pages that follow, I will try to distinguish between "conservatives," who are conscious of themselves as defenders of established institutions and as participants in the broad political movement that coalesced in the late 1950s, and the broader category of "the Right," which includes all of the thinkers and activists who define themselves in opposition to the political Left—and, in some cases, to the conservative movement as well.

Libertarians like Friedrich Hayek and Milton Friedman valued personal freedom above all. Traditionalists like Russell Kirk thought that freedom had to be balanced with order and justice. Majoritarians like Willmoore Kendall believed that communities had the right and responsibility to exclude ideas and individuals subversive of public order. Cold Warriors like James Burnham argued that the fight against communism was the preeminent issue of the twentieth century. Southern Agrarians such as Richard Weaver wanted to insulate the culture of the South from federal intrusion. Political philosopher Harry Jaffa said that conservatism needed to be anchored in the Declaration of Independence's proposition that all men are created equal. "Fusionists" like Frank Meyer thought that both libertarians and traditionalists could agree that true virtue is uncoerced. Radical traditionalists such as L. Brent Bozell thought virtue was more important than freedom. Neoconservatives such as Irving Kristol believed in retaining many of the programs of the New Deal and even some of the Great Society. Religious neoconservatives such as Michael Novak said that capitalism and Christianity were not opposed but complementary. New Right activists such as Phyllis Schlafly sought political power to block and reverse liberal social change. Originalist judges like Antonin Scalia gave deference to legislatures based on strict adherence to the constitutional text. Paleoconservatives such as Thomas Fleming blamed neoconservatives for polluting the Right with immigration, free trade, and intervention overseas.

These are only a few of the varieties of conservatism that you will encounter in these pages. These are only a few of the writers who have argued for a century about the relationship between the Declaration of Independence and the Constitution, the place of minority rights in a majoritarian democracy, the tension between a populist desire for liberty and an elitist commitment to institutions, and the choice between isolationist protection and international involvement. Only rarely have all of these different "rights" coexisted peacefully.

This book provides a broader perspective. While it would have been tempting to begin the narrative at the moment when the self-consciously conservative movement began to take shape, I found that beginning in the 1920s, when the Republican Party rejected Progressivism for the philosophy of individualism and economic freedom, brought into view some parallels with our own time. In other words, to understand the American Right in the third decade of the twenty-first century, you have to go back to the third decade of the twentieth century—when the modern Right seemed well entrenched and Presidents Warren Harding and Calvin Coolidge identified rapid economic growth with fidelity to limited, constitutional government, American patriotism, and religious piety. You must see how this conservative status quo was delegitimized twice over. First the Great Depression robbed the Right of its claim to prosperity. Then World War II discredited the Right's noninterventionist foreign policy.

Fierce opposition to communism made postwar American conservatism distinct. Anticommunism became the touchstone for the religious conservatives, economic conservatives, foreign policy realists, and ex-Communists who made up the Cold War Right. To really know conservatism, you have to watch as the bipartisan anti-Communist foreign policy of containment broke down in the jungles of Vietnam. Anti-Communist liberals and the "hard hat" working-class voters of the "silent majority" found themselves driven away from their party and into the GOP.

You have to understand that from 1947 to 1989, national security was the paramount concern of our national life. The Cold War loomed over American culture in ways that are difficult to relate to someone born after 1991. The slaughter of World War II was within living memory. The stakes were higher: nuclear war could end civilization, and political freedom stood on a precipice. The world was less free and less rich than it is today. For most of the men and women I will discuss in this text, there was no greater threat than the prospect of a Communist world. That danger conditioned responses to events. It required compromises. And it could lead to extremes.

The Cold War revived the anti-Communist American Right. It provided the impetus for conservatism's growing network of intellectual, financial, and political institutions. This book traces the rise of this conservative establishment. It began as a response to New Deal liberalism at home and to Soviet totalitarianism abroad. It grew in strength as crime, inflation, and national humiliation discredited the Democratic Party in the eyes of voters. It culminated in a Republican governing class under the administrations of Ronald Reagan and George H. W. Bush.

What happened next came as a shock. The Soviet Union disintegrated in 1991. The Cold War ended. Not a shot had been fired. Deprived of anticommunism as a common denominator for the American Right, the conservative establishment found itself looking for a new purpose. But it could not settle on a unifying mission. And as this establishment wondered what to do with itself, it came under attack from a growing number of right-wing dissidents who objected to its internationalist economic and foreign policies. With the Cold War over, the Right was tempted to return to its pre–World War II state. Isolationism, protectionism, and immigration restrictionism made a comeback.

If the Vietnam War splintered the Democratic coalition, then the 2003 Iraq War fractured the Republican one. Conservatism was never the same after the first improvised explosive device detonated in Baghdad. The public's rejection of the war, the economic calamity of George W. Bush's final year in office, and the Republican Party's continued support for an amnesty of illegal immigrants delegitimized the conservative establishment in the eyes of the populist independents, conservative Democrats, and disaffected voters who had been crucial to GOP victories in years past.

The dissidents were emboldened. The Tea Party became their vehicle to remove pro-war, pro-immigration, pro-trade Republicans from office. Then Donald Trump became their battering ram. The same talk radio, cable news, and digital and social media that conservatives had used to question liberal viewpoints turned inward. Now they undermined the authority of the conservative establishment. By the time the actual demolition crew showed up for work at 1150 Seventeenth Street, the intellectual and policy culture that the building symbolized had already collapsed under pressure from this new, national populist Right.

In its protectionism, immigration restrictionism, religiosity, and antipathy to foreign entanglements, Donald Trump's Make America Great Again movement resembled the conservatism of the 1920s—but with a significant difference. In the 1920s, the Right was in charge. It was self-confident and prosperous. It saw itself as defending core American institutions. One century later, in the early 2020s, the Right had been driven from power at the federal level. It no longer viewed core American institutions as worth defending. It was apocalyptic in attitude and expression. It resembled more closely the populist Democrats of William Jennings Bryan— who rallied under one banner all those who felt excluded from or dispossessed by the economic, social, and cultural powers of his time—than the business-friendly Republicans of Warren Harding.

THERE HAD BEEN WARNINGS THAT THIS MIGHT HAPPEN. WHEN you study conservatism from the vantage point of the 1920s, you see that every so often the Right has embraced a demagogic leader who pulls it toward the political fringe. From Tom Watson to Henry Ford, Father Coughlin to Charles Lindbergh, Joseph McCarthy to George Wallace, Ross Perot to Pat Buchanan, Ron Paul to Donald Trump, these tribunes of discontent have succumbed to conspiracy theories, racism, and anti-Semitism. They have flirted with violence. They have played footsie with autocracy.

Such a temptation toward extremism is present on both sides of the political spectrum. Indeed, one reason conservatives assumed power in the last quarter of the twentieth century was that the electorate judged the radical Left to have abandoned seriousness and sobriety for its own fanaticisms. Think of the segregation-supporting Southern Democrats (including Wallace himself), the rage-filled bombings of the antiwar, revolutionary Weathermen, the mayhem associated with many of the Black Panthers, the beyond-the-mainstream politics of George McGovern, and the anti-Semitic bigotry of Louis Farrakhan. What matters is the willingness of intellectuals and politicians to confront and suppress the extremes. One way to think about the hundred-year war for the Right is to conceive of it as a battle between the forces of extremism and the conservatives who understood that mainstream acceptance of their ideas was the prerequisite for electoral success and lasting reform.

I am not an entirely disinterested observer of this fight. Bonds of vocation, friendship, sentiment, ideology, and family connect me to many of the figures you will meet in this book. I believe American conservatism's commitment to the American political tradition of constitutional self-government and individual rights makes it unique. But there is, I think, a certain value in sharing an insider's perspective on a much-discussed and -debated topic. Since the day I set foot in 1150 Seventeenth Street, the conservative movement has been for me more than an abstraction. It has been my life. The long and winding road on which the various bands of conservatives have traveled over the last century has brought them, at the time of this writing, to a fair amount of political power but also to cultural despair. The Right is confused, uncertain, anxious, and inward looking. The building at 1150 Seventeenth Street and the self-confident conservative ruling class it represented are gone. But the story does not end there. When you study conservatism's past, you become convinced that it has a future.

CHAPTER ONE

NORMALCY AND ITS
DISCONTENTS

O N THE COLD AFTERNOON OF MARCH 4, 1921, WARREN Gamaliel Harding swore an oath to preserve, protect, and defend the US Constitution as the twenty-ninth president of the United States of America. His taciturn vice president, former Massachusetts governor Calvin Coolidge, stood nearby on the east side of the Capitol building. A mass of people surrounded them. When Harding spoke to the crowd, his remarks directed at the wounded veterans in the audience drew the biggest applause.

Four months earlier, Harding had defeated the Democratic nominee, Ohio governor James Cox, by one of the most lopsided margins in American history: 60 to 34 percent in the popular vote and 404 to 127 in the Electoral College. After eight years of Democratic rule under Woodrow Wilson, the Republican Party was returning to power.

For a generation, American politics had been carried aloft by the currents of Progressivism. This belief in reform through expert deliberation, government activism, and moral uplift dominated Washington to varying degrees throughout the presidencies of Republicans Theodore Roosevelt and William Howard Taft. It reigned supreme under Wilson, who in 1912 had won a three-way race against Taft, the incumbent, and former president Roosevelt, who ran as the nominee of the Progressive Party. Wilson captured more than 80 percent of the Electoral College but less than 42 percent of the popular vote.

By the time of Harding's inauguration, Wilsonian Progressivism had become associated with war, inflation, and civil unrest. Harding and Coolidge stood for a restoration of something like the pre-Progressive status quo. They did not seek to embody the people or steer the direction of the country from the White House. They oversaw a limited, noninterventionist government that promoted national pride and economic prosperity.

Nor did Harding and Coolidge think of themselves as "conservatives." They were spokesmen for Americanism. They embodied the mainstream. They identified economic growth with social well-being. The 1920s may have been a "conservative" decade when Progressivism found itself out of power, but it did not feel that way to either its most successful politicians or its most outspoken critics. To them, the 1920s were "normal."

A stroke incapacitated Wilson in his final months in office. But he already had realigned the world. The former president of Princeton University was a believer in technical expertise, scientific administration, and an organic and evolutionary society. He shared the view of historian Charles Beard, who in 1913 had written in *The Economic Interpretation of the Constitution* that the nation's founding document was the product of a group of selfish men primarily interested in shielding themselves from revolt. Beard's history was not meant to inspire gratitude toward the past. He wanted his readers to shape the future. Wilson agreed. "The modern idea," he said, "is to leave the past and press onward to something new."[1]

Novelty filled Wilson's first years in office. He delivered his State of the Union message to Congress in person. He signed the Federal Reserve Act. He applauded the ratification of the

Sixteenth Amendment establishing the progressive income tax. He championed consumer protection and antitrust measures. He increased federal spending. Further Progressive amendments to the Constitution established the direct election of US senators, the prohibition of alcohol, and a guarantee of voting rights for women (who helped put Harding into office).[2]

Nor did Wilson limit himself to the United States. His administration intervened throughout Latin America and the Caribbean basin. He legitimated his policies on the basis of universal principles. "We have gone down to Mexico to serve mankind if we can find out the way," he said. "We want to serve the Mexicans if we can, because we know how we would like to be free."[3]

Most Americans were unenthused. (Most Mexicans were too.) Wilson's entanglement in the Mexican Revolution and punitive expedition there in 1916 caused him embarrassment. Meanwhile, the public looked on with horror at the trench warfare ravaging Europe. As late as January 1917, Wilson had pledged, "This country does not intend to become involved in war." His opinion changed after the British naval blockade of Europe and the unrestricted German submarine warfare against US merchant vessels that resulted. "Neutrality is no longer feasible or desirable," he said to Congress on April 2, 1917, "where the peace of the world is involved and the freedom of its peoples, and the menace to that peace and freedom lies in the existence of autocratic governments backed by organized force, which is controlled wholly by their will, not by the will of their people."[4]

Wilson smashed the barrier that separated the United States from great power conflict in Eurasia. He recast a clash of empires as an ideological crusade. This was not a war for mere national interest. It was a confrontation between autocracy and democracy. America sent men into the conflagration in defense of its universal ideals. "We desire no conquest, no dominion," Wilson said. "We seek no indemnities for ourselves, no material compensation for the sacrifices we shall freely make. We are but one of the champions of the rights of mankind." So long as autocracies existed, Americans could not feign indifference to the world. Congress declared war four days after Wilson's speech. He even sent eleven thousand troops to aid the White Russians in their attempt to topple the revolutionary Communist regime in Moscow. That engagement ultimately ended in vain nearly two years after the conclusion of the Great War.[5]

American intervention in World War I fractured the Progressive movement. Wilson's secretary of state, populist firebrand William Jennings Bryan, had resigned in protest two years before America declared war rather than endorse the president's harshly worded note to Germany after the sinking of the *Lusitania*. Antiwar populists and Progressives joined forces. They assailed the intervention. They said that shadowy business and political interests were behind it. They lamented the changing demographic makeup of the nation caused by immigration from eastern and southern Europe. Their writings were often anti-Semitic.[6]

Harding and his administration were left to pick up the pieces. Soured by its war experience, weakened by the influenza pandemic that had lasted from 1918 to 1920, plunged into turmoil by Wilson's Red-hunting attorney general A. Mitchell Palmer and Justice Department official J. Edgar Hoover, and staggered by postwar recession, the American electorate was ready for change. Harding pledged normalcy. He promised to reduce social tensions. "Our supreme task," he said in his inaugural address, "is the resumption of our onward, normal way."

The new president disavowed internationalism. He withdrew US occupation forces from postwar Germany. His secretary of state, Charles Evans Hughes, pursued disarmament treaties with the great powers. He and Coolidge opposed Wilson's League of Nations but nevertheless supported American involvement in the World Court (the Senate blocked US participation). Their secretary of commerce, Herbert Hoover, organized relief efforts for the famine that resulted from agricultural policy in the Soviet Union, established by the Communists after the Bolshevik Revolution in 1917. At the same time, the Republican administrations of the 1920s raised tariffs and restricted imports. Normalcy meant nation-building at home.

Harding also rolled back Wilson's domestic program. Wilson had governed more in the spirit of his old rival, Theodore Roosevelt, than he would have liked to admit. In his Progressive mood, Roosevelt had come to believe that businesses and local communities established and maintained inequalities that prevented the lesser-off from exercising their freedom to the utmost. The federal government, Roosevelt said, would be "an efficient agency for the practical betterment of social and economic conditions throughout the land." Wilson followed his lead. The Progressives reconceived Washington, DC, as the headquarters of corporate regulation and economic management. The war accelerated this process of bureaucratic centralization.[7]

Progressivism rebelled against the economic, social, and constitutional doctrine of laissez-faire that shaped the public policy of the post–Civil War Republican majority. A lavish banquet held at one of New York City's most famous restaurants on November 9, 1882, had exemplified the philosophy of unregulated enterprise. The dinner honored British philosopher Herbert Spencer, who was known for his application of Darwinian insights to economy, society, and politics. According to Spencer, the "survival of the fittest" that Charles Darwin had described in *On the Origin of Species* also characterized business and trade. Individual entrepreneurship, initiative, capacities, and attributes determined success in the jungle of the marketplace, where the well adapted flourished and the maladapted perished.

The preeminent American analog to Spencer in the late nineteenth and early twentieth centuries, Yale sociologist William

Graham Sumner, similarly advocated for unrestricted trade and maximum individual freedom. In an era when the predominant domestic issue was the protective tariff, Sumner wrote that government should keep in mind the forgotten man who lost out from collective efforts to improve public life. Social Darwinism complemented the Gilded Age celebration of limited government, personal liberty, rugged individualism, and rags-to-riches stories exemplified by the work of Horatio Alger. The Americans who gathered at Delmonico's Steakhouse that night in 1882 assumed that Spencer's thought legitimized the social relations of the era. The celebrants were somewhat embarrassed when Spencer rebuked them for America's culture of overwork. The American industrialists and politicians were more Spencerian than Spencer.[8]

Harding drew inspiration from this earlier period. He wanted government to get out of the way. Crucial to his efforts were his vice president, his secretary of the treasury, Andrew Mellon, and his secretary of commerce. They cut government spending, slowed the pace of regulation, and oversaw a reduction in the top marginal tax rate from 73 to 25 percent.[9]

Harding's repudiation of the Wilson years extended to judicial affairs. He and his supporters venerated the Constitution. In a speech delivered in 1920, Harding declared, "The Federal Constitution is the very base of all Americanism, the 'Ark of the Covenant' of American liberty, the very temple of equal rights." Not long after taking office, Harding released from prison Eugene V. Debs, the Socialist Party's presidential candidate in 1912 and a supporter of the Bolshevik Revolution, who had spent two and a half years in confinement on a charge of sedition that the Wilson administration brought against him for opposing the war. Harding also nominated former president William Howard Taft to become chief justice of the Supreme Court. Associate Justice George Sutherland interpreted the Fourteenth Amendment of the Constitution as a guarantee of economic and legal rights not mentioned specifically in the text of the document. He joined majorities that struck down state and federal legislation that violated liberty of contract.[10]

When Harding died in office in 1923, his successor, Coolidge, did not depart from this constitutionalist path. In Coolidge's rhetoric, the Declaration of Independence and the Constitution offered the final words in a centuries-long argument over popular sovereignty. "If all men are created equal, that is final," he said. "If they are endowed with inalienable rights, that is final. If governments derive their just powers from the consent of the governed, that is final. No advance, no progress can be made beyond these propositions." Coolidge argued that success in self-government was related to religious piety. Political freedom depended on traditional morality and self-control. He urged his audience to preserve the inheritance of the Founders and to "follow the spiritual and moral leadership which they showed."[11]

The Republican Party of the 1920s stood for a popular mix of untrammeled commerce, high tariffs, disarmament, foreign policy restraint, and devotion to the constitutional foundation of American democracy. But the GOP was also just one part of a roiling and fractious political landscape where economic bounty, technological innovation, and newfound social and cultural freedom coexisted with some of the most atavistic and conspiratorial tendencies in the national psyche. And many of these atavisms had been spawned in reaction to the same Progressive ideas that mainstream Republicans opposed.

One example was the second Ku Klux Klan. President Ulysses S. Grant had suppressed the first iteration of this racist, anti-Semitic, and anti-Catholic secret society, created in the aftermath of the Civil War, during Reconstruction. In 1915 it was reorganized under the leadership of William Simmons, a Georgia preacher who was the son of a member of the first Klan. Radicalized by the influx of immigrants and by the beginning of the

Great Migration of black Americans from the South to the North, the Klan grew massively in size and geographic reach. Between 1920 and 1925 it was estimated to include anywhere from three to six million Americans of every economic class and trade in every corner of the United States. Its aims were unabashedly nativist and white supremacist. One Klan leader said that the group represented "the great mass of Americans of the old pioneer stock." Violence was the Klan's means of policing its ethnoracial conception of national identity.[12]

The era of normalcy was less than five months old on May 31, 1921, when mobs of white men rampaged through a black district in Tulsa, Oklahoma, killing at least three dozen people and injuring thousands more. The Dallas Klan, meanwhile, was known for its beatings and whippings of black victims. Members of the "invisible empire" sometimes aimed their wrath at bootleggers and other violators of the prohibition on the sale of alcohol. For a secret society, the Klan in the 1920s flirted with the mainstream: Klan members held public office as judges, congressmen, governors, and senators. The organization became so pervasive in the Sooner State that in 1923 Oklahoma governor J. C. Walton placed Tulsa under martial law. In July 1925 some ten thousand people, including women and children, participated in a "karnival" on Long Island. Entertainment included a rodeo. When night fell, they burned a forty-foot cross.[13]

The next month, some forty thousand Klan members marched down Pennsylvania Avenue in Washington, DC. One marcher held a banner reading, "Keep Kongress Klean." One day after the parade, a group of Klansmen gathered across the Potomac River in Arlington, Virginia, to burn an eighty-foot cross. When the Klan returned to the nation's capital the following year, the *New York Times* seemed somewhat relieved to find that its numbers had dwindled. "There were only two floats in the parade, one with the Paterson (N.J.) Klan, and the other with the Klan of Lemoyne," wrote its correspondent. On the first float a young woman holding a Bible stood next to an American flag. Beneath her the legend read, "100 percent American girl." The second float carried a schoolhouse, symbolizing the Klan's opposition to Catholic schools and its desire to create a federal department of education to better obstruct Catholic teaching. The Klan was the most visible representation of the anti-Catholic bigotry that endured as a political force for close to another four decades.[14]

Anti-Semitism was also pervasive. Colleges and universities imposed surreptitious quotas on admissions to reduce Jewish enrollment. Car manufacturer Henry Ford was the most prominent anti-Semite in the country. His magazine, the *Dearborn Independent*, circulated anti-Semitic literature throughout the many Ford dealerships nationwide. He compiled the most vicious of its contents into a four-volume book, *The International Jew: The World's Foremost Problem*. More than half a million copies of *The International Jew* were distributed in the United States. Ford later repudiated these views. He claimed, implausibly, that the anti-Semitic journalism of the *Independent* had been published without his knowledge. In the 1920s Ford began thinking about applying his talents for management and routinization to government. He toyed with the idea of running for president. In May 1923 media mogul William Randolph Hearst said that he would support a Ford candidacy. But Ford decided against entering the race. Instead he endorsed Coolidge, who went on to trounce his two challengers the following year.[15]

Both Harding and Coolidge opposed immigration. Harding's campaign manager liked to brag that his client had "the finest pioneer blood, Anglo-Saxon, German, Scots-Irish, and Dutch." The losers in this ethnic competition were Slavs, Poles, Italians, Greeks, Jews, and "Orientals," as Asians were then called. Harding and Coolidge supported two major immigration-restriction acts that shut off entry to the United States for the next forty years.

Even as he closed the door to mass migration, however, Coolidge celebrated the contribution of earlier waves of immigrants. "Whether one traces his Americanism back three centuries to the Mayflower, or three years of the steerage," he told the American Legion in 1925, "is not half so important as whether his Americanism of today is real and genuine. No matter by what various crafts we came here, we are all now in the same boat." But the vessel had no room for additional passengers.[16]

Civil rights were a different story. The Republican presidents of the 1920s tried to uphold their party's legacy of black emancipation. They tried to live up to the memory of Abraham Lincoln. Harding and Coolidge supported antilynching laws but could not get them past Southern Democrats in the Senate. Their public rhetoric stressed black people's rights to education and economic advancement. "When I suggest the possibility of economic equality between the races, I mean it in precisely the same way and to the same extent that I would mean it if I spoke of equality of economic opportunity as between members of the same race," Harding told an audience in Birmingham, Alabama, in 1921. Three years later, running for reelection, Coolidge delivered the commencement address at Howard University, the historically black college in Washington, DC. He told the graduates, "The nation has need of all that can be contributed to it through the best efforts of all its citizens."[17]

In August 1924 the black newspaper the *Chicago Defender* reprinted a letter Coolidge had sent to a man disgusted at the sight of a black candidate for Congress. "Our Constitution guarantees equal rights to all our citizens, without discrimination on account of race or color," Coolidge wrote. "I have taken my oath to support that Constitution. It is the source of your rights and my rights. I propose to regard it, and administer it, as the source of the rights of all the people, whatever their belief or race."[18]

Coolidge's commitment to the governing institutions of the United States led him to consider black advancement the inevitable

consequence of economic and political freedom and quality education. But that same commitment to the Constitution, as Coolidge
understood it, prevented him from using the federal government
to guarantee the very freedom and educational quality that he said
he desired. The Republicans of the 1920s were caught in a bind
between their belief in equality and their belief in limited government. This contradiction would ensnare the Right for ages.

EQUALLY STRIKING IS THE DISTANCE IN THE 1920S BETWEEN THE
popular Republicanism of Harding and Coolidge and the elitist
contempt for democracy expressed by both traditionalist and libertarian intellectuals. As a mass-membership organization, the
Republican Party directed its appeals to the largest possible number of voters. It embraced women's suffrage and Prohibition while
struggling to thwart the growth of the Klan. The GOP associated
itself with rising incomes and employment and the civil religion of
patriotic Protestantism.

Yet the main figures of the intellectual Right scorned politics.
They feared the dilution of the individual in a mass society. The
best-selling *Education of Henry Adams* lamented the withering
away of ancient wisdom and virtue. Far removed from the ins and
outs of partisan bickering, traditionalists wanted to recover the
spiritual element missing from the consumer marketplace. They
stood apart from their times but eventually shaped the perceptions,
ideas, and attitudes of a younger generation of individualists and
conservatives.

The "New Humanists," for instance, were a group of literary
critics who urged their audience to return to the "great tradition" of
Western civilization. The leaders of the movement, Irving Babbitt
and Paul Elmer More, had met during graduate school at Harvard, where they studied Asian languages and literature. Babbitt
and More were philosophical rather than political. The fate of the
Republicans and Democrats was not their concern. They were

interested more in problems of the spirit than in questions of distributive justice. They sought a deeper understanding of the origins of social decay and disruption. In numerous books and essays, they elevated humanity's metaphysical nature over its material needs and desires. Respect for tradition and authority, an appreciation of self-restraint, a fondness for ancient wisdom—these were the hallmarks of the humanist sensibility.

Beginning in the second half of the nineteenth century, Christian authorities found themselves under attack. Liberal theology attempted to reconcile Christian thought and teaching with modern scientific and technological knowledge. Historical criticism of the Bible undermined belief in textual authority. Darwinian theories of natural selection removed the need for a creator. The creative destruction of industrial capitalism unsettled family life, social patterns, and received opinion. Mainstream Protestants no longer felt themselves wedded to a literal interpretation of scripture.

With the realm of the supernatural and an eternal afterlife seeming remote, theologians became more interested in actualizing God's grace in the here and now. Baptist minister Walter Rauschenbusch, for instance, promoted a Social Gospel whose goal was the establishment of God's kingdom on earth. Rauschenbusch denied the reality of original sin. He preached that the main obstacle to a Christian society was the maldistribution of wealth. The task of reform was to change the environment so that man's good nature could express itself.

Not every Protestant was ready to join a settlement house. Between 1909 and 1919 a pair of Presbyterian brothers from Chicago—Lyman and Milton Stewart—began editing and publishing essays attacking developments in Protestant theology. The essays were gathered in four volumes and distributed to churches nationwide. They were called *The Fundamentals*—hence the name for Christians who agreed with them: Fundamentalists.

The Fundamentalists read the Bible as the inerrant word of God. They were theological cousins of Evangelical Christians, who also rejected liberal theology and the Social Gospel. The differences between Fundamentalists and Evangelicals were subtle. Both groups believed in inerrancy. But Fundamentalists, in the eyes of Evangelicals, tended to read the Bible more literally than necessary. Fundamentalists also tended to be dispensationalist: they believed that history proceeded according to a divine plan and that the end times were imminent. They walled themselves off from popular culture. To the Fundamentalists, liberal Protestants had abandoned scripture for the Social Gospel. Speaking at a World Christian Fundamentalist Association meeting in Philadelphia in 1919, Fundamentalist leader William Bell Riley labeled liberal understandings of the Bible a form of "social service Christianity." Before long, Fundamentalists would interpret the Social Gospel as a vehicle for Marxism.[19]

For Fundamentalist theologian J. Gresham Machen, liberalism could not be reconciled with Christianity. It was an alternative dogma. In 1925, in his book *Christianity and Liberalism*, Machen anticipated later critiques of "secular humanism." Liberalism, he wrote, "differs from Christianity in its view of God, of man, of the seat of authority and of the way of salvation. And it differs from Christianity not only in theology but in the whole of life."[20]

Fundamentalism, then as now, was a response to the secularizing tendencies of the time. It had its first test in the public square during the very year that Machen released his book. In May 1925 a teacher in Dayton, Tennessee, named John Scopes was arrested for violating a recently passed state law outlawing instruction in Darwin's theory of evolution through natural selection. Scopes became the poster boy for the five-year-old American Civil Liberties Union (ACLU), which had wanted to test the Tennessee bill as soon as it went into effect. The ACLU paid Scopes's legal fees. And it hired his attorney, Clarence Darrow, who was still famous for defending the murderers Nathan Leopold Jr. and Richard Loeb the year before.

The lawyer for the prosecution was William Jennings Bryan, Wilson's former secretary of state and a three-time Democratic Party presidential nominee. The trial lasted eight days—forty-eight hours more than it took the God of the Bible to create the universe. The jury needed just nine minutes to find Scopes guilty. (The ACLU paid his fine too.) Bryan had won the case but at the cost of his name. On the seventh day of the trial, Darrow had put him on the stand. Their exchange was riveting. But it also ended in embarrassment for the "Great Commoner," who struggled to answer Darrow's questions and became a figure of fun in the national press. He died in Dayton four days after his victory.[21]

The Scopes trial was a media sensation. It featured celebrity antagonists. It pitted the metropolis against the countryside. It had a profound effect on the trajectory of Fundamentalism, which for the next several decades rejected social and political engagement. The press continued to portray the Fundamentalists as hillbilly rubes and did not hesitate to cast the two sides of the trial as either heroes or villains in a prefabricated narrative. Darrow stood for enlightened modernity, Bryan for regressive superstition. The long-lasting mutual antipathy between the media and Fundamentalist Christians got its start. And one parent of this enmity was a correspondent for the *Baltimore Sun* named Henry Louis Mencken.

Then America's most famous writer, Mencken modeled for generations of journalists—including many writers who would go on to form the conservative movement—a highbrow attitude of irony, scorn, invective, and wit. He was a misanthrope, an iconoclast, a scourge of do-gooders and true believers. He adopted a critical stance toward American democracy and materialism. His libertarianism prevented him from embracing either Democrats or Republicans. Harding, Coolidge, Bryan: Mencken thought them all fools. "All government, in its essence, is a conspiracy against the superior man," Mencken wrote in his *Chrestomathy* (1949). "Its one permanent object is to oppress him and cripple him." How? By censoring ideas, taxing incomes, regulating alcohol, and conscripting men into military service.[22]

Mencken had a friend and ally in Albert Jay Nock, a former Episcopalian priest who had abandoned his family for a life of bohemian letters in New York City. From 1920 to 1924 Nock helped edit the *Freeman*, a political and cultural journal that was elitist and libertarian. Nock took classical liberalism—the philosophy of individual rights, equality before the law, and limited government—to the border of anarchism.

During the 1920s Nock wrote the essays collected in 1935 under the title *Our Enemy, the State*. There he distinguished between "the economic means" of private production and the "political means" of coercive expropriation. The state was the institutionalization of the political means. According to Nock, if liberty were to endure, the "economic means" had to be favored over the "political means." Like Mencken, Nock did not think much of "the forgotten man." He dwelled on the natural inequalities that separated individuals from one another. He scoffed at the idea that all men and women can benefit from education. He preferred the classical methods of instruction and formulated a teaching program of his own. If he had his way, Nock wrote, enrollment would be limited to the "educable."[23]

Nock's and Mencken's exacting standards were meant to expose the inadequacies of their nation and its citizens. They were snappy and memorable writers, but they also were oddballs estranged from the beliefs and behaviors of their countrymen. They pined for a departed age of aristocratic chivalry and Nietzschean self-assertion that never existed in the United States. The generalized form of right-wing politics during the 1920s—the public philosophy of institutional reverence shared by Harding and Coolidge—was both widely accepted and more appealing than either the speculations of the New Humanists or the badinage of Mencken and Nock.

ON MAY 21, 1927, NEWS BROKE THAT CHARLES LINDBERGH'S transatlantic flight from Long Island to Paris had been a success. The dashing Lindbergh, whose father had opposed both entry into World War I and establishment of the Federal Reserve during his tenure as a congressman from Minnesota, was an air mailman and an army reservist. He was transformed instantly into a national hero. Coolidge dispatched a battleship to France to retrieve him.[24]

On June 11, in a ceremony held on the grounds of the Washington Monument, Coolidge awarded Lindbergh the Distinguished Flying Cross. Hundreds of thousands of onlookers gathered before the stage. In his speech, Coolidge happily noted that Lindbergh's plane, the *Spirit of St. Louis*, had been built from American products and financed through private investment. The next day the Coolidges and the Lindberghs went to church together.

Everywhere you turned in Lindbergh's America, you saw material abundance, artistic expression, and dreams of international peace. Cars, radios, and homes became accessible to the public. Women and youth became more visible in society and culture. Jazz and modernism infused art with new forms and styles. The world was at peace. When Coolidge announced that he would not run for a second term, the 1928 Republican nomination went to Herbert Hoover, who defeated the Democratic nominee, New York governor Al Smith, in a landslide—58 to 41 percent. Coolidge, however, was not Hoover's biggest fan. "That man has offered me unsolicited advice for six years," he remarked, "all of it bad."[25]

Still, Coolidge thought, the continuance of Republican rule was a good thing. As he prepared to leave office, he was more than satisfied with the condition of the nation. "No Congress of the United States ever assembled, on surveying the state of the Union, has met with a more pleasing prospect than that which appears at the present time," he wrote in December 1928. The last embers of Progressivism seemed to be burning out. The pro-business, constitutionalist GOP was triumphant. The critics of "normalcy" were isolated and dyspeptic. They lacked an institutional base.[26]

Hoover was sworn in the following March. A little more than five months later, the world fell apart. The economy collapsed— and the Republican consensus went with it.

CHAPTER TWO

THE REVOLUTION OF 1932

THE STOCK MARKET CRASHED IN OCTOBER 1929. BETWEEN 1929 and 1933, gross national product and personal disposable income sank by one-third. The unemployment rate soared to 24 percent. President Herbert Hoover chose not to follow the precedent that Warren Harding and his secretary of the treasury, Andrew Mellon, had set eight years before. At the outset of the 1920s, the Republicans had cut spending and taxes and otherwise stood aside while industry and the market settled accounts. Faced with the destruction of so much wealth and employment at the beginning of the 1930s, Mellon urged Hoover to hold fast to the principles of laissez-faire. "Liquidate labor, liquidate stocks, liquidate the farmers, liquidate real estate," Hoover recalled Mellon advising him.[1]

Hoover did not listen. Trained in engineering, he had more confidence in government than his predecessor. The application of force directed by reason, in his view, could alter the world. Hoover saw the executive branch as a conduit, distributing and channeling energy for particular ends. In the spring of 1930, he and Congress embarked on a public works program to boost jobs and wages. That June, he signed into law the Smoot-Hawley Tariff Act to protect

US markets from foreign competition. Neither effort was enough to save the Republican House in the fall midterm elections.

The scale of public discontent was visible from the White House the following year. In December 1931, Hunger Marchers petitioned Hoover for relief. In January 1932, Hoover signed into law an act establishing the Reconstruction Finance Corporation (RFC). The RFC was a government-financed independent agency tasked with lending money to states and to industry. Risk was socialized; gains were privatized. Hoover expanded the RFC and spent more on public works. Nothing seemed to fix the economy.

Hoover's challenges multiplied. The impoverished veterans and unemployed workers who called themselves the Bonus Army began to assemble in Washington in late May 1932. They demanded the benefits that government had promised them. At the end of July, Hoover ordered the armed forces to evict the Bonus Army from its encampments in the nation's capital. It took two days for US Army chief of staff General Douglas MacArthur, who had risen to prominence during Woodrow Wilson's Mexican campaign, and his aides, Majors Dwight D. Eisenhower and George S. Patton, to do the job. The violent clash demonstrated the tenacity of government beneficiaries in claiming their entitlements.[2]

Hoover emulated the pro-business, hands-off ethic of his former bosses before turning to the state-centered activism that followed him in office. He mixed references to emergency actions, government programs, and alliances between the public and private sectors with odes to individualism and the market. For example, in October 1930, when he commemorated the 150th anniversary of the Revolutionary War's Battle of Kings Mountain in South Carolina, Hoover sang the praises of American exceptionalism. He extolled the "American system" against its Depression-era challengers: socialism, Soviet "Bolshevism," anarchism, and "despotism or class government." Like Calvin Coolidge, Hoover drew a causal link between the religious fidelity of the people and awe for the nation's founding institutions. But he also recognized—it was impossible not to notice—the dimming popularity of business amid the economic calamity.

Hoover grew defensive as the 1932 presidential election came into focus. He became alarmed by the measures his opponents embraced. "I may say at once that the changes proposed from all these Democratic principles and allies are of the most profound and penetrating character," he told a campaign rally in Madison Square Garden in late October 1932. "If they are brought about this will not be the America which we have known in the past." Public works and subsidized loans were one thing, but a quantum leap in government involvement in the economy and society was different. If the Democrats won, the "true liberalism" or "Americanism" that Harding, Coolidge, and Hoover associated with love of the founding, religious piety, personal responsibility, individual initiative, and self-reliance would disappear. "This election is not a mere shift from the ins to the outs," Hoover pleaded. "It means deciding the direction our Nation will take over a century to come." Eighteen days later, the electorate decided. Hoover lost, 40 to 57 percent.

The man who defeated him, Franklin Delano Roosevelt, was Theodore Roosevelt's cousin. He had studied President Wilson while serving as assistant secretary of the navy during World War I. He had supported unemployment insurance, pensions, and aid to farmers during his term as governor of New York. As a presidential candidate, however, FDR was intentionally vague about his plans. Using his powerful rhetorical skills, FDR framed the Progressive mind-set of government-directed improvement as fully consonant with American history and tradition. Wily, boisterous, and charming, Roosevelt was a natural politician with a common touch despite his patrician background.[3]

FDR's cleverness was evident in a radio address he delivered on behalf of the Democratic National Committee in the spring of 1932. He began by renouncing partisanship and describing his government service under Wilson, when "a whole nation mobilized for war," gathering "economic, industrial, social, and military resources . . . into a vast unit capable of and actually in the process of throwing into the scales 10 million men equipped with physical needs and sustained by the realization that behind them were the united efforts of 110,000,000 human beings." He went on to say that a similar effort, this time in the domestic arena, would end the Great Depression.

Then Roosevelt made a jujitsu-like oratorical move. No longer was the "forgotten man" the citizen whose interest was overlooked when government redistributed taxes to favored groups. For FDR, the forgotten man resided "at the bottom of the economic pyramid." And FDR said that his agenda would deliver "permanent relief from the bottom up," unlike Hoover's administration, "which can think in terms only of the top of the social and economic structure." Recasting government as an ally of the downtrodden in a struggle with vested private interests, Roosevelt undermined the long-standing Republican argument that what was good for business was, in the end, good for everyone. Only intermittently in the years since has the electorate found the GOP rebuttal persuasive.[4]

In September 1932, in a speech to the Commonwealth Club of San Francisco, Roosevelt redefined the American social contract. Developing the themes of Teddy Roosevelt's "New Nationalism" address two decades earlier, FDR called "for a reappraisal of values." Economic growth, industrial leadership, factory production—these concepts, which had figured so prominently in the pre-Depression Republican presidencies, were no longer as important to national renewal. The task that awaited Americans, FDR said, was "the soberer, less dramatic business of administering resources and plants already in hand, of seeking to reestablish foreign markets for our surplus production, of meeting the problem of underconsumption, of adjusting production to consumption, of distributing wealth and products more equitably, of adapting economic organizations to the service of the people." Laissez-faire was passé. "The day of enlightened administration has come."[5]

FDR's administration may or may not have been enlightened. But it was certainly improvisatory. In a May 1932 speech at Oglethorpe University in which he had called for "bold, persistent experimentation," Roosevelt said, "It is common sense to take a method and try it: If it fails, admit it frankly and try another. But above all, try something." His experiments tended to run in only one direction. The federal bureaucracy expanded, and government entangled itself in finance, agriculture, and industry. From his administration's first hundred days came a procession of agencies, commissions, associations, and bureaucracies: the National Recovery Administration, the Civilian Conservation Corps, the Tennessee Valley Authority, and the Securities and Exchange Commission. In 1935 the National Labor Relations Board and the Works Progress Administration joined the list of newborn government entities.[6]

Roosevelt built the federal government into an ever-present behemoth that regulated American life and dispensed benefits—from unemployment compensation to farm subsidies to income maintenance to Social Security. This transformation in the size and scope of government was not uncontested. FDR's expansion of the powers of the executive branch became the central topic of debate between conservatives and liberals.

Within a year of Roosevelt's inauguration, his opponents formed the American Liberty League to resist the New Deal. The Liberty League joined the National Association of Manufacturers, founded in 1895, and the US Chamber of Commerce, established in 1912, in a constellation of pro-business associations and pressure groups dedicated to opposing and, if possible, overturning Roosevelt's achievements. The league's purpose, wrote one of its organizers, was "to protect society from the sufferings which it is bound to endure if we allow communistic elements to lead the people to believe all businessmen are crooks." Another of the league's founders, Democratic attorney John W. Davis, who had served as Woodrow Wilson's solicitor general, wrote in a fund-raising appeal, "I am opposed to confiscatory taxation, wasteful expenditure, socialized industry, and a planned economy controlled and directed by government functionaries." Davis also oriented the league toward the fixed reference point of 1920s Republicanism: "I believe in the Constitution of the United States; I believe in the division of powers it makes."[7]

The GOP maintained its adherence to the doctrines of Harding, Coolidge, and Mellon even after the elections of 1932 and 1934 reduced the party to a mere nuisance in Congress and the states. "The only useful purpose of the Republican party," wrote Republican National Committee powerbroker Charles Hilles in 1934, "is a resolute resistance to economic heresies and the offer of substitute proposals that are sound and constructive." Coolidge, who had died in 1933, was out of the picture. The defeated Hoover cast off his vestigial Progressivism and became the most prominent spokesman for the anti–New Deal faction within the GOP. His public profile may have pleased FDR.[8]

In his books, speeches, and articles in the 1930s, Hoover elaborated on the themes of his presidency and losing campaign. Back in 1922, he had written that American individualism was unique because it was twinned with the idea of equality of opportunity. The New Deal, as Hoover put it in the title of his first postpresidential book, was a "challenge to liberty." A believer in the "true liberalism" of the nineteenth century, Hoover nonetheless resigned himself to an uncomfortable—for him—political label: "The New Deal having corrupted the label of liberalism for collectivism, coercion, [and] concentration of political power," he wrote to one correspondent, "it seems 'Historic Liberalism' must be conservatism in contrast." Hoover remained active in national politics from his base in Palo Alto, California, where over the years the Hoover War Library, which he had endowed at his alma mater, Stanford University, after the Great War, would turn into the Hoover Institution on War, Revolution, and Peace. This influential think tank continues to promote his ideas of free enterprise and limited government.[9]

For the Liberty League, the Republican old guard, and figures such as Hoover, the New Deal was not an extension of freedom; it was freedom's nemesis. What remained of the polity, economy, and society prior to FDR had to be preserved against the alternatives of socialism, communism, and fascism. This was a novel situation for the advocates of constitutionalism and private enterprise. Until 1932, they had been believers in "normalcy." They wanted to continue the inheritance of a limited federal government and a friendly environment for business activity. In effect, however, the New Deal created an entirely new government—the bureaucratic and regulatory structure formed by FDR and his "Brains Trust" of economic advisers. Unlike the Right elsewhere, which attached itself to established institutions such as throne, altar, and aristocracy, the American Right had no power base other than pockets of industry and parts of the enfeebled GOP. It tended to adopt an adversarial and catastrophizing attitude toward the government that it never quite shook off.

For example, by the end of Roosevelt's first term, journalist Albert Jay Nock had all but given up on politics. Nock understood the appeal of the New Deal. He was familiar with the longing for economic security and the ease with which the individual's identity could become subsumed by the anonymity of an interest group or a crowd. In 1936, in an article for the *Atlantic Monthly*, he told his readers that preserving what remained of Western civilization was the job of a minuscule number of enlightened men and women. American social, political, cultural, and intellectual life, he wrote, was pitched to the masses. "The Remnant," he went on, "are those who by force of intellect are able to apprehend these principles, and by force of character are able, at least measurably, to cleave to them; the masses are those who are unable to do either." Nock cast himself as a sort of prophet who scorned the crowd but understood two things: that the Remnant existed and that it would recover his wisdom. His mix of nostalgia, melancholy, and pessimism became a constant temptation for the American Right.[10]

For Nock, the New Deal resembled fascist governments in Europe. He was not alone in thinking so. Garet Garrett, editor of *American Affairs*, the publication of the pro-business Conference Board, wrote that FDR had initiated a "revolution in the state, within the form of law." Rose Wilder Lane, daughter of Laura Ingalls Wilder, wrote that FDR betrayed America by adopting the intellectual fashions of Europe. The president's enemies pointed out the similarities between the cartelization of the economy under the National Recovery Administration and the bureaucratization and centralization of Adolf Hitler's Germany and Joseph Stalin's Soviet Union. They said that FDR was a dictator in the making. "Fascism," wrote prolific anti–New Deal journalist John T. Flynn, "will come at the hands of perfectly authentic Americans."[11]

Republicans fought the New Deal on the grounds that it was a radical restructuring of America's government and market. But these dissenters made up a dwindling crowd. Their numbers were small compared with the writers, activists, and politicians who opposed the New Deal on the basis that it was not radical enough. In 1930, for instance, "twelve Southerners" associated with the "Fugitive" poets and literary critics of Vanderbilt University published *I'll Take My Stand: The South and the Agrarian Tradition*, an essay collection meant to counteract the erosion of southern distinctiveness caused by waves of economic development and proliferating mass media. The contributors worried that elements within southern society were all too eager to become part of an undifferentiated national culture.[12]

They came to be known as the Southern Agrarians. They took the Great Depression as additional evidence of the industrial

North's spiritual desolation. Finance, manufacturing, and conglomeration were a dead end. Wage labor did not satisfy psychological needs. And the job market was inherently unstable. But socialism wasn't any better, and Progressivism's centralizing impulses eroded regional and individual independence.

Agrarianism was more like European conservatism in its desire to preserve ancient social patterns against the upheavals wrought by industrialism and centralized government. This attachment to a vanished means of subsistence gave agrarianism a Romantic, literary character. Its poetic models of chivalric aristocracy, however, did not dwell on, if they mentioned at all, the chattel slavery that had been the basis of the southern economy for so many centuries.

This failure to reckon with the racist legacy of the South diluted the movement's impact. The Agrarians could not make up their minds on a political program or on civil rights for black people. The disparity between the Agrarians' beautiful rhetoric and philosophical sophistication and southern politics as actually conducted day to day was a brutal example of the difference between intellectual theory and democratic practice. Worse still, some of those who traveled in the same intellectual circles as the Agrarians flirted with another danger implicit in radical critiques of America: an openness to authoritarianism.

In 1933 socialite litterateur Seward Collins founded a journal called the *American Review*. It was a harbinger of the coming radicalism. The *Review* was a home for critics of New Deal America: it published Agrarians and New Humanists; Distributists, who followed Anglo-Catholic writers Hilaire Belloc and G. K. Chesterton in advocating for the widest possible distribution of private property; and neo-Scholastic philosophers such as Jacques Maritain, who sought refuge from the flux of modernity in the constancy of Thomist natural law. "The magazine," Collins wrote in the first issue, "is a response to the widespread and growing feeling that the forces and principles which have produced the modern chaos are incapable of yielding any solution; that the only hope is a return to fundamentals and tested principles which have been largely pushed aside."[13]

These "fundamentals and tested principles" shared a single quality: antimodernism. In other words, these writers opposed the fluidity, creative destruction, secularism, and individualism of modern society. The Agrarians saw the conflict between North and South over the growth of corporations, national interconnectivity, the status of Fundamentalism, and legal equality for black people as cultural warfare. Progressivism, liberalism, modernism in the arts and literature, and Darwinism—these were imports. The Agrarians sought a native tradition. A newly minted PhD from North Carolina named C. Vann Woodward, for instance, wrote a critical but sympathetic biography of Thomas Watson, the Populist Party candidate for president in 1904, who had denounced socialism and promoted the values of rural America.[14]

The Agrarian perspective had innate limitations. Not everyone could be a son of the South. Not everyone *wanted* to be. Not everyone wanted to be like Watson, who eventually promoted anti-Catholicism, anti-Semitism, and white supremacy. So opposed were the Agrarians to the shape of American society since Appomattox that they fell into the sinkholes of nostalgia, pessimism, and fecklessness. Like the Marxists, they took as their enemies "finance capitalism" and the political system of liberal democracy that perpetuated it. To follow the logic of such a systemic critique would lead to revolutionary violence. The political fringe beckoned.

The limitations of Southern Agrarianism were both regional and ideological. Natural law, by contrast, was eternal and universal. The neo-Scholastic Catholic critique of modernity had gained ground in America. It had been adopted by figures such as Mortimer J. Adler, who held a doctorate in psychology from Columbia University. Adler found a professional ally in Robert Maynard Hutchins, president of the University of Chicago, established in

1890. There the twin strands of American conservatism—criticism of economic collectivism and rejection of philosophical naturalism, a school of thought that denied the existence of supernatural phenomena—intersected.

Together Hutchins and Adler provided Chicago undergraduates with the option of enrolling in a great books program with a core curriculum modeled on the one adopted by Columbia in 1919. St. John's College in Annapolis also established a great books curriculum in 1937. For Adler and Hutchins, intellectual currents were responsible for carrying Western civilization to the abyss of fascism and communism. In 1941, their university established the Committee on Social Thought, a graduate program that would play a key role in promoting alternatives to the liberal understanding of politics and society.

At the same time, Chicago became the center of a free market revival. The first Chicago school of economics was more measured in its defense of the market than its descendants. Its founder, Jacob Viner, joined the faculty in 1916. Canadian born and of Jewish heritage, Viner had graduated from McGill and Harvard. He was a classical liberal who, like Adam Smith, believed that government had functions to perform in situations where the market failed. Public education, public health, and antitrust enforcement were legitimate functions of the state. While government should not interfere with the price system, Viner believed, it also could run budget deficits to sustain demand and provide liquidity to the financial sector.

Frank H. Knight joined Viner at Chicago in 1927. He was the first of eleven children born to a Fundamentalist family living in poverty in rural Illinois. He rebelled against the theology of his parents at an early age. Throughout his career, Knight instructed his pupils to question everything. One of those students, Henry Simons, followed Knight to Chicago, where Simons began to teach as well. In 1934, Simons published *A Positive Program for*

Laissez-Faire, a broadside against the wage and price controls in FDR's National Recovery Act.

Reading Simons's pamphlet in the twenty-first century, one is struck by both its similarities to and departures from the free market economics now associated with the University of Chicago. Like his students who followed him, Simons was an empiricist who understood there was a role for government in fiscal and monetary policy. He believed that the Great Depression was the result of government malfeasance. He emphasized the connection between economic and personal freedom. Years later, his students abandoned his diatribes against inequality, his promotion of nationalization of enterprises that could not be limited through competition, and his advocacy of high progressive income and estate taxes.[15]

Chicago was not the only site of free market thought. For decades, a number of economists based in Vienna, Austria, had waged a war against their counterparts in Germany who denied the existence of uniform economic laws. "Austrians" such as Ludwig von Mises and Friedrich Hayek studied individual behavior as well as the nature of the business cycle. Both, they believed, operated according to fixed principles. They rejected Karl Marx's labor theory of value, which stipulated that the worth of a commodity was the result of the labor put into it. They held that the subjective preferences of individuals determined prices. A capitalist could employ dozens of men working hundreds of hours to manufacture a brand of cigarettes, but if demand for that brand fell to zero, so would its price.

Though the Austrian and Chicago schools of economics both supported private property, voluntary exchange, limited government, the rule of law, and free trade, they also diverged on some points. The Austrians were theoretical, the Chicagoans empirical. The Austrians supported a strict gold standard; the Chicagoans embraced flexible or floating exchange rates. The Austrians tended to be more antigovernment; the Chicagoans believed that the state could justifiably intervene to break up monopolies and address negative "externalities"—costs not borne by the producers who caused them, such as environmental pollution or overfishing. The Austrians largely rejected the terminology and aims of macroeconomics and abhorred inflation; the Chicagoans were comfortable with macroeconomics and argued that a steady increase in the money supply, even directed by a central bank, would create a stable environment for savings, investment, and growth.[16]

In the 1930s the Austrian school migrated west. Friedrich Hayek moved to the London School of Economics and, later in the same decade, became a British subject. Ludwig von Mises left Vienna for Geneva in 1934 and went to the United States in 1940. A third member of the Austrian school, trade economist Gottfried Haberler, became the first resident scholar at the free market American Enterprise Association, now the American Enterprise Institute, founded in 1938.

Mises's works had been translated into English only a few years before his arrival in New York. His *Theory of Money and Credit*, outlining the Austrian theory of the business cycle as a function of investment, was published in 1912, but it wasn't translated into English until 1934. His *Socialism*, arguing that socialist central planning was doomed to failure because planners could not possibly account for all of the variables in an economy, was published in 1922, but it wasn't released in English until 1936. One essay collection, which began to sketch out the principles of "praxeology," or Mises's universal laws of human action, remained untranslated.[17]

Mises taught at New York University's graduate school of business. The Volker Fund, a nonprofit that supported libertarian causes, and other foundations financed his position. He carried on the weekly seminars he had conducted in Vienna. He wrote broadsides against government interference in the market. In 1944 he published two books: *Bureaucracy* and *Omnipotent Government*. He was against both.

Mises's commitment to a priori reasoning led him to frame the choice between liberalism and socialism as either-or. For Mises, any expansion of government's limited responsibilities was a surrender to bureaucracy and statism. He had little use for the empirical methods and real-world nuance of the Chicago scholars. Deviation from his views resulted in ostracization. After his student and friend Fritz Machlup endorsed the idea of floating exchange rates, Mises did not speak to him for three years. His rigid doctrines isolated him from the economics profession even as they attracted a devoted American following that would profoundly shape the postwar American Right.[18]

LIKE THE PHILOSOPHICAL SCHOOLS OF NEW HUMANISM AND Southern Agrarianism, the Chicago and Austrian critiques of FDR's economic policy were removed from everyday life. New Deal liberalism, populism, radicalism, and Marxism consumed the politics of the 1930s. For example, the Black Legion, a Michigan-based successor to the Ku Klux Klan, had tens of thousands of members, some of whom committed murder and assault against Catholics, Jews, and blacks. From his base in Kansas, a Fundamentalist minister named Gerald B. Winrod organized something called the Defenders of the Christian Faith and promoted the conspiracy theories surrounding the forged *Protocols of the Elders of Zion* and the fantastical Illuminati. He accused FDR of furthering the aims of Jews and Communists.[19]

A third group, the Silver Shirts, were up-front about their fascism. Strong on the West Coast, especially in Southern California, they envisioned a Christian nation based on the theory of corporatism: the formal organization and integration of the major social sectors—industry, labor, and state. This corporatist governance, the Silver Shirts said, would preside over a racial caste system, with Jews, blacks, and other racial and religious minorities subservient to white Protestants. Their journal was called *Liberation*.[20]

Two of FDR's radical opponents mixed left-wing economics with social conservatism. They exemplified the eventual convergence of the Far Left and the Far Right. One was a Catholic priest, Father Charles Coughlin of Royal Oak, Michigan, outside Detroit, who had attached a microphone to his pulpit and begun broadcasting his sermons in 1926. Four years later, his program was aired nationwide. Coughlin turned his attention from religion to politics. Attuned to the beliefs, ambitions, anxieties, and resentments of his lower-middle-class parishioners, Coughlin mixed anti-Communist diatribes with attacks on the "international bankers," primarily Jews, whose supposed machinations on Wall Street ripped off the little guy.[21]

Initially supportive of Roosevelt, Coughlin advocated better pay and working conditions for laborers, as well as aid for the unemployed. His radicalism and his aims grew with the size of his audience. In the fall of 1934, he established the National Union for Social Justice, demanding the nationalization of banks, a jobs guarantee at living wages, and corporatist arrangements between management and labor that would reduce strikes. The next year, he broke with FDR.

Senator Huey Long of Louisiana, known as "the Kingfish," embodied the fusion of traditionalism and antimonopoly, soak-the-rich economics that threatened Roosevelt. Long had won the governorship of his home state in 1928 on the slogan "Every man a king, but no one wears a crown." It took him two years to centralize economic and political authority in the state, making Louisiana, according to historian David M. Kennedy, the "closest thing to a dictatorship that America has ever known."[22]

In 1930 Long was elected to the US Senate. For the next five years, he held both offices at the same time. There seemed to be no limit to the power that Long could accumulate, so long as enough Louisianans felt that he stood for them against the coastal elites who endangered their patrimony. Like Coughlin, Long broadcast over the radio. He also sold books—the first used his famous motto, "Every man a king," as its title.[23]

Long created the Share Our Wealth Society in 1934. Its redistributionism was far-reaching. He said he would confiscate the wealth of the rich and transfer it to the people through cash benefits, guaranteed minimum incomes, subsidies, and retirement funds. He hired Gerald L. K. Smith, a former Fundamentalist minister who belonged to both the Klan and the Silver Shirts, as a surrogate speechmaker. Smith's presence in the Share Our Wealth Society offered additional evidence that the authoritarian-leaning Right easily could embrace a far-left economic program.

When a disgruntled Louisiana physician shot Long in the stomach inside the state capital in 1935, Smith tried to replace the Kingfish as head of Share Our Wealth. He didn't succeed. Smith's failure demonstrated the personal nature of Long's hold over his followers—and the potential risk to FDR if Huey Long had survived and followed through with his pledge to run for president in the next election.

Equally important to the future of both the country and the Right was the path traveled by members of the radical Left during the 1930s. Throughout the "Red Decade," intellectuals both inside and outside the US government looked up to the Soviet Union as a force for modernization and the embodiment of egalitarian ideals. Writers, artists, activists, and dilettantes fell for Soviet propaganda that contrasted Communist autarky with the failures of the Great Depression. Members of the Communist Party USA and their fellow travelers held jobs in journalism, publishing, the labor movement, and, with the beginning of the New Deal, government.

Meanwhile, a second and smaller group of intellectuals married their belief in Marxist doctrines with a dissident stance toward the Soviet Union and its grip over the Communist Party USA. Philosopher Sidney Hook, editor Elliot Cohen, journalist Max Eastman, and literary critic Lionel Trilling, among others, opposed Soviet dictator Joseph Stalin for betraying their revolutionary ideals and for extinguishing freedom within the territory under his control. The intellectuals' estrangement from Stalinism and its allies grew as news reached America of the Russian dictator's purges and show trials.

The anti-Stalinist Left coalesced around the little magazine *Partisan Review*, which published radical social criticism alongside modernist analyses of art and literature. *Partisan Review* was affiliated with the Left Opposition, the Communist dissenters to Stalin led by Soviet exile Leon Trotsky and émigré organizer and journalist Max Shachtman. In 1938, Hook and his mentor, John Dewey, led an independent Commission of Inquiry that acquitted Trotsky of Stalin's charges of treason. The investigation provided further evidence of a growing disenchantment with Soviet communism among a tiny but intellectually significant portion of the Left. This estrangement intensified as the left-wing enemies of Stalin fought against Soviet infiltration of American labor unions and cultural organizations and against Communist imperialism abroad.

To head off the racists, populists, Marxists, and Communists, FDR moved left and amped up his rhetorical barrages against business. In 1936, during his speech accepting the Democratic presidential nomination at Franklin Field in Philadelphia, Roosevelt declared war on "economic royalists." He proclaimed that "necessitous men are not free men." In previous centuries, liberalism had established a realm of individual autonomy free from government interference. Under FDR, however, liberalism also became a doctrine of government provision to satisfy ever-expanding human needs.

The Republican Party continued to stand for a restoration of the pre-1932 consensus. The GOP nominated Kansas governor Alf Landon, whose supporters called him "the Kansas Coolidge." The party platform announced, "America is in peril." The Republicans pledged "to maintain the American system of Constitutional and local self-government" and "to preserve the American system of free enterprise, private competition, and equality of opportunity." To end the Depression, the platform endorsed the "abandonment of all New Deal policies that raise production costs, increase the cost of living, and thereby restrict buying, reduce volume, and prevent reemployment." Notably, the platform did not disavow the idea of Social Security but suggested an alternative means of providing it.

What remained of the anti-Roosevelt financial and media establishment rallied behind Landon. One scholar estimated that around 80 percent of US newspapers endorsed the Republican ticket. "Governor Landon's mind has not been warped," Henry Ford said in a statement after hosting the nominee for lunch in Dearborn, Michigan. "My judgment would be that he would be a hard man to turn from the American way of doing things."[24]

That was not the electorate's judgment. FDR crushed Landon. In the end, the Kansas Coolidge won two states, Vermont and Maine, for a total of eight Electoral College votes. The "American way of doing things" was not as solid as Republicans believed.

In 1937, having become master of both the White House and Congress, FDR turned his attention to the Supreme Court. It remained stocked with judges who believed that the Fourteenth Amendment to the Constitution guaranteed both economic and political liberty and whose jurisprudence found the New Deal unconstitutional. In May 1935, the Court had struck down FDR's National Recovery Administration. The next year it nullified the Agricultural Adjustment Act. Thus the Court removed the underpinnings of FDR's strategy to inflate prices and wages artificially through anticompetitive government measures. He was furious.

Roosevelt launched his counterattack less than a month into his second term. On February 5, 1937, he submitted a bill to Congress that would have allowed him to appoint to the Supreme Court at least six new judges whose views of the New Deal aligned with his own. FDR's opponents knew what he was trying to do. Like the critics of Progressive jurisprudence two decades earlier, they described themselves as constitutionalist defenders of the Founders' legacy.[25]

And they had resources at their disposal. Publisher Frank Gannett began the National Committee to Uphold Constitutional Government, which used direct-mail marketing techniques to expand its membership. Gannett told audiences that Roosevelt was engaged in "a poorly camouflaged attempt to destroy the Constitution by undermining the people's confidence in their judiciary and in lawyers." An independent judiciary that restricted federal power, believed in liberty of contract, and was unafraid to strike down state laws that infringed on individual freedom and property rights had been a goal of the American Right since the nineteenth century. FDR's challenge to the constitutional order was direct and audacious.[26]

It was also unpopular. What became known as "court packing" annoyed more than just the economic royalists and the Liberty League. It disturbed the electorate. And the South, so important to FDR's coalition, was especially suspicious of anything that might endanger the legal structure of Jim Crow. A Democratic senator from North Carolina named Josiah Bailey became an outspoken opponent of FDR's proposal, claiming FDR wanted an enfeebled Court that, like the Democratic supermajorities in Congress, would permit the executive to impose his whims on the people. "A subservient Congress means a dependent Court," Bailey said in Maine in June 1937. "And the two together mean government by presidential decree and without restraint."[27]

FDR's plan was defeated in the Senate. But the president had the final victory. On March 29, 1937, the Court upheld a minimum wage law for women in Washington State. In April it upheld the constitutionality of FDR's labor agenda. By January 1938, with the retirement of Justice George Sutherland, a champion of

unenumerated rights to economic freedom, the constitutionalist flame inside the Supreme Court had dimmed. FDR won the
Court's grudging acceptance of the New Deal—but at a high cost
in popularity and momentum.[28]

The recession of 1937 made his troubles worse. Corporations
and business associations urged the president to lessen the burden
of taxes, expenditures, and regulations in order to improve growth.
Josiah Bailey and other Southern Democrats critical of the New
Deal decided to use this opportunity to broaden their network.
Bailey invited conservative Republicans to join him and his colleagues in a united front against Roosevelt.

The gambit was controversial. One GOP senator, who was not
part of the group and feared that Republicans would lose seats in
the midterm election if they came across as too oppositional, gave
the *New York Times* a document that Bailey had been circulating
within the chamber. Its ten points became known as the "Conservative Manifesto." Here was a distillation of the pro-business constitutionalism that Harding, Coolidge, and Hoover had preached
to the masses a decade earlier. Now it was considered antiquated,
aloof, and suspect.

The manifesto demanded cuts in the capital gains tax, a balanced budget, an end to compulsory union membership, "home
rule and local self-government," a reduction in welfare payments,
and the preservation of "the American system of private enterprise
and initiative, and our American form of government," all words
with contemporary resonance. In language similar to Hoover's, the
manifesto proclaimed that individualism, equality of opportunity,
and limited government did not throw workers to the wolves of
Wall Street but granted them "the priceless content of liberty and
the dignity of man."[29]

After the leak to the *Times*, anti–New Deal media outlets and
business groups publicized the manifesto. It was widely circulated but horribly ineffective. Bailey was unable to convince his

colleagues to sign on. FDR took no heed of it. The New Deal barreled on.

Then, in 1938, a combination of economic slump and residual bad feelings over court packing handed FDR his first electoral setback. Republicans picked up eighty-one seats in the House and gained eight seats in the Senate. While far from a majority, these Republicans allied with anti–New Deal Democrats in the manner Bailey had foreseen. Bipartisan opposition was strong enough to quash the most far-reaching New Deal legislation, but the prospects of reversing FDR's revolution were nil. "Republicans in Congress," wrote one member of the National Committee to Uphold Constitutional Government in 1939, "thus far have made little headway in undermining confidence in the major objectives of the New Deal." Eight decades later, the situation had not changed.[30]

THE CONTOURS OF A POST–NEW DEAL POLITICS WERE APPARENT as FDR approached the end of his second term. On one side there was a majority Democratic Party invested in broadening the welfare state to provide economic security, with a large faction of conservative Democrats opposed for various reasons to different forms of government intervention. On the other side was a minority Republican Party that could not make up its mind whether the New Deal should stay or go. One outcome of the 1938 campaign, however, was that the anti–New Deal faction of the GOP found a leader. His name was Robert Alphonso Taft.

The son of the deceased twenty-seventh president had been raised to uphold the constitutionalist and free market traditions of his party. A graduate of Yale and Harvard Law School, Robert Taft had apprenticed under Herbert Hoover at the American Relief Administration during the final years of the Wilson administration. What he saw amid the rubble of World War I confirmed his anti-European prejudices. For Taft, the Continent was a ruin of nationalism, monarchical squabbles, and class struggle. The United States ought to avoid it.

Taft spent the 1920s rising in Ohio politics. But he was swamped by the Democratic deluge of 1932 and lost his seat in the state senate. Then, from his law firm in Cincinnati, he watched FDR with growing alarm. The growth of state power and its concentration in the executive branch reminded him of the new authoritarian governments in Europe. The New Deal, Taft said in 1935, was "absolutely contrary to the whole American theory on which this country was founded." Taft's philosophy contained all the principles of his father, of Harding, of Coolidge, and of Hoover. "The regulation of wages, hours, and prices and practices in every industry is something which is, in effect, socialism; which is government regulation of the worst sort; which means a totalitarian state," he said in 1938.[31]

By then Taft was on his way to the US Senate. Once he was in Washington, his forceful criticisms of Roosevelt quickly established him as a leading conservative. So identified was he with his party that Taft became known as "Mr. Republican." His constitutional rectitude and budgetary restraint overshadowed a prudential view of politics that led Taft to adopt unexpected positions. He was for relief programs, for example, but thought the states should administer them. He supported an old-age pension but believed it should be financed on a pay-as-you-go basis. He supported the right to strike but abhorred the closed shop and labor violence. He found most offensive Roosevelt's accumulation of decision-making authority and government's advance into areas, such as electric power generation, where it had not gone before.

For Taft, FDR's preparations for war against Germany were the foreign policy equivalent of the New Deal. They deserved opposition as such. Soon after he was sworn into office, Taft warned against mobilizing American armed forces too rapidly. "Our armament program should be based on defending the United States and not defending democracy throughout the world," he said in response to FDR's 1939 State of the Union address, in which the president warned of the rise of Nazism and called for increased defense spending.[32]

In late August 1939, Germany signed a nonaggression treaty with the Soviet Union that alarmed not only governments across Europe but also left-wing intellectuals disgusted by the reality of Communist despotism. Here was Stalin putting the lie to the "antifascism" of the Soviet Union—and preparing to carve up a neighboring country. When Germany invaded Poland on September 1 and partitioned it with the Soviets, Robert Taft remained committed to American neutrality. He was not against spending more on defense—or even aiding the United Kingdom, which had declared war on Germany in support of Poland—so long as the aid did not give Adolf Hitler a reason to declare war on America. Intervention in defense of ideals, he argued, would produce the same mess that had been left at the end of the Great War. "The basic foreign policy of the United States," he said, "should be to preserve peace with other nations, and enter into no treaties which may obligate us to go to war."[33]

In the view of Taft and other noninterventionist conservatives, war would expand government, lead to rationing, and invest FDR with greater authority. "I do not agree that under our Constitution the executive can bring about a state of war without usurpation," Taft wrote to a friend. "He may have the power to get us into war, but he certainly has not the right." The United States should defend the mainland and the Caribbean basin, Taft said, but otherwise it should leave the conflagration in Europe to burn itself out. "Even the collapse of England is to be preferred to participation for the rest of our lives in foreign wars," he wrote in another letter. Taft's priority was the home front. "There is a good deal more danger of the infiltration of totalitarian ideas from the New Deal circle in Washington," he told a Saint Louis audience on May 20, 1940, "than there will ever be from any activities of the communists or the Nazi bund."[34]

Taft hoped that the GOP would nominate him to challenge Roosevelt in 1940 and thwart the president's unprecedented gambit for a third term. In 1936, Taft's ambitions for high office as Ohio's "favorite son" had been something of a lark. Now a US senator, with war raging in Europe and the economy still mired in a funk, Taft believed his opportunity had arrived. He was disappointed. His resistance to intervention on behalf of the Allies was too strident for many in the upper echelons of his own party. There was also the problem of Taft's personality: he didn't have much of one. He was cerebral, cold, and withdrawn. He didn't enjoy shaking hands, chitchatting, or listening to advice. He decided on his own course and stuck to it.

The GOP went with New York–based corporate lawyer Wendell Willkie, a former Democrat who generally favored FDR's approach overseas. Willkie had turned against the New Deal when the Tennessee Valley Authority threatened the private utilities he represented in court. Taft and the conservatives resented the easterners' embrace of a standpatter who more or less agreed with FDR. In conservative eyes, Willkie's nomination was the birth of Republican "me-tooism": the rush of GOP elites to embrace whatever reforms liberal Democrats had come up with. Willkie lost, of course, but he put up better numbers than either Hoover or Landon.

Taft recognized that he lacked some of the personal attributes necessary for presidential success. "I'm afraid you won't find much color in me," he once told a reporter. "I'm too damned normal." He resented the politicians, press lords, and financiers on the East Coast who clamored for intervention and backed Willkie's nomination. He was suspicious of journalists who portrayed him as a dullard and isolationist. "If isolation means isolation from European war," he once said in frustration, "I am an isolationist."[35]

Taft neither joined nor spoke for the antiwar America First Committee, but according to his biographer, he was "quietly encouraging" of it. The organization had been established in 1940 in Chicago. Its founders included graduates of some of the nation's elite educational institutions, and it drew support from Republicans, Democrats, Progressives, conservatives, and even figures within FDR's government. One of the chief organizers was a Yale Law student named Gerald R. Ford. A Harvard student named John F. Kennedy contributed a $100 check. The Buckleys, a wealthy oil family living in Sharon, Connecticut, named one of their sailboats *Sweet Isolation*.[36]

America First wanted four things. First was an "impregnable" national defense. Second was preparedness to thwart an attack on America. Third was neutrality in the war in Europe. Fourth was resistance to providing England "aid short of war." Its demands were like Taft's. But the committee had something that eluded him: widespread appeal.[37]

Its spokesman, Charles Lindbergh, was an aspirational figure whose triumphal (and, after the murder of his child, tragic) story commanded respect. Lindbergh was an icon to noninterventionists in the Midwest but a villain elsewhere. His refusal to condemn the moral depravity of the Nazis polarized audiences. He rubbed shoulders with fascist sympathizers and anti-Semites.[38]

Proud of his service in the US Army, Lindbergh resigned his commission after Roosevelt likened him to a pro-Confederate copperhead Democrat. He drew a moral equivalence between the governments of the United Kingdom and Nazi Germany. He singled out for blame scapegoats who he said agitated for American intervention. He became the symbol of an unfeeling and sinister isolationism.[39]

America First could not escape the stench of Nazism. The committee spent much of its time distancing itself from pro-Nazi groups and figures, including Huey Long's former minion Gerald

L. K. Smith. Violent anti-Semitism was rare in American history, but it seemed to follow in the footsteps of Hitler's defenders. In 1939, Nazi supporters had rallied in Madison Square Garden. When a Jewish reporter rushed the stage, he was beaten senseless.

Lindbergh's infamous speech in Des Moines, Iowa, on September 11, 1941—"Who Are the War Agitators?"—marginalized the antiwar cause and forever associated it with anti-Semitism. Lindbergh singled out "the British, the Jewish, and the Roosevelt administration" as the three groups "who have been pressing this country toward war." His wife had urged him to include a statement of opposition to anti-Semitism, but Lindbergh refused. "I am saying that the leaders of both the British and Jewish races, for reasons which are understandable from their viewpoint as they are inadvisable from ours, for reasons which are not American, wish to involve us in the war," he told the cheering crowd. By defining Jews as "not American," Lindbergh effaced more than a century of American religious toleration.

Some of Lindbergh's allies recognized the danger of his incendiary rhetoric. A Jewish noninterventionist wrote Lindbergh, complaining that the pilot had fueled anti-Semitic conspiracy theories. Socialist leader Norman Thomas, who belonged to America First, told Lindbergh that his speech had done "great harm." Herbert Hoover defended Lindbergh in public but admonished him in private. Lindbergh wrote in his journals, "I told him I felt my statements had been both moderate and true. He replied that when you had been in politics long enough you learned not to say things just because they are true."[40]

The noninterventionists were so busy trying to stop war in Europe that they gave little thought to events in the Pacific. The Imperial Japanese Army had been making territorial gains since its conquest of Manchuria in 1931. The surprise Japanese attack on US naval forces in Pearl Harbor on December 7, 1941, ripped the carpet from under the feet of Robert Taft and the America First

Committee. Lindbergh understood immediately that his cause was lost. "Our country has been attacked by force of arms, and by force of arms we must retaliate," the committee said in a statement released on December 8.

In his diary Lindbergh wrote that if he were in Congress, he would vote to authorize war against Japan. Taft, who was in Congress, voted yes. (Hitler declared war on America on December 11.) America First disbanded soon after the attack. Lindbergh made several attempts to have his army commission reinstated. He was denied.[41]

Yet America First opened up possibilities for a Right that had been marginalized throughout the Roosevelt years. For a time, foreign policy emerged as one area where the noninterventionist Right was on the same wavelength as a considerable segment of the population. Whereas social and economic criticisms of the New Deal had little effect on policy outcomes, the congressional and public attacks on FDR's prewar diplomacy had much greater force. They limited the president's ability to aid Great Britain and, after June 1941, the Soviet Union. They hampered his domestic preparations for conflict. And though Pearl Harbor rendered the campaign for neutrality moot, conservatives stumbled upon a grassroots constituency for an anti-FDR, anti-interventionist politics.

This durable isolationist strain in the electorate was not large enough for the Right to surmount the appeal of Roosevelt and the popularity of the war effort. To succeed, the Right would have to harmonize its nationalist sentiments and appeals with a public that accepted the necessity of overseas military engagements. It would have to join forces with the anti-Communist or ex-Communist Left whose antipathy for tyranny was as strong as its own. The rise of Soviet power in the aftermath of the war would give it the opportunity to do so.

CHAPTER THREE

FROM WORLD WAR
TO COLD WAR

WORLD WAR II ENDED THE GREAT DEPRESSION. IT TRANS-formed the American economy, created demands for equality for women and blacks, and handed an empire to a most reluctant colossus. The war boosted the GOP's popularity as both conservatism and the nation underwent radical shifts. The Right adopted a new ground for its arguments against government regulation and taxation. It coalesced around opposition to Communist subversion at home and Soviet expansion abroad. Meanwhile, an antitotalitarian Left supported policies to counteract Communist influence in the labor movement and intellectual life. By the beginning of the Cold War era, the constituent parts of the conservative movement had moved into place.

Ironically, as the US government assumed incredible new powers during the war, it also rolled back many elements of the New Deal. Some agencies were no longer relevant because the war brought full employment. Some were lost in the shuffle of bureaucratic reorganization. Some were hacked to pieces by an energetic political opposition. In 1942 the Republicans gained forty-seven

House seats and seven Senate seats. *Fortune* magazine dubbed the victors "normalcy men."

Isolationists paid no price for opposing intervention before Pearl Harbor. One scholar identified 115 isolationist candidates headed into the 1942 midterm elections; only 5 lost. By the last year of the war, Republicans had won a net twenty-one seats in the House and fifteen in the Senate. And the Right had new heroes: Generals Douglas MacArthur, who commanded US forces in the Southwest Pacific; George S. Patton, who led troops in the Mediterranean and European campaigns; and Curtis LeMay, who organized the strategic bombing of Japan.[1]

The populism of Father Charles Coughlin came to a halt. The Detroit priest had become more authoritarian in the run-up to war. In March 1938, he said he favored a "corporate state for America" where interest groups as well as geographic sectors would have representation in the legislature. A few months later, his newsletter published the anti-Semitic conspiracies of the *Protocols of the Elders of Zion*. Beginning in 1939, he blamed the war on the Jews and lobbied against intervention. Pearl Harbor ended his movement just as it extinguished America First. Radio networks ended their contracts with Coughlin. The US Postal Service labeled *Social Justice*, his periodical, as seditious. In May 1942 the archbishop of Detroit ordered Coughlin to cease his rabble-rousing. Coughlin obeyed, and his following dissipated.

The war also fulfilled some of Robert Taft's gloomy predictions. The empowered federal government marshaled tremendous resources and, in cooperation with corporate America, produced the technology and matériel that drowned the Axis. But the same government, under a Democratic president, also rounded up more than one hundred thousand of its own citizens—Japanese American men, women, and children—and forced them to relocate to camps far from their homes for no reason other than their ethnicity. There was little protest. Columnist Westbrook Pegler, a right-wing populist who loathed Franklin D. Roosevelt, nonetheless cheered the president's executive order on relocation, writing, "The Japanese in California should be under armed guard to the last man and woman right now, and to hell with habeas corpus until the danger is over."[2]

The experience of the Nisei, or second-generation Japanese Americans, was a rallying cry for libertarians. The *Santa Ana Register*—which later became the *Orange County Register*—reprinted an article condemning the treatment of the Japanese as a violation of liberty. Black writers were understandably sensitive to the harsh treatment of fellow minorities. Black conservative journalist George Schuyler wrote that the denial of equal rights to the Nisei might result in their being stripped of citizenship and sent back to Japan. Once that precedent was set, Schuyler warned, a similar fate could befall other disfavored groups, especially black Americans. At the same time, H. L. Mencken argued for lifting Roosevelt's restrictions on Jewish refugees seeking asylum.[3]

Even so, Mencken and Albert Jay Nock opposed this world war like they had the last one. Aging and pessimistic, the two authors retreated into autobiography. They attempted to set down in print the world in which they matured—a vanished landscape of distinct individuals, high culture, classical education, free enterprise, and limited government. Mencken released his three-volume memoir between 1940 and 1943. The title of Nock's autobiography, *Memoirs of a Superfluous Man*, revealed the nature of his relationship with his times. For Nock, the war did not vindicate American democracy. It proved America's unworthiness.[4]

Published in 1943, the *Memoirs* found its way into the hands of servicemen equally skeptical of FDR and the arsenal of democracy. A twenty-five-year-old soldier stationed in Utah named Russell Kirk wrote Nock a fan letter after finishing the book. A thirty-year-old professor of sociology at Berkeley named Robert Nisbet said that he "practically memorized" the *Memoirs* while serving in the South Pacific. Readers such as Kirk and Nisbet responded deeply to Nock because he represented a human type that no longer existed amid strategic bombing, million-man armies, concentration camps, and centralized planning.[5]

As the war neared its end, there was a growing rejection of state interference in the economy. In 1944 a pair of America Firsters, Frank Hanighen and Felix Morley, founded *Human Events*, a free market, antiwar weekly newsletter inspired by Albert Jay Nock's *Freeman*. *Human Events* carried on the anti-Roosevelt tradition of denying any difference between American liberalism and European totalitarianism. The next year the duo became a trio when an Illinois businessman named Henry Regnery joined the enterprise.

FDR's opponents got an assist from overseas. When the war began in 1939, the London School of Economics had moved its operations to Cambridge, where Friedrich Hayek lived with his family from 1940 to 1945. He decided to expand on an argument he had made in an essay titled "Freedom and the Economic System." Writing in English, which he felt (not quite accurately) that he had mastered, Hayek dedicated his new book "to the Socialists of all Parties." In 1944 it was published in England as *The Road to Serfdom*.[6]

Hayek wrote that Germany had abandoned the true liberalism of the nineteenth century for national socialism and that England was in danger of abandoning liberalism for socialism as well. Hayek was not against economic planning per se. Rather, he opposed "planning against competition." This was Hayek's phrase for the central direction of social and economic activity according to a rationally constructed blueprint. Such planning, he wrote, eroded the foundations of both democracy and the "rule of law" because economic and political liberty are intertwined. Allowing individuals the space to determine their own ends is the essence, Hayek said, of the philosophy of individualism. And individuals deserved such a sphere of autonomy because of the radical ignorance that is a fact of human existence.[7]

Hayek was no anarchist. He saw a role for the state and for minimal, simple, and transparent government regulations. Some provision of welfare did not violate his principles "so long as the organization of these services [was] not designed in such a way as to make competition ineffective over wide fields." Hayek understood that collective social action was often undertaken with the best of intentions. But humanitarian schemes of reform deserved a higher level of skepticism precisely because they held such emotional appeal. Hayek opposed the widespread trends toward bureaucratic centralization, nationalization of industry, and comprehensive government control of wages and prices.[8]

Hayek's critics did not acknowledge the nuances of his argument. They were instead preoccupied with his idea that the New Deal and the incipient British welfare state were the first steps toward tyranny. Not one but two book-length denunciations of Hayek were published in the United Kingdom. He was denounced as a defender of privilege and an advocate of the status quo. In fact, he had written the precise opposite.[9]

Hayek's popularizers tended to neglect his caveats and exceptions. In 1945 a cartoon version of his book was published by General Motors and reprinted in *Look* magazine. The same year, former Trotskyist Max Eastman commissioned an abridgment of *The Road to Serfdom* for *Reader's Digest* that was distributed in the United States through the Book-of-the-Month Club. It became a sensation.

One of *The Road to Serfdom*'s most positive reviews appeared in, of all places, the Communist *New Masses*, where a party organizer in his midthirties named Frank Meyer admitted that Hayek's arguments had merit. Encountering Hayek's polemic set Meyer on the path away from communism and socialism. In the meantime, Philadelphia-born financial journalist Henry Hazlitt wrote a rave front-page notice in the *New York Times Book Review* that contributed to *The Road to Serfdom*'s best seller status. Hazlitt was not the most objective reader. He had been converted to Austrian economics by Ludwig von Mises years before *The Road to Serfdom* was published. Mises's widow recalled that when her husband first called Hazlitt on the telephone, the young man reacted as if John Stuart Mill himself were on the line. In 1946 Hazlitt distilled the Austrian teaching into a short book of his own. *Economics in One Lesson* sold more than a million copies in the subsequent decades.[10]

In March 1945 Hayek arrived in New York to begin his book tour. His publishers told him that his speaking engagements would send him as far west as Oklahoma City. His first appearance, however, was scheduled for the next morning at town hall in Manhattan. Hayek was mortified. He had never lectured in public. The audience had been told he would speak for an hour on law and international affairs. It was a subject to which he had given little thought. "And then I discovered that American audiences are extremely grateful audiences," Hayek recollected. "You can watch on their faces their interest—completely different from, say, an English audience; and gradually I worked them up into great excitement, and I got through this lecture with great success." When he returned to England in May, Hayek was an academic celebrity.[11]

Yet he was no less concerned by the intellectual trends pushing liberal democracies toward socialism. When the war ended in 1945, Hayek tried to jump-start a conversation in which he had participated before the German invasion of Poland. In August 1938, he and Mises had hosted the prominent American journalist Walter Lippmann in Paris to celebrate the French edition of Lippmann's *The Good Society* (it had come out in English the previous year). At that time, Lippmann had abandoned his youthful relativism and sought a foundation for democracy in natural law. For five days, some two dozen economists and philosophers from across Europe debated the strengths and weaknesses of classical liberalism. The participants referred to the gathering as the Walter Lippmann Colloquium.[12]

Seven years later, Hayek began building an institution dedicated to the promotion of individualism. In December 1946 he wrote to Austrian philosopher Karl Popper and suggested that the new group be called the Acton-Tocqueville Society after British historian John Dalberg-Acton and French aristocrat and philosopher Alexis de Tocqueville. These two nineteenth-century Catholic liberals, Hayek said, ought to be the "agreed foundation from which such a common effort may start."[13]

Hayek wanted to establish a global network of classical liberals. He turned to the Volker Fund for help. Swiss economist Albert Hunold raised additional monies for a separate project that was folded into Hayek's. Hayek also decided, against Mises's objections, that the group should be open to a wide range of members. Its first meeting would be held in Mont Pèlerin, Switzerland.

When the conference opened on April 1, 1947, about three dozen economists, historians, philosophers, and journalists were present. They included some of the attendees of the Walter Lippmann Colloquium a decade before, representatives from the Foundation for Economic Education, Felix Morley of *Human Events*, Frank Knight of the University of Chicago, and several of Knight's students, including George Stigler, Aaron Director, and Director's brother-in-law, Milton Friedman.

Hayek delivered the opening remarks. "The basic conviction which has guided me in my efforts," he said, "is that, if the ideals which I believe unite us, and for which, in spite of so much abuse of the term, there is still no better name than liberal, are to have any chance of revival, a great intellectual task must be performed." First it was necessary to "purge" liberalism of "certain accidental accretions which have become attached to it in the course of time." Then liberals could face up to "some real problems which an over-simplified liberalism has shirked or which have become apparent only since it has turned into a somewhat stationary and rigid creed."[14]

On April 10 the conference adopted a "Statement of Aims." It left no doubt that these beleaguered liberals felt themselves engaged on the losing side in a battle of ideas that had been raging for more than a century. "Over large stretches of the earth's surface the essential conditions of human dignity and freedom have already disappeared," the statement began. "The position of the individual and the voluntary group are progressively undermined by extensions of arbitrary power." Together the participants resolved to study, among other things, "the problem of the creation of an international order conducive to the safeguarding of peace and liberty and permitting the establishment of harmonious international economic relations." At this point, however, the group still hadn't settled on a name. The debate grew so intense that one economist suggested they just refer to themselves by the location of the meeting. No one had a better solution, so the Mont Pèlerin Society was born.[15]

Hayek articulated his overall strategy in a 1949 essay in the *Chicago Law Review* titled "The Intellectuals and Socialism." Ideas drive history, Hayek believed, and thus intellectuals, "professional secondhand dealers in ideas," were far more important than most people assumed. "In every country that has moved towards socialism," he wrote, "the phase of the development in which socialism becomes a determining influence on politics has been preceded for many years by a period during which socialist ideals governed the thinking of the more active intellectuals." It was ironic, he said, that "parties of the Left" so often interpreted public affairs as a clash of economic interests, despite the overwhelming influence that ideas exercise over the climate of opinion.[16]

To revive liberalism, Hayek wrote, it was necessary to inspire the secondhand dealers of ideas. His approach was elite driven. A change in the ideological perception, and then in political reality, would come about only after enough intellectuals became convinced of the liberal ideal. In 1950 the Volker Fund sponsored Hayek's appointment to the Committee on Social Thought at the University of Chicago. For the next decade, America would become his base of operations.[17]

The death of FDR on April 12, 1945—a few weeks before victory in Europe and a few months before victory over Japan—brought the New Deal era to its conclusion. The American Right's wiliest domestic adversary had left the stage. The electorate was eager to pursue a new direction. In the 1946 midterm elections, the GOP ran on the slogan "Had Enough?"

The answer was yes. Republicans took control of Congress for the first time since 1928. In an acknowledgment of the Republican upsurge, President Harry Truman appointed Herbert Hoover to chair a commission on government reorganization. On Capitol Hill, Robert Taft found himself chairing committees. Mr. Republican devoted himself to his namesake legislation: the Taft-Hartley Act made major revisions to the New Deal–era Wagner Act, outlawing the closed shop and allowing states to pass right-to-work laws.

The postwar years gave Taft an opportunity to promote his idiosyncratic views. Rather than massively redistribute income and tightly regulate the economy to equalize outcomes, he wanted the government to guarantee a minimum standard of benefits for men and women unable to work. To move beyond this minimal welfare state, Taft said, would result in "creeping socialism" of the sort that Hayek had analyzed in *The Road to Serfdom*.

Republicans eager to concentrate on domestic policy discovered that the world had other plans. The Soviet Union emerged from World War II far more powerful than when the conflict began. Having defeated Nazi Germany on the eastern front, the Soviet Union extended its rule over the Baltic and Balkan states, half of Germany and Berlin, and most of eastern Europe. The world was a different place in 1945 than it had been in 1920. Aircraft carriers, air forces, ballistic missiles, and atomic weapons had reshaped the strategic landscape in ways that left America vulnerable. Communism, which in 1920 had been weak and restricted to an autarkic Russia in the middle of a civil war, was now a strong worldwide movement. World War II had come close to ending civilization. A third world war involving nuclear weaponry might finish it off.

The postwar years witnessed multiple setbacks and defeats to the cause of liberal democracy. The Western Allies had vanquished Nazi totalitarianism in the war but now confronted Soviet totalitarianism across the breadth of Europe. American officials scrambled to respond as Communist parties under the direct control of Moscow grew in western Europe and in the rapidly shrinking dominions of the British Empire.

Communist rebellions broke out across the globe. The full-scale demobilization that had followed America's previous wars did not occur. America was being reorganized, with institutions reformed or created; in preparation for a protracted conflict against communism waged across the globe in the air, on sea and land, and in space. This permanent war footing to avert a potential nuclear exchange between the two superpowers transformed American government, economy, and society. It changed both the American Right and the American Left in ways that would give rise to the postwar conservative movement.

Beginning in 1947, President Truman created multiple institutions and programs to preserve freedom in Europe by creating "situations of strength" and "counterforce" that would contain communism. Broadly popular, Truman's policies encountered opposition only from the pro-Soviet Left and the isolationist Right. The experience of World War II had changed the minds of some noninterventionist Republicans, including Michigan senator Arthur Vandenberg, who became chairman of the Foreign Relations

Committee in 1947 and recognized the importance of alliances, mobilization, and overseas deployments to contain the Communist menace. A bipartisan consensus formed around the Truman Doctrine, which the president announced on March 12, 1947. "It must be the policy of the United States," Truman told Congress, "to support free peoples who are resisting attempted subjugation by armed minorities or by outside pressures."

Truman aided the governments of Greece and Turkey in their fights against Communists. He authorized the Marshall Plan of reconstruction funds for western Europe. He signed into law the Selective Service Act providing for a peacetime military draft. He engineered the National Security Act of 1947, which created the modern defense and intelligence apparatus. He committed the United States to the United Nations—replacing the ineffective League of Nations, which America had not joined.

In 1948 Truman recognized the Jewish State of Israel against the advice of his own State Department, which feared destabilizing the Middle East. In 1949 he signed the North Atlantic Treaty, a mutual-defense pact with western European nations that established the North Atlantic Treaty Organization (NATO) alliance. These moves defined a foreign policy consensus of American anticommunism—called "containment"—that lasted for years until it was undermined by Joseph McCarthy, the assassination of John F. Kennedy, and the Vietnam War.

Taft was a lone voice in opposition to Truman. NATO, for example, was exactly the sort of permanent entanglement in European affairs that Taft had dreaded ever since his experiences with Hoover after World War I. He argued that NATO would make American foreign policy not less but more venturesome. "It is easy to slip into an attitude of imperialism," he said, "where war becomes an instrument of public policy rather than its last resort." He was among thirteen senators to oppose NATO when the treaty came to a vote in 1949.

Other Republicans agreed with Truman that the alliance system, foreign aid, and forward positioning of American forces secured liberty by upholding a structure of freedom and providing the nation with strategic depth. "My friend from Ohio has given me a first class headache tonight," Senator Vandenberg said one evening after Taft delivered a broadside against the North Atlantic Treaty.[18]

Taft's no on NATO demonstrated how far his foreign policy was from the mainstream. A year before the treaty vote, he had lost the GOP presidential nomination to Thomas Dewey for the second time. The youthful and debonair Dewey, elected governor of New York in 1942, inherited the mantle of eastern, establishment, internationalist Republicanism from Wendell Willkie, who had withdrawn from politics on account of illness before his death in October 1944. If Willkie's and Dewey's nominations confirmed that Republican powerbrokers no longer thought the public philosophy of Warren Harding, Calvin Coolidge, Herbert Hoover, Alf Landon, and Robert Taft could win the presidency, Dewey's surprise loss in the general election of 1948 was also a reminder of the limits of me-tooism. The GOP nominees who believed in foreign policy internationalism and a go-slow approach to domestic reform seemed to be competitive with the architects of FDR's New Deal and Truman's Fair Deal. But they also came up short—perhaps because they did not excite more conservative voters.

Truman had weaknesses of his own in 1948. His party divided over both its approach to the Soviet Union and its handling of race relations. Former vice president Henry Wallace ran on the Progressive Party ticket, and South Carolina governor Strom Thurmond led the State's Rights, or Dixiecrat, Party. Truman rolled over them both, though Thurmond did capture four southern states.

As fears of Communist subversion grew, the American Right began to feel in sync with majority American opinion. The touchstone of this connection was anticommunism. The postwar era was notable for the migration of ex-Communist intellectuals into the ranks of the American Right. These writers brought a missionary zeal to the crusade against the Soviet Union even as they maintained some of the habits of thought and argument that they had picked up during party debates. They gave national security priority over domestic policy and shaped the Right's thinking on foreign intervention. They privileged the ideological over the economic, and they saw the Cold War fundamentally as a contest of willpower. The anticommunism of these former radicals injected the Right with intellectual seriousness and political purpose.

There were plenty of reasons to oppose communism. For one thing, it didn't work, which Mises had pointed out back in the 1920s. It was also "godless" and materialist. Communist governments suppressed political and religious freedom. Moreover, communism was a national security threat to America's allies as well as to the American homeland. Anticommunism provided a shelter where free marketers, traditionalists, foreign policy realists, and Cold Warriors united to oppose Communist activities and bureaucratic centralization. Eventually all these groups would find themselves on the side of the GOP.

The ex-Communist with the most important influence on the postwar right was James Burnham. Born in Chicago in 1905 and educated at Princeton and Oxford, he had joined Leon Trotsky's Fourth International in 1934. In April 1940 he and a few comrades split from the Socialist Workers Party and formed the Workers Party. Trotsky, one of Burnham's political heroes since he had first read *The History of the Russian Revolution*, castigated him for denying the "science" of dialectical materialism. This dispute with his idol scarred Burnham. It led him to reconsider his already unorthodox brand of Marxism. He found that he could no longer identify as a Marxist.[19]

Yet Burnham did not book a one-way ticket to Ludwig von Mises's seminar in laissez-faire. "Having come to know something of the gigantic ideology of Bolshevism," he wrote later, "I knew that I was not going to be able to settle for the pigmy ideologies of Liberalism, social democracy, refurbished laissez-faire, or the inverted, cut-rate Bolshevism called 'fascism.'" Instead, Burnham contended that neither capitalism nor socialism would win the future because both systems were defunct. They had been replaced by managerialism.[20]

Burnham had been convinced by the work of Adolf Berle, a Communist fellow traveler who held a position in FDR's State Department, and Harvard economist Gardiner Means, who together analyzed the separation of ownership in joint-stock corporations from actual control of enterprises. He combined their insights with the thought of Italian Trotskyist Bruno Rizzi, who argued that Stalinism and Nazism were similar because both systems governed through bureaucracy and administrative diktat. In the managerial society, decisions were made not by voters (owners) but by bureaucrats (managers).

In 1941 Burnham explained his theory in *The Managerial Revolution*. The revolution was global. Elements of the transition to managerialism were present in every society, no matter the ideology professed by ruling elites. Nazi Germany, the Soviet Union, and even the New Deal United States were under managerial rule. "'Laws' today in the United States, in fact most laws, are not being made any longer by Congress," Burnham wrote, "but by the NLRB, SEC, ICC, AAA, TVA, FTC, FCC, the Office of Production Management (what a revealing title!), and the other leading 'executive agencies.'"[21]

Majorities had no power. Managers co-opted, manipulated, or vetoed them. Elites operated autonomously from the public. Burnham's approach to politics avoided abstractions and airy generalizations. He was concerned with facts, circumstances, and above all relations of power that enabled him, he said, to predict the course of events. He was drawn to the works of Italian sociologists

Gaetano Mosca, Robert Michels, and Vilfredo Pareto because they abjured ideology. He called his new intellectual models the Machiavellians.

His book of that title appeared in 1943. The Machiavellians were antiutopian and anti-illusion, but Burnham was not without values. Human beings were owed at least some dignity and freedom, he believed. "There is a responsibility," he wrote many years later, "to encourage others to promote those elements in society during this transition [to managerial rule] that promise at least the minimum of liberty and justice that distinguish human society from a merely animal existence." Liberty and justice were secured through what Burnham, following Mosca, called "juridical defense." The fundamental right was the right to oppose. And the right to oppose was protected only by the dispersion and diffusion of countervailing economic, social, and governmental power.[22]

The grandeur of Burnham's vision, the clarity of his expression, the force of his argument, and the iciness of his prose were overpowering. *The Managerial Revolution* became a best seller. Still a radical, Burnham joined the advisory board of the anti-Stalinist *Partisan Review*, where, in his 1945 essay "Lenin's Heir," he argued that Joseph Stalin's totalitarianism was not an aberration but the terminus of Marxism-Leninism. "Stalin is communism."

Burnham became one of America's most famous writers on foreign affairs. In 1947 he published *The Struggle for the World*, in which he declared that America was engaged in World War III whether it liked it or not. "You can get along with communism in only one way: by capitulating to it," he wrote. The historical situation required America to exercise global leadership. Burnham worried that the United States lacked the will to fight. Victory did not depend on weapons. It was a function of spirit. "All history makes clear that an indispensable quality of any man or class that wishes to lead, to hold power and privilege in society, is boundless self-confidence," he said in *The Managerial Revolution*. And the most blatant sign of confidence and strength was the willingness to use force.[23]

The Struggle for the World was published around the time that President Truman announced his foreign policy doctrine. It expressed many of the arguments of both conservative and liberal anti-Communists. And it won Burnham additional renown and acclaim. He lectured at the National War College, the Air War College, the Naval War College, and the Johns Hopkins School of Advanced International Studies. He served as a trustee of the "Free Europe University in Exile" for expatriate anti-Communists. And he consulted for the Central Intelligence Agency. Burnham's ideas found a receptive audience in Washington, DC, among both Democrats and Republicans.

In March 1947, President Truman created a loyalty program to weed Communists out of the federal bureaucracy. That same year the House of Representatives' standing Committee on Un-American Activities held hearings on Communists in Hollywood. Among the witnesses was Screen Actors Guild president Ronald Reagan, who had clashed with Communists attempting to influence his union. "Ronnie classifies himself as a liberal politically," Hollywood gossip columnist Hedda Hopper wrote after his testimony. "He is opposed to all forces that seek to curb or destroy individual liberty. 'Our highest aim,' said he, 'should be the cultivation of freedom of the individual, for therein lies the highest dignity of man. Tyranny is tyranny, and whether it comes from right, left, or center, it's evil.'"[24]

Though Reagan was by no means a typical labor boss, his anticommunism was not unusual. Through the efforts of ex–Communist Party members such as James Cannon and Max Shachtman of the anti-Soviet Socialist Workers Party, as well as the American Federation of Labor's George Meany, Jay Lovestone, and Lane Kirkland, America's union leadership had been insulated from Communist interference. These radicals and liberals opposed communism precisely because Soviet-style regimes outlawed independent unions and the right to strike. Their background in radical politics and commitment to liberal values of freedom and equality gave them a native understanding of communism that the Right did not possess.

For example, Reagan told Hopper that he opposed efforts to outlaw the Communist Party USA and said he recognized that many of the people drawn to communism had humanitarian sympathies and aims. "You can't blame a man for aligning himself with an institution he thinks is humanitarian," he said. "But you can blame him if he deliberately remains with it after he knows it's fallen into the hands of the Reds."[25]

Soon a witness appeared before the committee who was neither as famous nor as telegenic as Reagan. Whittaker Chambers had been born in Philadelphia in 1901 to a family addled by mental illness. He was a haunted soul. He had read *Crime and Punishment* at the age of eleven, and Fyodor Dostoyevsky's influence on him was profound. He began adulthood as Ivan, the rebellious, atheistic son in Dostoyevsky's epic *The Brothers Karamazov*. He ended it as Alyosha, Ivan's pious sibling.[26]

Chambers attended Columbia University from 1921 to 1924. There he met literary critic Lionel Trilling, who became the first tenured Jewish professor in the Columbia English Department and whose 1947 novel, *The Middle of the Journey*, is based on his friendship with Chambers. During his student days Chambers fell in with Communist circles and joined the party. He became a passionate revolutionary. He trained to spy for the Soviet Union and was sent to Washington to courier information from a network of Soviet spies within the Roosevelt administration.

Sometime in the late 1930s, however, Chambers had an epiphany. He was watching his baby daughter eat in his family's Baltimore apartment. "My eye came to rest on the delicate convolutions of her ear—those intricate, perfect ears," he wrote. "The thought passed through my mind: 'No, those ears were not created by any chance coming together of atoms in nature (the Communist view). They would have been created only by immense design.'" And "Design presupposes God." And if God existed, then the materialistic doctrines of Marxism-Leninism were false.[27]

Chambers began to doubt communism. In 1938 he severed his connection with the party, just as other disillusioned Marxists such as Lovestone, Cannon, Shachtman, Eastman, and Burnham had done. For a year he hid from his former comrades and from Soviet agents. Then he joined *Time* magazine. He ascended to the position of books editor. He was a brilliant journalist with a newfound sense of mission. From his perch at *Time*, Chambers promoted anti-Communist writers and tradition-minded philosophers. One faith—Christianity—replaced another.

In September 1939 Chambers informed Adolf Berle, the fellow-traveling State Department lawyer whose writing had influenced James Burnham, that during his time as a Soviet agent he had worked with Alger Hiss, another State Department lawyer and scion of Baltimore patricians. But Chambers was ignored. Then, almost a decade later, on August 3, 1948, Chambers repeated the accusation in a public hearing of the House Un-American Activities Committee. This time the allegation could not be dismissed. Hiss—who had advised FDR during the infamous Yalta Conference with Joseph Stalin, at which the president acquiesced to Soviet dominion over eastern Europe—appeared before the committee two days later. He denied not only being a spy but also ever knowing Whittaker Chambers. He sued Chambers for libel. And Chambers countersued.

Chambers and Hiss could not have been more unalike. Chambers was disheveled, rumpled, squat, tormented, bohemian, given to drink and depression, and conflicted about his sexuality, his loyalties, and his allegiances. Hiss was elegant, eloquent, dapper, composed, connected, and established. Chambers was born to suffer. Hiss was made to excel.

And Richard Nixon saw an opportunity. The ambitious lawyer and navy veteran of World War II had been elected to the House from California in 1946. He used his position on the committee to pursue the charge of Hiss's treason. Nixon cleverly maneuvered Hiss into admitting that he had lied when he said that he didn't know Chambers. Nixon's questioning turned the bulky, hesitant, shy Chambers into a sympathetic witness. In December 1948, Nixon told the grand jury investigating Hiss that Chambers had hidden microfiche confirming Hiss's identity as a spy in a pumpkin patch on his property in Westminster, Maryland. These "Pumpkin Papers" corroborated Chambers's testimony. But a myth grew up around them: the papers had been hidden in the patch only for a short while, not since Chambers had been a spy.[28]

The press sensationalized the duel between Chambers and Hiss. It was said that the case put a "generation on trial"—the generation of liberals and radicals who, in the 1930s, believed that Communists were not a bother at home and that the Soviet Union could be a force for peace abroad. Implicitly on the stand alongside Hiss were New Dealers the Right blamed for Soviet gains, such as Adolf Berle and treasury official Harry Dexter White. These stalwarts had not abandoned communism or sympathy for the Soviets even as an earlier generation of radicals had moved to the right because of Stalin's persecution of Trotsky, murderous purges, and show trials.

Hiss's perjury trial embarrassed such figures. Hiss was found guilty on January 21, 1950, and sentenced to five years in prison. (He was released after three years and eight months.) When the verdict was announced, Herbert Hoover sent Nixon a telegram saying, "At last the stream of treason that has existed in our government has been exposed in a fashion all may believe."[29]

Chambers was not so sure. One of the lessons he took from his ordeal was sociological. He said that the trial had exposed "the jagged fissure" between the "plain men and women of the nation, and those who affect to act, think, and speak for them." The social gulf between the patrician Hiss and the outsider Chambers was visible in reactions to the verdict. President Truman called the case "a red herring." Secretary of State Dean Acheson said after the conviction, "I do not want to turn my back on Alger Hiss." Many progressives professed Hiss's innocence as an article of faith until the 1990s, when decrypts of intercepted Soviet communications demonstrated the truth of Chambers's claim.[30]

Chambers was a pessimist. He thought that when he turned against communism, he joined the losing side. His penchant for self-dramatization may have distracted from his argument that only religious commitment or its secular equivalent drove men and women to make the ultimate sacrifice. "Communists are that part of mankind which has recovered the power to live or die—to bear witness—for its faith," he wrote. "And it is a simple, rational faith that inspires men to live or die for it. It is not new. It is, in fact, man's second oldest faith. It is the vision of man's mind displacing God as the creative intelligence of the world." With stakes this high, anti-Communists were prepared to make great sacrifices. And some were willing to support even the most unscrupulous of leaders.[31]

THE BACKDROP OF THE HISS SCANDAL WAS AMERICA'S DETERIO-rating security posture. In October 1948 financier Bernard Baruch, who had advised Democratic presidents since the Woodrow Wilson era, told Congress, "We are in the midst of a Cold War which is getting warmer." In late September 1949, President Truman informed the press that the United States possessed evidence that the Soviet Union had tested a nuclear device. Before two weeks had passed, Mao Tse-tung announced the formation of the

People's Republic of China. Generalissimo Chiang Kai-shek and his Nationalist army fled to the island redoubt of Taiwan.

At the same time, insurgents backed by North Korean dictator Kim Il-sung waged war against the non-Communist South Korean government of Syngman Rhee. It was not clear, however, that the Truman policy of "containment" of communism applied to the Korean Peninsula. Secretary of State Dean Acheson had said in January 1950 that he did not consider Korea to be within the US security perimeter. His remark would have grave consequences.

On February 9, 1950—not long after the Hiss verdict—the freshman Republican senator from Wisconsin, Joseph R. McCarthy, traveled to Wheeling, West Virginia, for a speech to the local Republican Women's Club. In some ways, McCarthy exemplified the American dream of a career open to talent and drive. The fifth of seven children, he had been born in 1908 to a poor, anti-Roosevelt farm family living in Grand Chute, Wisconsin. He went to Marquette University for his bachelor's and law degrees. After admittance to the bar, he served as a district judge. When World War II broke out, he joined the marines and was sent to the Pacific, where he became an intelligence officer for a bombing squadron, accompanied a dozen bombing runs, and acquired the nickname "Tailgunner Joe." McCarthy returned to Wisconsin after the war, took back his seat on the court, and entered the Republican Senate primary in 1946. He won. Then, in the general election, caught up in the postwar Republican wave, he defeated Democrat Howard McMurray.

McCarthy's first years in the Senate were uneventful. He supported NATO accession and did not record a vote on funding for the Marshall Plan. He must have grown tired of anonymity. He told the ladies in West Virginia, "While I cannot take the time to name all the men in the State Department who have been named as active members of the Communist party and members of a spy ring, I have here in my hand a list of 205—a list of names that were made known to the Secretary of State [Dean Acheson] as being members of the Communist Party and who nevertheless are still working and shaping policy in the State Department."[32]

McCarthy's math was incorrect. He based his figure on a letter from the secretary of state to Congress that said 285 "security risks" had been identified within the department, 79 of which had been dismissed. That left 206 risks, which McCarthy garbled into 205. He made matters still more confusing when he entered his speech into the congressional record and replaced the number 205 with 57 for no discernible reason other than perhaps a lack of confidence.[33]

Such dishonesty was characteristic of McCarthy. To his supporters, the specific content of his accusations mattered less than the general sense that a government infiltrated by subversives had failed to stop communism. The subsequent outbreak of war in Korea in June 1950 and the arrests of Julius and Ethel Rosenberg in July and August for espionage and treason on behalf of the Soviet Union created an environment in which McCarthy's accusations held tremendous power.

As had happened with the Hiss case, McCarthy's charge that the government continued to harbor Communist agents reversed the symbolic position of figures such as President Truman. "Give 'Em Hell Harry" was supposed to be the tribune of the people. He had presided over internal security measures designed to remove Communists from official positions. He had launched manifold alliances and endeavors to thwart the Red menace. But McCarthy turned Truman into the protector of a corrupt establishment. McCarthy redirected the rhetoric of populism, which typically blamed Jews or Catholics or bankers for the country's problems, toward the hidden Communists in America and their liberal Democratic protectors. And he did so without regard for the procedural norms that institutionalists such as Taft held dear.

McCarthy's celebrity grew. He did not wither under criticism. He doubled down. As his accusations multiplied, they became more outrageous, more galling, and more disconnected from reality. No part of the American government, including the military, was immune from charges of aiding, abetting, or participating in the Communist conspiracy. His Republican colleagues disliked him personally but were happy to indulge his destructive fantasies so long as Democrats were the target. "The pro-Communist policies of the State Department fully justified Joe McCarthy in his demand for an investigation," said Robert Taft. Another conservative senator, John Bricker of Ohio, told McCarthy, "There are times when you've got to have a son of a bitch around, and this is one of them."[34]

One of the few Republican dissenters was a first-term senator from Maine named Margaret Chase Smith. She delivered her "Declaration of Conscience" speech only a few months after McCarthy's diatribe in Wheeling. McCarthy sat in silence as Chase Smith extolled "the basic principles of Americanism": the rights to criticize, to have unpopular beliefs, to protest, and to think independently. She persuaded half a dozen of her colleagues to sign a statement of principles. Part of the statement read, "Certain elements of the Republican Party have materially added to this confusion in the hopes of riding the Republican Party to victory through the selfish political exploitation of fear, bigotry, ignorance, and intolerance."[35]

Her words fell on deaf ears. McCarthy derided Chase Smith and her colleagues as "Snow White and the Six Dwarfs." He was a political steamroller. He crushed most everyone in his path. When, in July 1950, Democratic senator Joseph Tydings of Maryland issued a report saying that McCarthy's charges had no basis in fact, McCarthy made sure to play a part in Tydings's defeat that November. Setbacks for US forces and dissension in the ranks in Korea empowered him further.

It had been assumed that Douglas MacArthur's audacious landing at Inchon in September 1950 would lead to North Korea's swift defeat. However, when MacArthur's forces approached the Yalu River separating North Korea from the People's Republic of China, the Communist Chinese launched a massive invasion of the peninsula. By April 1951, the Americans were fighting a war of attrition. The president was desperate for an exit strategy. Disturbed by news that the Truman administration might pursue peace talks, congressional Republicans leaked correspondence from General MacArthur, who had written that an American defeat on the peninsula could trigger a Soviet invasion of western Europe. Truman removed him from command on April 11.

A crisis in civil-military relations ensued. The general returned home to uproarious crowds. To his fans, MacArthur symbolized the resolute fighting spirit that Truman and the other liberals who "lost China" to communism had betrayed. He addressed a joint session of Congress on April 19. In an unprecedented display, MacArthur acquitted himself of blame for the status of the war. He scolded Truman for not unleashing Chiang Kai-shek and opening a second front against the Communists on the Chinese mainland. "It has been said, in effect, that I was a warmonger," MacArthur told his rapt audience. "Nothing could be further from the truth." MacArthur said that he desired the abolition of war. "But once war is forced upon us, there is no other alternative than to apply every available means to bring it to a swift end. War's very object is victory, not prolonged indecision. In war there is no substitute for victory."[36]

In the eyes of the Right, MacArthur was an anti-Communist martyr. He was an old soldier forced to fade away because of Democratic perfidy. He testified against the administration and, later in the spring, went on a speaking tour in Texas. His speeches were not as outrageous as McCarthy's. Nor were they so different either. The threat to America, he told audiences, came from "insidious forces working from within which have already so drastically altered the character of our free institutions."[37]

84

Around the same time, McCarthy swung a hammer at Secretary of Defense George Marshall. He accused the World War II hero and architect of European economic recovery of participating, along with Acheson, in "a great conspiracy, a conspiracy on a scale so immense as to dwarf any previous such venture in the history of man." Truman was a patsy, McCarthy said. The president "is a satisfactory front. He is only dimly aware of what is going on." But McCarthy's eyes were open. Stalemate in Korea hadn't come about because of error on the part of the allies or cunning on the part of the Communists. It had been planned.[38]

The few conservative periodicals backed McCarthy's crusade. In addition to the *American Mercury* and *Human Events*, there was the *Freeman*. A group of libertarian writers had relaunched Albert Jay Nock's magazine to promote "traditional liberalism and individual freedom." To do that, its writers believed, required an aggressive anticommunism. In this battle, McCarthy was the Right's champ. Hollywood screenwriter Morrie Ryskind, who wrote for the Marx Brothers, put it this way in a poem: "So here's to you, Joe McCarthy, you're a swell A-mer-i-can; / You're a terror to the traitors, an' a first-class fighting man."[39]

Even in the pages of *Commentary*, a liberal anti-Communist journal of opinion published by the American Jewish Committee, a young editor named Irving Kristol wrote a backhanded assessment of McCarthy that castigated liberals for conflating the defense of civil liberties with apologies for Soviet conduct. Born in 1920 in Brooklyn, Kristol was a graduate of City College where, in Alcove One of the dining hall, he had spent hours arguing with fellow undergraduate Trotskyists and radicals. His experience as a soldier in World War II cured him of socialism and utopianism. Kristol had no patience for cant. His scathing piece reverberated among the Left for decades.

Back in 1946, Robert Taft had said the Democrats were "divided between communism and Americanism." He sided with

MacArthur after the general's dismissal. Somewhat contrary to his stated principles of nonintervention, he backed the widening of the Korean War to include Taiwan. However, when McCarthy libeled Marshall, Taft demurred. He said that while administration policy might be incorrect, "I do not agree with Senator McCarthy's accusations of conspiracy or treason."[40]

By 1952, though, Taft was in Wisconsin saying, "Senator McCarthy has dramatized the fight to exclude Communists from the State Department. I think he did a great job in undertaking that goal." Taft's careful generosity—note that he did not say McCarthy had actually *accomplished* anything—was somewhat self-interested. He wanted McCarthy's endorsement to carry him to the Republican presidential nomination on his third and final try.[41]

Taft entered the 1952 cycle from a position of strength. He had spent the years since 1948 rallying his supporters on the Republican National Committee. He had won reelection to the Senate by a large margin while campaigning heavily for GOP candidates in 1950, when Republicans picked up twenty-eight seats in the House and five in the Senate. His successful defense of Taft-Hartley, as well as the nation's rightward drift, enhanced his reputation. He entered the presidential race on October 16, 1951. Once again he would have to contend with Dewey and the me-tooers. But the party was growing tired of the New York governor. As Illinois Republican senator Everett Dirksen would put it to Dewey supporters at the 1952 party convention, "We followed you before, and you took us on the road to defeat!"

This was Taft's chance. His problem was General Dwight Eisenhower. The World War II hero had recently left his position as supreme commander of NATO for the presidency of Columbia University. Eisenhower hadn't committed to an election campaign. But if he did, he would be a formidable presence. A Gallup poll in June 1952 had Taft trailing Eisenhower but leading him among the GOP county chairs who could swing a nomination.[42]

Eisenhower officially launched his presidential campaign on June 4. His opposition to Taft's foreign policy was no secret—it was why Eisenhower had opted to run for the Republican nomination. "If Taft had been president," one of Ike's staffers wrote in a campaign memo, "we wouldn't have to worry about bringing General Eisenhower back from Europe—Europe would have fallen long ago to the Communists without the Marshall Plan, etc." The title of the memo was "Demolish the Enemy." The writer wasn't referring to the Soviets.

Taft was just as alarmed at the prospect of an Eisenhower nomination. It would be a replay, he thought, of the last three GOP campaigns. "E. guided by me-tooers," he wrote. "No attack on New Deal—or T-A [Truman-Acheson] foreign policy . . . No cuts in foreign spending means no cuts at home. E. has gone along with whole foreign policy."[43]

Not entirely. Eisenhower would signal his disappointment in Truman's inability to conclude the war when he pledged in late October 1952 that, if elected, he would "go to Korea." Taft wrote his sole book, *A Foreign Policy for Americans* (1951), in an unsuccessful attempt to match Eisenhower's knowledge of and experience in foreign policy. His best hope for the nomination was party loyalty. Perhaps GOP insiders would choose the tested son of a Republican president over a political neophyte whose governing philosophy was a mystery.

Taft did not account for Eisenhower's craftiness. The general's beguiling smile was cover for a strategic genius and master of indirection. At the party's convention, Eisenhower's campaign disputed the validity of Taft's delegates from Texas, Georgia, and Louisiana, saying that the roster had been selected improperly. Taft thought that a compromise might allow him to keep some of the delegates and bring him closer to victory. He assumed wrong. His proposal was quashed. The hopes that conservatives would reclaim the nomination after a sixteen-year drought were dashed—partly because of Ike's planning and partly because of Taft's clumsiness and unpopular foreign policy.[44]

McCarthy did not repay Taft's favor with an endorsement. Tail-gunner Joe was celebrated at the convention and gleefully skewered Democrats throughout the fall campaign. At one point he deliberately confused the name of the Democratic nominee, former Illinois governor Adlai Stevenson, with that of an imprisoned spy: "Alger—I mean Adlai," he said in a radio address.[45]

There was no stopping Eisenhower. In order to shore up his western flank, the general selected Richard Nixon, elected to the Senate two years before, as his running mate. "The plan was for General Eisenhower to stress the positive aspects of his 'Crusade to Clean Up the Mess in Washington,'" Nixon wrote. "I was to hammer away at our opponents on the record of the Truman administration, with particular emphasis on Communist subversion because of my work on the Hiss case."[46]

It was a job Nixon relished. Eisenhower also won support from some members of the rising generation of anti-Communist conservatives, who preferred what historian Allan Lichtman called an "engaged nationalism," comfortable with military action and commitments abroad, to the "disengaged nationalism" of Taft. One of these engaged nationalists, an Arizona Republican running for Senate named Barry Goldwater, endorsed the general.

A disappointed Taft did his best to present a united front. He met with Eisenhower twice—once in private at the convention and again in September to offer a public endorsement at Eisenhower's headquarters in Morningside Heights in Manhattan. When Taft visited the general's hotel room during the July convention, he found Eisenhower shaken by the large crowds of supporters chanting his name. The general who had orchestrated the largest amphibious assault in world history was intimidated by the challenges ahead. "I was telling my wife," Eisenhower said, "that when I really have a nightmare it's when I imagine I have been nominated—and elected."[47]

"You'll win the election all right," Taft replied. This rueful comment encapsulated the senator's frustrations with his party's nominating procedures, with the public's continued embrace of New Deal liberalism, and with his own career. Taft seemed to recognize that his moment had passed. His version of conservatism was fading. And a new generation of conservative hawks was about to rise.

CHAPTER FOUR

IKE, MCCARTHY, AND THE NEW CONSERVATISM

DWIGHT EISENHOWER WAS THE FIRST REPUBLICAN PRESI-
dent in twenty years. His coattails brought in GOP control
of Congress for the first time since 1948, and his successful presidency inaugurated a conservative cultural and intellectual revival.
His conservatism was cautious, gradual, consensus based, and internationalist. He stood in a tradition of moderate Republicanism
that stretched back through Thomas Dewey and Wendell Willkie
to the pre–New Deal Herbert Hoover. And he was popular.

But not everyone on the Right liked Ike. The founders of
what became known as "movement conservatism" harshly criticized Eisenhower's domestic and foreign policies. They accused
Eisenhower of retaining the dreaded New Deal and not acting
aggressively enough against the Soviet Union. They rejected his
continuation of Harry Truman's "containment" strategy and counterposed their own strategy to "roll back" Communist gains abroad
and the welfare state at home.

It was during Eisenhower's administration that libertarians, traditionalists, and ex- and anti-Communists found common ground.
It was during his administration that the groups and journals

associated with this anti-Communist conservative movement co-alesced into a self-conscious whole. This "movement conservatism" was a network of institutions, publications, and individuals that sprang up during the Eisenhower years to defend political and economic freedom against the challenges of bureaucratic centralism and Soviet totalitarianism. To movement conservatives, Eisenhower belonged to the go-with-the-flow establishment.

Movement conservatives were a minority within the GOP. Indeed, at this time, they were often associated with the political fringe. By the end of Eisenhower's second term, however, they had attained some measure of intellectual credibility and political self-confidence. At the very least, they could not be ignored.

Religion was central to this anti-Communist revival. The baby boom coincided with resurgent Christian faith. Religious affiliation and attendance increased during the Eisenhower years. Protestant and Catholic church membership rose in the 1950s. Eisenhower made a point of attending religious services at the National Presbyterian Church in Northwest Washington. The words "under God" were added to the Pledge of Allegiance in 1954. Two years later, Congress adopted "In God We Trust" as the national motto and added it to the currency.

Public expressions of religious sensibility were common during the fight against "godless communism." Evangelical preacher Billy Graham launched his first "crusade" in 1947, led an eight-week revival in a Los Angeles parking lot in 1949, and founded *Christianity Today* in 1956. Dutch Reformed pastor Norman Vincent Peale preached a gospel of success on radio and television and in best sellers such as *The Power of Positive Thinking* (1952). The fascist demagogy of Father Charles Coughlin gave way to the ecumenism of Bishop Fulton Sheen, the host of *Life Is Worth Living*, whose Catholic anticommunism fit comfortably in the American mainstream.

Protestant theologian Reinhold Niebuhr expounded a teaching of human imperfectability. Niebuhr had abandoned socialism after concluding that human beings were too flawed and limited to plan economies or attain social perfection. The centrality of original sin in Niebuhr's thought led him to eschew idealism and ground his foreign policy in the reality of power politics. He always kept in mind the fallenness of the world and the unpredictable consequences of human action.[1]

This wave of religiosity crested in the spiritual, philosophical, and moral ruminations of several traditionalist writers. The cataclysm of World War II shocked and terrified these intellectuals. They wanted to know the causes of the war, of the movements that incited it, of the revolutions and politics that had given rise to authoritarian leaders and regimes. For the philosophical descendants of the New Humanists and Southern Agrarians, the brutality and trauma of the war reinforced a belief in the spiritual roots of modern decadence. The early Eisenhower years saw an outpouring of such assessments of the modern condition. The conservative movement was born when these classics of philosophical reflection joined with free market thought and the take-no-prisoners intellectual style of the anti-Communists.

The first example of this conservative literary renaissance arrived in 1948. That year the University of Chicago Press released *Ideas Have Consequences*, a book that blamed the war on the philosophical rejection of absolutes. Denying the existence of God, the reality of good and evil, and transcendent, unconditional standards of right and wrong was a one-way ticket to the charnel house of Europe and the ruins of Japan. *Ideas Have Consequences* was unique in that it did not locate these intellectual errors in the recent past. The mistakes had been committed much earlier. The book's author, a thirty-eight-year-old lecturer in rhetoric at the University of Chicago named Richard Weaver, blamed the fourteenth-century philosopher William of Ockham. Weaver, a native of North Carolina who had gone from socialism to agrarianism, rejected the notion of moral progress. He held up the American South as the "last non-materialist civilization in the Western world."[2]

Weaver was the first in a series of writers who saw history as a tableau of intellectual and moral derailments. For these critics of modernity, liberalism weakened the bonds of society and sapped the authority of ancient codes of behavior. Liberty, they wrote, was different from license. As Weaver put it, "Man, then, perfects himself by discipline, and at the heart of discipline lies self-denial."[3]

Many of the contributors to this growing body of literature came to be known as "new conservatives." In 1949, a year after *Ideas Have Consequences* was published, poet and essayist Peter Viereck released *Conservatism Revisited*—his attempt to rescue the label of conservatism from disrepute. Viereck defined conservatism as "the political secularization of the doctrine of Original Sin" and said it drew from the "four ancestries of Western man": Hebraic, Hellenic, Roman, and Christian.[4]

Viereck was an idiosyncratic thinker. His pantheon of conservatives included Franklin Roosevelt and Adlai Stevenson. His intellectual model was Klemens von Metternich, the Austrian diplomat who in 1814–1815 chaired the Congress of Vienna and negotiated the Continent's boundaries after the defeat of Napoleon. For Viereck, tradition, historical development, aristocratic bearing, and the maintenance of order were essential to conservative politics. He was not the last thinker to turn to European conservatism in search of answers for American problems.

In 1951 émigré philosopher Hannah Arendt published *The Origins of Totalitarianism*, in which she drew parallels between Nazism, fascism, and communism. A former student of German philosopher Martin Heidegger (with whom she had an affair), Arendt had fled Nazism for refuge at the New School for Social Research in New York. In *The Origins of Totalitarianism*, she detailed the crimes of Adolf Hitler and Joseph Stalin. How, she wondered, had these terrible men come to power? Her explanation was that masses of alienated and deracinated individuals had invested their hopes in totalitarian governments that collapsed the distinction between public and private life.

Arendt's blockbuster provided a vocabulary for the anti-Communist Left to oppose the Soviet Union. By demonstrating that Nazism and Bolshevism drew from the same well, manifested themselves in the same ways, and committed similar crimes, Arendt demolished the arguments of fellow travelers and Red sympathizers that the Soviet Union was an antifascist force. Her work demonstrated that anticommunism was not some right-wing fantasy or a "reflexive," "knee-jerk" "hysteria" but a considered position among intellectuals across the political spectrum. She was part of the *Partisan Review* crowd—some of whom, like James Burnham, moved right, while others stayed left.

In 1952 Friedrich Hayek got into the game. His work *The Counter-revolution of Science* blamed scientism—the application of the scientific method to human society—for ignoring all phenomena that could not be reduced to equations and for giving intellectuals the false sense that the world could be reconstructed along rational lines. That same year, Whittaker Chambers published *Witness*, his epic account of the Alger Hiss scandal. "The crisis of the Western world," Chambers wrote in the "Letter to My Children" that opens the memoir, "exists to the degree in which it is indifferent to God."[5]

Also in 1952, an obscure middle-aged professor at Louisiana State University named Eric Voegelin, who had fled the Nazis for the American South, wrote *The New Science of Politics*. According to Voegelin, Western thought and politics had been corrupted by Gnosticism, a Christian heresy of immanent redemption, since the twelfth century. Voegelin thought along the same lines as influential philosopher Hans Jonas, like Arendt a former student of

Heidegger's who wound up at the New School. For Jonas, Gnosticism was the belief in religious salvation through radically dualistic and secret knowledge. His studies of the Gnostic religion were part of the intellectual mainstream.

Two other important traditionalist books were published in 1953. Sociologist Robert Nisbet brought out *The Quest for Community*, in which he explained that the growth of the centralized state had eliminated the intermediary social formations from which human beings derive meaning and direction. For Nisbet, freedom was the result of the overlapping circles of authority emanating from the institutions of family, neighborhood, church, and voluntary association. The alternative to such authority, Nisbet wrote, was the coercive power of the state. Like other new conservatives, Nisbet believed that freedom could be preserved if it was sheltered from the growing demands of the state. This opposition to centralized government was the nexus between traditionalism and libertarianism.

Henry Regnery, the Chicago businessman who collaborated in the founding of *Human Events*, had formed a nonprofit publishing company in 1947 to publish conservative books. He turned it into a for-profit business the following year. And in 1952 he received a letter from a thirty-four-year-old doctoral candidate at the University of St. Andrews in Scotland named Russell Kirk.

The budding scholar had composed a massive, 450-page dissertation that he called *The Conservatives' Rout*. Alfred Knopf was interested in publishing it, Kirk said, but only if the author made substantial cuts to the manuscript. Kirk wanted to know if Regnery might publish the whole thing instead. Regnery was eager to do so, but only if Kirk changed the title. *The Conservatives' Rout* was too pessimistic, he thought. Regnery and Kirk settled on *The Conservative Mind*.

Kirk was a young fogey. He was in love with old things, mythic folkways, ancient practices, and dusty tomes. He ventured from his family homestead in rural Mecosta, Michigan, to study at Michigan State College (now Michigan State University), to earn a master's degree at Duke University, to serve in the war, and to learn and brood in Scotland. Then he returned home.

Kirk fell in love with the South while at Duke. The romanticism of the Southern Agrarians appealed to him. He liked lost causes, exercises in imagination, and haunted houses. For Kirk, partisan politics was debasing and bewildering. His master's thesis, devoted to the eccentric Jeffersonian statesman John Randolph of Roanoke, Virginia, was published as a book in 1951.

In Scotland, Kirk said, he had witnessed "the metaphysical principle of continuity given visible reality." He ransacked the collected works of Edmund Burke, the eighteenth-century Anglo-Irish parliamentarian and philosopher known for his opposition to the French Revolution (and his support for the American one) for quotations in defense of inherited institutions, traditional prejudices and prescriptions, classical standards of learning, and Christian definitions of moral behavior.[6]

The Conservative Mind was a stuffed stocking of a book. It was filled to bursting with intellectual and literary portraits of figures from Burke to Alexis de Tocqueville, John Stuart Mill to Karl Marx, Lord Acton to T. S. Eliot, John Adams to John Calhoun. Kirk assimilated the American Right into a broader Anglo-American tradition. He minimized the differences between Burkean, European-style conservatism, with its preference for monarchy, aristocracy, and established churches, and American constitutionalism, with its belief in enumerated powers, individual natural rights, and religious pluralism.

Kirk defended the Constitution, but as a historical artifact rather than as the political structure designed by the Founders to instantiate the principles of the Declaration of Independence. Thomas Jefferson disappeared from his narrative. In almost five hundred pages, Kirk makes one passing reference to James Madison, the chief theorist of constitutionalism in the United States. To Kirk, the text of the Constitution and Bill of Rights was less important than unwritten, untaught ideas about manners, etiquette, and conversation. Kirk valued intuition, inspiration, sympathy, and spirit. With *The Conservative Mind*, he gave conservatives an identity, an intellectual genealogy, and a point of view.

The book was a critical and commercial success. *Newsweek* called Kirk "one of the foremost intellectual spokesmen for the conservative position." On July 6, 1953, *Time* magazine devoted its entire book section to *The Conservative Mind*. Kirk was no longer an eccentric author from an academic backwater. He was the face of the new conservatism. He quit his job at Michigan State and became a full-time writer and lecturer.[7]

Kirk's output was Olympian. One count puts his collected works at twenty-six nonfiction books, three novels, three short story collections, and somewhere around six thousand pieces of journalism. He also founded two journals: *Modern Age* in 1957 and the *University Bookman* in 1960. He entertained and instructed anyone who took the trouble to visit his ghost-inhabited dwelling. There would be no conservative movement without Russell Kirk, even if the movement evolved in ways that Kirk came to deplore.[8]

Kirk also had critics. The most blistering response to Kirk from the libertarian Right came in the July 16, 1955, issue of the *Freeman*. Its author was Frank Meyer, whose devotion to Hayek had become as fierce as his former loyalty to Marx. Meyer applauded Kirk's historical and literary knowledge. But he also wrote that *The Conservative Mind* did not advance right-wing thought and might even be a step backward. The belief that every individual is created in the image of God and therefore an end in him- or herself may be "the first principle of any philosophy of freedom," Meyer wrote. But, he continued, "it is not by itself sufficient to guarantee the freedom of men in society."[9]

Meyer's review of *The Conservative Mind* foreshadowed the tensions between Russell Kirk's traditionalism, which privileged virtue, and libertarianism, which prioritized individual freedom. It also vividly illustrated that, despite Kirk's literary panache and widespread popularity, the traditionalism he espoused was too antagonistic toward other groups on the right and too divorced from everyday American life to serve as the basis for a mass movement.

The American Right needed a leader without Kirk's rural eccentricities who could include under a broad ecumenism the squabbling camps of traditionalists and libertarians. It so happened that exactly such an individual had recently graduated from college.

IN 1951 REGNERY PUBLISHED AN ATTACK ON THE STATE OF higher education called *God and Man at Yale*. Its author, William F. Buckley Jr., had graduated in 1950 at the age of twenty-four. He was the son of William Buckley, a devout Catholic oilman who had settled his large family in Connecticut after misadventures fighting for mineral rights with revolutionary governments in Latin America. Bill Jr. was the sixth of ten children Buckley had with his wife, Aloïse, a southern belle from New Orleans.

Buckley's parents taught him the catechism of the Catholic Church, fervent anticommunism, and steadfast opposition to government interference in the economy. His family also encouraged his boisterous, rebellious spirit. In 1957 Buckley told broadcaster Mike Wallace, "I am already a revolutionary against the present liberal order. An intellectual revolutionary."[10]

Through his father, Buckley met Albert Jay Nock, who often visited the Buckley home in Sharon, Connecticut. Bill Jr. read Nock's *Memoirs of a Superfluous Man* during his senior year of high school. He thrilled to Nock's ideas of individualism, anti-statism, and the Remnant—those few souls who could preserve the wisdom and practices of Western civilization during the approaching dark age. This view of the state as enemy was ingrained in Buckley.

Like his father, young Buckley opposed American entry into World War II before Pearl Harbor. He was drafted into the army in November 1943 and inducted in July 1944. He hated it. He was happy when the war ended. But he was also grateful for what military service had taught him. Life in the army exposed Buckley to religious, ethnic, and racial minorities. It showed him the wide variety of peoples inhabiting the United States. The army socialized Buckley. It did not domesticate him.[11]

By the time Buckley matriculated at Yale, his older brother James had graduated from there and was enrolled in the law school. The undergraduate class that entered Yale in 1946 was huge, swelled by the ranks of veterans who had deferred study until after the war. Even so, Buckley stuck out. He joined the *Yale Daily News* and the debate team, where his partner was Brent Bozell, a Nebraskan convert to Catholicism who had served in the merchant marine. The two embraced a polemical style that alternated between Bozell's dramatic oratory and Buckley's sarcastic wit. Bozell was stentorian and commanding, while Buckley was full of quips and jests that deflated his opponents. They became drinking buddies and boon companions. The relationship went from friends to family after Bozell married one of Buckley's sisters, Patricia, in 1949.[12]

Buckley and Bozell were sophomores in 1948 when they enrolled in the politics seminar of a new professor named Willmoore Kendall. Born in Oklahoma in 1909, Kendall was a child prodigy who had taught himself to read by telling his father, a blind pastor, the baseball box scores. He quickly became Buckley's first nonparental intellectual role model. "I attribute whatever political and philosophical insights I have to his tutelage and friendship," Buckley said of Kendall in a 1954 letter to Henry Regnery. He referred to Kendall as "my late mentor." No reader of Buckley's long sentences, rigorously structured arguments, and parenthetical asides can fail to detect the stylistic tics he absorbed from his teacher.[13]

Kendall was wild. He loved to drink. He fooled around. He chased after faculty spouses. And he wrote letters at a stunning pace. Buckley estimated receiving one thousand missives from Kendall during the 1950s alone. Kendall is said to be the only professor to have had his tenure bought out by Yale. When that happened, six years before his death in 1967, he went to teach at the University of Dallas.[14]

A college graduate at the age of sixteen, at eighteen Kendall published his first book, *Baseball: How to Play It and How to Watch It*. Then a Rhodes scholarship took him to Oxford. Journalistic trips to Spain during its civil war in the 1930s impressed on him a fear that anarchy might lead to communism. Authoritarian rule under Francisco Franco, Kendall thought, was preferable to Stalinist totalitarianism. He flirted with prairie socialism but abandoned it by the time he wrote his dissertation at the University of Illinois. When Yale hired him, Kendall described himself as a Truman Democrat. He retained a close identification with the Midwest and called himself an "Appalachians to the Rockies patriot."

Kendall was neither an elitist nor a libertarian. But he was not quite a traditionalist either. He believed in the necessity of communal standards, in popular sovereignty, in majoritarianism, and in the US Constitution as a finely wrought machine through which the "deliberate sense of the community" could be determined and legitimized. His literary style was as novel as his personality and thought. His writing was circuitous, dexterous, and capacious. He loved winding sentences and itemized lists.

Buckley ate this up. Kendall shared his impish spirit. Together with Bozell, they reveled in campus controversy. Debates and scandals were opportunities to expound their convictions. Buckley always sought the highest-profile platforms for his arguments. He became chairman of the *Yale Daily News* and used his leadership position to torment the faculty. He debated professors over the school curriculum and the Communist threat. He said that Yale had lost its religious and intellectual moorings.

Buckley took revenge on Yale after graduation. First, though, he married Patricia Taylor, the Anglican daughter of a Canadian lumber tycoon, in July 1950. He also had to deal with the outbreak of the Korean War. Kendall advised him to join the Central Intelligence Agency (CIA). He put Buckley in touch with a friend whom he had met while working for the precursor of the agency during World War II: James Burnham. Then Burnham introduced Buckley to a CIA operative named E. Howard Hunt, who arranged an assignment for the young man in Mexico and whose long-lasting friendship would haunt Buckley many years later.[15]

Before his departure for Mexico City, Buckley finished a manuscript that distilled the arguments he had made against the Yale administration. The relativistic doctrine of academic freedom, Buckley said, had undermined the foundations of the university and liberal education. "I consider this battle of educational theory important and worth time and thought even in the context of a world-situation that seems to render totally irrelevant any fight except the power struggle against Communism," he wrote. Then, in a few sentences suggested by Kendall, Buckley continued, "I myself believe that the duel between Christianity and atheism is the most important in the world. I further believe that the struggle between individualism and collectivism is the same struggle reproduced on another level. I believe that if and when the menace of Communism is gone, other vital battles, at present subordinated, will emerge to the foreground. And the winner must have help from the classroom." In this brief passage, Buckley united conservative themes of religion and classical education with libertarian ideas about the market and anti-Communist fears of subversion and domination. This ability to see where the joints of the American Right lined up was one reason that Buckley's leadership of movement conservatism was such a success.[16]

Buckley applied Kendall's ideas about majoritarianism and public orthodoxy to the problem of educational institutions that, in his opinion, failed to inculcate traditional values. He arrived at the unconventional solution of not less but more popular control over places like Yale. For Buckley, academic elites had betrayed and revised the purposes of college. The consumers of education—the parents and students who paid to learn—would do better.

Henry Regnery heard about Buckley's project. In April 1951 he wrote the recent graduate asking to take a look. Buckley sent him a draft on May 7. As Regnery put it, "No long time was needed to make up our minds that this was a book we very much wanted to publish, as I wrote to Buckley on May 14." The book was rushed into print so that it would come out as Yale celebrated its 250th anniversary in October. It featured an introduction by journalist John Chamberlain. A former left-winger who participated in Sidney Hook and John Dewey's Commission of Inquiry that acquitted Trotsky of Stalin's charges of treason in the 1930s, Chamberlain had embraced the market, worked as an editor of the *Freeman*, and penned the foreword to the first US edition of *The Road to Serfdom*.[17]

"The response of the academic community to the book was instantaneous, and violent to the point of irrationality," Regnery wrote. Buckley reveled in the outrage. The president of Yale demanded that Buckley withdraw *God and Man at Yale* from publication. Buckley refused. McGeorge Bundy, a professor of government at Harvard who would go on to serve as national security adviser to Presidents John F. Kennedy and Lyndon B. Johnson, attacked Buckley viciously in the pages of the *Atlantic*. Buckley replied in equal measure. "When I sat down to review Mr. Buckley's book," Bundy said in rebuttal, "I was somewhat concerned lest my readers refuse to believe that so violent, unbalanced, and twisted a young man really existed."[18]

Not only did Buckley exist; he thrived. In March 1952 the Buckleys returned from Mexico and settled in Stamford, Connecticut.

They bought a waterside home on the Long Island Sound at Wallacks Point. It would be Buckley's primary residence for the rest of his life. His son Christopher was born that September.

In May 1952 Buckley had joined the staff of the *American Mercury*. He found the *Mercury* an unpleasant place to work. His rebelliousness manifested itself. He clashed with the editor and soon quit. He began to freelance from his garage, which he converted into an office. He wanted to write another book. This time he would collaborate with Brent Bozell, by then a student at Yale Law. Kendall would help them analyze another institution they considered broken by secular liberals: the US government in the era of Joe McCarthy.

At that point, the Wisconsin senator was at the height of his power. In 1952 he targeted William Benton of Connecticut, who had tried to expel him from the Senate. McCarthy called the Democrat a "mental midget." Benton lost reelection. Nor was McCarthy interested in bullying just one political party. In February 1953 he said that the Voice of America had "sabotaged" Eisenhower's foreign policy. The next month he tried, and failed, to block Eisenhower's nominee for ambassador to the Soviet Union. The execution of the Communist spies Julius and Ethel Rosenberg in June highlighted the issue of Soviet infiltration and espionage. And the death of Robert Taft from cancer in July left McCarthy as the leader of the anti-Communist Right.

In November 1953 McCarthy said that the Truman administration had been "crawling" with Commies. He was now head of the Senate's Permanent Subcommittee on Investigations, which gave him additional resources and personnel to unearth Communist subversion. His office became an alternate power center to Ike's White House.

Eisenhower noticed. He began a sly campaign to subvert the countersubversive. In the spring of 1953, when McCarthy sent his aides Roy Cohn and David Schine to investigate US-government-funded libraries in Europe, Eisenhower warned the public, "Don't join the book burners." That May, when McCarthy called upon federal employees to send his office evidence of Communist infiltration, Eisenhower was enraged. The president saw it as a direct challenge to the independence of the executive branch of government. "McCarthy is making exactly the same plea of loyalty to him that Hitler made to the German people," he said during a White House meeting on May 27.[19]

Meanwhile, liberal opposition to McCarthy was driving figures such as James Burnham further right. In November 1953 Burnham resigned from the editorial board of *Partisan Review*, believing his fellow anti-Stalinist intellectuals had fallen for Soviet propaganda and political warfare. The letter he wrote announcing his departure warranted the attention of the *New York Times*. "I believe 'McCarthyism' to be an invention of the Communist tacticians, who launched it and are exploiting it, exactly as they have done in the case of their previous operations of what might be called *diversionary semantics*," Burnham declared.[20]

The following year Burnham quit another liberal anti-Communist organization, the Congress for Cultural Freedom, a nonpartisan institution created during the Truman years that included a broad spectrum of intellectuals, from Bertrand Russell and Arthur Schlesinger Jr. to Raymond Aron, Arthur Koestler, and Sidney Hook. Burnham charged that it, too, was more concerned with McCarthy than with the Soviet Union. (The CIA's sponsorship of the congress was revealed to the public in 1967.) Suddenly Burnham found himself aligned not with the left-wing intellectuals with whom he had spent his life but with conservative Red hunters.[21]

The rising generation of engaged nationalist conservatives backed McCarthy, even as they occasionally squirmed over his vulgar contempt for institutional manners. Many of the traditionalist "new conservatives," however, were appalled by the senator's antics. Peter Viereck, who had rehabilitated "conservative" as a political label, rejected McCarthy outright. But Russell Kirk was more ambivalent. The usually loquacious Kirk avoided the subject of McCarthyism. He wrote only one piece concerning the Wisconsin senator, and for a relatively obscure journal. "Senator Joseph McCarthy, whatever one thinks of him, is not undemocratic, being the gift of the Congress of Industrial Organizations to America (which supported him against La Follette) and immensely popular in his own state," he wrote. "Neither does he have any totalitarian program; he has no program at all; he is, instead, in the old line of destructive critics in the American Congress whose function it is to bedevil the executive arm of government for good or ill." So Kirk withheld judgment—at least publicly.[22]

Buckley and Bozell completed their manuscript, titled *McCarthy and His Enemies*, in December 1953. A Gallup poll taken a month later showed that McCarthy retained the support of half the public, with only 29 percent disfavoring him. Regnery sent the galleys to Whittaker Chambers, hoping the anti-Communist witness would endorse it. But Chambers refused. "As the picture unfolds," he wrote in response, "the awful sense begins to invade you, like a wave of fatigue, that the Senator is a bore, for the same reason that Rocky Marciano (if that is his name) is a bore to people who are not exclusively interested in fist-throwing." Regnery forwarded the correspondence to Buckley, who asked his publisher's publicity department to ask Chambers directly for a jacket blurb. Again, Chambers denied the request. "None of us are his enemies," Chambers wrote to Buckley regarding McCarthy, "but all of us, to one degree or another, have slowly come to question his judgment and to fear acutely that his flair for the sensational, his inaccuracies and distortions, his tendency to sacrifice the greater objective for the momentary effect, will lead him and us into trouble."[23]

Although Chambers would not sanction Buckley's work, he nevertheless befriended the young author. He worried that Buckley would end up as discredited as the Wisconsin senator. "I am urging a decent prudence, unstinting but firm, because I believe that the tighter the Right clings to a myth which does not justify itself, the farther and faster it will be swung away from reality, will be carrying not a banner but a burden," he wrote in one letter to his anti-Communist protégé.[24]

The burden was not going away. In a February 1954 speech, McCarthy referred to "20 years of treason"—a time span that included the first year of Eisenhower's presidency. In response, Adlai Stevenson charged that McCarthy, not Eisenhower, controlled the GOP. Eisenhower selected Richard Nixon to rebut Stevenson on television. Nixon was not looking forward to the speech. He understood that Ike had chosen him because of his anti-Communist reputation. Plus, Nixon enjoyed McCarthy's company. "I found him personally likable, if irresponsibly impulsive," Nixon wrote. Eisenhower reminded his vice president to smile for the camera.[25]

Nixon addressed the public on March 13, 1954. He did not mention McCarthy by name. But the message was unmistakable: the senator had gone too far. "The president, this administration, the responsible leadership of the Republican Party insists that whether in the executive branch of government or the legislative branch of government the procedures for dealing with the threat of communism in the United States must be fair and they must be proper," Nixon said. In one of the many rhetorical questions that filled his speeches, Nixon raised the objection that McCarthy's techniques might be justified because his targets were "rats." "I agree that they're a bunch of rats," Nixon said. "But just remember this. When you go out to shoot rats, you have to shoot straight, because when you shoot wildly it not only means that the rat may get away more easily, you make it easier on the rat."[26]

The speech was well received. Nixon separated "responsible Republicans" from McCarthyites while maintaining his credibility as an opponent of Communist "rats." Eisenhower called to congratulate him. It was part of the general's careful marginalization of McCarthy—pushing Tailgunner Joe to the sidelines even as Eisenhower appropriated the issue of Communist subversion for himself.

Buckley and Kendall traveled to Westminster, Maryland, to visit Chambers around the time *McCarthy and His Enemies* was published on March 30, 1954. Then McCarthy himself, along with his chief counsel, Roy Cohn, attended a reception for the authors in New York City. The young men had grown close to the senator. Bozell ghostwrote some of McCarthy's speeches. Buckley told friends that he had taken McCarthy's financial advice—and lost money on the stock market as a result.[27]

McCarthy thought the book was too critical. In several passages, when they judged he had gone too far and spoken incorrectly, Buckley and Bozell distanced themselves from McCarthy. But they also said that McCarthy's instincts were correct. They accused Democrats of being as dishonest as liberals held McCarthy to be. And in language that could (and may well) have been written by Kendall, they argued that it was entirely justified for a majority to decide that it did not want certain ideologies represented in governing institutions. "Not only is it *characteristic* of society to create institutions and to defend them with sanctions," they wrote, but "societies *must* do so—or else they cease to exist."[28]

Buckley and Bozell had bad timing. A few weeks after *McCarthy and His Enemies* was published, the senator began his hearings into Communist infiltration of the US Army. Henry Cabot Lodge Jr., Eisenhower's ambassador to the United Nations, told the president, "Investigation of the Army, while ostensibly aimed at making sure that the Army is secure against Communist penetration, is actually a part of an attempt to destroy you politically." But Eisenhower didn't really need the advice. McCarthy was clearly targeting an institution that Ike loved, that molded Ike's character, and that Ike had belonged to all his adult life.[29]

A few days after the army-McCarthy hearings began, Buckley addressed a Republican women's group in New York. The audience numbered in the thousands. Buckley spoke with his usual verve. He reversed the conventional narrative: In Buckley's telling, Mc-Carthy was the victim, and the national media were the bullies. "Far from suffering a reign of terror," Buckley said, "it is my contention that we are living in an age when particularly the cowards speak up. Men who have never had the spirit to face up to their mothers-in-law are suddenly aware that they can now earn a badge of courage by denouncing Senator McCarthy and what is more, their heroism is sure to be immortalized in the *New York Times*."[30]

This was the minority view. The army hearings capsized McCarthy's popularity. The shift in public opinion was exemplified during the famous moment in June 1954 when army chief counsel Joseph N. Welch exploded at the senator, asking, "Have you no sense of decency, sir, at long last? Have you left no sense of decency?" By the end of the summer, a Senate committee had been empaneled to determine whether McCarthy deserved censure. His approval rating fell to 30 percent.[31]

The anti-Communist conservatives did not abandon him. A month after Welch demanded evidence of McCarthy's decency, some two thousand people attended a dinner for Roy Cohn at the Astor Hotel in New York City. Buckley was among the speakers. Among the dozens of awards Cohn received that evening was one from Rabbi Benjamin Schultz, who handed McCarthy's chief aide a plaque "in recognition of his battle for his God and country, which has inspired America." Or at least a shrinking part of it.[32]

In September the censure committee, led by Utah Republican Arthur Watkins, issued its findings. The committee judged that McCarthy deserved rebuke for failing to testify before the Senate and for harassing a witness. Again the anti-Communist Right came to the senator's defense. On November 11, seven hundred conservatives—including Buckley, Burnham, anti–New

Deal pamphleteer John T. Flynn, and black journalist George Schuyler—published an open letter against censure in the *New York Times*.[33]

The McCarthyites cast their champion as the lone figure who, whatever his faults, had the boldness and tenacity to raise the issue of subversion. In the McCarthyite imagination, the senator was an innocent child. His pure motivations and totemic significance served as automatic rebuttal to any criticism. "In some charismatic way that cannot be explained by his own often inept acts and ignorant words," James Burnham wrote, "McCarthy became the symbol through which the basic strata of the citizens expressed their conviction—felt more than reasoned—that Communism and Communists cannot be part of our national community, that they are beyond the boundaries, that, in short, the line must be drawn somewhere."[34]

McCarthyism reinforced the sense of the anti-Communist Right that it was participating in an embattled counterrevolution. Buckley, Bozell, Kendall, and Burnham believed that McCarthy stood for the ability of civilization to proscribe some opinions as beyond the pale. "What McCarthy was all about," Buckley wrote in 1968, "was the effort to affirm an American consensus which excluded certain things. Certain things as, yes, un-American."[35]

In reality, McCarthy's demagogy pushed the political system to the limit. It united both Democrats and a majority of Republicans against him. McCarthy had enveloped the Right in his elaborate conspiracy theory. He fed off conservative alienation from government, from media, from higher education. For a time, it seemed as though this strategy of condemning American institutions as irrevocably corrupted was popular and might succeed. It could not, of course. Ultimately fantasies cannot withstand the pressures of reality.

McCarthy threatened the entire edifice of anticommunism by associating it with crackpot theories and embarrassing theatrics.

So much disgrace did McCarthy bring to the cause of anticommunism that Richard Condon used him as the model for an unwitting dupe of the Communists in his novel *The Manchurian Candidate* (1959). The Senate censured McCarthy in a vote of 67–22 on December 2, 1954. Politically marginalized and spiritually broken, he sank into alcoholism and died in 1957.

McCarthy's main legacy, in retrospect, may have been accelerating the departure of ex-Marxists such as Burnham from the Left—and into the waiting arms of William F. Buckley Jr. McCarthy's self-immolation once again deprived the Right of leadership. In the years to come, Buckley and his allies would reconstruct and expand the conservative movement in preparation for its launch into presidential politics.

CHAPTER FIVE

A MOVEMENT GROWS

T HE DEATH OF ROBERT TAFT AND THE CENSURE OF JOSEPH McCarthy left the American Right confused and rudderless. In the Senate, the most prominent conservative during the Dwight Eisenhower administration was William Knowland of California, who shared Taft's dourness but had yet to attain Taft's stature. Knowland was no match for Eisenhower or for Lyndon Johnson, the Texas Democrat who became majority leader after Republicans lost the Senate in 1954.

William F. Buckley Jr. was acutely aware of this conservative weakness. The intellectual work performed by Friedrich Hayek and Russell Kirk had yet to be connected to political institutions and translated into a political program. Conservative intellectuals had plenty to say, but too few self-consciously conservative politicians could amplify those messages into popular support.

The McCarthy episode reminded conservatives of the importance of mass media. Besides the *Chicago Tribune*, William Randolph Hearst's chain of newspapers, and *Reader's Digest*, three right-leaning periodicals existed when Buckley put pen to paper: *Human Events*, the *Freeman*, and the *American Mercury*. None was a weekly journal of opinion like the *New Republic* and the *Nation*.

None had the same influence among intellectual elites. In November 1951 Buckley had written a letter to his successor as chairman of the *Yale Daily News*, expressing his amazement at the storm over his first book. "I should have known better, of course," Buckley confessed, "for I had seen the Apparatus go to work on other dissenters from the Liberal orthodoxy, and I respected the Apparatus and stood in awe of it."[1]

Living as a freelance, without professional commitment, Buckley perceived that conservatism lacked a structure to advance its ideas in public life. "The few spasmodic victories conservatives are winning are aimless, uncoordinated, and inconclusive," he wrote in a November 23, 1954, letter. "This is so . . . because many years have gone by since the philosophy of freedom has been expounded systematically, brilliantly, and resourcefully." Gradually putting conservatives into key positions in the bastions of liberalism would require time and effort, so Buckley chose another option. He spent the 1950s building counterinstitutions—an "Apparatus" for conservatives—from which he could attack liberal strongholds in a bid to shift elite opinion rightward.[2]

His first project was a student group. In 1953 he and Frank Chodorov, the libertarian journalist associated with the Foundation for Economic Education, set up the Intercollegiate Society of Individualists (ISI), a vehicle for conservative student activism and scholarship. Buckley was its first president. ISI established a network of young conservatives on campuses and distributed the growing literature of the Right. It experienced explosive growth and would continue to influence the conservative movement well into the twenty-first century. As successful as ISI was, however, it was not enough for Buckley. He still wanted to match the superior articulation of the Left.[3]

In 1952 he had met William S. "Willi" Schlamm, a forty-eight-year-old Austrian émigré and ex-Communist who rose to a high position in Time Inc. and befriended Whittaker Chambers.

Schlamm persuaded Buckley to found a magazine to serve as a platform for the growing number of conservative writers. The project was imperative: two of the largest-circulation right-leaning journals were cracking up. The *Freeman* had lost staff after a fight over the magazine's direction and now limited its content to doctrinaire lessons in the value of economic freedom. The *American Mercury*, under new ownership, was anti-Semitic.[4]

"I propose to found a magazine, which will be called *National Weekly*," Buckley wrote to potential investors in 1954. He knew exactly what he wanted: the magazine that launched in 1955 as *National Review* competed for influence with liberal journals of politics, literature, and ideas. Its premise was that ideas mattered above all else. Just as Friedrich Hayek had argued in "The Intellectuals and Socialism," Buckley believed that long-term political success depended on intellectual ascendancy and mainstream credibility. *National Review*, said attorney William Rusher, who joined the magazine as publisher in 1957, was engaged in a "radical operation" to "redesign the intellectual premises of the modern world."[5]

Schlamm insisted that Buckley serve as editor in chief and that Buckley own a controlling stake in the enterprise. "I had the advantage of owning all the stock in this company," Buckley once said. "There was never any question of who ran the organization. It's amazing how many fights are avoided when you have total control." (Ironically, Schlamm was one of the first people to leave after a fight with Buckley.) He and Schlamm recruited a staff that drew heavily from the ranks of ex-Marxist anti-Communists. They took in several refugees from the *Freeman*. Willmoore Kendall, James Burnham, and Frank Meyer also signed on. Chambers and Kirk did not want to join.[6]

Chambers's concerns were philosophical. He worried the magazine would be too beholden to the ideology of laissez-faire. "A conservatism that cannot face the facts of the machine and mass production, and its consequences in government and politics, is foredoomed to futility and petulance," he wrote Schlamm. He considered himself not a conservative but a man of the Right. And he worried, correctly, that the magazine would align itself against President Eisenhower and Vice President Richard Nixon, the latter of whom had done so much for him and remained a friend.[7]

Kirk's reluctance was personal. He did not want to be on the same masthead as Meyer, his harshest critic. He was also wary of Buckley, who already was upstaging him as the voice of American conservatism. Kirk agreed to write a monthly column for the magazine but otherwise kept his distance from the periodical and its editor. "In the course of twenty-five years' association," he wrote in his memoir (penned in the third person), "Kirk visited the shabby offices of *National Review* not more than six or seven times—and then usually on business with the publisher, William Rusher." In 1957, when Kirk founded *Modern Age*, no ex-Communists sat on its editorial board. And in 1982, when Kirk assembled an anthology of conservative writing for Penguin Books, he omitted Buckley.[8]

The first issue of *National Review* had a cover date of November 19, 1955. It sold for twenty cents. It was a flimsy thing: some thirty-two pages long, no advertisements, few illustrations or cartoons. The layout was pinched and difficult to read. There were several typos. In truth, it was more of a newsletter or a direct-mail solicitation than a periodical. Kendall, Burnham, and Meyer were fully themselves, but the voice of Buckley, only thirty years old, was still developing.

The magazine was forthrightly oppositional. *National Review*, its editors wrote, "stands athwart history, yelling Stop." There was an ambiguity as to whether Buckley opposed all change—"history" with a lowercase *h*—or the deterministic theory of capital *H* "History" that ends in world communism. Buckley was fine with the uncertainty. He was eager to roll back not only communism but also the "effronteries" of the twentieth century. The magazine was "out of place," he said, "because, in its late maturity, America rejected conservatism in favor of radical social experimentation." Thus *National Review* defined conservatism as the set of beliefs dominant in the age of Warren Harding, Calvin Coolidge, and Herbert Hoover.[9]

Buckley said that conservatives, "at least those who have not made their peace with the New Deal, and there is serious question whether there are any others," were "non-licensed nonconformists." The editors of *National Review* described themselves as "radical conservatives." They advocated the "restoration" of Coolidge's understanding of Americanism. The "tradition of fixed postulates having to do with the meaning of existence, with the relationship of the state to the individual, of the individual to his neighbor, so clearly enunciated in the enabling documents of our Republic," the editors wrote, had been abandoned for positivism and relativism. Liberals had fooled a generation of students. "And since ideas rule the world, the ideologues, having won over the intellectual class, simply walked in and started to run things." This attack on relativism and on the universities as the source of ideological corruption would persist throughout *National Review*'s life.[10]

Just as he had done in *God and Man at Yale*, Buckley synthesized the discordant notes of the Right. *National Review*'s editorial credo mentioned libertarian opposition to the "growth of government," traditional defenses of "the organic moral order," anti-Communist combat against "coexistence" with communism, Nockian elitism in education and culture, distaste for Eisenhower's middle-of-the-road Republicanism, and antiunionism and antiglobalism—by which the editors meant opposition to multilateral organizations such as the United Nations and the "One World" aspirations of GOP me-tooers such as Wendell Willkie.

One reason the staff could agree on most subjects was that many of them were Buckleys. *National Review* was a family affair. Buckley's sister Aloïse contributed a feature story on Ivy League fund-raising. Brother-in-law Brent Bozell was an associate and contributor. And in 1960 another of Buckley's sisters, Priscilla, joined as managing editor, a position she would hold for the next twenty-five years.

The editors had certain preoccupations. They devoted five of the first issue's thirty-two pages to books and arts. Not one but two columns discussed higher education: Kirk's "From the Academy" and Buckley's "The Ivory Tower." Burnham's column, "The Third World War," was a remorseless and mesmerizing dissection of the latest developments in US foreign policy. And Kendall's column, "The Liberal Line," took on the latest arguments from the "liberal establishment." Kendall's majoritarianism posited an American public that was basically conservative in its instincts but had been led astray by a ruling elite—the "establishment" whose existence *New Yorker* writer Richard Rovere would credit *National Review* with introducing into political debate. The founders of *National Review* considered themselves the leaders of an intellectual army that could compete on the same battlefield as the best troops of the academic Left.[11]

THE FIRST TASK OF *National Review* WAS TO GAIN SOME SORT OF intellectual respectability. The press mocked the magazine when it first appeared. It was considered amateurish and sophomoric. Its funding was meager. It was meant to be a weekly, but for budgetary reasons it quickly adopted a biweekly publication schedule. The change was another reminder that self-conscious intellectual conservatism did not appeal to a large market.

The movement conservatism of William F. Buckley Jr. was fringe. Back in 1950, prominent literary critic Lionel Trilling had written, "The conservative impulse and the reactionary impulse do not, with some isolated and some ecclesiastical exceptions, express themselves in ideas but only in action or in irritable mental gestures which seek to resemble ideas." This sense of liberal supremacy—though it should be noted that Trilling was *lamenting* the absence of a serious conservatism—was commonplace.[12]

In a critique of Russell Kirk in the *American Political Science Review*, for example, Samuel P. Huntington of Harvard University wrote, "Liberals must be the conservatives in America today." The year *National Review* arrived on the scene, political scientist Louis Hartz published *The Liberal Tradition in America*, arguing that the classical liberalism of John Locke and Thomas Jefferson was uniquely suited to the United States. Historian Clinton Rossiter chimed in with *Conservatism in America*, which made the case that conservatism's sole purpose was to strengthen this liberal tradition. Daniel Bell, a friend of Irving Kristol's from City College and a former radical turned sociologist who was now a journalist at *Fortune* magazine, edited a collection titled *The New American Right*. It argued that conservatism was nothing more than the expression of political extremism and social status anxiety, the result of an inability to cope with the modern world. Theodor Adorno wrote *The Authoritarian Personality*, where he came up with the pseudoscientific "F Scale"—*F* for "fascist"—by which certain character traits indicated susceptibility to autocratic rule. Later in the decade, political scientist Herbert McCloskey wrote that the "uninformed, the poorly educated" filled the ranks of the American Right.[13]

This intellectual snobbery, ignorance, derision, and contempt for conservatism was, Buckley said, confirmation of *liberal* status anxiety. "If one dismisses *a priori* the possibility that there are rational grounds for resisting the Liberal view of things," he wrote, "one necessarily looks elsewhere than to reason for explanation of such discomfiting phenomena as, e.g., the great popularity of the late Robert Taft." Buckley exaggerated Taft's popularity, but his point was that conservatives with reason, logic, and wit held an advantage over liberals, who were not used to defending their ideas and were puzzled by conservatism's very existence. Conservatives would have to define themselves in terms no liberal could dismiss or ignore. This process of self-definition required Buckley to mark the boundaries of his worldview.[14]

His first target was anti-Semitism. He attacked Gerald L. K. Smith, who'd gone from Huey Long surrogate to rabid America Firster to Holocaust denier, as a man "with an *idée fixe*, namely, the role of the Perfidious Jew in modern society." Buckley's conservatism dissociated itself from the Liberty Lobby—not to be confused with the defunct Liberty League—whose founder, Willis Carto, peddled a white supremacist, anti-Semitic ideology that blamed Jews for manipulating the "ruling elite in Washington" into appeasement of "an aroused, armed Russian-Asiatic threat." The Liberty Lobby's most popular pamphlet was called *America First*.[15]

When the *American Mercury* endorsed the *Protocols of the Elders of Zion* in 1959, Buckley said that no one who appeared on its masthead could appear on his and that his editors would not write for H. L. Mencken's old magazine until its ownership changed hands. The decision was controversial. *National Review* lost subscribers as a result. But it pleased those inside the Buckley circle who wanted him to move away from the extreme. "How good, and how strong, it is to take a principled position," Whittaker Chambers, who by this time had come aboard *National Review*, wrote to Buckley. "It defines, and in defining, frees."[16]

Then Buckley excluded the libertarian heroine Ayn Rand for her "rhetorical totalism." Born in 1905, the indomitable Russian émigré had become a best-selling author in the years since she fled the Soviet Union at the age of twenty. She wrote her first novels, *We the Living* (1936), *Anthem* (1938), and *The Fountainhead* (1943), in opposition to both Soviet communism and the collectivist conformism she saw in the New Deal. Her early supporters included Mencken.[17]

Rand was an atheist and materialist who, following Friedrich Nietzsche, celebrated the individual will and scorned altruism as morally corrupting. She called her philosophy "Objectivism." In the Randian cosmology the dollar replaced the crucifix. Christianity, she said, is "the symbol of the sacrifice of the ideal to the nonideal." She gathered around her a coterie of worshipful acolytes, including an economist in his twenties named Alan Greenspan, who would become chairman of the Federal Reserve in 1987. In 1964 Rand told *Playboy*, "I am challenging the cultural tradition of two-and-a-half thousand years." But it was precisely this tradition—the cultural legacy of Western civilization, including its religious heritage—that *National Review* existed to uphold.[18]

Chambers lowered the hammer on Rand. He reviewed her magnum opus, *Atlas Shrugged*, under the headline "Big Sister Is Watching You," in *National Review*'s December 28, 1957, issue. He wrote that there was no difference between Objectivism and Marxism: "Randian Man, like Marxian Man, is made the center of a godless world." The novel had no literary merit. "Its shrillness is without reprieve," Chambers went on. "Its dogmatism is without appeal . . . From almost any page of *Atlas Shrugged*, a voice can be heard, from painful necessity, commanding: 'To a gas chamber—go!'"[19]

Rand bristled at the insolence of Buckley and his crew. She had met Buckley three years prior. He often told the story of her first words to him, in her Russian accent: "You ahrr too intelligent to believe in Gott." Buckley sent her postcards written in Church Latin. *National Review* attacked her, Rand said, because she was a skeptic who disavowed religious authority. "There are religious magazines which one can respect," she wrote in a 1960 letter to Barry Goldwater, "even while disagreeing with their views. But the fact that the *National Review* poses as a secular political magazine, while following a strictly religious 'party line,' can have but one purpose: to slip religious goals by stealth on those who would not accept them openly, to 'bore from within,' to tie Conservatism to religion, and thus *to take over* the American conservatives." For the rest of her life, Rand refused to be in the same room as the editor of *National Review*.[20]

Rand correctly perceived Buckley's linkage of American conservatism with religious faith. His conservatism incorporated the broad tendencies on the American right, from libertarianism to traditionalism to engaged anti-Communist nationalism. Historical necessity, he believed, required that anticommunism take precedence over the other two persuasions, even as he attempted to maintain them all within the coalition.

Buckley would not allow sectarianism. Achieving a viable consensus was hard going. The partisans of tradition and the champions of freedom, the committed institutionalists and the rowdy populists, retreated into their personal ideological quarters. "All that can be reasonably hoped for," Russell Kirk wrote in 1958, "so far as the immediate future is concerned, is a series of leagues and coalitions of anti-collectivist elements against the collectivist tendency of the times."[21]

The previous year Kirk had traveled to St. Moritz, Switzerland, for the tenth anniversary of the Mont Pèlerin Society. It was his (rather wishful) sense that Hayek's organization was shifting its emphasis from individualism to conservatism. "All in all," Kirk remembered, "a fair number of members seemed in 1957 to be moving away from the more extreme doctrines of nineteenth-century Benthamism, yet remaining strongly attached to liberal concepts of the free market and political liberty—although, in later meetings, they would not move very far."[22]

The highlight of the conference was the presidential address. Hayek read aloud his essay "Why I Am Not a Conservative." Lovers of freedom, Hayek began, were on the defensive. They needed allies. "In this," he acknowledged, "they find themselves much of the time on the same side as those who habitually resist change." He had Kirk in mind. But, Hayek added, any alliance between classical liberalism and conservatism was tactical and probably temporary. Unlike liberalism, conservatism had no alternative to the socialist ideal: "It has been regularly the conservatives who have compromised with socialism and stolen its thunder." He was referring to European conservatives, such as German chancellor Otto von Bismarck, who had built the welfare state to thwart revolution before it began.[23]

Conservatism's reliance on prejudice and tradition, Hayek went on, made it hostile to the growth of knowledge and the development of human potential. Its nationalism was separated by a hair from socialism and collectivism. But Hayek also acknowledged that the conservatism he described did not really exist in the United States "because what in Europe was called 'liberalism' was here the common tradition on which the American polity had been built: thus the defender of the American tradition was a liberal in the European sense." That was why "in the United States it is still possible to defend individual liberty by defending long-established institutions."[24]

Hayek placed himself in the Whig tradition of Edmund Burke, Lord Acton, and Alexis de Tocqueville. Whiggism, he said, "is the doctrine on which the American system of government is based. In its pure form it is represented in the United States, not by the radicalism of Jefferson, nor by the conservatism of Hamilton or even of John Adams, but by the ideas of James Madison, the 'father of the Constitution.'" According to Hayek, American "conservatism" was the same as the constitutionalism of James Madison, who secured individual liberty through the separation of powers, enumerated powers, federalism, and the Bill of Rights.[25]

When Hayek finished his remarks, Kirk was asked to respond. After all, he had done more than anyone to persuade Americans that the European form of conservatism was relevant, even necessary, in a nation with no legally established aristocracy, monarch, or church. In the audience sat Henry Regnery, who recalled that Kirk defended the arguments of *The Conservative Mind* "extemporaneously, without notes of any kind, and with great brilliance and effect." Privately, however, Kirk was no fan of the Austrian professor. "While I can't account fully for Hayek's distemper," he wrote Buckley some years later, "in general he is a vain and impractical person, rather doctrinaire, who thinks that he is the law and all the prophets, and that nothing is needed for the salvation of humanity but the obedient reading of Hayek's works."[26]

Hayek held fast to the banner of liberalism even as Woodrow Wilson and Franklin Roosevelt reformulated its substantive content into something quite different from his beliefs. *National Review* wanted both Hayek and Kirk inside its camp, along with the ex-Communist hawks, but it rejected the label "liberal" in favor of "conservative"—you could not be conservative and look to FDR and liberal Democrats for wisdom. In the eyes of *National Review*, the "new conservatism" of poet and essayist Peter Viereck, who took his cues from both Prince Klemens von Metternich and President Roosevelt, was no less compromised than liberalism itself. "Middle of the road" was the new me-tooism. That was why *National Review* soon collided with the architect of D-Day and the most successful Republican president in decades.

Dwight Eisenhower represented and advocated the traditional values of nineteenth-century America as he reinforced, and in some cases expanded, the architecture of the New Deal. Eisenhower's continuation of FDR's legacy was enough to inspire accusations from the Right that he was indifferent to, or perhaps welcoming of, creeping socialism. And his cautious foreign policy realism drove the anti-Communist Right to despair: he was more interested in avoiding war than in liberating the captive peoples of the Soviet Empire.

When the Soviet Union cut off West Berlin in 1948, President Harry Truman had directed US air forces in Europe, under the command of General Curtis LeMay, to airlift thousands of tons of food and supplies to the beleaguered city for over a year in defiance of Communist rule over East Germany. In 1954, however, during Eisenhower's second year in office, when the French suffered defeat at the hands of the Viet Minh Communist insurgency in the Battle of Dien Bien Phu, the new president was reluctant to become involved in the conflict between North and South Vietnam. The partitioned country was divided between pro-American authoritarians and pro-Soviet Communists, just as Korea had been after the armistice there a year earlier.

Early in Eisenhower's presidency, Republican senator John Bricker of Ohio had introduced an amendment to the Constitution that would have limited the president's conduct of foreign policy. The Bricker amendment would have required Congress to not only ratify treaties with other nations but also pass separate legislation authorizing a given treaty's provisions. The object was to prevent the loss of American sovereignty and freedom of action.

The Bricker amendment was a halfway house between the disengaged nationalism of Taft and the engaged nationalism of Senator Barry Goldwater and Buckley. Even the conservatives who wanted the United States to roll back communism had no desire to be ruled by the United Nations. "Should such treaties as the human rights covenants or the draft statute for an international criminal court be adopted by U.N. members," Bricker thundered, "we would have world government in fact if not in name."[27]

Eisenhower, however, saw the Bricker amendment as a needless shackle on the presidency. He made sure that it was defeated. And he fired a member of his Commission on Intergovernmental Relations, Notre Dame Law School dean Clarence "Pat" Manion, for campaigning on its behalf. That decision made Eisenhower inadvertently responsible for the modern conservative broadcast industry. Manion took to the airwaves, creating *The Manion Forum* radio program. "The present crisis," Manion said, referring to the growth of Soviet power, "is a judgment upon our tragic policy of always putting American interests last instead of first." Popularizers such as Manion—and publisher Henry Regnery—were the connective tissue between a group of anti-Communist eccentrics and a mass audience. He was a trailblazer for later right-wing radio hosts.[28]

National Review was unfriendly toward Dwight Eisenhower's foreign policy because, in the magazine's view, it was not anti-Communist enough. In late October 1956 the Suez crisis dealt a staggering blow to what remained of the British Empire. Then, right before the US presidential election, an emboldened Soviet Union crushed the anti-Communist Hungarian Revolution. For Catholic anti-Communists, the tragedy of Hungary was a double betrayal: not only of a captive nation but also of an embattled church. "I was furious at my government—the leader of the free world—for not responding," remembered Lee Edwards, a twenty-five-year-old just out of the army whose father, a journalist for the *Chicago Tribune*, was a friend of Joe McCarthy's.[29]

Still, James Burnham urged Buckley to endorse Eisenhower's reelection in *National Review*. Buckley was reluctant, even adding his name to a far-right scheme to vote in "independent" electors who would choose for president a "conservative All American" who could "defeat international Socialism which has captured both political parties." Buckley's concession to Burnham was to run a symposium titled "Should Conservatives Vote for Eisenhower-Nixon?" Its contributors mainly answered no. In November 1956, as if to remind the world of conservatism's political irrelevance, Eisenhower easily dispatched Adlai Stevenson for a second time, winning 57 percent of the vote. The Democrats captured just seven states—all of them formerly part of or sympathetic to the Confederacy.[30]

After his reelection, Eisenhower said he represented a "modern Republicanism" that combined the best of the New Deal with economic prosperity and military strength. Distraught conservatives were convinced that neither party was interested in ending the Communist threat. "The liberal ideology is programmatic in a sense in which the Republicanism of Mr. Eisenhower is definitely not," Buckley wrote near the end of the decade. For Buckley, the "blandness of Modern Republicanism" prevented Republicans from offering real alternatives—conservative alternatives—to liberal programs.[31]

Another issue on which *National Review* distinguished itself from Eisenhower was civil rights. The president had carried out the desegregation of the armed forces and of Washington, DC, but he was no radical on race. He rarely discussed the subject. He did not comment publicly on the Supreme Court's 1954 desegregation ruling in *Brown v. Board of Education of Topeka*. He met with black leaders only once during his presidency. He followed the Republican precedent of abstract support for civil rights combined with deference to congressional inaction. Republicans stuck to a gradual approach to civil rights. They did not want to alienate their southern allies or violate the principles of federalism. At this time, the seniority system of committee leadership gave control of Congress to Southern Democrats, which meant that the advance of black political equality was slow and painful.[32]

The Supreme Court and the nascent civil rights movement forced Eisenhower to act. In 1957 he ordered federal troops to Arkansas to guarantee nine black students safe passage into Little Rock's Central High School, the first time the US armed forces had been sent to enforce a federal law since Reconstruction. In the same year—after Democratic senator Strom Thurmond filibustered against the legislation for twenty-four hours and twenty-seven minutes—Eisenhower signed the first of two civil rights acts during his presidency in an incremental bid to guarantee blacks the right to vote.

Buckley and *National Review* objected. In 1956 Regnery had introduced Buckley to James J. "Kilpo" Kilpatrick, editor of the *Richmond News Leader* and author of *The Sovereign States* (1957). Kilpatrick became one of Buckley's regular contributors. He attacked *Brown v. Board*, opposed the desegregation of schools, and criticized the civil rights leadership. Before long, he was *National Review*'s chief political correspondent, writing profiles of various presidential candidates. Kilpatrick's editorial presence tethered *National Review* to one of its traditionalist antecedents: Southern Agrarianism. And so, to the movement's enduring shame, conservatism's flagship journal aligned itself with the racist Southern Democrats who had supported the New Deal when it meant federal largesse for their states.

National Review criticized civil rights in the 1950s on two grounds. First, the editors wrote, the Constitution drastically limited the federal government's powers. Second, civil disobedience, no matter how nonviolent, eroded the foundations of social order. But conservatives with southern roots went further. They valorized the South and minimized its mistreatment of African Americans. For traditionalist Richard Weaver, the South's racial hierarchy, religiosity, and historical memory of the Lost Cause were "strong barriers to *anomie*"—they prevented (for southern whites) feelings of alienation from self and community. In Weaver's eyes, these illiberal traditions were conserving forces. "Anyone who looks beneath appearance to reality," he wrote, "must see that the attack upon the Southern school system is but one front of a general attack on the principle of an independent, self-directing social order, with a set of values proper to itself."[33]

Buckley agreed. He wrote *National Review*'s infamous August 1957 editorial "Why the South Must Prevail," arguing that "the White community is so entitled [to continuing discrimination] because, for the time being, it is the advanced race." In *Up from Liberalism* (1959), he wrote that efforts to improve the lives of black people carried America along the road to serfdom. The problems of central power, he explained, "loom large in the minds of conservatives, many of whom would unhesitatingly vote for integrated schools in their own neighborhoods, but understand the distinctiveness of the Southern problem; and, in any case, hesitate to export their patented solutions to Southern dilemmas."[34]

Behind this sympathy for "Southern dilemmas" was Buckley's distrust of the democratic process. He retained the Nockian elitism that predicted the masses would opt for an oppressive state if given the chance. "Democracy," Buckley once said, "is not one of my absolutes." He drew a parallel between the empowerment of American blacks and the radical, often Marxist politics of anticolonial leaders in liberated Africa. "There was not a single of these African countries prepared for independence, educationally, socially, economically, or spiritually," wrote black journalist George Schuyler, an occasional contributor to *National Review*, who criticized much of the civil rights movement for what he called its refusal to accept and promote the economic gains blacks already had made.[35]

Buckley made opposition to civil rights and identification with the South part of the conservative movement. "I pray every Negro will not be given the vote in South Carolina tomorrow," he wrote privately in 1961. "The day after, he would lose that repose through which, slowly but one hopes surely, some of the decent instincts of the white man go to work, fuse with his myths and habits of mind, and make him a better and better instructed man, and hence a man more likely to know God." Around this time, Weaver sent Buckley a letter offering kudos for saying publicly that, as Weaver put it, "the doctrinaire position on integration is untenable, either in theory or practice."[36]

Buckley would repudiate these views. Kilpatrick, too, would disavow segregation. But the conflation of arguments against government expansion with defenses of white supremacy limited the reach of conservatism. And the ease with which figures such as Kilpatrick slid from segregationism into advocacy of color blindness and opposition to liberal positions on busing, housing, crime, welfare, and other issues made the conservative movement suspect in the eyes of Americans of all races, especially the elites to whom Buckley meant to appeal.

Resistance to civil rights crippled the argument for limited government by equating federal inactivity with the maintenance of white supremacy. Far from benefiting from southern "backlash," intellectual conservatism's position on race prevented it from winning the allegiance of an elite that saw civil rights as the full flowering of Abraham Lincoln's vision for America.

NOT EVERY CONSERVATIVE—OR EVEN EVERY MEMBER OF THE *National Review* editorial board—shared Buckley's positions. Brent Bozell chided Buckley in the pages of the magazine, scolding him for not limiting his arguments against civil rights to a strict interpretation of the Constitution. During the 1950s, moreover, a group of political thinkers emerged who both opposed modern liberalism and supported civil rights. They were called Straussians.

Leo Strauss was the son of Orthodox Jewish parents from the German state of Hesse. Philosophy was his lifelong vocation. In 1922, with a new PhD, he traveled to the University of Freiburg, where he studied under Edmund Husserl and listened to Husserl's assistant, Martin Heidegger.

Strauss was enthralled by Heidegger's mastery of philosophy. After Hitler's rise to power, however, he became disturbed by Heidegger's teaching. "The key term is 'resoluteness,' without any indication as to what are the proper objects of resoluteness," Strauss later wrote. It smacked of a relativism that could lead to nihilism. "There is a straight line," he said, "which leads from Heidegger's resoluteness to his siding with the so-called Nazis in 1933."[37]

Like Hannah Arendt and Eric Voegelin, Strauss fled the Nazis in 1937 at the age of thirty-eight for a teaching position at the New School for Social Research in New York. There he developed his critique of modern social science. As Strauss explained in his

Walgreen lectures at the University of Chicago, published as *Natural Right and History* in 1953, scientific "facts" had been severed from moral "values." Positivism—that bane of all traditionalists—was born. This separation of facts from values robbed Western civilization of its ability to distinguish good from evil. Why? Because social scientists limited their inquiry to "facts," which could be verified empirically, and dismissed everything else—including virtue and morality—as arbitrary and subjective. "The crisis of modernity," Strauss wrote, "reveals itself in the fact, or consists in the fact, that modern Western man no longer knows what he wants—that he no longer believes that he can know what is good or bad, what is right and wrong."[38]

Strauss had no interest in propounding dogmatic rules for political action. For him, circumstance, prudence, and moderation determined the right course of policy. Liberal democracy was not the ideal regime, because its focus on the satisfactions of the body left it vulnerable to corruption and outside attack. But it was better than the alternatives. Liberal democracy required supplementation. Its tastes needed elevating.

Strauss's work consisted of dense readings of philosophical texts. He wrote little about his adopted country. His frame of reference was continental Europe. His mind was concerned not with Democrats or Republicans but with Hellenes and Hebraists. The few mentions of America in his published work are complimentary. He chided positivists by referencing the Declaration of Independence and its self-evident truths: normative values of right and wrong, he observed, were woven into America's founding documents. He enjoyed pointing out that "one of the most conservative groups here calls itself Daughters of the American Revolution." For Strauss, the old conservatism of throne and altar was irrelevant in the United States. "The conservatism of our age," he wrote, "is identical with what originally was liberalism, more or less modified by changes in the direction of present-day liberalism."[39]

Strauss's students applied his methods of close textual reading and thick exegesis to the study of America. In 1944 a graduate student in political science named Harry Jaffa enrolled in one of Strauss's courses. "His presence was as unimpressive as the dilapidated classrooms provided by the New School," Jaffa remembered. "But he was pure overwhelming intellectual force." In 1949, when Strauss accepted a position at the University of Chicago, Jaffa went with him. There Jaffa completed his dissertation, published in 1952 under the title *Thomism and Aristotelianism*. Jaffa began contemplating his next project.[40]

A few years earlier, while shopping at a Fourth Avenue bookstore in New York, Jaffa discovered the debates between Abraham Lincoln and Stephen Douglas. He was captivated by the dialogue between the future president and the incumbent Democratic senator from Illinois. He thought that their exchanges read like a Socratic dialogue. He began working on a book about them.[41]

Meanwhile, two other students of Strauss published studies of American political institutions. In 1957 Walter Berns released *Freedom, Virtue, and the First Amendment*. The Supreme Court, Berns said, had misread the First Amendment as protecting an unlimited right to free speech. It elevated freedom above all other concerns. And this was terrible. For Berns, the object of politics was not freedom but virtue. "The solution to the problem," Berns wrote, "is the development of a moral character on the basis of which the good citizen will reject both the Communist and the depraved Republican or Democrat."[42]

In 1959, in his essay "Democracy and the *Federalist*," Martin Diamond overturned the dominant interpretation of the founding. Progressives had assumed that the Declaration of Independence stood for democracy and the Constitution for liberty—the liberty of property holders to retain what was theirs. Diamond said that the progressives had it backward: it was the Declaration that proclaimed liberty and the Constitution that protected democracy.

Diamond reached his conclusions through a detailed study of *The Federalist Papers*. He resuscitated a particularly American view of politics as the balancing of institutional prerogatives and individual ambition. And he was modest enough to suggest that the Founders still had something to teach political scientists.

Jaffa also read the Lincoln-Douglas debates as a work of political philosophy. In 1959 he brought out *Crisis of the House Divided*. The fight over popular sovereignty in the territories, Jaffa wrote, recapitulated the dispute in Plato's *Republic* over the nature of justice. Are there objective standards of right and wrong, or is justice merely the interest of the stronger? Through a brilliant analysis of Douglas's and Lincoln's positions, Jaffa demonstrated that Lincoln's appeals to the Declaration of Independence transcended the Constitution of the Founders and contributed to a new birth of freedom. "The crisis of the house divided had arisen," wrote Jaffa, "because a very considerable portion of the American people had turned its back on the truth upon which its own rights depended."[43]

The Straussians were anti-Communist. But they also kept their distance from *National Review* and from both traditionalism and libertarianism. In a review of Russell Kirk's *A Program for Conservatives* (1954), Berns wrote, "Despite the talk of class, order, church, and family, all Mr. Kirk can say (and he says it in numerous ways) is that the good is identical with the ancestral." The suspicion was mutual. Kirk rarely responded to the attacks of Straussians. He barely mentioned Jaffa and Berns by name. Instead he disagreed civilly with Strauss's reading of Burke and with the idea that Lincoln was anything more than a practical politician. Willmoore Kendall, for his part, agonized over the implications of a government not limited by the Tenth Amendment. In a *National Review* essay on *Crisis of the House Divided*, he worried that Lincoln was the progenitor of the powerful liberal chief executives who wielded centralized power in the service of egalitarianism.[44]

Kendall's piece was interesting because he, too, had become a disciple of Strauss. In late November 1956 he received a letter addressed to his office in the Yale political science department. "For some time I have been receiving *National Review*," Leo Strauss began. "You will not be surprised to hear that I agree with many articles appearing in the journal, especially your own." Yet Strauss could not comprehend the animosity of the editors toward the State of Israel. "I am, therefore, tempted to believe that the authors in question are driven by an anti-Jewish animus; but I have learned to resist temptations." In the paragraphs that followed, Strauss defended Israel as a conservative project.[45]

Kendall responded by saying that he agreed completely with Strauss. Buckley, he said, was no anti-Semite. And Kendall's explanation for *National Review*'s anti-Israel bias—a bias that would persist, to a lesser degree, for decades—was characteristic of his thought: certain editors, he wrote, were too beholden to liberal concepts of equality and freedom of speech. (In truth, much of the animus stemmed from Burnham's foreign policy realism: the Machiavellian, like many early members of the Central Intelligence Agency, had an Arabist bent and thought that Israel was outnumbered and doomed to fail.) Kendall asked if Strauss would consent to have his letter printed in an upcoming issue of the magazine. The answer was yes. That was how Leo Strauss made his first—and only—appearance in *National Review*, in his typical role as a friendly critic of both liberalism and conservatism.

THE 1958 MIDTERM ELECTIONS CRIPPLED THE GOP. SENATOR Bricker was defeated. Conservative Senate leader Bill Knowland, who had resigned his seat to run for governor of California, lost too. "The voters did not repudiate conservatism as philosophy and program; and neither did they endorse it," Brent Bozell wrote in an election postmortem for *National Review*. "They proved, however, that the Republican Party, the traditional vehicle of conservative political action, is dead." It was not the first, and far from the last, time the GOP was declared a corpse.[46]

Movement conservatives were not sanguine. They had lost Taft, McCarthy, Bricker, and Knowland in the space of five years. Neither party agreed with them on either domestic or foreign policy. Clearly the electorate was uninterested in what conservatives were selling. James J. Kilpatrick indulged in gallows humor. "My impulsive answer to the question, where do conservatives go from here," he wrote, "is down to Paddy's Grill to get falling down drunk." Buckley acknowledged "the failure of the conservative demonstration." Conservatism, he wrote, must "be wiped clean of the parasitic cant that defaces it, and repels so many of those who approach it inquiringly."[47]

In retrospect, the electoral reversals of 1958 helped usher in the younger and more energizing conservative leadership of Buckley and Goldwater. In the spring of 1959, Clarence Manion sent a letter to former America Firster General Robert E. Wood, asking, "Confidentially, what would you think about a committee to draft Goldwater for the Republican nomination for president? Such a movement may start a 'prairie fire.'"[48]

Goldwater, a Phoenix businessman who ran a department store and had flown cargo for the army during the war, had become a prominent conservative spokesman. The descendant of Jewish immigrants on his father's side, Goldwater had been brought up an Episcopalian. His politics were anti–New Deal. In 1952 his promotion of antiunion right-to-work legislation brought him to the Senate. An opponent of foreign aid and a reliable vote for Robert Taft, he took on a high-profile fight against Walter Reuther, head of the United Auto Workers, during his first term. The *Saturday Evening Post* began to speak of Goldwater's "leadership potential."[49]

The first step toward a Goldwater presidential candidacy, Manion thought, was to publish a book in Goldwater's name that could serve as a manifesto for the upcoming election. Manion even had a title in mind: *The Conscience of a Conservative*. What Manion did not have was a writer. He approached Brent Bozell to assemble a manuscript out of Goldwater's speeches, articles, columns, interviews, and conversation. At first Bozell was reluctant, but he accepted Manion's offer in July 1959. *The Conscience of a Conservative* was released in April 1960. Into its 127 pages Bozell poured the essence of postwar conservative thought.[50]

Goldwater grounded his conservatism in a particular reading of the Constitution and the American political tradition. "The conservative," he wrote, "looks upon politics as the art of achieving the maximum amount of freedom for individuals that is consistent with the maintenance of social order." Human liberty is the consequence of human dignity. "The conscience of a conservative," Goldwater said, "is pricked by *anyone* who would debase the dignity of the individual human being."[51]

The issue is how best to secure the rights of the individual. "Freedom," Goldwater wrote, "depends on effective restraints against the accumulation of power in a single authority." The Constitution disperses and diffuses power in defense of individual rights. Federalism, enumerated powers, checks and balances, the difficult but not insurmountable Article V process of ratifying constitutional amendments, and the Ninth and Tenth Amendments, which stipulate, respectively, that rights not mentioned in the Constitution are reserved to the people and to the states—these mechanisms also protect against the aggrandizement of the central government.[52]

The greatest threat to freedom was the Soviet Union. A quarter of *Conscience* is devoted to hard-line foreign policy. One of Bozell's innovations was in shifting the focus of conservative polemic from the internal danger of Communist infiltration to the external threat of Communist expansionism. Goldwater emerged from its pages as an upright, stolid, steely, flinty guardian of America. For him, the conservative project was essentially a negative one: rejecting liberal proposals, deconstructing the New Deal, and defeating communism. "I have little interest in streamlining government or in making it more efficient, for I mean to reduce its size," Goldwater declared. "I do not undertake to promote welfare, for I propose to extend freedom. My aim is not to pass laws, but to repeal them."[53]

The book was a publishing phenomenon. Its first hardcover edition quickly sold out. Within months, one hundred thousand paperbacks were in circulation. By 1964, *The Conscience of a Conservative* had sold 3.5 million copies. It elevated Goldwater to phenom status. The press dubbed him "Mr. Conservative." The difference between this nickname and that of "Mr. Republican" Robert Taft was telling. Goldwater was an ideological figure, the leader of a movement that transcended the GOP. Taft was a party man.[54]

Students loved Senator Goldwater's commitment to principle and his devotion to liberty. The only stumbling block to a conservative presidential candidacy was the favored candidate. Goldwater decided not to run in 1960 and backed Richard Nixon's bid. Nevertheless, Goldwater was furious when, during the convention, Nixon made a secret visit to Nelson Rockefeller, the liberal Republican governor of New York, and forged the "Compact of Fifth Avenue" to secure the nomination. In exchange for concessions in the party platform—including stronger civil rights language—and for selecting a nonconservative running mate, Rockefeller agreed to support Nixon.

When he learned of the compact, Goldwater told the press, "If the Fourteen Point agreement—both the substance of it and the process by which it was reached—is allowed to go unchallenged, it will live in history as the Munich of the Republican Party." He shared his fears with one of his friends from Arizona, an attorney named William Rehnquist. "I would rather see the Republicans lose in 1960 fighting for principle," he said, "than I would care to see us win standing on grounds we know are wrong and on which we will ultimately destroy ourselves."[55]

In choosing a vice presidential nominee, Nixon bypassed both Goldwater and anti-Communist congressman Walter Judd of Minnesota. To appease Rockefeller, he settled on former Massachusetts senator Henry Cabot Lodge Jr., whom Eisenhower had recommended. "While I was concerned that his domestic views were more liberal than mine," Nixon wrote, "I had no doubt that if the need ever arose he would be able to take over and serve as president."[56]

That did not lessen the disappointment of conservatives, who had been denied a place at the top of the Republican ticket for five elections in a row. When Goldwater addressed the 1960 Republican convention, it was as the favorite-son presidential nominee of Arizona. Following tradition—and not wanting to be the nominee in any case—he asked that his name be withdrawn from consideration. The audience exploded in anger and cries of no.

Goldwater wouldn't have it. "This country, and its majesty, is too great for any man, be he conservative or liberal, to stay home and not work just because he doesn't agree," he said to the crowd. "Let's grow up, conservatives! We want to take this party back, and I think some day we can. Let's get to work!"

And work they did. In September 1960, ninety students from forty-four colleges spread across twenty-four states met at Great Elm, Buckley's childhood home in Sharon, Connecticut. On September 11 they adopted the "Sharon Statement," an affirmation of "certain eternal truths" in "this time of moral and political crisis." The text mentioned integration of political and economic freedom, the triune conception of state power—limited to internal order, administration of justice, and national defense—constitutionalism, and anticommunism. The document's primary author was M. Stanton Evans, a Yale graduate who had recently been named, at the age of twenty-six, editor of the *Indianapolis Daily News*. The only serious disagreement among the signatories was whether to include the phrase "God-given free will." God prevailed.[57]

The Sharon Statement was the founding charter of a group called the Young Americans for Freedom (YAF). Buckley was thrilled at its inception. He gladly hosted the students and was pleased when they raised the age limit for membership to thirty-five. (He was then thirty-four years old.) Buckley saw the YAFers as idealists from the pages of Hayek's "The Intellectuals and Socialism." One of his friends and comrades, anti-Communist activist Marvin Liebman, provided office space for the organization in New York. The next year the YAFers started their own magazine, *New Guard*, and named Lee Edwards editor. Liebman hired a small staff, including a twenty-seven-year-old Texas Republican named Richard Viguerie, who became an expert in marketing through direct mail.

The fighting spirit of the ascendant Right was on display when Soviet premier Nikita Khrushchev arrived in the United States in mid-September 1960 to address the United Nations General Assembly. Just months before, the Soviet Union had shot down an American U-2 reconnaissance jet and imprisoned its pilot, Francis Gary Powers. On September 17, Buckley addressed a sold-out audience during an anti-Communist rally at Carnegie Hall. His speech displayed all his talents for sarcasm. He accused liberals of hypocrisy and vacillation in the face of Khrushchev's willfulness:

That he should achieve orthodox diplomatic recognition not four years after shocking history itself by the brutalities of Budapest; months after endorsing the shooting down of an unarmed American plane; only weeks since he last shrieked his intention of demolishing the West; only days since publishing in an American magazine his undiluted resolve to enslave the citizens of free Berlin—that such an introduction should end up constituting his credentials for a visit to America will teach him something about the West that some of us wish he might never have known.

Still, he concluded, there was no reason to despair. The traditions of Western civilization were a reservoir of spiritual strength from which Americans could draw the will to resist tyrants like Khrushchev. "Even out of the depths of despair, we take heart in the knowledge that it cannot matter how steep we fall, for there is always hope," Buckley said. "In the end, we will bury him."[58]

Buckley's defiance revealed both how far conservatism had come in the years since World War II and how far it had to go. He could command a crowd of mostly young people at a large venue. His magazine drew from a variety of libertarian, traditionalist, and anti-Communist thinkers. Other schools of thought, such as Straussianism, aligned themselves with the Right. His movement had a galvanizing spokesman in Barry Goldwater. And Buckley had done his part to ward off some of the Right's worst instincts, repudiating anti-Semitism and extremism and, in the aftermath of the McCarthy episode, emphasizing the international struggle against communism rather than countersubversion.

Yet Buckley was still viewed as an eccentric, not only by liberal tastemakers but also by liberal anti-Communists and the Republican Party elite. His reach was limited by the means of communication at his disposal and by the bipartisan anti-Communist consensus in the 1960 election that, in his opinion, did not go far enough. The Democratic nominee, Massachusetts senator John F. Kennedy, was both a Roman Catholic and to Richard Nixon's right on key foreign policy questions.

At this point in its twentieth-century odyssey, movement conservatism had recovered intellectually and institutionally from the nadir of the Great Depression. But it was still a minority political tendency. As he addressed the throngs in Carnegie Hall, Buckley could not have imagined that the coming decade would break the American Left and propel the Right toward the corridors of power.

CHAPTER SIX

NEW FRONTIERS

R ICHARD NIXON LOST IN 1960. THE PRESIDENTIAL RACE WAS close—a difference of fewer than 120,000 votes. Narrow victories for John F. Kennedy in Texas, where his vice presidential nominee Lyndon Baines Johnson controlled the state machine, and in Illinois, where Chicago mayor Richard J. Daley held similar power ("Vote early and vote often," he is thought to have said), generated Republican accusations of voter fraud. Nixon rejected pleas to contest the result. He thought Kennedy had engaged in dirty tricks, but it was better to take the loss and fight again another day. He went into private law practice and plotted a run for governor of California in 1962.[1]

William F. Buckley Jr. and *National Review* were ambivalent about the new president. Kennedy was a liberal, to be sure. But he also did not seem terribly interested in a rapid and grand extension of the New Deal. He had praised Robert Taft. Herbert Hoover once called Kennedy his "favorite senator." The Kennedys and the Buckleys also shared superficial commonalities. Both families were Catholic, and their foreign policies did not seem so different either. The new president's brother Robert, who would be named attorney general, had worked for Joe McCarthy's committee. His father was an America Firster who had donated to McCarthy's reelection. And Kennedy displayed a *National Review*–like resolve and self-confidence in his inaugural address when he pledged that America would "pay any price, bear any burden, meet any hardship, support any friend, oppose any foe to assure the survival and success of liberty."[2]

For the second presidential election in a row, the magazine did not endorse a candidate. The prospect of a choice between Kennedy's vigorous anti-Communist liberalism and Nixon's continuation of Dwight Eisenhower's legacy may have contributed to Buckley's sense of melancholy as *National Review* celebrated its fifth anniversary. One week before the election, friends, donors, and associates of *National Review* gathered for dinner at the Plaza Hotel in New York. Buckley addressed several prominent members of the audience: Hoover, General Douglas MacArthur, and Admiral Lewis Strauss, the former chairman of the Atomic Energy Commission whose nomination for secretary of commerce the Senate had rejected after he pulled nuclear physicist J. Robert Oppenheimer's security clearance. "We are all of us in one sense out of spirit with history," Buckley said. "And we are not due to feel those topical gratifications which persons less securely moored will feel as they are carried, exhilarated, in and out with the ebb and flow of events."

The task of *National Review*, Buckley went on, was to function as Albert Jay Nock's Remnant, keeping alive the sacred wisdom of the past. "And I expect," he concluded, "that they and all of you, my good and generous and devoted friends, must be happy, as I am, to know that for so long as it is mechanically possible, you have a journal, a continuing witness to those truths which animated the birth of our country, and continue to animate our lives." The next five years would bring Buckley's movement to political heights not achieved in three decades—and expose the internal fissures and paranoid dangers that would persist for decades more.[3]

The editors of *National Review* performed an ongoing balancing act. They tried not to lean in the direction of either too much libertarianism or too much traditionalism. They tried to maintain an equilibrium between principle and prudence. Some of the editors were more interested than others in theoretical questions. In demand as a public speaker, a television guest, and, beginning in 1962, a syndicated columnist, Buckley found himself too busy to indulge in philosophical speculation. For James Burnham, who with Priscilla Buckley shouldered most of the responsibility for putting the magazine out every other week, abstract thought was all too often an escape from political reality. More important was the analysis of discrete events in the real world and formulating responses to them.

Whittaker Chambers tried to push Buckley in the direction of the "Beaconsfield position." This was Chambers's way of describing the politics of nineteenth-century British prime minister Benjamin Disraeli, whom Queen Victoria named Earl of Beaconsfield in 1876. To Chambers, Disraeli was a conservative who recognized that the state could be a stabilizing influence on society. But Buckley resisted anything that resembled statism. Chambers resigned from the magazine in November 1959 on account of his deteriorating health. "Frank Meyer is emerging clearly as the Voice," he wrote to Buckley soon afterward. "I am not being sniffy: this, I gather from stray NR readers, is just what they want to hear."[4]

Like many of his colleagues, Meyer was something of an oddball. He lived with his wife and two sons in a book-filled farmhouse in rural Woodstock, New York. He was nocturnal, sleeping during the day and working through the night. He fought against postal zip codes. He grew alarmed at the totalitarian implications of the school lunch program. After nightfall he spent hours on the phone, in long conversations on politics, economics, literature, and philosophy. Willmoore Kendall joked that an emergency phone call between Meyer and Brent Bozell was one that interrupted an ongoing phone call between Meyer and Bozell.

Meyer did the most to harmonize freedom and virtue. He became *National Review*'s books and arts editor in 1957, after the departure of Willi Schlamm. He used his position to encourage up-and-coming writers such as Joan Didion, John Leonard, Robert Phelps, Guy Davenport, and Arlene Croce, even when they were not entirely on board with Buckley's editorials. Meanwhile, in his own articles, Meyer attempted to establish a conservative intellectual consensus. He articulated the concepts behind the practice of American democracy as he understood it. Using the techniques of ideological argumentation that he had picked up during his years as a Marxist, Meyer produced a theoretical framework for the sort of conservatism that men such as Warren Harding and Calvin Coolidge had practiced as a matter of course.

Freedom was the touchstone of Meyer's conservatism. But he grounded this freedom in what he called, appropriating the vocabulary of Eric Voegelin, a "transcendental moral order." Meyer wanted to reconstitute the political philosophy of the American founding, when "this simultaneous belief in objectively existing moral value and in the freedom of the individual person was promulgated in uncompromising terms."[5]

Meyer divided the world into two poles: one was the province of the individual; the other was the domain of social and governmental authority. Twentieth-century America, he said, had moved too close to the second pole. That was why he stressed the forces of freedom against collectivists, statists, and traditionalists who conflated means (free choice) and ends (virtue). "True, freedom, though it is the end of political theory and political action, is not the end of men's existence," he wrote. "It is a condition, a decisive and integral condition, but still only a *condition* of that end, which is virtue."[6]

Meyer distinguished between the purpose of politics and the purpose of morality. The end of politics, he said, must be freedom, because individual virtue cannot be attained if it is coerced. Meyer did not draw a rigid distinction, however, between government and society. He paid little attention to the intermediate institutions that lie between the individual and his government: the family, neighborhood, church, association, and vocation. Nor did Meyer address the possibility that emphasizing individual freedom over these social formations might *inhibit* one's ability to choose virtue or even to know what it is. This omission created a vulnerability in his position that critics never failed to exploit.

When the 1960s began, Meyer worried most about those libertarians whose opposition to the state led them to decry the security measures that *National Review* argued were necessary to defeat communism. In 1961, several of Friedrich Hayek's students at the University of Chicago had founded the *New Individualist Review*. In its third issue, associate editor Ronald Hamowy attacked Buckley. On foreign policy, internal subversion, and civil rights, Hamowy charged, *National Review* had traded the principle of individual liberty for communal standards. "Nowhere, any longer, does a rollback or repeal of the New Deal seem to be seriously contemplated," he lamented.[7]

Hamowy diverged most significantly from *National Review* in foreign policy. Unable to accept the existence of a standing army and national security establishment, he and his fellow radical libertarians were effectively anti-anti-Communist. They railed against *National Review*'s embrace of the military-industrial complex, its gradual approach to domestic reform, and its confrontational stance toward the Soviet Union. "Frank S. Meyer finds the vision of a total nuclear holocaust not entirely unappealing," Hamowy wrote.[8]

For *National Review*, the risk of war with the Soviet Union was necessary to the defense of freedom. And a life without freedom would not be worth living. "Senior Warmonger Frank Meyer argues that freedom is the meaning of life, that without freedom there is no life, that indeed that is why he would rather be dead than Red," Buckley wrote in a sarcastic response to Hamowy. "He does not know that to be a true libertarian you must love freedom but not *that* much—you must prefer to be Red than dead, or you cannot be in the libertarian tradition." Buckley could not allow the "extreme apriorism" of the libertarians to dominate the Right.[9]

In 1962, Meyer turned his attention to Murray Rothbard, an Austrian economist who despite his admiration for Joe McCarthy pursued an anti-anti-Communist foreign policy of military demobilization and disarmament. In his critique of Rothbard, Meyer described the conservative consensus.

> The common source in the *ethos* of Western civilization from which flow both the traditionalist and the libertarian currents, has made possible a continuing discussion which is creating the fusion that is contemporary American conservatism. That fused position recognizes at one and the same time the transcendent goal of human existence and the primacy of the freedom of the person, a value based upon transcendent considerations. And it maintains that the duty of men is to seek virtue; but it insists that men cannot in actuality do so unless they are free from the constraint of the physical coercion of an unlimited state.[10]

In his attack on the libertarian anti-anti-Communists, Meyer inadvertently provoked his friend Bozell. By this time, the Bozell family had moved to Spain, where Brent steeped himself in the religious culture and antimodern ideology of Generalísimo Francisco Franco's anti-Communist authoritarian regime. "Where before he was a dedicated Catholic," his wife, Patricia Buckley Bozell, said later, "he became a Catholic who believed that all thinking, all action, no matter where and when, should be rooted in Catholicism."[11]

This religious perspective convinced Bozell more than ever that liberalism, as Eric Voegelin had said, was a Gnostic heresy. It helped him understand that the state did not exist in opposition to the public but was a creation of the public. Bozell's traditionalist Catholicism intensified his anger at the US Supreme Court, which under Chief Justice Earl Warren had embarked on a series of decisions ruling school prayer unconstitutional. It also made him alert to the heretical impulses of those branches of the Right that stretched back to classical liberalism. Among them was Meyer's fusion.

Bozell's reply to Meyer was the longest article *National Review* published in its first seven years. He amplified an argument Meyer had had a few years earlier with Walter Berns over the place of virtue in political life. But Bozell's conception of virtue, unlike Berns's, was religious, not philosophical. And it was associated with a particular sect: Catholicism.

Bozell zeroed in on Meyer's idea that virtue coerced was not virtue at all. "If freedom is the *first* principle' of the search for virtue," he wrote, "if as Meyer writes at another point, it is 'the *precondition* of a good society,' then, by definition, there is no superior principle that can be invoked, at any stage, against the effort to maximize freedom—there is no point at which men are entitled to *stop* hauling down the 'props' which every rational society in history has erected to promote a virtuous citizenry."[12]

According to Bozell, Meyer's scheme was wrong because freedom and virtue did not actually inhabit distinct moral and political spheres. They were inseparable. Freedom was not an end in itself in either politics or morality. It was one of the means to virtue. And politics ought to modulate freedom if it became an obstacle to morality—if, to use the example Bozell mentioned in his piece, liberal no-fault divorce laws undermined the institution of marriage.

Bozell had a more sophisticated view than Meyer of the relationship between law, society, and culture. But he too assumed the existence of a homogenous society and a traditional culture that restrained libertinism and channeled freedom toward virtue. In the absence of such a culture, the state would be the sole arbiter of virtue. For this reason, Bozell was careful not to advocate a "fusion" of his own—a fusion of church and state.[13]

This disclaimer did not satisfy Meyer. No matter how loudly Bozell rejected theocracy, Meyer responded, the assumption that government is an "instrument" for "articulating and thus defending" the commonwealth's virtue results in theocracy. Committed to philosophical abstraction and inclined toward definitive judgments, neither Meyer nor Bozell recognized that there are different levels of government promotion of virtue and rejection of vice—not all of them authoritarian—and that the American civil religion offers a nonsectarian language for statesmen to exhort moral behavior and civic responsibility.

Bozell teased out a knot in Meyer's thinking, but in a way that could neither satisfy the libertarians inside the conservative coalition nor appeal to the majority of Americans who were not traditionalist Catholics. That was one reason the final victory in the dispute went to Meyer. Bozell's politics could not sustain a wide-ranging American Right, much less one that was viable at the polls.

"Fusionism"—the term was Bozell's, based on Meyer's original reference to "fusion"—also won out through default. By the mid-1960s, the writers who might have sustained the argument were either uninterested or unavailable. Chambers died in 1961. Russell Kirk held his fire for a blistering review of Meyer's book *In Defense of Freedom* in 1964, then dropped the subject and practically all mentions of Meyer from his writing. Richard Weaver had fused libertarianism and traditionalism in his own way in 1960, when he wrote that both groups felt "the same impulse to condemn arbitrary power." But Weaver—to whom Kirk, Meyer, and Kendall all looked for guidance—died in 1963. Around the same time, Kendall dropped his association with *National Review* and decamped to Texas. Bozell also grew distant, occupied by the problems, questions, and demands of Catholic thought. Finally, fusionism appealed to movement conservatives because it offered the most plausible theoretical explanation for their belief that the continuance of the American republic depended on a complex mixture of both freedom and virtue.[14]

If *National Review* was not religious enough for Bozell, it was too religious for Max Eastman, the ex-Communist journalist who had gone from translating Leon Trotsky to lunching with Buckley. After reading the Meyer-Bozell argument over fusionism, Eastman began to feel that *National Review* was overly religious and predominantly Catholic. He sent Buckley a note saying he could write for it no more. Buckley drew from Eastman's departure a lesson in the relationship between religion and conservatism. "Can you be a conservative and believe in God?" he asked. "Obviously. Can you be a conservative and not believe in God? This is an empirical essay, and so the answer is obviously, yes. Can you be a conservative and despise God, and feel contempt for those who believe in Him? I would say no."[15]

Here was another instance of Buckley seeking equilibrium. He offered a place for agnostics, even atheists, within his conservatism but on the condition that they not devote themselves to God hatred. Too much ballast on one side of *National Review* threatened to capsize the ship. Thus it was Frank Meyer who defined movement conservatism, for his theories alone created the space where libertarians and traditionalists could join in a common anti-Communist endeavor. Meyer kept a steady course. He maintained a semblance of order. Buckley called him "air traffic control."

THE REAL THREAT TO THE COHERENCE AND SUSTAINABILITY OF conservatism was not its intellectual debates but its more florid manifestations. Conservative doctrine needn't be worked out fully for the Right to prosper politically—so long as the general public considered it mainstream. That was why Buckley had to confront the John Birch Society (JBS).

Robert W. Welch Jr. was two years away from retiring as a candy magnate when Regnery published his *Life of John Birch* in 1954. The story of an American missionary to China killed by Communist partisans at the end of World War II, Welch's book was an anti-Communist martyrology and a call to arms against the Communist conspiracy. That conspiracy, Welch asserted with no evidence, was much broader and far deeper than even Joseph McCarthy had imagined.

Among his friends, Welch began to circulate an unpublished document, *The Politician*, detailing President Eisenhower's role in the Communist plot. When Welch showed *The Politician* to Barry Goldwater, the senator told him, "I want no part of this. I won't even have it around. If you were smart, you'd burn every copy you have." Needless to say, Welch did not take the advice.[16]

Regnery introduced Buckley to Welch, who wrote $1,000 checks to *National Review* in 1955 and 1957. In 1958, with support from some of the financial backers of America First, as well as Kansas industrialist Fred Koch, Welch founded the John Birch Society in Indianapolis. He sent Buckley a leather-bound edition of *The Politician*. So, early on, Buckley was aware of what the JBS founder truly believed. He wrote Welch to say that he rejected the theory. But he did not disavow the Birchers. For his part, Russell Kirk quipped, "Eisenhower isn't a Communist—he is a golfer."[17]

It became difficult to avert one's gaze from the JBS as it grew in size and strength. Chapters opened up around the country. The Bircher publication, *American Opinion*, enjoyed a wide circulation and shared a few contributors with *National Review*. It was hard to gauge the society's actual membership since its internal operations were opaque. But when Welch called for the impeachment of Earl Warren in 1961, phone calls, mail, and telegrams inundated Capitol Hill. And Bircher slogans became popular bumper stickers: "Impeach Earl Warren," "U.S. Out of U.N.," "Support Your Local Police."

Welch insisted on personal loyalty and top-down control. Birch Society chapters were rigidly organized. Members were directed in secret to pursue political office. Birchers were drawn not only to Welch's anti-Communist message but also to his description of a world where sinister elites were behind everything that had gone wrong in the country. The Birch Society became an outlet for the nation's antiestablishment energies. It drew strength from the millions of Americans who did not feel represented by the politics of JFK Democrats and Nixon Republicans.

The movement was an expression of antielitism. The JBS provided its membership with both a sense of community and a ghoulish framework through which to interpret current events. "The controlling order, which we have dubbed THE INSIDERS, has given more attention and ruthless enforcement to keeping its very existence a secret than to any other objective in the whole *satanic* program," Welch wrote. The insiders were behind everything: the betrayal of eastern Europe, the Communist takeover of China, the stalemate in Korea, even the deaths of prominent Republicans. "We don't know whether the peculiar cancer of which Bob Taft died," he said, "was induced by a radium tube planted in the upholstery of his Senate seat, as has been so widely rumored."[18]

It was impossible to say how many JBS members believed in every last bit of Welch's lunacy. But for some Birchers the conspiracy theories were unquestionably the point of the organization. And the myths were a launch pad for anti-Semitism and extrajudicial violence. One of Welch's lieutenants, a classics professor named Revilo Oliver who for a time contributed to *National*

Review, endorsed the *Protocols of the Elders of Zion* in a 1964 speech. In 1962 a Bircher exploded a bomb outside a journalist's home. "He was quietly dropped from the rolls when the bombing story hit the headlines," wrote ex-Bircher Gerald Schomp in his memoir *Birchism Was My Business.* Another Bircher, Robert Bolivar DePugh, formed the Minutemen, an armed group of between three hundred and four hundred people who trained in paramilitary exercises to prepare for the Communist invasion. The Minutemen newsletter was called *On Target.* DePugh ended up going to prison on gun charges.[19]

Robert Welch and the John Birch Society emerged as the successors to Joe McCarthy. But the JBS was better organized, more widely dispersed, and more difficult to defeat. McCarthy's demise ended neither the politics of countersubversion nor the appetite for groundless accusations of treason. In 1958, the year the society was born, FBI director J. Edgar Hoover published *Masters of Deceit: The Story of Communism in America and How to Fight It.* W. Cleon Skousen, a JBS member, published *The Naked Communist,* which claimed to reveal the Soviet plan for world domination and the way Moscow controlled the US government. The society also benefited from the continued appeal of disengaged nationalism to the Right. Welch opposed the North Atlantic Treaty Organization, foreign aid, and entanglement in Indochina.

The campaign to impeach Warren generated a huge amount of public scrutiny into Welch. A Democratic congressman from Ohio obtained a copy of *The Politician,* entered it into the congressional record, and called Welch "Hitler." Between February and December 1961 more than seven hundred articles on the JBS appeared in the nation's major newspapers. *Time* reported on the group in March. The *New York Times* followed up in April. Then the space flight of Soviet cosmonaut Yuri Gagarin displaced coverage of the society.[20]

It was not out of the news for long. Army general Edwin A. Walker was found to have distributed Birch material to soldiers under his command. While the JBS tried not to be overtly racist, Walker also embraced the conspiracy theories of Fundamentalist radio and television broadcaster Billy James Hargis, for whom the civil rights movement was a Communist plot. When Kennedy's defense secretary, Robert McNamara, relieved Walker of command, the general resigned and entered politics.

A MacArthur-like rupture in civil-military relations was imminent. Alarmed by the presence of the JBS inside the armed forces and knowing that the Bircher issue divided the Right and split the Republican Party, Kennedy delivered a broadside against the conspiracy mongers on November 18, 1961, shortly after Walker's resignation. The great American consensus, Kennedy said during his speech in Los Angeles, was under attack from "the discordant voices of extremism."

Kennedy reasserted his national security bona fides. He said that action, not talk, was "the most effective answer that [could] be made to those who would sow the seeds of doubt and of hate." He had spent more money on defense and taken an aggressive posture toward Communist threats. In 1959 Fidel Castro had established a Communist state in Cuba. Two years later, early in his term, Kennedy launched an American-sponsored invasion of the island by exiled Cuban paramilitary troops that ended in disaster at the Bay of Pigs. Then, in October 1962, Kennedy faced down the threat of Russian nuclear weapons based in Cuba—without resorting to the air strikes urged by the air force chief of staff, General Curtis LeMay.

A new breed of "defense intellectuals" supported Kennedy's resolve. Prominent among them, from the RAND Corporation think tank, was the married couple of Albert Wohlstetter, author of the influential essay on nuclear deterrence "The Delicate Balance of Terror," and Roberta Wohlstetter, author of the prize-winning study of intelligence failure *Pearl Harbor: Warning and Decision.* One of their former RAND colleagues was Herman Kahn, the futurist and nuclear strategist who cofounded the Hudson Institute and, along with Henry Kissinger and Werner von Braun, was satirized as Dr. Strangelove in the 1964 Stanley Kubrick film of the same name.

Kennedy's administration and his allies in the press went on the offensive against the Birchers—and anyone else who accused JFK of softness toward communism. The president tried to rein in J. Edgar Hoover. He had the Internal Revenue Service investigate twenty-two conservative nonprofits. He called on the Federal Communications Commission (FCC) to enforce the fairness doctrine, which mandated equal airtime for divergent viewpoints. The FCC revoked the license of a conservative broadcaster. A memo prepared by labor leader Walter Reuther for Robert Kennedy, titled "The Radical Right in America Today," mentioned none other than Barry Goldwater.[21]

America's most famous conservative was a friend of President Kennedy's who had been trying to broaden the conservative message in the wake of Nixon's defeat. On July 11, 1961, Goldwater delivered a speech on the Senate floor on "the forgotten American." Robert Novak, a reporter for the *New York Herald Tribune,* called it "The Goldwater Manifesto." In Goldwater's framing, conservatism stood for the "silent Americans" against the special interests seeking favors from Washington, DC. This was a gripping message—but also ahead of its time and in the hands of an unreliable messenger. For as much as Goldwater's advisers wanted him to include more Americans in his definition of conservatism and to temper his opposition to government programs, he happily fell back on the doctrines expounded in *Conscience of a Conservative.*[22]

Goldwater still had no interest in running for president. But he left some wiggle room. It was enough to inspire a small group of conservative Republicans, including *National Review* publisher William Rusher, to begin organizing a Draft Goldwater Committee. The project began in secret at a meeting in Chicago on October 8, 1961. Two months later, this inner circle divvied up chores. "Rusher's in charge of the kooks," someone said, referring to *National Review*.[23]

Rusher's colleagues at the magazine were far less enthusiastic about Goldwater. Burnham was open to Goldwater's rival, New York governor Nelson Rockefeller, who combined liberal stances on civil rights and the welfare state with strong anticommunism. But Burnham was alone. Buckley had no patience for Rockefeller, but he was not convinced Goldwater was up to the challenge. Others simply did not think Goldwater would run.

The John Birch Society presented another obstacle. Its members adored Goldwater, who said of the group, "I see no reason to take a stand against any organization just because they're using their constitutional prerogatives even though I disagree with most of them." In a presidential campaign, Goldwater's deflection might not be enough to distance the candidate or the conservative movement from Welch, who was busy charging Kennedy with treason. "The Birch Society represented to Buckley—and certainly to me and a few others—the absolute worst in American right-wing thinking," wrote conservative activist Marvin Liebman. "It was a resurrection of the know-nothing bigotry that largely made up the American right before Buckley came on the scene."[24]

Buckley was not prepared to make this argument in public. "I do not agree with some of the corporate projects of the Society," he wrote in the spring of 1961, "but I cannot think of one that is so scandalous or so mischievous as the call for nuclear disarmament, or world government, or what have you, upon which the press at large has yet to register its anxiety, or scorn." He said, "I hope [the JBS] thrives, provided, of course, it resists such false assumptions as that a man's subjective motives can be automatically deduced from the objective consequence of his acts." In other words, it was wrong to say Eisenhower was a Communist just because he did not risk a nuclear war to keep Hungary free.[25]

The entanglement of the Birch Society with both the conservative movement and the Draft Goldwater effort presented the Right with a dilemma. Conservatism could attain neither elite validation nor nationwide success if it was associated with Birchism. But it also could not sustain itself if Birchism was excised—it would have no constituency. The internal stress was most acute for conservatives who wanted to be taken seriously by liberal institutions. One was William Baroody Sr., the son of Christian Lebanese immigrants, who had worked in Eisenhower's Commerce Department and become president of the American Enterprise Association (AEA), which he renamed the American Enterprise Institute (AEI) in 1962. Another was W. Glenn Campbell, who had worked for Baroody at AEA before leaving to direct the Hoover Institution on War, Revolution, and Peace in 1960.

Baroody wanted to compete on the same turf as the Brookings Institution, AEI's liberal rival. He insinuated himself into Goldwater's circle. In January 1962 he called a meeting of prominent conservatives, including Buckley and Kirk, at the Breakers hotel in Palm Beach. The plan was to meet with Goldwater, who was visiting his sister, and discreetly advise him to distance himself from the JBS. As Buckley recollected many years later, Goldwater was loath to take on Welch directly—doing so would shatter his base of support. An indictment of Welch's followers would come across as condescension, snobbery, elitism, and disrespect for the hoi polloi. If Buckley and Kirk wrote articles of their own, however, they might provide Goldwater an opportunity to voice his disagreements with Welch, if not with Welch's fans.[26]

Buckley returned from Florida to New York, where he wrote a five-thousand-word essay, "The Question of Robert Welch." The issue with the Birch Society, he argued, was less the structure of the organization than the delusions of its founder. "The underlying problem," he wrote, "is whether conservatives can continue to acquiesce quietly in a rendition of the causes of the decline of the Republican Party and the entire Western world which is false, and, besides that, crucially different in practical emphasis from their own." Kirk followed up with a column on the subject. And Goldwater wrote in to *National Review*, "I believe the best thing Mr. Welch could do to serve the cause of anticommunism in the United States would be to resign." In language reminiscent of Nixon's speech against McCarthy ten years earlier, Goldwater continued, "We cannot allow the emblem of irresponsibility to attach to the conservative banner."[27]

This well-choreographed, intellectual-political pas de deux may have shaken the confidence of some Birchers in their leader Welch. It certainly put Buckley, Kirk, and Goldwater on the record against him. But its overall effect was minimal. Welch didn't go anywhere. And the media continued to portray the Right as fanatical and extreme.

The prospect of running against JFK attracted Goldwater. He hoped that the two candidates might hold a series of debates on the most important questions of principle and policy. In February 1963, Bill Rusher made the case for Goldwater in *National Review*. The essay, "Crossroads for the GOP," argued that the 1964 nominee would determine whether conservatism had a future in the Republican Party. Reprints of the article sold in great numbers. That spring, Goldwater recognized that the decision to run was not entirely his own. He told *Newsweek*, "I ask myself, 'What's my responsibility to conservatism?'"[28]

The Kennedy administration, the press, and liberal intellectuals continued to conflate Goldwater and Buckley with Robert Welch and General Walker. In 1963 Daniel Bell brought out a revised and expanded edition of his anthology *The New American Right*, this time under the title *The Radical Right*. "To understand the Manichean style of thought, the apocalyptic tendencies, the love of mystification, the intolerance of compromise that are observable in the right-wing mind," wrote historian Richard Hofstadter in his contribution to the volume, "we need to understand the history of fundamentalism as well as the contributions of depth psychology." But the Right was also a Rorschach test for liberals: they often saw in conservative politics exactly the worst tendencies they were looking for.[29]

Still, the Right was assisting in its own delegitimization. General Walker moved to Texas, where he continued to promote Welch and Hargis and ran unsuccessfully for governor. Elsewhere in the South, segregationists used violence to suppress the civil rights movement. Police unleashed fire hoses and dogs on nonviolent protesters, including children, in Birmingham, Alabama, in May 1963. Medgar Evers was murdered in Jackson, Mississippi in June. Domestic terrorists bombed a church in Birmingham, killing four black girls, in September. Buckley deplored the violence, but he also questioned Martin Luther King Jr.'s strategy of civil disobedience. And he remained convinced that desegregation should be a state responsibility. Buckley never quite explained how racist Democrats such as Bull Connor and George Wallace would ever volunteer for the task.

In Dallas in October, General Walker headlined a large and rowdy protest against Adlai Stevenson, now serving as JFK's UN ambassador. The rally spooked Stevenson. It also worried some of the president's advisers, who wondered whether he and Vice President Johnson should go ahead with a planned visit to Texas. JFK overruled their concerns and went ahead with the trip to meet with Governor John Connally. It never occurred to anyone that the actual threat to Kennedy might come from a Marxist-Leninist activist for Fidel Castro's Communist revolution in Cuba, who had previously defected to the Soviet Union and who had fired at General Walker (and missed) in the spring.

There followed one of the most extraordinary reversals in American history: the Right shouldered the blame for the actions of the Communist who assassinated JFK. Jacqueline Kennedy led the effort to shift public attention from Lee Harvey Oswald's communism to the atmosphere of right-wing extremism that surrounded Dallas. This was her way of turning her late husband, whose domestic agenda had been stuck in the Senate, into a martyr for civil rights, an issue on which he hadn't spent much political capital.

Prominent journalists assisted the widowed Kennedy. "The irony of the president's death is that his short administration was devoted almost entirely to various attempts to curb this very streak of violence in the American character," wrote James Reston of the *New York Times*. Walter Cronkite of CBS lied outright: he reported that Goldwater's reaction to JFK's death was "no comment." In fact, Goldwater had been stricken with grief.[30]

HARDLY ANYONE IN GOLDWATER'S CIRCLE BELIEVED THAT A Republican could win against Kennedy's heir, Lyndon Johnson, who surfed a wave of popularity after the gruesome killing of the young president. Goldwater met with his advisers in December. "The senator began by saying, 'Our cause is lost,' arguing that no Republican could win in 1964 because Americans would not want three different presidents in barely one year," recalled Goldwater aide Lee Edwards. "The idea of running against Johnson was abhorrent to him—Johnson was a wheeler-dealer, a hypocrite on civil rights, a dirty fighter."[31]

At the same time, Goldwater reasoned that if he let this chance slip by, Rockefeller would almost certainly win the nomination, and Eisenhower's "modern Republicanism" would embed itself within the GOP. That would dash the hopes of the thousands of activists who had rallied to Goldwater's cause. And it might inspire them to reject mainstream politics for the JBS. "All right, goddam it," Goldwater said. "I'll do it."[32]

He announced his candidacy on January 3, 1964. He offered, he said, "a choice, not an echo." He would not trim his sails to win this campaign. Americans would have to accept Barry Goldwater for what he was: gruff, determined, abrupt, and filled with conviction. One of his campaign posters read, "In your heart, you know he's right." Not every Republican felt that way. The primary campaign drew other contestants, including not only Rockefeller but also Governor William Scranton of Pennsylvania—two Republican exemplars of technocratic, problem-solving liberalism. The primary became a proxy battle between conservative Republicans of the West and South and moderate and liberal Republicans of the East.

The Rockefellers and Scrantons of the world stood for more than the disinterested application of policy expertise. They represented the liberal elite of both parties. Conservatives detested this bipartisan, "moderate" consensus. A forty-year-old mother of six was the voice of grassroots disgust. Phyllis Schlafly had graduated from Washington University in Saint Louis in 1944. She earned a master's degree from Radcliffe the next year and became involved in Republican politics in Illinois while raising her family. A devoted Catholic anti-Communist, Schlafly joined the John Birch Society, but she resigned when she self-published her first book, *A Choice, Not an Echo*, in support of Goldwater's candidacy. Schlafly acutely identified and described the sense of betrayal that conservatives felt toward party bigwigs.[33]

Schlafly portrayed Republican politics as a shadow play in which the true powers were the "kingmakers," who with "their propaganda apparatus have launched a series of false slogans designed to mask the failure of their candidates to debate the major issues." The kingmakers, in league with the Democrats, wanted to preserve FDR's New Deal. Eisenhower wasn't a Communist; he was a liberal. And that was reason enough to oppose figures such as Nelson Rockefeller. Schlafly believed that the market competition fueling American prosperity should also drive American politics. The two parties should stand for alternatives, not Kennedy's "great American consensus." Goldwater was the only choice that ensured ideological competition.[34]

The race for the Republican nomination came down to the June 2 California primary. When Rockefeller's second wife gave birth to a son a few days before voting began, traditionalist voters were reminded of the scandal surrounding his divorce. The story may have tipped the race in Goldwater's favor. When the results from California were in, Goldwater was victorious. His campaign had achieved its essential aim. For the first time since Alf Landon, the Republican nominee would be an unabashed, no-holds-barred conservative. At headquarters, Goldwater raised a toast to his staff and to his nation. "Here's to the greatest country in the world," he said. "As Harry Golden says, only in America would the first Jewish presidential nominee be an Episcopalian."[35]

Through the Goldwater campaign the intellectual Right made its presence felt in presidential politics for the first time since the Great Depression. The list of Goldwater's advisers was a roll call of movement conservatism. Russell Kirk drafted some early speeches. Baroody and Campbell populated the campaign with AEI associates such as speechwriter Karl Hess and national security expert Robert Strausz-Hupé. William Rehnquist served as counsel. A thirty-four-year-old Yale Law professor named Robert Bork offered legal analysis. And Milton Friedman gave advice on economic policy.[36]

Born to Jewish immigrants in Brooklyn, the elfin, mischievous, implacable Friedman grew up in Rahway, New Jersey. His early studies in technical economics won him the professional credibility that came in handy when he published *Capitalism and Freedom* in 1962 and *A Monetary History of the United States*, coauthored with Anna J. Schwartz, in 1963. In these works, Friedman defended the system of private ownership and exchange and argued that the monetary policies of the Federal Reserve had turned the stock market crash of 1929 into the Great Depression of the 1930s. Friedman was an advocate of "monetarism": he argued that the quantity of money in an economy determined prices and that the Federal Reserve should abandon discretion in favor of fixed rules of monetary policy, such as a gradual increase in the money supply, in order to avoid financial panics and recessions.

Friedman proudly identified himself as a nineteenth-century liberal. Like Hayek, he was wary of being called a conservative. He supported radical changes in the relationship of economy and state. In his mind, most of twentieth-century fiscal, monetary, and social policy was mistaken. "If we'd had minimum-wage laws and all the other trappings of the welfare state in the nineteenth century," he said in an interview with *Playboy* magazine, "half the readers of *Playboy* would either not exist at all or be citizens of Poland, Hungary, or some other country. And there would be no *Playboy* for them to read."[37]

Nor was Friedman content to criticize. He shot off ideas like sparks—which was why Goldwater was so close to him. Friedman proposed a range of substitutes for failed government initiatives: flexible exchange rates, a steady growth in the money supply, a negative income tax, an end to occupational licensure, education vouchers, and abolition of the draft. "Only a crisis—actual or perceived—produces real change," Friedman wrote. "When that crisis occurs, the actions that are taken depend on the ideas that are lying around."[38]

The Goldwater campaign allowed Friedman to publicize his alternatives. In an essay for the *New York Times Magazine*, "The

Goldwater View of Economic Policy," Friedman extolled an all-volunteer military, a 5 percent across-the-board annual tax cut for five years, a gradually balanced federal budget, and block grants to the states. Goldwater was no reactionary, Friedman wrote. "The irony is that the critics who charge him with retreating to the nineteenth century are themselves working hard as they can to turn the clock back to the mercantilism of the sixteenth and seventeenth centuries." From the perspective of the early twenty-first century, Goldwater's Friedman-inflected program does not seem regressive. It seems visionary.[39]

The only conservative intellectuals not associated with the Goldwater campaign were Buckley, Bozell, and the folks at *National Review*. Sometime after he had worked with Buckley on distancing Goldwater from the John Birch Society, Bill Baroody decided that Buckley was himself too extreme. In the months before the campaign officially began, he ambushed the magazine editor, leaking to the *New York Times* the story of Buckley's meeting with Goldwater aides. The article then became the pretext for excluding Buckley from Goldwater's operation. That was a bad choice. Goldwater needed all the help he could get.

The senator's fears proved true. LBJ used his vast resources and bully pulpit to realize the ambition of Rockefeller aide Stu Spencer: "Destroy Barry Goldwater as a member of the human race." The press corps had LBJ's back. Goldwater was tarred as a Nazi. A group of psychiatrists announced that he was psychologically unfit for the presidency. Goldwater was held up as proof of anti-intellectualism in American life, of what Richard Hofstadter deemed the paranoid style in American politics. The infamous "Daisy" television ad, aired only once, implied that the election of Goldwater would result in a nuclear holocaust. The dishonest fury of what Buckley had called the liberal "Apparatus" enraged conservatives. "The mass communication network," wrote Meyer, "solidly in Liberal hands, is even more formidable an opponent than conservatives had thought." Dislike of the media became one of the Right's signature traits.[40]

Still, Goldwater gave the press a lot to work with. He could not live down an offhand remark that perhaps low-yield tactical nuclear weapons could clear the jungle canopy obscuring Vietcong supply routes from American bombers. For all the earnestness of his fans—self-proclaimed "Goldwater Girls," kids in crew cuts and bold-rimmed glasses, collectors of Goldwater-themed merchandise—the candidate himself remained dyspeptic and irritable. Offered a sample of "Goldwater," a drink made for conservatives, the senator gagged and said, "This taste likes piss! I wouldn't drink it with gin!" He preferred Old Crow bourbon on the rocks.[41]

Nor could Goldwater shake his association with extremism. He hardly tried to. When he appeared on a talk show in May, host Steve Allen asked him about the JBS. "I don't worry so much about these people, frankly, as I do those people, again acting under their constitutional privileges, who subscribe to the idea that we can have a centrally controlled economy run by the government or that we can deprive the states of their powers and centralize the power of government in Washington," Goldwater replied. That wasn't a disavowal. It was a change of subject.[42]

Goldwater's July 16 convention address at the Cow Palace in San Francisco was a defiant restatement of his views. It was also a pungent rebuke of liberal elements within the GOP. Rockefeller had used his convention speech to attack the Birchers and other groups and gloried in the boos, hollers, and jeers from the crowd. Goldwater and his speechwriters, including Harry Jaffa, who had left Leo Strauss at Chicago to teach at Claremont Men's College in California, wrote a speech that answered Rockefeller in kind.

The nominee lambasted the liberal mentality. "Those who seek to live your lives for you, to take your liberties in return for relieving you of yours; those who elevate the state and downgrade the citizen, must see ultimately a world in which earthly power can be substituted for divine will," he said. "And this nation was founded upon the rejection of that notion and upon the acceptance of God as the author of freedom." Then, in a line supplied by Jaffa, he turned his sights on Rockefeller. "And let our Republicanism so focused and so dedicated not be made fuzzy and futile by unthinking and stupid labels," he said. "I would remind you that extremism in the defense of liberty is no vice. And let me remind you also that moderation in the pursuit of justice is no virtue!"[43]

The delegates went crazy. They loved it. But Goldwater's allies understood that the senator had played right into the media caricature. His fate was sealed. Lee Edwards overheard one reporter say, "My God, he's going to run as Barry Goldwater." A thirty-four-year-old public relations executive and Bill Scranton supporter named William Safire, raising a banner that read, "Stay in the Mainstream," kept an eye on Richard Nixon during Goldwater's speech. The former vice president was impassive. But inside he was roiling. "I felt almost physically sick," he recalled.[44]

It was no surprise that the general election did not go smoothly. For one thing, Goldwater's position on civil rights was tortured and difficult to explain. In language familiar to a subsequent generation of pro-choice politicians, Goldwater said that he personally opposed segregation but could not impose his views on the South. In truth, Goldwater did support racial integration. He did help found Arizona's chapter of the National Association for the Advancement of Colored People. He did work to desegregate the Senate cafeteria. He did vote for the Civil Rights Act of 1957 and for the Twenty-Fourth Amendment barring poll taxes. But he voted against the Civil Rights Act of 1964 because he believed Title II (mandating equality in public accommodations) and Title VII (prohibiting workplace discrimination) were unconstitutional and would lead to affirmative action and racial quotas.

Adding to the confusion was the fact that Goldwater presided over a convention whose platform committed its nominee to the "full implementation and faithful execution of the Civil Rights Act of 1964, and all other civil rights statutes, to assure equal rights and opportunities guaranteed by the Constitution to every citizen." The inclusion of this language, despite Goldwater's public opposition to the act, was one reason GOP leader Senator Everett Dirksen endorsed him. "Too long have we ridden the gray ghost of me-tooism!" Dirksen told the Illinois delegation. "When the roll is called, I shall cast my vote for Barry Goldwater!"[45]

Many of Goldwater's southern supporters were less interested in the reasoning behind his opposition to the Civil Rights Act than in its real-world consequences. On September 16, 1964, Democrat Strom Thurmond announced that he would join the Republican Party, thereby becoming the second GOP senator from the South (John Tower of Texas, elected in 1960, was the first). The alliance between the former head of the Dixiecrats and the Republican Party was an epochal event in American politics. It exemplified the slow realignment of the South away from the Democratic Party. But it signaled, in the politics of 1964, just how far from the mainstream Goldwater was. In welcoming Thurmond and standing athwart the Civil Rights Act, Goldwater alienated not only the GOP's black constituency, which had been shrinking since the Franklin Roosevelt administration, but also all of the white voters who hoped that the law finally would satisfy demands for political equality.

Goldwater addressed the civil rights issue in a speech on October 16, 1964. Drawing from the work of Robert Bork—who had argued in the *New Republic* the previous year, "If every time an intensely felt moral principle is involved, we spend freedom, we will run short of it"—Goldwater placed himself in the tradition of Justice John Marshall Harlan's dissent in *Plessy v. Ferguson*.[46]

"It has been well said that the Constitution is color blind," Goldwater began. "Our aim, as I understand it, is neither to

establish a segregated society nor to establish an integrated society. It is to preserve a *free* society." Goldwater said that he did
not disagree with the Civil Rights Act's intent but objected to the
powers it granted government. And he warned of unanticipated
consequences. Among them, he said, would be the forced busing
of students across school districts, because the Civil Rights Act
"reintroduces through the back door the very principle of allocation by race that makes compulsory segregation morally wrong and
offensive to freedom." This was an argument that few wanted to
hear. Goldwater's worries had not yet materialized. His arguments
simply confirmed that he was out of step with the moment.

Buckley recognized that the country was not about to embrace
Goldwater. He rejected the argument among many conservatives that a "hidden vote" would put the Republican in the White
House. On September 11, Buckley left the Young Americans for
Freedom in shocked silence by telling them the election was lost:
"A great rainfall has deluged a thirsty earth, but before we had
time properly to prepare the ground," he said. "I speak of course
about the impending defeat of Barry Goldwater." The next month
he told the New York Conservative Party, which he first conceived
in 1957 and had helped start in 1962, that despite Johnson's as-
sured victory, "In America there are those who are *dragging our
feet*; resisting, kicking, complaining, hugging tightly to the ancient
moorings. What do we cling to? Among other things, the individual, and the individual's role in history."[47]

A day later, on October 27, one individual stepped forward.

By the fall of 1964, Ronald Reagan's worldview was in full maturity. After his film career had dried up, the actor turned to television, hosting *General Electric Theater* and spreading the gospel
of free enterprise to workers at GE plants across the country. He
had met Buckley in 1961. They became fast friends. Reagan was
a veteran union man—he'd been president of the Screen Actors
Guild for six terms. FDR was his "hero." He chaired Democrats

for Eisenhower in 1952 and 1956 and Democrats for Nixon in 1960. But his increasing political activism discomfited his employers. GE dropped Reagan in 1962. That year he changed his registration to Republican.[48]

Shortly before Election Day, a group of California donors approached Reagan. They wanted him to record a speech for television in support of Goldwater. He agreed—on the condition that he deliver his remarks before a live audience. After the speech was taped, film was sent to the Goldwater campaign. Baroody resisted airing it because Reagan had criticized Social Security. Goldwater, Baroody feared, would come across as too conservative.

Reagan wondered why the speech hadn't aired. He called Goldwater to ask about the holdup. Goldwater said he would watch the speech for himself. He did. When the lights came up, Goldwater asked his aides, "What the hell is wrong with that?" Not long after, "A Time for Choosing" aired nationwide.[49]

Its content would not have surprised anyone who followed Reagan's career. Of interest was the way Reagan framed his remarks. He cast himself as a former Democrat who liked Barry Goldwater. The intended takeaway: that limited government and strong-willed anticommunism were not just for Republicans. Reagan warned that rising taxes and spending endangered American prosperity. He said that American troops were imperiled in Vietnam, where Kennedy and then Johnson had committed money, weapons, supplies, and finally numerous US troops since 1961.

Reagan's thoughts operated along unconventional axes. He did not conceive of a horizontal political axis stretching from left to right. "You and I are told increasingly that we have to choose between a left or right, but I would like to suggest that there is no such thing as a left or right," he said. "There is only an up or down—up to man's age-old dream, the ultimate in individual freedom consistent with law and order—or down to the ant heap of totalitarianism, and regardless of their sincerity, their humanitarian motives, those who would trade our freedom for security have embarked on this downward course."

Similarly, Reagan reversed the standard conception of progress. To him, progress was identical with the enhancement and expansion of human freedom. Reaction and regression took place when government pulled human beings back from the realization of their full potential. For this reason, Reagan believed that socialism and liberalism were reactionary philosophies—anachronisms. They came from the nineteenth century. Only freedom was future oriented.

A choice quotation highlighted the importance that Reagan placed on spiritual strength and self-confidence in the battle against the Soviet enemy. "Winston Churchill said, 'The destiny of man is not measured by material computations. When great forces are on the move in the world, we learn we are spirits—not animals.' And he said, 'There's something going on in time and space, and beyond time and space, which, whether we like it or not, spells duty.'" Reagan's cheerfulness, optimism, humor, and future orientation, along with his support for religion in the public square, were methods for instilling such confidence, spirit, and will in the public.[50]

What became known in the Reagan mythos as simply "The Speech" contrasted favorably with Goldwater's convention address. Where Reagan was inclusive, Goldwater was exclusive. Where Reagan was forward-looking, Goldwater was grim. Reagan bypassed the issue of ideological fanaticism by labeling his positions as common sense, whereas Goldwater's "extremism" line undid the work that he, Buckley, and Kirk had performed to stigmatize Robert Welch. Reagan also had the personal qualities of a film and television star that the irascible Goldwater did not. He upstaged his new party's presidential nominee. The press raved, but Goldwater stewed. He did not write Reagan a thank-you note—a slight that Reagan's wife, Nancy, never forgot.[51]

One week after the speech aired, Goldwater was crushed. LBJ was elected in a historic landslide, winning 61 to 39 percent and capturing every state except Arizona, Louisiana, Alabama, Mississippi, Georgia, and South Carolina. The repudiation of conservatism could not have been more definitive. After Goldwater's defeat, a liberal Harvard undergrad named Charles Murray, long before the career in social science that would make him famous, rushed to Lamont Library to read the postelection issue of *National Review*. He wanted to know how Buckley would deal with his candidate's humiliation.[52]

To the great surprise of many liberals, conservatives were less upset by the election result than they might have been. They finally had nominated one of their own for president. They had established a beachhead in the presidential selection process. They had marshaled intellectual resources to develop a serious policy platform. As some of their earlier heroes exited the scene—both Herbert Hoover and Douglas MacArthur died in 1964—a new champion, Ronald Reagan, entered from stage left.

Conservatives also launched new institutions, including the New York Conservative Party and the American Conservative Union. A Conservative Book Club, founded in 1964, grew to thirty-six thousand members by the end of the decade. *National Review*'s circulation swelled. Richard Viguerie, formerly of Young Americans for Freedom, had unearthed a continent-wide stratum of small-dollar donors eager to respond to direct-mail marketing and fund-raising appeals.[53]

Buckley and Reagan saw the Goldwater vote as a foundation on which to build. They attributed his loss to failures in message, to public ignorance of conservatism, and to fear of extremism. Goldwater did not hit conservatism's ceiling. He established its floor. "Conservatism wasn't defeated in this election," Draft Goldwater activist F. Clifton White told a puzzled *New York Times* reporter. "It was hardly even debated." A popular bumper sticker facetiously took pride in Goldwater's popular vote total: "27 Million People Can't Be Wrong."[54]

The personnel and infrastructure for a conservative comeback were in place. Johnson owned this moment of peace and prosperity. But the moment wouldn't last. Riots, crime, and the radical opponents of the Vietnam War were about to rip apart American liberalism and the Democratic Party.

CHAPTER SEVEN

THE GREAT DISRUPTION

A S EARLY AS MAY 1964, NOT LONG AFTER HE DECLARED "war on poverty" in his State of the Union address, Lyndon Johnson used the phrase "Great Society" to describe his goal of equality, prosperity, and peace. For a time it seemed as though the Great Society might be achieved. The murder of John F. Kennedy combined with LBJ's election landslide to propel the newly elected president to heights few chief executives have experienced.

Not since the New Deal had so much legislation flowed from Washington: the Kennedy tax cut, the Medicare bill, the Rent Supplement Act, the Economic Opportunity Act, the creation of Head Start, the Elementary and Secondary Education Act, an end to the restrictions on immigration that had been in place for forty years, and funds for public housing and urban renewal. LBJ saw the Civil Rights Act and Voting Rights Act not as the capstone to black aspirations for equality but as a base for far-reaching reform. In June 1965 he announced to graduates of Howard University the beginning of "the next and more profound stage of the battle for civil rights. We seek not just freedom but opportunity—not just legal equity but human ability—not just equality as a right and a theory but equality as a fact and as a result."[1]

LBJ also carried on JFK's anti-Communist legacy. He followed the course set by Dwight Eisenhower and Kennedy into further involvement and escalation in Vietnam. He had been warned not to do this. France's president, Charles De Gaulle, had told Kennedy in 1961 to beware an "endless entanglement" in Indochina, where America would "sink step by step into a bottomless military and political quagmire." Hans Morgenthau, dean of the "realist" school of international relations, which based its foreign policy on cold calculations of national interest defined as power, also argued against intervention in the pages of *Commentary*.[2]

LBJ would not relent. He told his biographer that he was just as concerned with the domestic consequences of an American defeat as he was with the global ones. He had seen how Communist gains set back the Harry Truman administration. He had seen how the Communist conquest of China empowered Joseph McCarthy. Losing Vietnam would shatter his administration, imperil his domestic agenda, and bring forth new demagogues. So, in addition to his surge of troops into South Vietnam, LBJ ordered the bombing of North Vietnam in February 1965. But his military strategy was self-constrained. He limited the air assault, sometimes choosing targets himself. He frequently "paused" the bombing to encourage reciprocal goodwill on the part of the Vietnamese Communists. That never happened. North Vietnam's strategy was to wait America out.[3]

LBJ saw the Vietnam War as a natural extension of the Great Society. But the connection worked both ways. If America was exporting its soldiers, humanitarian assistance, and democratic values to South Vietnam, it also seemed to be importing the polarization and endemic violence of that ill-fated land. The generosity of Lyndon Baines Johnson did not pacify. It inflamed.

In America, rates of violent crime began to soar. So did the number of births to unmarried women and divorce filings. Enrollment in Aid to Families with Dependent Children, the New

Deal–era welfare program for low-income families, grew from three million in 1960 to four million in 1965, six million in 1968, and ten million in 1970. Meanwhile, the fertility rate declined. The left-wing counterculture that had been building in the 1950s, drawing from the ideas of the Beat writers, Norman Mailer, Herbert Marcuse, James Baldwin, and others, burst into the public. Drug use, promiscuity, graffiti, truancy, and other acts of rebellion multiplied. A "New Left," emphasizing social and cultural liberation rather than political and economic equality, was born on America's campuses.[4]

There were frequent outbreaks of civil disorder. Clashes between police and black Americans triggered violent uprisings not only in the South but also in major urban centers across the country. In August 1965 the Watts neighborhood of Los Angeles erupted in violence. Thirty-four people were killed and more than one thousand injured. Twelve thousand National Guardsmen arrived to quell the riot.[5]

Watts was a taste of the chaos to come. It previewed a decade of social turbulence and upheaval that exacted a toll in lives and wasted resources that fell most heavily on racial and ethnic minorities. The New Left celebrated the violence as just, necessary, and beneficial. The public support that had sustained the civil rights movement melted under the heat of violent streets and radicalized demands. Nor did it take long for voters exhausted and upset over the disruptions of the 1960s to express themselves. Surprisingly, the first manifestation of this working-class backlash against the Great Society was support for a member of the Remnant: William F. Buckley Jr.

On April 4, 1965, Buckley addressed the Communion breakfast of Catholic policemen at the New York Hilton. His speech was a defense of policing and a broadside against media that publicized police abuse while downplaying criminal offenses. "The doctrine that a man is innocent until proved guilty seems to have been stretched to mean that the apprehending officials are guilty unless proved innocent," he said to laughter. He compared the press treatment of the murder of civil rights activist Viola Liuzzo with coverage of the killing of a policeman in Hattiesburg, Mississippi. Both events were terrible, Buckley argued. But the former death was, sadly, less shocking than the latter one. "Every age in which values are distorted—an age like our own—in which truths are thought either not to exist, or to exist only as quaint curios from the dead past—the wrath of the unruly falls with special focus on the symbols of authority, of continuity, of tradition," he continued. "It is no accident at all that the police should be despised in an age infatuated with revolution and ideology." Nor was it a surprise, he went on, that the Catholic Church should be singled out for "the brunt of the organized hatred of the principal agents of revolution."[6]

The response was overwhelming. Yet Buckley was shocked the next morning when he read media coverage of the event. The *New York Herald Tribune* and *New York Times* reported that he had praised George Wallace's police forces in Selma, Alabama, and that Buckley's audience had laughed and cheered when he mentioned Liuzzo. None of that happened. Buckley launched a public relations campaign to highlight the bias. The controversy provided the thirty-nine-year-old polemicist plenty of fodder. It also may have encouraged him to enter politics. His popularity at the Catholic police breakfast was undeniable. He said later that he decided to run for mayor of New York within forty-five minutes of delivering the speech. But he did not begin to organize his campaign for a few months.[7]

John Lindsay, the liberal Republican congressman from Manhattan's "Silk Stocking" district, entered the race on May 13. The media loved Lindsay. It treated him as another JFK. *Newsweek* called his announcement "the first chapter in *The Making of the President*, 1972." Buckley, however, worried that a Lindsay victory would reverse the gains conservatives had made within the

GOP. To counter the impression that only liberals had proposals for America's cities, he wrote a column outlining a conservative mayoral agenda: a crackdown on lawbreaking, drug legalization for adults with a doctor's prescription, tax-free zones for black entrepreneurs, restrictions on deliveries and parking to ease traffic, right-to-work legislation, legalized gambling, allowance for "anybody without a police record [to] operate a car as a taxi," work requirements for welfare recipients, an end to school busing, mandated vocational training for dropouts, and exemption of teenagers from minimum wage laws.[8]

When the column was reprinted in the next issue of *National Review*, managing editor Priscilla Buckley highlighted it on the cover with the headline "Buckley for Mayor?" It turned out to be a rare instance when the answer to a headline ending in a question mark was yes. Buckley, who maintained a secondary residence in New York City, announced his bid for Gracie Mansion on June 24. His opening press conference displayed his quick wit. "How many votes do you expect to get, conservatively speaking?" he was asked. "Conservatively speaking, one," he replied. A week later, a reporter asked him, "What would you do if you *were* elected?" Buckley's answer: "Demand a recount."[9]

Buckley ran for mayor on a lark. He became the nominee of the state Conservative Party. He wanted to resuscitate conservative spirits after Barry Goldwater's landslide defeat and to formulate "strong new programs distinctively Republican—bracing, realistic, courageous, strategically adventurous." But the campaign turned out to be much more satisfying and meaningful than he anticipated.[10]

Buckley put out well-regarded policy papers on a range of subjects, demonstrating the seriousness of his ideas. He needled Lindsay and the Democratic candidate, city comptroller Abe Beame, at every opportunity. And he discovered a new fan base through television. "This was a period in which it was supposed a conservative couldn't survive a confrontation with a liberal face to face," he said later. "A few collisions had a tremendous effect." Buckley the candidate was such a success on television that, after the election, he started his own program on, ironically, the Public Broadcasting System. *Firing Line* featured the counterrevolutionary in debate with his left-wing counterparts.[11]

This suave smart aleck with a polysyllabic vocabulary did not come across as either a far-right extremist or a gaffe-prone senator. Thus the mayoral campaign also helped Buckley to separate *National Review* conservatism from the extremist fringe. After Robert Welch's *American Opinion* called for US withdrawal from Vietnam in August 1965, Buckley decided to break with the group unequivocally. Weakness in the face of communism was the final straw. In October 1965, not long before Election Day, he devoted an entire issue of *National Review* to a condemnation of the John Birch Society (JBS).[12]

Buckley did not become mayor of New York, of course. He never expected to. But his 13 percent of the vote was a harbinger of the looming Democratic crackup. His strongest supporters were the ethnic Democrats from the city's outer boroughs who voted for Buckley in such great numbers that they capsized Abe Beame. Buckley had uncovered, quite by accident, the future electoral base of the Republican Party: white voters without college degrees, who belonged to traditional blue-collar unions, resented perceived liberal snobbery, and disliked the results of liberal governance.

This discovery put Buckley in an odd position. He was an ambivalent populist. In fact, he rejected the label. But he could not deny that the "establishment" that *National Review* poked, prodded, and lampooned was liberal in outlook. In his first two books, he argued that more popular control would improve the university and rid government of Communists. In his 1963 collection *Rumbles Left and Right*, he wrote that he would "sooner live in a society governed by the first 2,000 names in the Boston telephone directory than in a society governed by the 2,000 faculty members of Harvard University." Had he really meant it? Or was Buckley's antielitism really just his antiliberalism in democratic disguise? It was a question he never really answered.[13]

RONALD REAGAN WAS MUCH BETTER SUITED TO THE ROLE OF popular tribune. Born in Tampico, Illinois, on February 6, 1911, he seemed to embody an idealized vision of midwestern America that had receded into the past. His childhood and adolescence were closer in time to the nineteenth century than the twenty-first. His memories of small-town life were formed before Franklin Roosevelt's revolution. He recalled seeing a horse-drawn fire engine when the family moved to Chicago. From Chicago the Reagans moved to Galesburg, where young Ronald had memories of watching doughboys march off to fight in the Great War. Once Reagan complained about overregulation by saying that he'd driven a tractor without a license at the age of fourteen.[14]

The biggest influences on Reagan's life, his mother and father, were born in 1883. His father, Jack Reagan, was a Catholic, Irish American shoe salesman who suffered from alcoholism. His mother, Nelle Reagan, was a member of the Disciples of Christ Church into which Ronald, inspired by the 1903 novel *That Printer of Udell's*, was baptized when he turned eleven. Reagan's church emphasized personal destiny and free will. Nelle taught him to believe in the basic decency of human beings and to have confidence in the future. This conception of individual agency would guide Reagan always. If Nelle Reagan shaped her son's character, Jack Reagan molded his politics. "My dad believed passionately in the rights of the individual and the working man," Reagan wrote. Jack Reagan found these values best expressed in the Democratic Party—and his son, for much of his life, did too.[15]

Reagan was among the few in his generation to attend college. In high school he discovered football, lifeguarding, girls, and acting. Then he went to Eureka College, in Eureka, Illinois. The Disciples owned the school. The economics taught at Eureka at that time predated the Keynesian school of government management of demand. Reagan devoured the work of classical economists such as John Bright and Richard Cobden, the nineteenth-century liberal free traders who waged a successful campaign to repeal the protectionist Corn Laws in Great Britain. He read Frédéric Bastiat, Ludwig von Mises, and Friedrich Hayek. By the time he graduated, his individualistic, Christian, liberal democratic worldview was fully formed.[16]

The consistency of his principles was astonishing. From the Screen Actors Guild to General Electric, from commencement addresses to "The Speech," Reagan never wavered from his sense that America was the last, best hope for individuals to work out their personal destinies in freedom and peace. Over time, his conviction developed that government was the greatest obstacle to human flourishing. Reagan condensed these ideas into a few lines in a 1965 interview with the *New York Times*: "I think basically that I stand for what the bulk of Americans stand for—dignity, freedom of the individual, the right to determine your own destiny."[17]

Not long after the success of his televised endorsement of Goldwater, Reagan received many calls from Republican donors urging him to run for governor of California. He spent the next year mulling over the prospect. The popular reaction encouraged his spirits. He announced his candidacy on television in January 1966. "I'm not proposing an aimless hit-or-miss approach with government sitting back, hopefully waiting for a volunteer to recognize a problem and think of a solution," he said during the lengthy speech. "I am suggesting setting up a state-wide program on a systematic basis with government providing leadership and mobilizing the full creative abilities of the people, which in my opinion is the meaning of the phrase, 'government of and by the people.'" This was Reagan's vision of a "Creative Society"—his alternative to LBJ's Great Society. And his fans were ecstatic. "Everything he says is American," one woman enthusiastically told reporters.[18]

Like Buckley, Reagan made an issue of civil disorder. He focused on the campus disturbances that had started in 1964 at the University of California, Berkeley, home of the New Left. Speaking about Berkeley at a May 1966 rally in San Francisco, he said, "A small minority of beatniks, radicals, and filthy-speech advocates have brought such shame to a great university." When student activists "were allowed to assault and humiliate the symbol of authority, a policeman in uniform," he said, "that was the moment when the ringleaders should have been taken by the scruff of the neck and thrown off campus—personally." He cracked that a campus radical was someone who "looks like Tarzan, has hair like Jane, and smells like cheetah."[19]

Reagan held Goldwater's position on civil rights. But he tried to avoid the subject. He was extremely sensitive to the charge of racism. His church forbade it. His parents remonstrated against it. One of the few missteps in Reagan's political career took place during his first run for governor, when he left the state convention of the National Negro Republican Assembly in a huff after his primary opponent implied that he was a racist. (Reagan later returned to the meeting and apologized for storming out.) "Mostly Reagan shied away from the civil rights issue, distancing himself from segregationists and talking about riots and order instead," wrote historian Matthew Dallek.[20]

Reagan's opponents found that their attacks did not stick. That was how he came to be known as the "Teflon" candidate. The fact that elements of the John Birch Society in Southern California called him a sellout also strengthened Reagan's mainstream credentials. The incumbent governor, Democrat Pat Brown, grew so frustrated with his inability to land a punch on Reagan that he recorded an ad where he asked two black girls, "You know I'm running against an actor. Remember this, you know who shot Abraham Lincoln, don't you? An actor shot Lincoln."[21]

Reagan won by almost a million votes. The conservatives shed the stigma of the JBS not just by trying to dissociate themselves from it but also by putting forward candidates whom the public did not see as extreme. And the Republican Party, left for dead after 1964, had its best off-year result since 1946. The Goldwater supporters who had posted a billboard next to a Chicago highway that read, "In your heart, you know he's right," switched the message to "Now you know he was right." Pat Brown put it simply: "People can only accept so much," he said, referring to the whirlwind of civil unrest that had descended on California. "And then they regurgitate."[22]

In his inaugural address, Reagan explained his views on the relationship between elected officials and government. For Reagan, an officeholder was as much a guardian of the people as their agent, "chosen by them to see that no permanent structure of government ever encroaches on freedom or assumes a power beyond that freely granted by the people." Government powers are limited, but leaders can exhort, coordinate, encourage, and publicize the activities of free persons and voluntary associations. Reagan said that government should help the aged, disabled, orphans, and others who are unable to work through no fault of their own. It should coordinate and partner with the private sector. It should lead by example and by admonition. "But government must not supersede the will of the people or the responsibilities of the people," Reagan said. "The function of government is not to confer happiness but to give men the opportunity to work out happiness for themselves."[23]

That did not mean Reagan backed rule by plebiscite. "I think that we have to keep in mind that the purpose of the Bill of Rights was to forever put our right to control our own destiny beyond the reach of majority rule," he said. "It just does not follow that the majority is always right. In a lynch mob you have majority rule, and it doesn't make them right." This commitment to minority rights was a key qualification to Reagan's populism.[24]

George Wallace did not share it. At his January 1963 inauguration as governor of Alabama, Wallace had told the audience, "I say, segregation now! Segregation forever!" Five months later, he stood in the schoolhouse door to prevent black students from entering the University of Alabama. Now he was becoming a national political figure. In 1964 Wallace had entered several Democratic primaries and stunned the press with his strong showings: 34 percent in Wisconsin, 30 percent in Indiana, 43 percent in Maryland. "If it hadn't been for the n— bloc vote," Wallace growled, "we'd have won it all." It was the only time that journalists heard him use the slur.[25]

In 1965 Wallace unleashed hell on the voting rights activists marching from Selma to Montgomery. But as the next presidential election approached, he began to downplay his segregationism and stepped up his antielitism. (Voters whose sole motivation was racism knew where Wallace stood.) As he began to attack the federal government and its know-it-all politicians and bureaucrats, his support in the North grew. And his support among conservatives grew too.

Wallace attracted to his cause some of the worst specimens in American public life. Fans of Gerald L. K. Smith and George Lincoln Rockwell, head of the American Nazi Party, were part of his campaign machinery. Members of the John Birch Society joined his cause. "I am glad to have their support," Wallace said of the JBS in September 1968. "I have no quarrel with the Birch Society."[26]

The challenge that Wallace posed to the Right was unequivocal. Buckley called him "Mr. Evil," "a dangerous man," and a "great phony." Buckley deplored the "uncouthness that seems to account for his general popularity." Russell Kirk wrote in a letter that Wallace was "almost utterly ignorant of statecraft on any grand scale." Frank Meyer saw Wallace as the heretic in chief. "Populism is the radical opposite of conservatism," he wrote in 1967. Later in the same piece, Meyer wrote that Wallace's populist followers ignored that "there are other dangers to conservatism and to the civilization conservatives are defending than the liberal Establishment, and that to fight liberalism without guarding against these dangers runs the risk of ending in a situation as bad as or worse than our present one." Meyer and Buckley judged Wallace not just on his demagogic style but also on his willingness to embrace the welfare state.[27]

It was precisely the Wallace style, and what it conveyed, that many conservatives liked about him. Wallace's conservatism, wrote James Kilpatrick, "may lack intellectual depth, but it makes up for any absence of philosophy in the hard-driving ring of a salesman's conviction." Jeffrey Hart, a professor of literature at Dartmouth who had become a senior editor at *National Review*, saw Wallace as a rebel against the norms that liberals used to stifle the Right. "Wallace suggests freedom from the conventional taboos," he wrote. "The man *says* what he thinks. Wouldn't it be fun to do that? Even more impressive, he has actually *prospered* by saying what he thinks, by being abrasive and obnoxious. That reverses all of the conventional expectations."[28]

Whenever *National Review* criticized Wallace, readers would send the magazine angry letters. They would cancel subscriptions. "The two snidely ugly caricatures of the Wallaces on pages 402 and 405 are just too pointless and disrespectful for our 'lower middle class' minds," read one letter to the editor. "The thought has occurred to us that just as great a tyranny could come upon us if conservatives of your stripe 'won' the federal machinery." Wallace's pugnacity was contrasted favorably with the braininess of *National Review*. After all, he was a fighter. "Whether one approves of him or not," read another letter, "he *is* doing it and all you sissies do is stand around wringing your hands."[29]

Wallace was a master of the "I'm rubber, you're glue" rhetorical gambit. "The biggest bigots in the world are—they're the ones who call others bigots," he said. He fed his supporters a diet of grievances. Like Huey Long, he capitalized on their sense of being dispossessed and disrespected. "The average American is sick and tired of all those overeducated folks with the pointed heads looking down at us," he said. His fuel was the politics of racial polarization—of bitter animosity between whites and blacks, of interracial violence and hate.[30]

This hostility was growing worse. In June 1966 James Meredith led a march from Memphis, Tennessee, to Jackson, Mississippi, during which Stokely Carmichael, who had replaced John Lewis as the head of the Student Nonviolent Coordinating Committee (SNCC), was arrested. Released from jail, Carmichael began chanting, "We want black power!" He said, "Every courthouse in Mississippi ought to be burned tomorrow to get rid of the dirt." Later that year, in Oakland, Huey Newton and Bobby Seale formed the Black Panther Party and embraced violence as a means of destroying the white power structure. Newton killed a police officer in October 1967. This new generation of Black Power activists adopted Marxist philosophy. They saw themselves as the US equivalent of the anticolonial rebels who had chased Europeans out of Africa. The Panthers took on the trappings of a junta-like paramilitary organization. "Minister of Education" Eldridge Cleaver, a convicted rapist, was arrested after a shootout with police in 1968.[31]

Americans found themselves caught between the extremes of Wallace and Cleaver. When Americans watched the evening news, they saw large parts of their society enveloped in anarchy. By the end of February 1968, Gallup reported that "crime and lawlessness" was the public's number one concern. The rest of the year would do little to persuade it otherwise. Vietnam, the counterculture, and Black Power were shaking America to its foundations— within four years of LBJ's political apotheosis.[32]

THE PRESIDENTIAL ELECTION YEAR OF 1968 BEGAN WITH THE Tet offensive. In this massive surprise attack, coinciding with the Vietnamese New Year, the North Vietnamese army and the Vietcong insurgency struck US and anti-Communist forces throughout South Vietnam. For North Vietnam, Tet was both a tactical defeat and a strategic victory. The suddenness and ferocity of the military operation broke the confidence of the liberal establishment in Washington. When the US commander in Vietnam requested hundreds of thousands of additional troops to supplement the half million already there, LBJ and his advisers blanched. Johnson sent a paltry number instead. Tet was the final humiliation. The president wanted out.

As a result of Tet the media became much more adversarial toward both the war and LBJ. Members of the press had once thought of themselves as a bunch of hard-drinking, gossipy good old boys who were ready to look the other way when politicians behaved indiscreetly or invoked national security. Now the press took on a self-appointed role as the moral conscience of the nation, the arbiter of right and wrong, the pacesetter of the domestic and global agenda. When Walter Cronkite, who had smeared Barry Goldwater four years earlier, returned from Vietnam in the aftermath of Tet, he told his audience, "It seems more certain than ever that the bloody experience of Vietnam is to end in a stalemate." He should have checked first with Ho Chi Minh.[33]

Losing the support of his own advisers, demonized by antiwar demonstrators, assailed by the media, and bewildered by Minnesota senator Eugene McCarthy's strong showing in the New Hampshire primary, LBJ announced on March 31 that he would not seek a second term. It was a Sophoclean demise for the most effective agent of liberalism since FDR. Suddenly the Democratic primary turned into a three-way race between McCarthy, Robert F. Kennedy, now a senator from New York, and Vice President Hubert Humphrey.

Then on April 4, less than a week after Johnson's announcement, James Earl Ray assassinated Martin Luther King Jr. while the civil rights leader stood on a hotel balcony in Memphis. As word of the killing spread, violence broke out in cities across America. The previous year, riots had erupted in more than one hundred cities, with the worst destruction occurring in Newark and Detroit, where forty-three people died. SNCC leader H. Rap Brown had expressed the mentality of Black Power when, upon his release from imprisonment in Cambridge, Maryland, in July 1967, he urged supporters, "Burn this city down." That is exactly what happened after King's assassination a year later in Baltimore, Chicago, and Washington, DC. When the smoke cleared, fifty people had been killed nationwide.

LBJ's surrender and MLK's murder created a vacuum of leadership and authority. Those who used force commanded the streets. At Columbia University, student radicals occupied university administration buildings. By that time, Daniel Bell had become a professor of sociology on the Morningside Heights campus. He urged the dean of Columbia College not to call in the police. "I said, 'Look David, you can't assert authority, you have to earn authority,'" Bell recalled. "He said, 'Nonsense.'" More than one hundred people were injured in the clash that ensued. Bell was aghast at the violence. When he arrived home that night, he burst into tears. Soon after, he left Columbia for Harvard.[34]

William F. Buckley Jr. saw incipient fascism among the mobs. "One wishes, forlornly, that the Weimar Republic had had more policemen," he wrote, "and that they had succeeded, back when it might have worked, in rescuing those who were so permanently, so tragically, victimized by the uproarious students who fought and bled for Hitler." Russell Kirk blamed liberal education. "Schooling without discernible standards, from kindergarten through college, has left the typical collegian nowadays ignorant of principle, vague of aspiration, and imperfect in any intellectual discipline," he wrote. Ronald Reagan continued to emphasize law and order. "No community can long tolerate irresponsibility, the forerunner of anarchy," he said. "The rights of the majority of the community will be protected, even if, in the last resort, it requires public laws to do so."[35]

America did not lack statutes, edicts, and other proscriptions against antisocial behavior. It did, however, need recognition of their legitimacy. By 1968, America had become estranged from traditional understandings of deference and comportment. Both the antiwar students and the Black Panthers saw America as unredeemable and corrupt, worthy of destruction, kindling for a purifying fire. Political violence was normalized.

On June 4, the night of the California primary, a Palestinian nationalist named Sirhan Sirhan murdered Robert F. Kennedy. The Democratic National Convention, held in Chicago in late August, was dominated by violent clashes between student protesters and Mayor Richard J. Daley's police. The chaos outside the convention hall mirrored the tumult within. Liberals fought with the radical Left over their party's handling of war, civil rights, and the nominee selection process. The class lines dividing the majority party were exposed before the world: uniformed cops were on one side; affluent, college-educated "Yippies" were on the other. The media, already infuriated with the Democratic establishment for its conduct of the war, took the side of the kids.[36]

Hubert Humphrey emerged from the melee as the party's nominee. After Chicago, however, a great part of the Democratic leadership and the national press came to embrace the antiwar, antitraditional values of the New Left and "New Politics" that Gene McCarthy and RFK represented. The political landscape was altered in ways that forced conservatives into an alliance with some of the older liberals who rejected the counterculture and a precipitous withdrawal from Vietnam.

Back in 1964, James Burnham had written *Suicide of the West*, his diagnosis of what he called "the liberal syndrome." Liberalism, he argued, was the ideology of Western suicide—the way in which America's elite reconciled itself to decline. Four years later, Burnham came to believe that the radical Left presented an even greater challenge to civilization than the liberalism of FDR, Truman, JFK, and LBJ. "Fundamentally, conservatives criticize liberalism because its practices weaken the institutional defense against barbarism and its ideas sap the will to resist barbarism," he wrote. "But the real Left—the revolutionary, Communist Left, New as Old—is of a different order. Its specific objective is to overthrow, to destroy what it calls 'capitalism,' the 'establishment,' 'the status quo,' 'the consumer society'—all meaning the existing structure of such civilization as we have been able to manage." The magnitude of the threat required conservatives to forge new alliances and to endorse a candidate whom they might otherwise have spurned. This new alliance was with a group of intellectuals surrounding the *Public Interest*. The prodigal candidate was Richard Nixon.[37]

The *Public Interest* was a quarterly journal edited by Daniel Bell and Irving Kristol, who cofounded it in 1965 to gauge the success of the Great Society through empirical research. But the magazine became something more. Its changing political identity mirrored Kristol's intellectual journey from ex-radical to Republican thought leader. After leaving *Commentary*, Kristol had founded (with poet Stephen Spender) the liberal anti-Communist *Encounter* in London in 1953, sponsored by the Congress for Cultural Freedom. He and his family returned in 1958 to New York, where he took a job as editor of the *Reporter*.

Then Kristol left the *Reporter* to join Basic Books, where he rose to the level of executive vice president. His job was to expand Basic's catalog to include works of social science. That was not a problem. Many in Kristol's circle had become sociologists. Since their days at City College, Kristol's network had been fascinated by Robert K. Merton's 1936 paper "The Unanticipated Consequences of Purposive Social Action." His friends, including Bell, Nathan Glazer, and Seymour Martin Lipset, had followed Merton into various faculties of sociology. "If you can't subscribe to socialism," Kristol once joked, "you might as well be a sociologist. It's the next best thing."[38]

In 1960 Bell had published *The End of Ideology*. He argued that politics was becoming a nonideological process of piecemeal technocratic management. "There is today," he wrote, "a rough consensus among intellectuals on political issues: the acceptance of a Welfare State; the desirability of decentralized power; a system of mixed economy and of political pluralism." This rough consensus matched the preferences of the polymathic Bell, who self-identified as a "socialist in economics, a liberal in politics, and a conservative in culture." Four years after the publication of *The End of Ideology*, President Johnson appointed Bell to a commission on automation. Fear was widespread at the time that economic growth and technological advancement might render labor unnecessary.[39]

The report that Bell and Massachusetts Institute of Technology economist Robert Solow wrote for the commission concluded that the threat was overblown. They used social science to dispel erroneous conventional wisdom. Bell's work convinced him that Kristol was right in thinking the time was ripe for a journal to demystify some of the more exaggerated beliefs circulating within the upper echelons of the Great Society. Then Kristol's mentor, Sidney Hook, introduced them to Wall Street executive Warren Manshel, who offered to back the new magazine.

The *Public Interest* never enjoyed a high circulation. Making money was not its purpose. It aimed for nothing less than the assembly of an alternate faculty of social science. Its contributors applied the law of unintended consequences to the study of social programs. In issue after issue, they evaluated government not on its intentions but on its results. And more often than not, the results were lacking. The *Public Interest* was not an academic journal. Footnotes were rare. The prose was accessible. But its research, reports, and polemics proved devastating to the liberal shibboleth that government programs were always and everywhere the best ways to reduce inequality and promote social health and happiness.

As the decade of the 1960s went on, the always unconventional Kristol moved steadily right. The teaching of Leo Strauss influenced him deeply. "I cannot persuade myself that a democracy whose notions of public and private virtue are slowly being emptied of their substance can sustain itself," he wrote in 1966. "Democracy, after all, means self-government; and such self-government is, in the long run, utterly impossible without adequate self-definition, self-certainty, self-control." The *Public Interest* circle was made up of Democrats—but Democrats whose critiques of the welfare state under Lyndon Johnson sounded awfully conservative.

MOVEMENT CONSERVATIVES, MEANWHILE, HAD TO FIGURE OUT where they stood in relation to Richard Nixon. The former vice president had spent years brooding over his reputation as a loser, a has-been who announced his departure from politics altogether after his failure in the 1962 California governor's race. But the perceptive Nixon spied weakness where others saw only strength: Lyndon Johnson, he thought early on, would not be able to withstand the pressures of the White House. Johnson's ambitions were too great and his means of achieving them too small. From his law offices at 20 Broad Street in New York City, Nixon plotted his return to politics and a second presidential campaign.

Nixon recognized that he had to repair his relationship with conservatives. They associated him with the "middle-of-the-road" policies of the Eisenhower years and with the concessions he had made to Nelson Rockefeller in 1960. Nixon's support for Goldwater was not enough, especially after a newspaper column reported that he had called the "Buckleyites" a greater menace to the GOP than the Birchers.[40]

In December 1965 Nixon had hired a twenty-seven-year-old editorial writer for the *St. Louis Globe-Democrat* to serve as his political aide. Born to a large Irish Catholic family in Washington, DC, Patrick J. Buchanan inherited the values and traditions of his father, a descendant of Scotch-Irish and Irish immigrants who believed in the Lost Cause of the South and "whose trinity of political heroes consisted of Douglas MacArthur, General Franco, and the junior senator from Wisconsin they called Tailgunner Joe."[41]

Buchanan became Nixon's ambassador to *National Review*. He wrote a letter to the magazine explaining that Nixon's comments had been intended to suggest that Buckley, because of his strength as a mayoral candidate, was a greater threat to John Lindsay's chances than the Birchers might have been. *National Review* contented itself with Buchanan's spin. "So, all's well that ends well," the editors wrote. "And if Richard Nixon is willing to give personal leadership to the Republican conservatives, he will find them ready to follow him." Buchanan responded to this overture by bringing Nixon in front of conservative movement groups, such as Young Americans for Freedom and the American Conservative Union. And he arranged for the growing network of conservative columnists to interview Nixon.[42]

Goldwater's support for Nixon was not in doubt—he wanted to repay the favor from 1964. A similar calculus shaped party leaders' attitudes toward Nixon after his barnstorming campaign on behalf of sixty-six Republican House candidates in thirty-five states during the 1966 midterm. When two-thirds of them won, they felt that they owed Nixon too. At the very least, they deferred to him on foreign policy.

There was little question that Nixon was the GOP's leading foreign policy strategist. His status as a former vice president gave him access to world leaders during frequent international trips. When he returned from these fact-finding missions, he would deliver lengthy, impressive tours d'horizon on the geopolitical scene before audiences of policy leaders and campaign donors. The furor over LBJ's Indochina policy raised the salience of foreign affairs in a way that benefited Nixon politically.

Among Nixon's potential rivals for the 1968 nomination, Ronald Reagan lacked experience. Michigan governor George Romney's reputation lost luster after he told the press that he had undergone a "brainwashing" by US military personnel during a visit to Vietnam. Nixon, by contrast, spoke of an "honorable peace" in Indochina. He wrote in *Foreign Affairs* of a time "after Vietnam" when America would endeavor to include China in "the family of nations." On the basis of his foreign policy and his anti-Communist background, Nixon earned Strom Thurmond's endorsement.

As the domestic scene grew more shambolic, Nixon pointed to a middle ground. He endorsed civil rights legislation but also defended public order and the rule of law. "There can be no right to revolt in this society; no right to demonstrate outside the law, and, in Lincoln's words, 'no grievance that is a fit object of redress by mob law,'" he wrote in *Reader's Digest* in October 1967. When the students revolted on campuses nationwide in 1968, Nixon slammed the uprising as "the first major skirmish in a revolutionary struggle to seize the universities of this country and transform them into sanctuaries for radicals and vehicles for revolutionary and political goals."[43]

Following Buchanan's advice, Nixon sharpened his rhetoric. He attacked Humphrey for being a "conscientious objector" in the "war on crime." He selected as his running mate Maryland governor Spiro Agnew, who was notorious among his fellow liberal Republicans for upbraiding the black civil rights leaders who had allied themselves with Stokely Carmichael during riots in Baltimore that killed six and injured seven hundred.[44]

Nixon's style improved. Huge margins in early primaries dispelled the idea that he was nothing but a loser. He cleaned up his image by relying on a television producer in his late twenties named Roger Ailes. He went out of his way to attend Martin Luther King Jr.'s funeral. Still smarting from his performance against John F. Kennedy eight years earlier, he made sure that there would be no televised debates. For anti-Communist conservatives appalled at both LBJ's conduct of the war and what they perceived as the anti-American turn of left-wing radicals inside the Democratic Party, Nixon was, as Buckley said, "the most right, viable candidate who could win."[45]

At the time, Buckley needed to keep George Wallace from swallowing American conservatism whole. He invited Wallace onto *Firing Line* and promptly flayed the governor of Alabama. In an essay for *Look* magazine published the week before Election Day, Buckley warned, "Those conservatives who take sly pleasure from Wallace's techniques should reflect that that kind of thing is do-able against anybody at all; do-able for instance by the Folsomite Wallace of yesteryear, who roared his approval of his candidate's attack on the 'Wall Street Gotrocks,' 'the damned decency crowd,' and 'them Hoover Republicans.'"[46]

Buckley distinguished between the issues that animated Wallace's supporters and Wallace's unacceptable behavior and welfarist policies. Barry Goldwater was even more careful not to offend Wallace sympathizers. In a *National Review* article headlined "Don't Waste a Vote on Wallace," Goldwater praised the governor of Alabama for his straight talk, appeal to patriotism, call for law and order, antagonism toward liberal intellectuals, talent for public speaking, and mastery of "the dramatic, memorable gesture." Goldwater cautioned that his piece shouldn't be read as a personal attack on the governor. (He needn't have worried.) He never mentioned race. Instead Goldwater argued tactics. A vote for Wallace, he wrote, would be lost for Nixon. It would therefore help Humphrey. And a third party would be disastrous for the conservative cause.[47]

In the end, Wallace did himself in. He named retired general Curtis LeMay as his running mate and had to scramble for the high ground after LeMay raised the possibility of using nuclear weapons to end the war in Vietnam. The Alabama governor's poll numbers dropped, and LBJ's last-minute "October surprise" of a supposed breakthrough in negotiations with North Vietnam failed to put Humphrey over the top.

The election, like that in 1960, was close. This time Nixon won by half a million votes. Wallace and LeMay took only Georgia, Alabama, Mississippi, Louisiana, and Arkansas, but stole voters from both Nixon and Humphrey nationwide and came within forty-three thousand votes of throwing the election to the House of Representatives. The failure of LBJ's strategy against North Vietnam, his inability to reduce crime, and unrest at home had busted open the New Deal coalition. The Great Society was in shambles. Nixon was ascendant. His quest for a new majority was on.

CHAPTER EIGHT

NIXON'S CONSERVATIVES

THE PRESIDENCY OF RICHARD MILHOUSE NIXON OFFERED many opportunities for a changing American Right. It was a chance for conservative policy wonks to put their plans into action. The chameleonlike president incorporated a wide range of ideological styles into his speeches and initiatives. This variability was a consequence of his complex personality and a conservative movement in a state of flux.

Nixon's tenure coincided with the outbreak of a "street-corner," populist conservatism grounded in antagonism toward liberal elites, as well as a neoconservative movement composed of anti-Communist liberals who turned rightward as the Democratic Party embraced a policy of nonconfrontation with the Soviet Union and openness to nontraditional lifestyles. At the same time, the former insurgents of *National Review* found themselves incorporated into the governing establishment that they had assailed for two decades. By the time of Nixon's premature departure from office, the Republican Party had gained ground among key sectors of the New Deal coalition, including Catholics, ethnic voters, and blue-collar workers.

Nixon's staff reflected his desire for a broad menu of options and his long-standing interest in ideas. He relied on a troika of speechwriters that included one conservative (Pat Buchanan), one moderate (William Safire), and one liberal (Ray Price). By the time Nixon reached the White House, he understood that it was important to play nice with the Right. He appointed William F. Buckley Jr. to a UN delegation. He kept up a regular correspondence with Russell Kirk, whose *A Program for Conservatives* he admired and who once told him to read T. S. Eliot's *Notes Toward the Definition of Culture*. He put Milton Friedman on an economic advisory task force whose labor expert, University of Chicago business school dean George Shultz, became Nixon's secretary of labor, director of the Office of Management and Budget, and treasury secretary (and later Ronald Reagan's secretary of state). His economic counselor, Arthur Burns, hired an assistant named Martin Anderson, a thirty-two-year-old conservative policy wonk who had written, among other things, a well-regarded critique of urban planning and a proposal for an all-volunteer military force.[1]

Nixon's conservatism was more flexible and less doctrinaire than the theoreticians at *National Review* might have liked. He carefully studied his four-volume edition of Edmund Burke's parliamentary speeches. He read everything by Winston Churchill. But he also drew lessons from the careers of European conservatives who believed that a capable state could ward off revolution from below. He owned a well-worn copy of the memoirs of Charles De Gaulle, who in conversation first introduced Nixon to the term "détente" to describe a policy of balance-of-power negotiations with the Soviet Union. Nixon also enjoyed A. J. P. Taylor's biography of Otto von Bismarck.[2]

For domestic policy, Nixon called on Daniel Patrick Moynihan, a Democrat and Harvard professor known for his criticisms of fellow liberals. Moynihan was a controversial figure on the left.

One of his early works, a study coauthored with sociologist Nathan Glazer titled *Beyond the Melting Pot*, argued that ethnic groups retained certain cultural beliefs and practices years after their arrival in the United States and that these attributes were more determinative of a group's politics than its economic class. Moynihan had worked in the Labor Department for John F. Kennedy and for Lyndon Johnson before leaving in 1965, just as a report he had written, *The Negro Family: The Case for National Action*, was leaked to the press. The media zeroed in on Moynihan's finding that "the family structure of lower class Negroes is highly unstable, and in many urban centers is approaching complete breakdown." Mistaking it as the government's official explanation for the violence in Watts, black and white academics and activists took Moynihan's report as an exercise in blaming the victim. They hurled accusations of racism at its author.[3]

As social conditions worsened during the 1960s, Moynihan became more willing to antagonize the Left. "Liberals must divest themselves of the notion that the nation—and especially the cities of the nation—can be run from agencies in Washington," he told the Americans for Democratic Action, a group of prominent anti-Communist liberals, in a September 1967 speech revealingly titled "The Politics of Stability." His critical study of LBJ's "Community Action Program," a centerpiece of the war on poverty, cautioned social scientists against treating the world as a plastic object. When Nixon asked him for reading recommendations, Moynihan provided a list of ten political biographies, including Clinton Rossiter's life of Alexander Hamilton and Robert Blake's *Disraeli*. And Moynihan introduced Nixon to the *Public Interest*.[4]

Back in June 1968, Pat Buchanan had brought onto the Nixon campaign a congressional aide named Kevin Phillips, who recently had completed a manuscript on political trends that he shared with the staff. Phillips agreed with Buchanan that Nixon's path to victory ran through George Wallace voters and Catholic Democrats who flinched at social disorder. As the Democratic Party moved left, these voting blocs had nowhere to go but right.

In 1969 Phillips's manuscript was published as *The Emerging Republican Majority*. "Far from being the tenuous and unmeaningful victory suggested by critical observers," it began, "the election of Richard M. Nixon as President of the United States in November 1968, bespoke the end of the New Deal Democratic hegemony and the beginning of a new era in American politics." Several hundred pages of excruciatingly detailed election analysis followed. For the Republican majority to last, Phillips argued, the party would have to retain the 57 percent of the electorate that voted against Hubert Humphrey. The Wallace supporter, he wrote, was the key to this new majority. Buchanan convinced Nixon that the Wallace supporters were up for grabs. Nixon pursued these disaffected working-class voters in what became known, somewhat misleadingly, as the "southern strategy." He thus broadened the Republican Party's appeal and incorporated groups into his coalition that changed the nature of conservatism.[5]

Among the books that influenced Buchanan as he cultivated the Wallace vote for Nixon was Richard M. Scammon and Ben J. Wattenberg's *The Real Majority* (1970). These anti-Communist liberal Democrats had surveyed polling data and come away with two insights. First, economics was giving way in voters' minds to "law and order, backlash, anti-youth, malaise, change, or alienation," which Scammon and Wattenberg called the "Social Issue." Second, a majority of voters belonged to groups hardly represented at all in media discourse. The average voter was neither a student activist nor a Black Panther but "a forty-seven-year-old wife of a machinist living in suburban, Dayton, Ohio."[6]

The "Dayton Housewife," as the archetype came to be known, was not an acolyte of Friedrich Hayek or Russell Kirk. But her instincts drove her to support politicians who shared their concern for the rule of law. William Gavin, a Nixon speechwriter from

New Jersey, described the politics of the Dayton Housewife as "street-corner conservatism." It was, he wrote, "based on the discovery, usually in college (but rarely in college classes), that the unarticulated political and social beliefs of a working-class, Catholic family are not the foolish superstitions the liberal college professors believe them to be, but, instead, are the simple and specific examples of complex and universal principles which are at the root of order and progress in the Western world."[7]

In April 1970 an assistant secretary of labor named Jerome Rosow wrote a memo to the head of his department titled "The Problem of the Blue-Collar Worker." It detailed the empirical basis of street-corner conservatism. Rosow explained that a working-class wage earner's income peaked just when his personal cost of living—paying for a home mortgage and for his children's education—began to skyrocket. "The worker has some margin beyond his budget needs when he is young, but only if he saves and does not acquire a living standard commensurate with his pay," Rosow wrote. Inflation made things worse. What Rosow dubbed the "economic squeeze" and the "social squeeze" worked together to make the husband of the Dayton Housewife feel besieged and alone. He also suggested a plan of action for the federal government to lessen the burdens on working families. The political implication of his memo—left unsaid—was that the party that improved living standards would benefit at the polls.[8]

Keeping working-class families in mind, Nixon's domestic policy modified rather than attacked Great Society liberalism. To quell the student uprising, he empaneled a commission that included Milton Friedman to explore ways of ending the military draft. It released its final report in February 1970. Three years later, the military draft was no more.

On other occasions, however, Nixon embraced government activism in the spirit of moderate, New Deal Republicanism. He presided over the creation of the Environmental Protection Agency and the Occupational Safety and Health Administration. And he launched the Philadelphia Plan, an attempt to force unions to hire more black workers without the use of strict quotas.

Nixon did not deliver a televised domestic policy address until August 8, 1969. The policies he unveiled during that speech fit well with what Whittaker Chambers had called the "Beaconsfield position" of moderate reform. They did not roll back the welfare state so much as nudge it in a conservative direction. Nixon's "New Federalism," for example, involved revenue sharing between the federal government and states. He hoped that supplying money in the form of block grants would encourage fiscal restraint and experimentation. The Family Assistance Plan (FAP), Daniel Patrick Moynihan's brainchild, would have replaced the New Deal–era Aid to Families with Dependent Children and food stamps with a defined monthly cash benefit that required the recipient to work.

There was a noteworthy shift in the way that Nixon talked about welfare. Unlike Herbert Hoover and Robert Taft, Nixon did not focus entirely on the system's cost or on occasional cases of fraud. Under Moynihan's influence, Nixon emphasized the moral drawbacks of welfare dependency and its effects on personal responsibility and family structure. "It breaks up homes. It often penalizes work. It robs recipients of dignity. And it grows," he said that night in August.[9]

For Moynihan, FAP was a chance to launch a distinctly American family policy. "Its passage," he wrote, "would set a standard of social policy against which the world might measure itself." One of the inspirations behind FAP had been Milton Friedman's proposal for a negative income tax. In theory, the Friedman plan was a relatively easy way to replace the welfare system with a national income "floor" under which no one could fall. Moynihan tried to eliminate the disincentive to earn more if the next dollar one made resulted in more than a dollar of lost benefits. But the Democratic

House of Representatives nixed his solution. It tossed overboard the work requirement. And it retained food stamps.[10]

The FAP alienated both Left and Right. By May 1970, after it passed the House in an unrecognizable form, Milton Friedman was writing in his *Newsweek* column that the FAP had become a "travesty" and that he would not vote for it. *National Review* and *Human Events* were against it as well. They called it the "mega-dole." Liberals in Congress opposed FAP because it wasn't generous enough. And by November, when the Senate Finance Committee killed the program entirely, Moynihan had left the White House. The story of FAP illustrated the inherent risks when the Right co-opted the issues of the Left: the effort would more likely implode than succeed.[11]

Nixon's cultural politics were more effective. Liberals could not help falling into the chasm that separated the instincts of the counterculture from the sentiments of popular opinion. Once again, perceived weakness against Communists and criminals harmed the Democrats and helped the Republicans. On November 3, 1969, President Nixon defended his Vietnam policy in a televised appeal to the "great silent majority of my fellow Americans." They understood, Nixon said, that "North Vietnam cannot defeat or humiliate the United States. Only Americans can do that." Polls registered support for Nixon's position. The next day Republicans won the off-year gubernatorial elections in New Jersey and Virginia.[12]

Buchanan urged Nixon to designate the vice president as an attack dog and sic Spiro Agnew on the major newspapers and broadcast networks. Nixon gave his approval. Agnew had already deployed some of the phrases with which he would long be associated. During an appearance in New Orleans in October 1969, for instance, he called the media "an effete corps of impudent snobs." Now Buchanan wrote for him a rip-roaring screed against the television networks to deliver in Des Moines on November 13.[13]

"The purpose of my remarks tonight," Agnew said, "is to focus your attention on this little group of men who not only enjoy a right of instant rebuttal to every presidential address, but more importantly, wield a free hand in selecting, presenting, and interpreting the great issues of the nation." The time had come, Agnew went on, for media to respond to and reflect the opinions of Americans throughout the country. As soon as Agnew finished speaking, Nixon later wrote, "telegrams began arriving at the White House." They were positive. Agnew discovered that not only Barry Goldwater supporters and the Nixon administration disliked the media.[14]

And the media was just one institution against which Nixon hoped to rally the silent majority. Another was the Supreme Court. To replace Earl Warren as chief justice, Nixon nominated Warren Burger, who had backed "law and order" in a 1967 speech to a group of moderate Republicans called the Ripon Society. Burger was confirmed without incident. Nixon's next nomination for the Court was Judge Clement Haynsworth Jr. of Richmond. It was not a success. Haynsworth was instantly skewered for having upheld segregation prior to *Brown v. Board of Education of Topeka*. The Senate rejected the nomination, infuriating Nixon.[15]

He next put up G. Harrold Carswell, a Georgia native who lived in Florida and was a member of the Fifth Circuit Court of Appeals. It was soon discovered, however, that as a candidate for the Georgia legislature in 1948 Carswell had said, "Segregation of the races is proper and the only practical and correct way of life in our states." In a televised interview, an embarrassed Carswell said that he had been wrong and that he no longer believed in segregation. But it was too late. The Senate rejected him too.[16]

Nixon denounced the Senate for blocking his southern nominees. He sent up Harry Blackmun of Minnesota, who was confirmed. Nixon got two more appointments the following year: Lewis Powell, a corporate lawyer from Virginia, and William

Rehnquist, Goldwater's attorney and friend and a reliable judicial conservative.

In addition to the media and the courts, Nixon went after the academy. College campuses, he believed, incubated anti-Americanism. They were sites of antiwar resistance. Racial quotas and open admissions violated liberal principles of merit and contributed to radicalism. Weak administrators midwifed chaos. Professors transmitted radical values to their students, who then assumed high positions in law, administration, and media.

Campuses were on fire in part because the liberal establishment no longer felt responsibility for Vietnam. Former high-ranking Democratic officials joined with the national print and television media to portray the war as lost. They said that a unilateral withdrawal was the only answer. They characterized domestic violence as an understandable response to social oppression. A threatening, unappeasable radicalism swept elite campuses, pushing old-school liberals and the population at large toward the Nixon Republicans.

Political philosopher Walter Berns, for example, had been teaching at Cornell University when the black nationalist Afro-American Society took over the student union building and demanded, among other things, a ban on whites entering their organization, a slush fund, and control over black admissions. The heavily armed radicals bent the administration to their will. "In effect," Berns recollected, "they took control of the university." One of Berns's colleagues, a fellow student of Leo Strauss named Allan Bloom, noticed disturbing parallels with what had happened on campuses an ocean away and a generation before. "The American university in the sixties was experiencing the same dismantling of the structure of rational inquiry as had the German university in the thirties," he wrote. Berns and Bloom resigned from the faculty and went to Canada, where they taught at the University of Toronto.[17]

The war also strained the political Right. In April 1969, in the pages of *New Guard*, a publication of the Young Americans for

Freedom (YAF), Milton Friedman's son David tore into Buckley for describing drug addiction as a contagion. For Buckley, the younger Friedman was engaging in libertarian "extreme apriorism." "I love and adore Milton Friedman," Buckley wrote in response, but "the articulation of libertarian theory to such lengths as Mr. Friedman is able to take it ought to be understood to be a form of intellectual sport." Libertarian speculations might be fun, Buckley wrote. They were not serious.[18]

War was serious. At the outset of the 1960s, Young Americans for Freedom had narrowly escaped takeover by the John Birch Society. Now, at decade's end, it risked splitting over Vietnam. One faction represented the conservative mainstream of Buckley and *National Review*. It supported the war but believed that LBJ had mismanaged it disastrously. The other faction consisted of anti-anti-Communist libertarians.

The matter came to a head in late August 1969 at YAF's annual convention in Saint Louis. Buckley found himself opposite Karl Hess. The former Goldwater speechwriter had joined forces with Murray Rothbard to create a "Radical Libertarian Alliance" that they hoped would rival YAF. One libertarian burned his draft card before the assembled crowd. Cries of "Kill the Commies!" resounded in the hall. The libertarians replied with chants of "Laissez-faire! Laissez-faire!" When the dust settled, the conservatives had expelled the libertarian heretics. These outcast followers of Rothbard, Hess, Ayn Rand, and Ronald Hamowy poured their energies into the year-old *Reason* magazine and into the Libertarian Party, which held its first presidential convention in 1972.[19]

Not only the libertarians took issue with *National Review*'s support for the war. Brent Bozell had left *National Review* in September 1966 to begin his own magazine, *Triumph*. What started as a *National Review*–like publication devoted exclusively to issues surrounding the Catholic Church became a self-described "radical

Christian" journal. On many questions, the editors of *Triumph* found themselves on the same side as the New Left. They opposed American foreign policy, derided capitalism, and explained away violence in the cities as legitimate protest against the oppressive racist culture of materialism.

In February 1968 Bozell wrote of "the death of the Constitution" and repudiated his own book, *The Warren Court*, an attack on judicial flouting of communal norms. "The American commonwealth no longer *wishes* to restore the constitutional republic," he declared. Bozell offered examples of public debate that had been conducted without reference to the nation's founding document. The problem, he went on, did not stem from elites or even from the people. It was a consequence of the founding. The constitutional machinery had no purpose outside itself. It performed whatever function the people desired of it. "The Constitution has not only failed; it was bound to fail."[20]

Dismayed by Buckley's endorsement of Nixon, Bozell wrote that the conservative movement had failed too—it had ended with Goldwater's defeat. By Nixon's inauguration, he said, conservatism was unequivocally dead. Bozell's elegy, "Letter to Yourselves," scored a few points. It accurately described the compromises that conservatives had made with power. It mapped the distance they had traveled from the amalgam of anti-statism, nationalism, anticommunism, and constitutionalism that animated *The Conscience of a Conservative*. But Bozell wrote with an air of finality that could lead him astray.

The same sort of catastrophic reasoning that had led Bozell to describe the Republican Party as done for after the 1958 election made him argue that the American conservative movement was over because *National Review* hadn't supported the nomination of Ronald Reagan in 1968. "On every front where your program has confronted secular liberalism's," Bozell told conservatives, "you have been beaten." Judged against his impossible standard, that may well have been the case. Seen through the lens of a gradualist rather than apocalyptic politics, however, conservatism had made great institutional and political strides since World War II.[21]

The *National Review* crowd remained friendly with Bozell. It tended to overlook his attacks. In this instance, though, the magazine responded with an unsigned editorial paragraph. "We feel a great personal tenderness for the editors of *Triumph* magazine, and in any case we prefer absolutists who say that kind of thing, to absolutists who say other kinds of things," the editors wrote. "But we decline to accept either their analysis, which we dismiss as morbid; or their remedies, which are angelistic."[22]

The expulsion of the libertarians from YAF and the alienation of *Triumph* from movement conservatism reinforced the integral role of hawkish anticommunism in the self-understanding of the American Right. It was also further evidence that Buckley and his circle were becoming part of, and to some degree replacing, the mainstream that they had ridiculed for so long. The war, the counterculture, the breakdown of social order, and partisan politics had the unpredictable consequence of turning Buckley, the crusading journalist who had been mocked fifteen years earlier as a "scrambled egghead on the right," into a member of the establishment.

For example, on the subject of civil rights, Buckley sounded more like the pro-Lincoln Harry Jaffa than the Southern Agrarian Richard Weaver. Buckley thought of himself primarily as a defender of America, of its traditional principles and political and economic systems. He came to understand that the people who believed the South would rise again were in their own way just as dangerous to the constitutional order as the Yippies and the Panthers. "The historical responsibility of the conservatives is altogether clear," he wrote. "It is to defend what is best in America. At all costs. Against any enemy, foreign or domestic."[23]

Nowhere was this shift plainer than in James Buckley's election in 1970 to a US Senate seat from New York on the Conservative

Party ticket. A corporate lawyer who had managed his younger brother's mayoral campaign, James Buckley shared the conservative views of his family. The Buckleys were now insiders. And yet, as Buckley grew more comfortable in his new role as a member of an intellectual and governing elite, the Republican Party became more populist in orientation.

NIXON'S EXPANSION OF THE VIETNAM WAR INTO CAMBODIA triggered a revolt. On April 10, 1970, "Yippie" leader Jerry Rubin appeared at Kent State University and said, "The first part of the Yippie program is to kill your parents. And I mean that quite literally, because until you're prepared to kill your parents, you're not ready to change this country." On May Day, law professor Robert Bork and his wife felt the thud of an explosion when radicals dynamited the Yale University hockey rink. "Kingman Brewster, the president of Yale, announced the next day, on no evidence he ever cared to disclose, that the sabotage was done by right-wing terrorists," Bork recalled. "That was a particularly penetrating insight since no one knew of any right-wingers, much less right-wing terrorists, anywhere near New Haven, or Connecticut, or New England." The more likely perpetrator, Bork suspected, was one of the thousands of left-wing activists who flooded the town common to protest the trial of a Black Panther on murder charges.[24]

The situation spun out of control on May 4, 1970, when National Guard troops opened fire on student protesters at Kent State, killing four. Washington, DC, became an armed camp. Upward of one hundred thousand protesters marched outside a White House ringed by police and barricades of large buses. In New York on May 8, clashes broke out between antiwar protesters and counterprotesters working downtown at the World Trade Center construction site. The construction workers, cabbies, and tradesmen who backed the Nixon policy in such confrontations with the students dramatically illustrated America's social, economic, and class divides, as well as working-class support for tough anticommunism. When Nixon heard about the riot in New York City, he said, "Thank God for the hard hats!"[25]

The new American radicalism did not fault America for failing to live up to its ideals. It criticized the ideals themselves as bogus. In the view of the extreme Left, American society was bankrupt and deserved liquidation. A comment by one student rebel at Columbia in 1968 haunted Irving Kristol. "He said, 'You don't know what hell is like unless you're born in Scarsdale,'" Kristol recalled. "Now, Scarsdale is a really nice place. All the world wishes it was born in Scarsdale." For Kristol, the young man's inability to find satisfaction in the New York suburbs evinced a growing spiritual vacuum within American society that the New Left was trying to fill.[26]

In the fall of 1970 the *Public Interest* published a special issue, titled "Capitalism Today," devoted to this nationwide rebellion. Daniel Bell wrote of "the cultural contradictions of capitalism." Commercial society's emphasis on instant gratification, Bell argued, eroded the moral principles at the basis of its economy. The waning of inherited and authoritative values coincided with rising public demands for entitlements. Material expectations were becoming more hedonistic. Political demands threatened to overwhelm the system. Not only did people want more stuff, but more groups of people wanted more rights. "Just about *all* grievances now get dumped into the lap of government," Bell wrote in a separate article for *Fortune* magazine, "while the voluntary associations that once furthered the claims of different groups are withering." The circuits of government were overloaded. Asked to do too much, government ended up doing little well.[27]

Around this time, Irving Kristol's old employer, *Commentary* magazine, enlisted in the battle against the counterculture and the left-wing teachers, social workers, journalists, bureaucrats, and politicians who put its values into practice. After taking the helm of the magazine in 1960 at the age of thirty, *Commentary*'s editor, Norman Podhoretz, a native of Brownsville, Brooklyn, who had studied literary criticism with Lionel Trilling at Columbia, initially moved in a radical direction. He opposed the war in Vietnam and published counterculture icons such as Paul Goodman, Norman Mailer, and James Baldwin.

Events drove Podhoretz to the right. It was his contention that the New Left endangered the Jewish people. In 1967, after Israel's victory over the armies of Egypt, Jordan, and Syria in the Six Day War, the radical Left adopted the Soviet line of comparing the Jewish state to Nazi Germany. The following year, a dispute over the racial allocation of teaching jobs led to a crippling New York City teachers' strike. "Somewhat to our own surprise," Podhoretz wrote, "we found that we simply could not stomach the hatred of 'Amerika' that increasingly pervaded the New Left and the counterculture. And this revulsion led to a process of reflection and reconsideration that gradually brought us to a new appreciation of the virtues of the American political system and of its economic and social underpinnings."[28]

In January 1970, after a day of work at his second home in upstate New York, Podhoretz had something like a religious epiphany. "Judaism," he realized, "was true," and therefore the unchosen obligations of faith, family, community, and nation needed to be defended. He snapped out of a long spell of writer's block and began writing a column for the magazine called "Issues." Each installment took on another sacred cow of his multiplying ex-friends on the left. He began commissioning essayistic takedowns of liberal "types": radical professors, activist clergy, the clique of intellectuals behind the New Left *New York Review of Books*. *Commentary* served up a monthly supply of intellectual ammunition aimed directly at the counterculture.[29]

Like many of the intellectuals who became known as "neoconservatives," Podhoretz developed an appreciation of interest group politics, religion, and ethnicity as bulwarks of freedom. "If the Jewish community were to act, as I was, controversially, urging it to do, on the basis of the old question, 'Is it good for the Jews?'" he wrote, "it would soon find itself defending the traditional liberal idea according to which justice is best served when individuals are treated as individuals and not as members of a group." That is because pluralism disperses power in such a way as to prevent the majority from infringing on minority rights. Podhoretz aired these arguments in an address to the American Jewish Committee, *Commentary*'s sponsor, in the spring of 1971. As he turned to the right, the magazine's February issue featured several articles on "revolutionism and the Jews."[30]

The editors of *National Review* were pleased. They published a short editorial on *Commentary* with the headline "Come On In— the Water's Fine"—which was exactly what, ever so slowly and reluctantly, many of the contributors to *Commentary* and the *Public Interest* did. The anti-Communist liberals Nathan Glazer and Seymour Martin Lipset, who had penned essays for Bell's 1955 anthology *The New American Right*, now appeared in William F. Buckley Jr.'s magazine. Political scientist John P. Roche, a former adviser to JFK and LBJ and onetime president of Americans for Democratic Action, had once mocked Buckley. In 1970 he showed up in the pages of *National Review*.[31]

"How," asked Glazer, "does a radical—a mild radical, it is true, but still someone who felt closer to radical than to liberal writers and politicians in the late 1950s—end up by early 1970 a conservative, a mild conservative, but still closer to those who now call themselves conservatives than to those who call themselves liberal?" It was a good question. For Kristol, the answer was not that complicated. Someone who understands that "social reform is a long, difficult, complex, and, at best, imperfect affair," he said, "cannot be a man of the left."[32]

Nixon's diplomacy exhibited the same realism as his domestic agenda. He formed an intense relationship with his national security adviser, Henry Kissinger, a Harvard professor and friend of Buckley's whose tragic worldview stemmed in part from his family's escape from Nazi Germany in the summer of 1938. Kissinger had fought for the United States in World War II and, after the war, enrolled at Harvard, where he received his PhD in 1954. His dissertation, later published as *A World Restored* (1957), studied the efforts of the early-nineteenth-century Holy Alliance diplomats Charles Maurice de Talleyrand-Périgord and Klemens von Metternich, as well as British foreign minister Viscount Castlereagh, to establish international order through the balance of power after the conclusion of the Napoleonic Wars. By 1968, Kissinger was advising Nelson Rockefeller on foreign policy. He was as surprised as anyone when, after the election, Nixon elliptically asked him to join the White House.[33]

Nixon's foreign policy had three elements. The first was withdrawal from Vietnam. The second was driving a wedge between China and the USSR through "triangular diplomacy." And the third was détente, or "coexistence," with the Soviet Union through arms control. The goal was to get America out of Indochina and to reduce tensions with Communist powers by ending China's diplomatic isolation and demonstrating that America could negotiate with the Soviets.

The opening to Red China was crucial. On July 15, 1971, in a televised address from Los Angeles, Nixon announced that he would visit China as a guest of Chairman Mao Tse-tung. As it happened, Bill Buckley was also in California that day, watching Nixon's speech from Ronald Reagan's living room. He had just finished recording *Firing Line* interviews with the governor and with his brother, Senator James Buckley. The group was silent as they listened to Nixon commit the anti-Communist heresy of recognizing the People's Republic. Reagan had to leave for a moment to take a call from Kissinger. "The balance of the evening," Buckley remembered, "was given over only glancingly to the great catharsis, which not many months later, by compound interest, would emerge as a Long March jointly undertaken by the United States of America and the People's Republic of China."[34]

Nixon's deviation from the anti-Communist cause was a breaking point for the Right. He had recognized one tyrannical regime while negotiating an arms-control agreement with another. To *National Review*, these moves did not diminish the Communist threat. They enlarged it. Within two weeks, Buckley, James Burnham, Frank Meyer, and William Rusher joined with eight other leaders of the Conservative Book Club, the Conservative Party of New York, the American Conservative Union, and the Young Americans for Freedom to issue the "Manhattan Declaration." It suspended their support for Nixon's reelection.

"The defection of the twelve [signatories to the Manhattan Declaration] proved of great benefit to me," recalled Nixon's political aide, Patrick Buchanan. "For two years I had been warning Nixon of problems on the right. Now the breach was public." It was Buchanan's job to keep the conservatives on board. They wanted Nixon to keep Agnew as his running mate, spend more on defense, and abandon the FAP.

Then Nixon veered left on domestic policy with the same enthusiasm as he had in recognizing China and shoving aside Taiwan. On August 15, 1971, he announced his "New Economic Policy," ending the dollar's link to gold and imposing wage and price controls. Every strain of American conservatism opposed him. Milton Friedman wrote that Nixon's price controls did "far more harm to the country than any of the later actions that led to his resignation."[35]

In the space of a month, Nixon upended the financial and security arrangements of the postwar world. Conservative intellectuals may have held their support for Nixon, but conservative politicians, importantly, did not. Neither Goldwater nor Reagan signed the Manhattan Declaration. Nor did the senator closest to *National Review*. "Important to note—James Buckley's people did not participate," Buchanan wrote to White House chief of staff H. R. Haldeman on July 28. "If any of those three broke with us, however," Buchanan warned in September, "the whole conservative revolt would be in the national media on a regular basis and we would, as I say, be in deep kimshee."[36]

The limited reach of the Manhattan Declaration was an unwelcome reminder to conservatives that the Republican Party remained the only viable—and unreliable—political instrument for their ideas. Some of the signatories backed John Ashbrook, a conservative congressman from Ohio, in his 1972 primary challenge to Nixon. But after Ashbrook performed dismally in New Hampshire—receiving fewer votes than Nixon's antiwar challenger Representative Pete McCloskey—Buckley withdrew his support. The conservatives had never trusted Nixon. By the summer of 1971 he had justified their worries. But they were also stuck with him.[37]

WHEN NIXON TOUCHED DOWN IN BEIJING IN FEBRUARY 1972, Buckley was there as part of the traveling press. He came away disgusted. The amorality of triangular diplomacy kindled in him a renewed appreciation for the idealism of the Cold War against Communist regimes. Some forms of government were better than others, Buckley thought, and America's was better than the rest. There was a moral distinction between American freedom and Communist totalitarianism. At the very least, Buckley wrote, American officials should be willing to say unapologetically that the former was superior to the latter.[38]

As Buckley was making his way to Asia, Irving Kristol traveled to Europe. He went to Montreux, Switzerland, to address the Mont Pèlerin Society on "capitalism, socialism, and nihilism." The subject allowed him to critique the classical liberalism of Friedrich Hayek and the libertarianism of Milton Friedman. At this moment, Kristol was in the intellectual ascendancy. His first essay collection, *On the Democratic Idea in America*, had been published to favorable reviews. In May a thirty-five-year-old *Wall Street Journal* writer named Robert L. Bartley profiled him and the *Public Interest* for an article titled "Irving Kristol and Friends." The piece was reprinted—along with an interview with Kristol, an appreciation written by Nathan Glazer, and a positive assessment of *On the Democratic Idea in America*—in the pages of the twenty-seven-year-old R. Emmett Tyrrell Jr.'s magazine *The Alternative*. The pugnacious campus monthly was published in Bloomington, Indiana, and later changed its name to the *American Spectator*.

Kristol was at the center of an expanding circle of writers and publications. When the socialists at *Dissent* magazine labeled him and his allies "neoconservatives," he decided that the name was as good as any. Kristol's neoconservatives were grounded, empirical, and skeptical of large endeavors. One of their heroes was Harvard political scientist Edward C. Banfield, author of *The Unheavenly City* (1970). There was no urban "crisis," Banfield argued. There were just problems concentrated among the "present-minded" residents of lower-class neighborhoods. And urban renewal and public housing made these problems worse. Banfield exemplified the neoconservative ideal: he was a toughminded scholar whose research was unassailable but anathema to liberals. His academic colleagues treated him as a pariah. The situation became so unbearable that Banfield briefly took a job at the University of Pennsylvania.[39]

Robert Bartley ended up becoming the most influential neoconservative acolyte. The native of Ames, Iowa, had majored in journalism at Iowa State University and earned a master's degree in political science from the University of Wisconsin at Madison. After a brief stint in the army, he joined the *Wall Street Journal*, where he went from the Philadelphia bureau to the editorial board in New York. At first, Bartley was reluctant to opine. "I don't know how to write editorials," he told legendary *Journal* editor Vermont Royster. "It's just like writing book reviews," Royster replied. "Except you don't have a book."[40]

There was no need for Bartley to fret. He excelled at his job. By 1972, he had been named editor of the editorial and op-ed pages. One of his first hires was Kristol, who joined the paper's board of contributors and wrote a monthly essay for the next twenty-eight years. More important, however, was the fact that the editorials themselves—many of them written by Bartley—began to reflect a neoconservative cast of mind. The editorial pages of the nation's financial newspaper of record were not just a home for defenses of free markets. They also publicized neoconservative thought.[41]

In August 1972 Kristol helped organize an advertisement in the *New York Times* on behalf of "Democrats for Nixon." These Democrats, including Sidney Hook, were repulsed by their party's nominee, South Dakota senator George McGovern, who called for unilateral withdrawal from Vietnam and allied himself with the counterculture. "I found myself getting more and more disillusioned with what then was regarded as the official liberal position," Kristol recalled. "Even on the basis of what works, one was forced to become more conservative."[42]

Kristol's embrace of Nixon led Daniel Bell to resign as coeditor of the *Public Interest*. Glazer, who along with Bell and Moynihan remained a Democrat, replaced him. (Bell and Kristol stayed life-long friends.) Buckley, for his part, credited the neoconservatives with infusing the Right with newfound energy. "The conservative message at that point had become so platonic," he said. Burnham also detected a waning of intellectual energy and political realism on the right. "No serious politics in our time," he wrote, "can be based on a simplistic anti-welfarist doctrine." The neocons, Buckley added, "taught the conservatives—they certainly taught me—methods of the organization of social data, which I wasn't familiar with."[43]

Differences remained between neoconservatism and *National Review*. The neoconservatives had grown up poor, were mostly from New York, and were more interested in urban problems than traditionalists who idealized rural life. Paradoxically, while neoconservatives came from modest circumstances, they spoke from within prestigious academic and journalistic institutions. Another difference was that *National Review*, despite backing away from segregation, remained committed to the doctrine of states' rights and opposed the exercise of federal power outside the enumerated powers of the Constitution. Neoconservatives accepted the New Deal and supported both the 1957 and 1964 Civil Rights Acts. They believed federal power was necessary to secure political equality under the law but that judges and bureaucrats had misread the 1964 Civil Rights Act to mandate something that the law expressly prohibited—an affirmative action of racial quotas and busing of students to achieve an arbitrary racial mix in public schools.

National Review remained skeptical, at best, toward the Israeli government. The neocons unabashedly supported Israel not only as the national home of the Jewish people but also as a fellow democracy amid a sea of Soviet-allied despotisms. *National Review* was also critical of the labor movement, but many neoconservatives traced their roots to the social democratic activism of the 1930s and 1940s. They continued to support the role of labor in political and civil society and applauded the opposition of the American Federation of Labor and Congress of Industrial Organizations (AFL-CIO) to communism. *National Review* also held a restrictionist position on immigration, whereas neoconservatives, who descended from immigrants to the United States from southern and eastern Europe, supported the free movement of peoples.

Neoconservatives were not so much pulled to the right as pushed there by the New Left. The neoconservatives believed that they were defending liberalism, not negating it as more traditional conservatives sought to do. This attitude toward liberalism might have been the key distinction between neoconservatism and *National Review*. It was also how neoconservatives changed the tonality of the American Right. The economics of balanced budgets gave way to the economics of growth and full employment. The anticommunism of countersubversion was transmuted into a defense of democracy. Philosophical support for tradition in the abstract was overshadowed by concrete social policies that addressed the demoralization of welfare recipients.

If any candidate could unite *National Review* and the *Public Interest* and was sure to annoy the Dayton Housewife and the "hard hats," it was George McGovern. Two days after he won the Massachusetts Democratic primary on April 25, 1972, a devastating quote from a fellow liberal senator appeared in the syndicated column of journalists Rowland Evans and Robert D. Novak. "The people don't know McGovern is for amnesty, abortion, and legalization of pot," the anonymous senator told the reporters. "Once middle America—Catholic Middle America, in particular—finds this out, he's dead."[44]

The Nixon forces were happy to spread word of McGovern's views. "We ought to set this early that McGovern is not the candidate of the people, but of a small elite, of New Leftists, the elitist children, etc.," Buchanan wrote to Nixon advisers H. R. Haldeman and Clark MacGregor after the 1972 Democratic convention. Ironically, the senator Evans and Novak quoted was Missouri's Thomas F. Eagleton, who served as McGovern's running mate for eighteen days before dropping out when news broke that he had undergone shock therapy during the 1960s. (Eagleton was replaced by Sargent Shriver, the first director of the Peace Corps.)[45]

Even though Norman Podhoretz could not bring himself to support Nixon, he found himself appalled by McGovern. Following the well-trod path of others in the anti-Communist labor

Left, Podhoretz and his wife, social critic Midge Decter, joined forces with the Social Democrats USA, a remnant of the old Socialist Party of America whose members included Sidney Hook, veteran civil rights activist Bayard Rustin, and a younger generation of anti-Communist labor organizers such as Penn Kemble, Carl Gershman, and Joshua Muravchik. "To be a social democrat in those years," Decter wrote, "meant to be to the right of the Democratic Party and to the left of the Republican Party: a very narrow place, where neither we nor the labor movement could permanently remain."[46]

The most famous representative of this contracting Democratic center was Senator Henry M. "Scoop" Jackson of Washington. Jackson was an environmentalist and a defender of the welfare state, but he also opposed forced busing to integrate de facto segregated schools. And he was an unapologetic Cold Warrior who supported Nixon's Vietnam strategy. He remained suspicious of détente with the USSR and favored strong nuclear deterrence. He was also the coauthor, with Ohio Democratic congressman Charles Vanik, of the Jackson-Vanik amendment, a rider to the 1974 trade bill that "linked" trade with nonmarket economies to liberalized emigration. The amendment was aimed at the Soviet Union, which had made it next to impossible for its persecuted Jewish minority to emigrate to Israel.

Jackson's 1972 bid for the Democratic nomination had crashed against the shoals of McGovernism and the "New Politics" of cultural radicalism and anti-anticommunism. But Jackson's campaign and staff became fixtures of the capital's foreign policy scene. They included Ben Wattenberg; Richard Perle, who had been a classmate of Albert Wohlstetter's daughter; Paul Wolfowitz, who had been a student of Allan Bloom's at Cornell and of Wohlstetter's at the University of Chicago; and Elliott Abrams, a Harvard-trained lawyer who later became Midge Decter and Norman Podhoretz's son-in-law.

In December 1972, a month after McGovern was crushed at the polls, Wattenberg set up the Coalition for a Democratic Majority to rally what remained of liberal anticommunism. "By the time McGovern had gone down to one of the worst defeats in the country's history," Decter wrote, "we were ready with a publicized statement of purpose which said in effect that we were opposed to the left and to all those legislative and judicial measures—for a primary example, affirmative action—whose intent was to overturn the country's essential philosophical and political underpinnings." Neoconservatives, *National Review*, and street-corner conservatives agreed: America needed defending against the curses of the Left.[47]

The outcome of the 1972 election was anticlimactic. "No doubt future textbooks on how to score landslide victories will begin with the injunction: Get George McGovern nominated by the opposite party," Buckley quipped. Nixon won 61 percent of the popular vote and every state but Massachusetts. He outperformed the anti-Humphrey vote from 1968 that Kevin Phillips had made a benchmark for the GOP nominee in *The Emerging Republican Majority*. "The adversary culture that had captured the Democratic Party had been rejected and the radical left so repudiated that the discredited remnants were turning to acts of terror," Buchanan wrote. "At his second inaugural, Nixon would reach the apogee of his approval, 68 percent, in Gallup."[48]

Nixon's success was personal. It did not translate to the rest of his party. Republicans gained House seats, but Democrats netted two seats in the Senate, including a seat in Delaware won by a thirty-year-old councilman named Joe Biden. Nixon was strong in the South and among Catholics. But the election was more a personal rejection of McGovern than an endorsement of the new majority. No one issue dominated the election.

Watergate certainly did not. The break-in at the Democratic National Committee headquarters inside the Watergate office, hotel, and residential complex along the Potomac River in Washington, DC, occurred in the middle of the campaign, on June 17, 1972. For months, the crime was overshadowed. First there was the election. Then, on January 23, 1973, came the announcement of the Paris Peace Accords with North Vietnam. And then, after Nixon's second inauguration, came the return of American prisoners of war.

This benign neglect of Watergate soon ended, however. In February 1973 the Senate authorized a joint select investigative committee into the Watergate break-in and a potential White House cover-up. Its chairman was Democratic senator Sam Ervin of North Carolina. Then, in an April 30 televised address, Nixon announced the resignations of Haldeman and other key aides, including White House counsel John Dean, because of fallout from Watergate. And in May, the Justice Department appointed its own special prosecutor to investigate the matter.

Through the criminal activities of his Committee to Reelect the President (CREEP) and his attempt to hide his involvement in the White House cover-up, Nixon once again presented conservatives with a choice between principle and partisan necessity. Buckley kept his distance from the scandal. His close friend Howard Hunt, who had arranged for his brief job with the Central Intelligence Agency, was one of Nixon's "plumbers," charged with fixing White House leaks, and helped plot the break-in. In January 1973, Buckley removed himself "from editorial discussion involving the Watergate affair." He would bring it up in his columns over the next two years, but always warily and with a noticeable hesitation to pronounce categorically on the question of Nixon's guilt.[49]

At first, *National Review* lambasted media coverage of Nixon and took the position that the wrongdoing was limited to the burglars themselves. Irving Kristol wrote in his May 1973 *Wall Street Journal* column that Nixon's "evident lack of puzzlement over these bizarre events" disturbed him. The next month, Kristol incorrectly predicted that Nixon would not resign. But he also correctly grasped that Watergate's consequences would be far-reaching and would damage the cause of a free society. The scandal, he wrote, made "a mockery of the efforts of those—I am one of them, and here declare my interest—who have been trying to counter the extremist impulse in American politics and to make an intellectual case for political moderation." For his part, Russell Kirk blamed Watergate on a lack of "moral imagination" on the part of the Nixon lieutenants at CREEP. He also believed that his defenses of Nixon throughout the scandal caused newspapers to drop his syndicated column, which he decided to end.[50]

Kirk more likely lost papers to a thirty-one-year-old named George F. Will. This former professor of political philosophy had fallen in love with journalism by reading the sports pages and the *New York Post* columns of liberal writer Murray Kempton. He had studied at Oxford and Princeton and briefly taught at the university level before joining the staff of conservative senator Gordon Allott of Colorado.

Will moved to DC in January 1970. He freelanced for *National Review* and the *Alternative* while working as a congressional aide. When Allott was defeated in Nixon's reelection year, Will called Buckley and suggested himself for the position of *National Review*'s Washington editor. Buckley agreed. He also made Will the book editor, replacing Elsie Meyer, who had been filling in for her husband, Frank, since his death the previous April.

Will's first "Capitol Issues" column appeared in the magazine's February 2, 1973, issue. He never forgave Nixon for snubbing Allott during the final weeks of the campaign. "A year ago the reigning philosophy was survival of the fittest, and Mr. Nixon and his agents were feeling remarkably fit," Will wrote in November 1973. "Today Mr. Nixon has all the friends he has earned and deserves."[51]

Will's criticism of both Nixon and Agnew drew fire not only from *National Review*'s readers but also from its staff. Bill Rusher could not stand him. Both Rusher and Stan Evans, who wrote a column for the biweekly *National Review Bulletin*, hadn't really supported Nixon *until* Watergate. Now both men accused Will of serving liberal interests. Evans said he would not write for the *Bulletin* so long as Will was a part of *National Review*. Rusher waged a guerrilla campaign to have Will fired. Their disdain grew in intensity when, in addition to his *National Review* duties, Will began writing a column for the *Washington Post*—whose reporters had done so much to advance the Watergate story—in 1974.

If conservative intellectuals were divided on the subject of Watergate, conservative politicians were not. The scandal was a replay of the fight over Nixon's recognition of China. "I can't say publicly but feel very deeply we are witness to a lynching," Reagan wrote in a May 1973 letter. "I still have confidence that when the smoke clears we will find the president was not involved," he wrote in June. In October, Buckley quietly asked conservative leaders whether they were ready to call on Nixon to resign. Reagan's response was two words long. "HELL NO," he wrote.[52]

October 1973 was a critical month—a moment when the entire world might well have flown apart. Agnew resigned as vice president over corruption charges. Nixon fired both his attorney general, Elliot Richardson, and his deputy attorney general when they refused to dismiss the Watergate special prosecutor. Robert Bork, who had joined the administration as solicitor general earlier in the year, was now in command of the Justice Department. He carried out the president's order, but the "Saturday Night Massacre" did not help Nixon at all. When the dust settled, another special prosecutor was appointed. The Watergate investigations rolled on.

In the meantime, Arab nations led by Egypt and Syria launched a surprise attack against Israel on Yom Kippur, the holiest day of the Jewish calendar. As his presidency began to crumble, Nixon and Kissinger led a heroic effort to resupply the unprepared Israeli forces, even threatening nuclear retaliation if the Soviet Union, which stood behind the Arab armies, became directly involved.

By the end of October, Israel had turned the tide of battle. But it was a far more difficult campaign than the Six Day War of 1967, which had established Israeli control of Gaza, the West Bank, and the Golan Heights. The Arabs, furious at American support for their sworn enemy, embargoed oil exports to nations they deemed overly supportive of Israel. They wanted to starve the United States of fuel. The resulting gas shortages also contributed to price inflation. The "first oil shock" unleashed economic havoc throughout the world.

In November, during the question-and-answer period after a speech at Kansas State University, Buckley said that Nixon would resign before he was impeached, and "by doing that, rather than hanging by his fingernails onto power, he would both relieve a Republic that is sorely vexed, and ingratiate himself with it, as no other act of his at this point would succeed in doing." Buckley also wrote to Reagan again. He worried that Congress was too slow in confirming Agnew's replacement, House minority leader Gerald Ford. "I think the moment has come delicately to insist, in declarations aimed *urbe et orbe*, that Congress must proceed to confirm the Vice President just in case," he wrote. "Following that, a patient, cautious disassociation would appear to be prudent." (Ford became vice president on December 6, 1973.) But neither Reagan nor Goldwater wavered in support for Nixon. In January 1974 the Arizona senator said, "I don't think it's the prerogative of one man to put himself above 46 or 47 million Americans who voted for Mr. Nixon or the 23 or 24 percent of the American people who still believe he should be president."[53]

By the spring of 1974, James Burnham was convinced that Nixon would set back the conservative cause just as Joe McCarthy and the John Birch Society had done. Both Bill and James Buckley agreed. On March 19, Senator Buckley, in a statement written by Burnham, called on Nixon to resign. He said that Watergate had become a "crisis of the regime," spilling over into every aspect of American society and debilitating the government at a time of global conflict and economic crisis. While he had not determined whether Nixon was guilty of a crime and did not want to lend the impression that Nixon's resignation would be an admission of wrongdoing, Senator Buckley argued that Nixon's withdrawal would uphold the office of the presidency and check Congress from steamrolling the executive branch and vastly expanding the welfare state. "I hope and pray he will realize," Buckley concluded, "that the greatest and culminating action he can now take for his country is the renunciation of the world's highest office."[54]

The dam broke on July 24. The Supreme Court issued a unanimous ruling that ordered Nixon to deliver all tapes of his recorded White House conversations to the special prosecutor. Within seventy-two hours, the House Judiciary Committee approved the first article of impeachment against the president. "To remove Mr. Nixon from office must now be done," Buckley wrote in his August 7 syndicated column. The *Wall Street Journal* editorial board came out for the president's removal the same day. Also on August 7, Goldwater visited the Oval Office and told Nixon that "at most" ten senators would vote to acquit him. Four of those senators were firm, Goldwater said. "The others are undecided. I'm one of them."[55]

On the evening of August 8, Nixon announced that he would resign at noon the next day. After the televised address, an exhausted Kissinger returned to his office. One of Nixon's lawyers was there, feeling morose and inadequate. Kissinger told him that he had done the best he could. "It was not a legal case," he said. "It was a Greek tragedy. Nixon was fulfilling his own nature. Once it started it could not end otherwise." Nixon's attempt to govern as a moderate conservative, to extract America from Vietnam by splitting the Sino-Soviet alliance, and to weld working-class white voters to the Republican coalition had ended in personal disgrace. The next few years would see the growing influence of the neo-conservatives, the return of religion in politics, and the rise of Ronald Reagan.[56]

CHAPTER NINE

THE PRAIRIE FIRE

G ERALD FORD WAS PRESIDENT OF THE UNITED STATES FOR A little more than two years. He was an accidental president— the only man to hold the office who was elected to neither the presidency nor the vice presidency. On paper, he was not the best fit for the job. Ford was a creature of the House of Representatives, where he had served from 1949 to 1973, when he replaced Spiro Agnew as vice president. For most of his political life, his constituency had been limited to the borders of Michigan's Fifth District. A college football star and decorated naval veteran of World War II, Ford was personable, modest, and well liked. But he was never associated with any particular ideology or agenda. In 1965, after the Barry Goldwater debacle, he won the job of minority leader. The moderate Republicanism he brought to the Oval Office had a role in his undoing.

Ford set for himself the difficult task of repairing the damage of Watergate and Vietnam while maintaining the policies of Richard Nixon. Conservatives were unhappy when he selected as his vice president neither Ronald Reagan nor Barry Goldwater but their longtime enemy Nelson Rockefeller. Then Ford's popularity with the broader public took a hit in September 1974, when he

pardoned his former boss. It was a decision from which he might
have recovered—had not global and national conditions taken such
a turn for the worse during his administration.

Ford was unable to arrest the decline of American power following the collapse of South Vietnam in April 1975. Nor could he
stop the erosion of consumer confidence from rising inflation. He
did not know how to navigate the polarized politics generated by
new social issues such as abortion, gay rights, and the Equal Rights
Amendment (ERA), which would have prohibited discrimination
on the basis of sex. These collective blows to American prestige,
self-confidence, and civil peace knocked out not only Ford's presidency but that of his successor, Jimmy Carter.

Ford was not helped when the Democrats made tremendous
gains in the 1974 midterm elections, leaving them with huge
margins in both the House and Senate. By the end of that year,
the GOP was at a demoralizing low. The predictions of imminent doom for conservatives and Republicans that accompanied
every electoral setback sounded once more. This time, however,
not just liberals in the Republican Party were shedding crocodile
tears. The Right believed that Republicans had lost not only because of Nixon's personal flaws but also because he had rejected
conservatism. "The Republican Party is dead," warned Reagan,
"unless it stands up and erects a set of principles around which
people can rally."[1]

For neither the first nor the last time, conservatives wondered
whether the GOP was the best political vehicle for their ideas. "If
Mr. Ford's reluctant warriors determine that their guiding principle should be to take those actions least displeasing to the greatest
number, if their objective is to enjoy as long as possible the unanticipated gift of the gods, then their claim upon the conservatives
is nonexistent," Pat Buchanan wrote in *Conservative Votes, Liberal
Victories* (1975). "At the very least," Kevin Phillips concluded in
Mediacracy (1975), "the easygoing political traditions of the past

are in for a massive strain; at most, America may be on the verge of an epochal shift in the nature of her political and governmental institutions." Bill Rusher held that conditions were ripe for the emergence of a third major party.[2]

This new party would be unified by a total rejection of the status quo. Its base of support would be the Old South and the rapidly growing West, along with blue-collar counties in the North. It would combine the Sun Belt with the Golden State, Canarsie with Cuyahoga. Its pop culture heroes would be cowboys and renegades such as John Wayne and Clint Eastwood. It would conceive of itself as an oppositional force, antagonistic to all aspects of the eastern establishment, Republican and Democrat, liberal and conservative, cultural and economic. It would unify the supporters of Ronald Reagan and George Wallace.

Richard Viguerie, who had built his direct-marketing company into a business empire, popularized the term "New Right" to describe the increasing number of political activists fighting lax divorce and abortion laws, the gay rights movement, ERA, school busing, tax increases, media bias, the return of the Panama Canal to Panama, threats to the nonprofit status of churches and religious institutions, and other perceived misdeeds of the establishment. In 1975 Viguerie founded a magazine, *Conservative Digest*, to advance this populist, social conservative agenda. Phillips was his star columnist.

The New Right, Phillips wrote, was different from both *National Review* and the neoconservatism of the *Public Interest*, *Commentary*, and the *Wall Street Journal* editorial pages. Their New York–based writers were too removed from Middle America. They were too academic, too upper-middle-class, too closely associated with the Republican Party to be trusted. The conservative intellectuals, Phillips believed, were too interested in maintaining respectability among liberals. The New Right did not care about elite validation. It wanted results. Its aim was a dramatic reduction in the reach of the state. "99 percent for Defense—keep America strong—and 1 percent on delivering the mail. That's it," said activist Terry Dolan. "Leave us alone."[3]

The enemies of the New Right were compromise, gradualism, and acquiescence in a corrupt system. Partisan identification had little to do with the antagonisms of New Right activists. William F. Buckley Jr. and George Will were just as much targets of their criticism as CBS and the *New York Times*. To the New Right, conservatives and Republicans with Ivy League degrees were sellouts. They were weak. "We're interested in ideology," said Dolan. "We're not interested in respectability."[4]

In a contribution to a symposium held in *Commentary*, Phillips distinguished between two types of conservatives. One was more effective in real-world politics than the other. "There are conservatives whose game it is to quote English poetry and utter neo-Madisonian benedictions over the interests and institutions of establishment liberalism," he wrote. "Then there are other conservatives—many I know—who have more in common with Andrew Jackson than with Edmund Burke. Their hope is to build cultural siege-cannon out of the populist steel of Idaho, Mississippi, and working-class Milwaukee, and then blast the Eastern liberal establishment to ideo-institutional smithereens." Phillips repudiated the cornerstone of Burkean conservatism—the protection of established order against radical change—in favor of upheaval, demolition, and power.[5]

Support for George Wallace and for the fight against crime and busing was not just about racial antagonism. Something else was going on. Before he ran for the Senate in 1972, Joe Biden had written that busing was an unpopular and ineffective solution to de facto residential segregation. Busing might backfire. Later, during Biden's second Senate term, he told a witness at a committee hearing, "Sometimes even George Wallace is right about some things."[6]

Biden was suggesting that by characterizing all opposition as racism, liberals had blinded themselves to the growing rebellion among their own voters. The ability to send a child to the school of your choice, to live in a safe neighborhood, to rely on a fixed income and maintain a consistent level of purchasing power at the grocery store and the gas pump, to grow angry at national dishonor—such concerns were reasonable and legitimate. For liberals to ignore, pathologize, or wave them away was more than risky. It was foolish.

The New Right believed in aggressive political combat. Its politics of conflict required new institutions. In 1973 the National Right to Life Committee and the American Legislative Exchange Council were incorporated and the first Conservative Political Action Conference was held. The National Conservative Political Action Committee started in 1975. Concerned Women for America and the Free Congress Foundation launched in 1977. That same year, Harlan Bronson "Bullethead" Carter, a fifty-four-year-old former border patrol agent, assumed control of the National Rifle Association. He turned the sportsmen's organization into a powerful lobby against gun control.

"If we are to build an enduring Republican majority, then we need to construct institutes that will serve as the repository of its political beliefs," Pat Buchanan had written in a memo to President Nixon in 1972. "The [American Enterprise Institute (AEI)] is not the answer." AEI was too scholarly, too detached from everyday politics. A new think tank, Buchanan went on, "could serve many purposes: a) a talent bank for Republicans in office; b) a tax-exempt refuge for Republicans out of office to stay at work and stay together; c) a communications center for Republican thinkers the nation over."[7]

The idea was picked up the following year. With support from beer tycoon Joseph Coors, two congressional aides incorporated the Heritage Foundation on February 16, 1973. Its job was to deliver policy analysis and recommendations to congressmen before votes were cast. The aides were Ed Feulner, who worked for conservative Illinois congressman Phil Crane, and Paul Weyrich.

"I can think of no one who better symbolizes or is more important to the conservative movement than Paul Weyrich," Viguerie wrote in *The New Right: We're Ready to Lead*. Like George Will, Weyrich had worked for Senator Gordon Allott. But the resemblance ended there. "Paul typifies the political philosophy of the New Right," Viguerie went on, "which parallels the military philosophy of Douglas MacArthur, 'There is no substitute for victory.'" The New Right embraced the rhetoric of combat over conciliation, disruption over stability. "The New Right does not want to conserve, we want to change," Weyrich told Viguerie. "We *are* the forces of change."[8]

In an essay for *The New Right Papers*, Samuel T. Francis, an aide to Senator John East of North Carolina, described the New Right as the political manifestation of "Middle American Radicals" working to overthrow the ruling liberal elite. To succeed, Francis explained, the New Right would have to shed its association with the conservatism of *National Review*. According to Francis, the rather pessimistic and anti-statist conservatism of *National Review* had few adherents beyond burdened businessmen and lovers of old books.

For Francis, the conservative movement was too Catholic, too Jewish, too urban, and too comfortable with liberalism. "Middle American Radicals" were Protestant whites in the South and Midwest without college degrees—so-called real Americans. And the ranks of voters opposed to what the New Right called "social engineering" were growing. Of course, the founders of *National Review* didn't believe in social engineering. On the contrary, they opposed it as yet another extension of the overbearing, centralized state. The New Right and *National Review* held opposing views on how politics should be conducted and divergent attitudes toward government institutions.[9]

The situation on the left was similar. Substantive fissures over foreign and domestic policy divided the Democratic coalition. And they persisted throughout Ford's administration. As Senator Henry M. Jackson and his team of neoconservatives assailed Nixon and Ford's grain deal with the Soviets, concessions on arms control, and reluctance to link trade to human rights—especially the right of Soviet Jews to emigrate to Israel—Secretary of State Henry Kissinger encountered a sharp and wily critic from within his own administration.

Since February 1973, Daniel Patrick Moynihan had served as ambassador to India, where he became alarmed at the anti-American tendencies of the United Nations. He spent December 1974 working on a long paper explaining why he felt America needed to press its case in global forums. He finished the piece during Christmas week and sent it to Norman Podhoretz.[10]

Some sixty pages of triple-spaced typescript arrived in the *Commentary* editor's mailbox early in 1975. Podhoretz reorganized parts of the argument, inserted transitions, cut material, and showed it to the author. Moynihan was pleased. His essay appeared in the magazine's March 1975 issue. Podhoretz arranged a press conference—the first in *Commentary*'s history—to mark the occasion of what was clearly a landmark article. The *New York Times* covered the event. "Moynihan Calls on U.S. to 'Start Raising Hell' in U.N.," read its headline.[11]

That was one way of putting it. In his essay, titled "The United States in Opposition," Moynihan observed that the newly decolonized nations of the Third World constituted a majority in the UN General Assembly hostile to American interests. To prevent the collapse of these diplomatic institutions into proxies of the Soviet Empire, Moynihan argued, the United States should start behaving like a parliamentary minority. "*This is our case*," Moynihan concluded. "We *are* of the liberty party, and it might surprise us what energies might be released were we to unfurl those banners."[12]

"The United States in Opposition" was the clearest statement yet of *Commentary*'s ongoing case for an assertive US foreign policy. In a pair of articles that ran in April and July 1976, Podhoretz and longtime contributor Nathan Glazer broadened Moynihan's argument to include the general conduct of American statecraft. Podhoretz pointed to America's refusal to involve itself in the struggle between Communists and the military in Portugal and between Communist and anti-Communist factions in Angola. And he excoriated America's dilatory response to the rise of the Italian Communist Party. "If it should turn out that the new isolationism has indeed triumphed among the people as completely as it has among the elites," he warned in "Making the World Safe for Communism," "then the United States will celebrate its two hundredth birthday by betraying the heritage of liberty which has earned it the wonder and envy of the world from the moment of its founding to this, and by helping to make that world safe for the most determined and ferocious and barbarous enemies of liberty ever to have appeared on the earth."[13]

In "American Values and American Foreign Policy," Glazer described the "great struggle" to define America's self-image. "If it sees itself as a good country and a strong country—the way I would say the overwhelming majority of Americans did between 1945 and 1965—and if it is seen by others in the same way, it will feel confident in playing a large role in the world," he wrote. "If it sees itself as a good though weak country (one present-day image of ourselves), or as wicked and strong (another), or as wicked and weak, there will be a tendency to retrench and redraw." For *Commentary*, America was both good and strong.[14]

"The United States in Opposition" was condensed for the mass-circulation *Reader's Digest*—another first for *Commentary*. Moynihan appeared on television talk shows. He received a compliment from Secretary of State Kissinger, whose tenure in office was at something of a low point. Kissinger did not share the same rapport with the new president that he had enjoyed with Nixon. "With Ford," Kissinger wrote, "what one saw was what one got." Kissinger saw a mixed bag.[15]

In March 1975 North Vietnam invaded South Vietnam. And in April the genocidal Communists of the Khmer Rouge took over Cambodia. That month, Ford asked Moynihan if he would like the job of US ambassador to the United Nations. Moynihan said yes. Before assuming the post, he developed his argument for the "party of liberty" in lectures at the City University of New York and the University of Chicago. "Postwar American diplomacy," he said in Chicago, "has failed to see that the presentation of the American case is a task that requires professional competence, especially as addressed to the new nations. Mere empathy is not enough." The Senate confirmed Moynihan on June 10. The president swore him into office on June 30.[16]

He wasted no time causing trouble. After the ceremony, Moynihan left the White House to attend an AFL-CIO gala in honor of Alexander Solzhenitsyn. The Nobel Prize–winning author had been expelled from the Soviet Union on February 13, 1974—the same year that the first volume of his reconstruction of the horrors of Soviet prison camps, *The Gulag Archipelago*, was translated into English with galvanic effect.

Solzhenitsyn's careful examination of the dehumanization of the Soviet population exploded any pretense of morality on the part of Communist leaders and fellow travelers. Solzhenitsyn was an anti-Communist hero: a literary giant with the courage to defy the prison wardens of the Soviet Empire. He had the voice of a prophet and the stern presence of a man who had suffered greatly but whose strength of will allowed him to survive. In his public pronouncements he warned the West that no amount of negotiation would change the evil nature of the Soviet regime.

At dinner, Moynihan sat on the dais as the Russian exile mesmerized the crowd. "Whether you like it or not," Solzhenitsyn told his audience, "the course of history has made you the leaders of the world." Without mentioning names, Solzhenitsyn contrasted Nixon-Ford policies with what he called "true détente." "From our experience I can tell you that only firmness makes it possible to withstand the assaults of Communist totalitarianism," he said. While the West was conceding too much, Solzhenitsyn went on, a new generation within the Soviet Union was growing tired of oppression. "Let us try to slow down the process of concessions and help the process of liberation!"[17]

On July 2, Senators Jesse Helms and Strom Thurmond requested that Ford meet with Solzhenitsyn. The meeting was denied—the White House said it interfered with the president's schedule. This excuse inflamed Kissinger's critics. "The episode ennobles Solzhenitsyn," William F. Buckley Jr. commented. Ford's chief of staff, Donald Rumsfeld, and Rumsfeld's deputy, Dick Cheney, urged Ford to meet with the dissident. But the president sided with Kissinger. In his memoirs, Kissinger conceded that the rebuff was a mistake, but he never forgave the conservatives and neoconservatives for the embarrassment. "Our neoconservative critics," he wrote, "wanted to prevail in the name of ideology, not superior tactics—indeed, they saw no other way for America to prevail."[18]

What Kissinger condemned as "ideology" was in fact an alternative strategy of anti-Communist resistance. This strategy based its confrontation on human rights. It resembled the "psychological" and "information" warfare that James Burnham had advocated decades before. "Those of us in the 'neocon' camp refused to subordinate human rights concerns to what [the Nixon and Ford] administrations saw as far more important and 'serious' matters like trade and détente," remembered Elliott Abrams. Senator Scoop Jackson, for instance, called for a "linkage" between a nation's human rights record and its treatment by the United States. Moynihan personified neoconservative forthrightness in his confrontations with Ugandan dictator Idi Amin and in his stirring protest of a UN resolution declaring Zionism a form of racism. During the Zionism controversy, Moynihan relied on Podhoretz to help draft the opening of his famous message. "The United States rises to declare before the General Assembly of the United Nations, and before the world, that it does not acknowledge, it will not abide by, it will never acquiesce in this infamous act," he said.[19]

Moynihan was the most popular member of the Ford administration (competition was light). His statements transfixed anti-Communists of both parties. "At the U.N.'s barbarous parliament, the barbarians, because of Moynihan, are no longer getting a free rhetorical ride," *National Review* gushed. The editors floated Moynihan for president: "Daniel Patrick Moynihan is our 1975 Man of the Year."[20]

This embrace of Moynihan indicated a change in movement conservative attitudes. *National Review* found itself allied to the last holdouts of FDR-Truman-JFK liberal anticommunism. Where once the magazine had dismissed "containment" of the Soviet Union in favor of "rollback," it now thought the strategy defensible. The New Right, for its part, continued to view the neoconservatives with suspicion, even as it agreed with their anti-Communist policies.

By the beginning of 1976, however, Moynihan's influence within the Ford administration had faded. Kissinger reasserted control over America's diplomacy at the United Nations. He scratched a speech Moynihan had prepared that criticized the participation of the Palestine Liberation Organization in UN activities. Moynihan was not bitter. "I was 40 before I had any real idea what [Edmund] Burke was about," he wrote. "Kissinger knew in his cradle. On the other hand, I knew what [Woodrow] Wilson was all about." He left his post in February. As soon as he was out of a job, Moynihan flew to Massachusetts to campaign for Scoop Jackson in the Bay State's presidential primary. In New York in June, he announced his candidacy for the US Senate.[21]

Scoop Jackson won the Massachusetts primary, but the 1976 Democratic presidential nomination went to a relative unknown: former one-term governor of Georgia James Earl Carter Jr. Carter was a pro–civil rights Southern Democrat, a soft-spoken naval veteran who wanted to be all things to all people. Moynihan tried to steer the political novice toward a foreign policy of tough-minded support for human rights. Working with Ben Wattenberg, he inserted a plank into the 1976 Democratic platform that read, in part, "America must continue to stand as a bulwark in support of human liberty in all countries. A return to the politics of principles requires a reaffirmation of human freedom throughout the world."[22]

Both Democrats and Republicans held competitive presidential races in 1976. After leaving the office of California governor in January 1975, Ronald Reagan had returned to the speaker circuit and was broadcasting radio commentaries. Bill Rusher made a personal appeal to Reagan to run as the third-party candidate of the American Independent Party (AIP), which had nominated George Wallace in 1968. Reagan politely refused. Instead the AIP nominated Lester Maddox, the notorious bigot who bracketed Carter as governor of Georgia.

In November 1975 Reagan announced that he would challenge Ford for the Republican nomination. He anchored his campaign in New Right themes: détente endangered America, inflation harmed workers, and the family was under siege. He said that affirmative action amounted to reverse discrimination. He noted that majorities of black and white Americans opposed court-ordered school busing. He believed that "interrupting a pregnancy is the taking of human life and can only be justified in self-defense—that is, if the mother's own life is in danger." He decried "other decisions of government—some still pending—which strike at basic values and, indeed, at the very heart of the family."[23]

For all his grasp of the issues animating conservatives, Reagan's campaign did not start off well. He lost the first six contests. Ford successfully defined Reagan's tax and budget proposals as a threat to entitlement spending. In the days before the Illinois primary, which Reagan lost by nineteen points, Fred Barnes of the *Washington Star* watched the ex-governor drop his notecards and lose his place. "His speech that day was dreary and incoherent," Barnes wrote. "He looked like a loser."[24]

Out of money and ready to retire, Reagan stayed on for one more contest. His campaign made its last stand in North Carolina, where Senator Helms and political consultant Tom Ellis formulated a turnaround strategy. On primary day Reagan left North Carolina for California, thinking his political career was at an end. Midflight he got word that he had won by six points. The race went on.

By the convention, Reagan was within 120 delegates of Ford. There was no presumptive nominee. As the incumbent, Ford had the advantage, but Reagan might win if he could force a second ballot on the convention floor. An ill-considered gambit to name liberal GOP senator Richard Schweiker of Pennsylvania as his running mate backfired on Reagan. Ford, meanwhile, in a concession to pro-life activists, replaced Rockefeller on the ticket with Kansas senator Bob Dole. In the end, Ford became the Republican nominee.

But Reagan became the soul of the GOP. Helms led the successful effort to insert a plank in the party platform supporting "morality in foreign policy." The text was an indirect rebuke of Kissinger and détente. "We recognize and commend that great beacon of human courage and morality, Alexander Solzhenitsyn, for his compelling message that we must face the world with no illusions about the nature of tyranny," it read in part. "Ours will be a foreign policy that keeps this ever in mind." The platform singled out for criticism the 1975 Helsinki Accords—an international agreement signed by thirty-five nations, including the United States and the Soviet Union. For the Ford administration, Helsinki was proof that détente worked: Washington could negotiate with Moscow (and other nations) as equals. For conservatives, Helsinki legitimated the Soviet presence in Eastern Europe.

On the last night of the convention, Ford graciously invited Reagan onstage and asked him to make impromptu remarks. Reagan highlighted the achievements of his supporters. "I believe the Republican Party has a platform that is a banner of bold, unmistakable colors with no pale pastel shades," he told the convention hall. Reagan said that recently he had been asked to contribute an essay for a time capsule that would be opened in the year 2076. As he wrote the contribution, he said, he thought about the dangers confronting the country, especially the threat of nuclear war with the Soviet Union. "And suddenly it dawned on me," Reagan told the transfixed crowd. "Those who would read this letter a hundred years from now will know whether those missiles were fired. They will know whether we met our challenge. Whether they had the freedom that we have known up until now, will depend on what we do here." The audience was rapt. Some people were in tears. The contrast between Reagan's eloquence and Ford's stolidity was plain.[25]

The general election between Ford and Carter was close. It was notable for the first televised presidential debate in sixteen years. At one point during the exchange, Ford said, "There is no Soviet domination of Eastern Europe and there never will be under a Ford administration." Whatever Ford was trying to get at—he probably meant that the captive peoples of Eastern Europe maintained their national pride despite Communist oppression—the gaffe was a remarkable lapse in judgment. It also played into the impression, created in part by comic Chevy Chase on *Saturday Night Live*, that Ford was a bumbling klutz.

Carter, on the other hand, was a southern Evangelical Christian who played up his conservative values. He promised to a post-Watergate country, "I will never lie to you." He said that he was proud of his grandfather Jim Jack, who had "unswerving allegiance" to the Agrarian populist Tom Watson, the onetime champion of workers of all races who wound up a racist and anti-Semite. Carter won every southern state except Virginia and the election by 50 to 48 percent of the popular vote.[26]

The results left conservatives with mixed feelings. They had come close to recapturing the GOP. They had forced the party to repudiate the "Nixonger" foreign policy of détente with the Soviets. And Ford nearly had secured a full term in which he would have been careful to pay attention to the Right. On the other side of the ledger, the conservatives' favorite son—Ronald Reagan—had lost the presidential nomination. And James Buckley had lost his Senate seat in the general election—to Daniel Patrick Moynihan.

Still, there was little doubt that the country was turning right. Reagan's successor as governor of California, Democrat Jerry Brown, was a fiscal hawk. The neoconservative Moynihan was no one's idea of a woolly-headed liberal. Nor did Carter fit the progressive mold. It seemed that, finally, America was syncing up with the conservative movement. "Certainly, within the Republican Party, conservatism—understood as the anti-statist impulse—is stronger than at any time in the last half-century," George Will wrote in his final *National Review* column before starting at *Newsweek*.[27]

THE CARTER PRESIDENCY CATALYZED THIS RIGHTWARD SHIFT. IT allowed the GOP to move beyond the Nixon-Ford years. Its failures against inflation, crime, and the Communists boosted Reagan's fortunes in 1980. Perhaps most significantly, the Carter years created the space for conservatives and neoconservatives to formulate new approaches to contemporary problems.

A lot of this work happened inside the conservative infrastructure that was slowly taking shape in Washington. Think tanks long had been safe havens for policy wonks whose party was out of the White House. The American Enterprise Institute was unique in the late 1970s in that, in addition to Republican veterans of the Nixon and Ford administrations, including President Ford himself, neoconservatives began to fill its offices.

AEI president Bill Baroody and Irving Kristol had become fast friends. They shared an interest in philosophy and religion. And this interest motivated Baroody to enlarge AEI's fields of study beyond economics and foreign policy and into political and social thought. That was why Kristol spent a sabbatical at AEI during the 1976–1977 academic year and why Baroody began to recruit Democratic intellectuals, such as Ben Wattenberg and Georgetown political scientist Jeane Kirkpatrick, whose dissent from the counterculture had left them politically homeless.[28]

AEI was a meeting ground for intellectuals and policymakers. When President Ford had wanted to use the nation's bicentennial to remind Americans of the republic's enduring principles, he turned to his friend and adviser Robert A. Goldwin, a former dean at St. John's College in Annapolis who had a close affiliation with AEI. The think tank held a symposium on America's founding that brought together Irving Kristol, Martin Diamond, Ed Banfield, Robert Nisbet, and others for lectures at Independence Hall in Philadelphia. In a memo to Ford's staff, Kristol recommended that they review the transcripts of the symposium, in particular his and Diamond's emphasis on the distinctiveness of the American revolution. It was the one modern change of regime, Kristol said, that did not end in nihilist terrorism. Kristol also urged Ford's staff to emphasize the exceptional nature of American government and society, especially its openness to immigration. "The success of this enterprise," he wrote, "reveals both the *universality* of the political ideas on which the U.S. was founded, and their *realism*."[29]

The neoconservative network centered on AEI grew quickly. Among Kristol and Baroody's recruits was theologian Michael Novak. Born to immigrant Slovak parents in Johnstown, Pennsylvania, Novak had attended a Catholic seminary but decided against a vocation. He studied at Catholic University and then at Harvard. He covered the Second Vatican Council as a journalist, leading to his book *The Open Church* (1964). But as he delved into radical thought and politics, Novak never lost sight of his roots in the ethnic working class.

Novak was a dashing, thirty-three-year-old Stanford professor of religion when he traveled to Cuernavaca, Mexico, in 1966. There he taught alongside Richard John Neuhaus, the activist Lutheran pastor of a majority black church in Brooklyn, and Peter Berger, the conservative-leaning sociologist who also participated in the antiwar movement. This trio of left-wing intellects wound up imbuing capitalism with moral and religious substance. That was not their intent. As was the case with other neoconservatives, their experience with the counterculture left them reeling.

In 1968, for instance, Novak left Stanford to teach at the State University of New York's experimental college in Old Westbury. The radicalism of the students petrified him. He set up a school within the college that maintained traditional academic standards. It did not go over well. "We were said by some to be—what else?—fascists."[30]

In 1970 Sargent Shriver, the former director of the Peace Corps and brother-in-law to the Kennedys, asked Novak to serve as his traveling writer and counselor during a cross-country jaunt in support of Democratic congressional candidates. Five months with Shriver reminded Novak of the enduring qualities of the American people. Out of his travels came *The Rise of the Unmeltable Ethnics* (1972), a celebration of hybrid identity similar to the "politics of interest" Norman Podhoretz had articulated from a Jewish standpoint. The book led to a break with Neuhaus, who criticized it in a stinging review. The two did not speak for almost a decade.[31]

In 1972, as he began to think seriously about the disparity between radical ideology and American reality, Novak picked up a copy of Irving Kristol's *On the Democratic Idea in America*. It influenced him greatly. He learned from Kristol that "the American experiment, rooted in Aristotelian prudence and a sense of human fallibility and evil, is a bracing corrective to the ideological and utopian thinking of Europe." He lit up after reading Friedrich Hayek's "Why I Am Not a Conservative." He studied Alexis de Tocqueville and took from the French aristocrat the principle of association as a middle way between atomistic individualism and state control.[32]

Neuhaus was finding his own way to a similar place. He was the seventh of eight children born to a Lutheran pastor in rural Pembroke, Canada. He studied at Concordia Seminary St. Louis, presided over St. John the Evangelist in the Williamsburg neighborhood of Brooklyn, and was active in both the civil rights and antiwar movements as part of Clergy and Laymen Concerned About Vietnam (CALCAV). He had become friends with Peter Berger and with Berger's wife and fellow sociologist, Brigitte, shortly after the publication of Berger's landmark *Social Construction of Reality* (1966). The uprising at Columbia University in 1968, when student chants echoed slogans he had heard as a child in Vienna during the Nazi Anschluss, drove Berger to resign from CALCAV and become a Republican. He remained friends with Neuhaus. In 1970 they released a collaboration, *Movement and Revolution*, and Neuhaus ran for Congress. He lost in the Democratic primary.[33]

Neuhaus moved right. His book *In Defense of People* (1971) criticized the antihuman implications of environmentalism and population control. In 1974, while attending a memorial for Rabbi Abraham Joshua Heschel, Neuhaus found himself disgusted by the "strident, leftist cliché" with which fellow activists recalled his mentor. He broke ranks with the Left the following year, when he failed to persuade CALCAV to adopt a resolution condemning the human rights abuses of the newly unified Communist Vietnam.[34]

In the winter of 1974, Neuhaus spent time with the Bergers in their Brooklyn home. Inspiration struck. "Neuhaus and I thought it would be fun to make a list of the major themes in mainline Protestantism that irritated us," Berger recalled. Berger organized a meeting at the Hartford Seminary in January 1975 to discuss these annoyances further. The result was the "Hartford Appeal for Theological Affirmation," published as a book in 1976. The signatories argued that the mainline churches had become obsessed with politics at the expense of spirituality.[35]

Neuhaus's contribution anticipated his future work. "What passes for modern thought has largely robbed religious claims of their public potency," he wrote. "It has relegated religious truth to the realm of the private and subjective, and has established as dogma the notion that all assertions that cannot be empirically verified by conventional scientific method are at best irrelevant and, more likely, dangerous to public discourse." The Hartford Appeal stood for widening the aperture of religion in public life. That made it controversial.[36]

Novak was embroiled in controversy of his own. On March 14, 1976, the *Washington Post* published his article "A Closet Capitalist Confesses." "I first realized I was a capitalist when all my friends began publicly declaring that they were socialists, [Michael] Harrington and John Kenneth Galbraith having called the signal," he wrote. "How I wished I could be as left as they." But Novak could not bring himself to want to live in any socialist society, "even Sweden." He found it funny that his socialist friends did not actually want to live in such places either. "I realized that socialism is not a *political* proposal, not an *economic* plan. Socialism is the residue of Judeo-Christian faith, without religion. It is a belief in community, the goodness of the human race and paradise on earth." Capitalism worked because it was attuned to the fallen human condition. "A system built on sin is built on very solid ground indeed," Novak went on. "The saintliness of socialism will not feed the poor." The Christian press savaged Novak's piece. Surprised at the reaction, he defended himself by elaborating his arguments for capitalism. And in 1977 he accepted a position at AEI.[37]

Berger and Neuhaus became involved with AEI as well. Berger had spent several years studying development in East Asia. "The intellectual result of these peregrinations can be stated in one sentence," he said. "*I discovered capitalism.*" Another living room conversation got him thinking. "Brigitte, who had increasingly concerned herself with questions of family policy, was the one who suggested to Neuhaus and me that some radical reformulations of social policy were much needed." AEI provided the institutional backing to think seriously about this reformulation. The final product was *To Empower People: The Role of Mediating Structures in Public Policy*, a forty-five-page pamphlet released in 1977.[38]

Building on theories of association developed by Burke, Tocqueville, and Robert Nisbet, Berger and Neuhaus argued that policy should be directed to the "institutions standing between the individual in his private life and the large institutions of public life." They examined family, neighborhood, church, and voluntary associations as means of empowerment. Government, they said, should refrain from interfering with and damaging these mediating structures. And perhaps—Berger and Neuhaus were hesitant on this point—government might also consider using the mediating structures as instruments of social policy.[39]

The pithy document amounted to a field reversal. Prior to its publication, most conservatives had emphasized individual initiative, while American liberals viewed the state as an agency of social uplift. "The Berger-Neuhaus concept of mediating structures suggested that both these approaches had become outmoded as they were increasingly ineffectual," Novak observed some years later. "Both approaches, they said, rested on misdiagnoses of social reality." Associations mattered most.[40]

Meanwhile, a misdiagnosis of economic reality occupied Irving Kristol's attention. In 1975 he had published in the *Public Interest* an essay titled "The Mundell-Laffer Hypothesis" by Jude Wanniski, an editorial writer for Robert Bartley at the *Wall Street Journal*. For some time, Wanniski, Bartley, and others had been meeting with Columbia University economist Robert Mundell and his protégé Art Laffer of the University of Chicago business school. The discussion aimed at potential solutions to the combination of unemployment and inflation, or stagflation, that ailed the economy and pushed Americans into higher tax brackets.

Mundell believed that, in a stable monetary environment, tax cuts would incentivize production and growth. They would boost supply. And as classical economist Jean-Baptiste Say had predicted, supply would create its own demand. Mundell called for "effective market classification": he wanted to fight inflation with monetary policy and induce growth through fiscal policy. Not only was Mundell's theory unlike Keynesian economics, which could not explain the combination of inflation and unemployment, but it also differed from the monetarist economics of Milton Friedman because, unlike Friedman, Mundell called for a fixed currency.

Wanniski was an evangelist for Mundell's ideas. On September 16, 1975, he had met with Ford chief of staff Don Rumsfeld and his deputy, Dick Cheney, at a restaurant across the street from the US Treasury, where he pressed the cause of tax cuts. Wanniski drew a graph on a napkin illustrating the so-called Laffer Curve. It depicted a theoretical point at which tax cuts generate enough revenue from economic growth to pay for themselves. Inside the Ford administration, Wanniski's pleas fell on deaf ears. But they made an impression not only on Bartley, whose editorials began reflecting the Mundell-Laffer thesis, but also on former Nixon aide Jeffrey Bell, then working for Ronald Reagan, and on Jack

Kemp, the former Buffalo Bills quarterback elected to Congress in 1970.[41]

In 1976 Wanniski met Kemp, and the Mundell-Laffer hypothesis got a new name: supply-side economics. The phrase came from economist Herb Stein, who dismissed the ideas of "supply-side fiscalists" at a conference attended by Wanniski and Bartley. Wanniski liked the sound of "supply-side" and ran with it. He convinced Kemp that growth mattered more than deficits. The New York congressman then introduced a bill calling for a 30 percent across-the-board tax cut, rechristened the following year as "Kemp-Roth" (William Roth of Delaware sponsored the bill in the Senate). In 1978 a watered-down version of the tax cut passed Congress. Carter vetoed that bill but later signed into law Representative Bill Steiger's reduction in the capital gains tax from 49 to 28 percent.

The breakthrough year for supply-side economics was 1978. Wanniski published his magnum opus, *The Way the World Works*, in which he introduced the concept of the "tax wedge," or the bite that government takes from each worker's earnings. The intent of tax cuts was to incentivize production on the margin. Wanniski's vision encompassed more than tax cuts, however. For him, supply-side theory was a way of understanding history and winning elections.

For too long, Wanniski argued, Democrats had played the part of Santa Claus. They bestowed gifts on the electorate. The moment was ripe, he thought, for Republicans to become Santa Claus as well. That would give the country two political Santa Clauses, one bearing income transfers and the other tax cuts. Wanniski possessed something close to a religious belief in the creative potential of human beings. What in Mundell and Laffer's hands was a dry reading of the economy took on ebullience and populism in Wanniski's. "No individual, no philosopher king, could possibly be a superior judge of the interests of the electorate than the electorate itself," he wrote. The politician's job was to find out what the electorate wanted and deliver it.[42]

And the electorate was rebellious. Bell, who had left Reagan to enter politics in his home state of New Jersey, upset incumbent liberal Republican Clifford Case in the Senate primary by running on the Kemp tax cut. (Bell lost to Bill Bradley in the general election.) The passage of Proposition 13 in California, limiting property taxes, had a more lasting impact. Laffer, who had moved to the University of Southern California, was one of the few public figures supporting Howard Jarvis, the antitax crusader behind the initiative. For Wanniski, Proposition 13 revealed the true nature of politics. "The world is divided not into Communists or Capitalists, or Republicans and Democrats, or liberals and conservatives," he wrote. "It is divided into Populists and Elites, the ruled and rulers."[43]

Kristol saw a new politics emerging from the tax revolt. He wrote that Proposition 13 "was a new kind of class war—the people as citizens versus the politicians and their clients in the public sector." He mentored Kemp in the hopes that the congressman would run for president in 1980. He promoted Kemp's book *An American Renaissance* when it was published in 1979. "There could be no book, nor could there be an American renaissance, without Irving Kristol," the congressman inscribed in the copy he gave to Kristol. "Many thanks from the Kristolian wing of the GOP."[44]

It is instructive to compare *An American Renaissance* with Barry Goldwater's *Conscience of a Conservative*. Goldwater condemned taxation and the welfare state as infringements on individual freedom. Kemp's problem with high marginal tax rates was that they reduced growth. Rather than cutting government programs, Kemp wanted to "draw people out of the [safety] net by expanding attractive opportunities in the private sector." Goldwater said he wanted to repeal laws, not pass them. Kemp wrote, "The federal government should provide some sort of coverage for catastrophic illnesses, maintain adequate health services for the poor and the old, and concentrate on encouraging private health insurers to expand their regular coverage, which now touches nearly 90 percent of the people." Linking the two books was a hard line against the Soviet Union. Even here, though, Kemp included a chapter titled "Exporting the American Idea," in which he argued that the promotion of economic growth "can win victories without risking lives."[45]

Kemp also had good things to say about Franklin Roosevelt and John F. Kennedy. Just as cuts in marginal tax rates had been a Kennedy policy, the supply-siders appropriated the liberal ends of progress, inclusivity, and compassion. They differed from liberals in their preferred means. "If the government of any nation is not committed to dynamic politics, growth, general expansion, and consensus rather than coalition thinking," Kemp wrote, "then whatever policies it advances or attempts to advance will inevitably be halted by factional strife." As he told the International Longshoremen's Association in July 1979, "With economic growth, there is room for everyone to get ahead. Without it, the country tears itself apart competing for pieces of a smaller and smaller pie."[46]

Reagan was reluctant to embrace supply-side economics. But he and his advisers worried that Kemp might enter the 1980 Republican primary and hit him from the right. So he adopted Kemp's program in exchange for the congressman's endorsement and named Kemp one of his economic spokesmen. Over the objections of many conservative economists, Kemp-Roth became the centerpiece of Reagan's economic program. Milton Friedman, for instance, said he supported Kemp-Roth not because he agreed with the supply-siders but because any tax cut that denied revenue to the treasury was good.

Conservatism was beginning to possess the intellectual seriousness and elite credibility that had eluded it for so long. Friedrich Hayek had won the Nobel Prize for Economics in 1974. Milton

Friedman received it in 1976. That same year the Nobel Prize for Literature went to Saul Bellow, whose 1970 novel *Mr. Sammler's Planet* dramatized the neoconservative critique of social disorder and urban decay.

The persistence of stagflation was a boon for free market critics of government economic policy. The inability of liberal economists to either explain or solve the combination of unemployment, inflation, and recession gave new legitimacy to capitalism's defenders. In 1970, for example, Milton Friedman had first aired his argument that a corporation's primary responsibility was to its shareholders. He was famous for saying that inflation was "always and everywhere a monetary phenomenon" that would not abate until the money supply was brought under the control of a defined rule.

Back in 1971, before he joined the Supreme Court, Lewis Powell had urged business leaders to take proactive measures to defend themselves from environmentalists, consumer protection advocates, and government regulators. In his 1978 book *The Anti-trust Paradox*, Robert Bork wrote that monopolies should be broken apart only if they did not benefit the consumer—a lot of government antitrust activity simply hobbled the market, prevented business formation, and hurt efficiency and output. Economist James Buchanan, meanwhile, formulated his theory of public choice, explaining that interest groups thrived off a government that concentrated benefits and dispersed costs and that government itself was a special interest. And political scientist Mancur Olson, in his *Logic of Collective Action* (1965), stated that the American economy had a free-rider problem: the majority benefited from public goods whose full cost they did not pay.[47]

In the 1978 midterm elections, Republicans netted three seats in the Senate and gained fourteen seats in the House. The incoming GOP freshman class included former White House aide Dick Cheney, as well as a history professor from Georgia named Newton Leroy Gingrich, who had won a suburban Atlanta district on his third try. High taxes, inflation, gas lines, rampant crime, and the loss of authoritative values were beginning to align vast sectors of the public with the American Right.

Reagan welcomed these newcomers. In his speech to the Conservative Political Action Conference in Washington in February 1977, he sided with "a majority trying to assert its rights against the tyranny of powerful academics, fashionable left-wing revolutionaries, some economic illiterates who happen to hold elective office, and the social engineers who dominate the dialogue and set the format in political and social affairs." He wanted a "New Republican Party" that would not be "limited to the country club big business image" but would "have room for the man and woman in the factories, for the farmer, for the cop on the beat, and the millions of Americans who may never have thought of joining our party before, but whose interests coincide with principled Republicanism," including the "majority of social conservatives" abandoned by the Democrats.[48]

As Reagan took the spotlight, Buckley moved aside. The *National Review* editor, disappointed by Watergate and by his brother's election loss, turned in 1976 to writing his Blackford Oakes series of spy novels and his sailing travelogues. He still edited his magazine, wrote his syndicated column, and hosted his television show, but he found himself at odds with the New Right. Buckley had come out for decriminalizing marijuana in 1972, putting him at odds with social conservatives. Nor had his distaste for George Wallace abated. Buckley recognized that Wallace supporters might be necessary to complete the new majority, but he opposed any "concession to George Wallace of a philosophically disreputable kind: on the issue, for instance, of metaphysical human equality."[49]

Buckley and *National Review* had adopted political philosopher Harry Jaffa's view of the founding and of Abraham Lincoln. In 1979 Buckley commissioned a twenty-three-year-old Harvard graduate student named Charles Kesler to write an article on Jaffa for *National Review*'s Fourth of July issue. And Jaffa's influence on Buckley was apparent many years later when, in 1988, the latter reissued his anthology of conservative thought under the title *Keeping the Tablets*. He appointed Kesler his coeditor and swapped out one Jaffa essay, "On the Nature of Civil and Religious Liberty," for another Jaffa essay, "Equality as a Conservative Principle."[50]

By the late 1970s, Wallace was no longer a significant danger to the Right. The Alabama governor's star power had faded since a would-be assassin shot him during a campaign stop in Laurel, Maryland, in 1972, leaving him paralyzed. His moment had passed; he was yesterday's news. Reagan now spoke for the voters who felt ignored or disrespected by bureaucrats, judges, professors, and journalists. He did so in uplifting, soothing tones. And he did not dwell on race.

In 1978 a special episode of *Firing Line* displayed the differences between *National Review* and the New Right. Buckley debated Reagan over the treaties that relinquished US control of the Panama Canal. Buckley, seconded by James Burnham and George Will, argued for ratification. Reagan, seconded by Pat Buchanan and Admiral John S. McCain Jr., repeated the mantra he had told audiences to great applause: "We built it, we paid for it, it's ours."

Buckley, the enfant terrible of the Dwight Eisenhower era, found himself on the same side of an issue as President Carter. Buckley had mainstreamed American conservatism, but it was now flowing in directions he often would not follow. Conservatism was becoming more political, more topical, more journalistic, less philosophical, and above all more populist. In the end, Buckley's side in the Panama Canal dispute prevailed as a matter of policy. But the controversy illustrated that *National Review* was no longer, as he had put it in his publisher's statement in 1955, "the only game in town." Worse, not long after the debate, Burnham suffered a stroke that prevented him from writing. All at once, Buckley was the last of the original editors of *National Review*.[51]

REAGAN'S POPULISM CARRIED OVER INTO HIS RELATIONSHIP with the Christian Right. In 1970 the Internal Revenue Service (IRS) had changed the criteria for granting religious schools tax-exempt status: no longer would their religious affiliation allow them to violate civil rights law without forfeiting their tax exemption. A series of court fights erupted between Fundamentalist Bob Jones University and the IRS.

The Supreme Court was the main engine of religious discontent. Beginning in the 1960s, its decisions had led to the end of prayer and religious education in public schools, nationwide legalization of contraception, and most controversially, in 1973 in *Roe v. Wade*, a constitutionally protected right to abortion on demand. "What both the legal revolutionaries and the marketing experts forgot," wrote Nathan Glazer, "is that we are not one culture, but many cultures."[52]

Phyllis Schlafly had not forgotten. After Congress authorized the Equal Rights Amendment in 1972, she founded STOP ERA to prevent its ratification. "Within a year after Phyllis Schlafly entered the battle," wrote biographer Carol Felsenthal, "the ERA bandwagon started losing steam."[53]

Schlafly targeted state legislatures where pro-ERA forces were diffuse and weak. In her speeches and in the pages of her monthly newsletter, the *Phyllis Schlafly Report*, founded in 1967, she rallied the grass roots against gender neutrality. She warned that ERA would transform schools, the military, prisons, hospitals, and the family itself. For Schlafly, ERA represented the revolutionary challenge of the "women's lib" movement. It threatened the special privileges American women received from the institution of the family, the ethic of chivalry, and the time-saving innovations spawned by free market competition. "The claim that American women are downtrodden and unfairly treated is the fraud of the century," she wrote in the February 1973 *Report*. "The truth is American women never had it so good." Thirty states ratified ERA prior to Schlafly's campaign. Eight years later, only five additional states had signed on.[54]

Schlafly's dynamic presence invigorated a pro-family counterrevolution. She was fearless. She debated feminists, withstood campus hecklers, gave political speeches, published columns and articles, and recorded radio commentaries and television appearances. In 1975 she established the Eagle Forum as a headquarters for her expanding operations. A Catholic, Schlafly took up the issue of abortion after *Roe v. Wade* and connected it to the assault on the family. There was no constitutional right to abortion, she said, only a legal right conferred by the Supreme Court. But, Schlafly warned, ERA would write abortion into the Constitution.

Social conservatism was everywhere. When abortion was legalized in Washington, DC, in 1970, Brent Bozell had led a demonstration in front of the George Washington University Hospital's abortion clinic, where he addressed members of the "Sons of Thunder," a fringe group dressed in uniforms inspired by a Catholic militia that had fought in the Spanish Civil War. After speeches and prayer at a nearby park, Bozell led the crowd, shouting, "Viva Cristo Rey," toward the hospital. The demonstrators clashed with police. Bozell was arrested. Legalized abortion was genocide, he wrote in a *New York Times* op-ed after his release, and neither party was truly discomfited by the barbaric practice.

Not long after *Roe*, Senator James Buckley had introduced a Human Life Amendment banning abortion. In 1974 the original March for Life was held in Washington. In 1975, with Bill Buckley's blessing, an editor of *National Review* founded the quarterly *Human Life Review*. In 1976 an Illinois congressman named Henry Hyde successfully sponsored an amendment that banned the use of taxpayer funds for abortion. And in *How Should We Then Live?*, a book and movie released in 1976, Presbyterian minister Francis Schaeffer traced the decline of Christian culture to relativism and materialism.

Pop star Anita Bryant announced for Christ and launched the "Save Our Children" campaign in 1977 to support a referendum banning gay rights in South Florida. To Bryant's surprise, her cause won in a landslide. That same year, child psychologist Dr. James Dobson created his *Focus on the Family* radio program. *The 700 Club*, hosted by Pat Robertson, had been in national syndication since 1972. It debuted on cable TV in 1977.

Elected officials did not make the decisions that so upset the daily lives of the traditional Democratic base. Judges and bureaucrats did. And the failure of the bureaucracy to deliver on its grand promises of racial harmony and general uplift severed the Democratic Party from the bulk of its support. Television producer Norman Lear, for example, thought he was spoofing bigoted and sexist working men when he created the role of the father in his sitcom *All in the Family*. Little did he realize that Archie Bunker would become the show's most popular character. Voters could take only so much condescension and contempt. Then they looked elsewhere. Then they looked right.

The phenomenon of resurgent Fundamentalism was novel because it presented a united front against secularism. Fundamentalists found themselves on the same side as Evangelicals, Episcopalians, Catholics, and Orthodox Jews. "In terms of current conflicts involving religion, Jews, Catholics, and Protestants are no longer the principal combatants," wrote Nathan Glazer. "The combatants are, rather, traditionalists against liberals of whatever religious background."[55]

Though a "born-again Christian," President Carter was unable to capitalize on his personal connection to these religiously inspired activists. The furor over his interview with *Playboy* in October 1976 was a sign of things to come. Reverend Jerry Falwell, founder of Thomas Road Baptist Church and of Liberty University in Lynchburg, Virginia, and host of the *Old Time Gospel Hour* broadcast, criticized the article on national television. Falwell was scandalized that Carter would appear in the same pages as nude centerfolds. One of Carter's assistants scolded Falwell over the phone, telling him to stop criticizing the president. Falwell was shocked. Where he had once said that a preacher's place was in church and that Martin Luther King Jr. was too political, he now devoted himself to political activism.

That same month, in a speech before the National Conference of Catholic Charities, Carter said that the family was "the cornerstone of American life" and pledged to hold a conference on the family at the White House. It turned out to be a debacle. None of the participants could agree on what a family actually was. Liberals alienated traditional Catholics, who had been such an important part of the Democratic coalition. Michael Novak witnessed the chaos. Conference planners, he wrote, spoke of "the nostalgic family," the supposedly outmoded unit of mother and father and 2.5 children. "They did not seem anxious to exclude any arrangement," Novak regretted.[56]

Social conservatism was the rallying cry of the New Right. In 1977 Schlafly organized a "pro-family" rally in Houston that drew some fifteen thousand people. The next year a district court overruled the 1970 IRS policy revoking the tax-exempt status of educational institutions, such as Bob Jones University, that the government deemed to be segregated. (The Supreme Court would reverse this decision in 1983.) Religious conservatives were outraged and stepped up the tempo of their activism. And in 1979 Paul Weyrich persuaded Jerry Falwell to form a group, Moral Majority, to register voters and campaign for candidates such as Reagan. Membership exploded.[57]

Moral Majority cast a wide net. The organization had four tenets. It was pro-life. It was pro-family—the "nostalgic family" criticized by the cultural Left. It was "pro-moral" and against pornography and drugs. And it was pro-American. That meant it lobbied for increased defense spending, a strong posture vis-à-vis the Soviet Union, and support for anti-Communist allies, including the State of Israel.

The audience for these principles was vast. Falwell launched *Moral Majority Report* in January 1980; by October, close to half a million copies were in circulation. More than five hundred thousand Evangelicals attended a "Washington for Jesus" rally in the capital before the election. A rally in Dallas in August drew more than eighteen thousand people. And the 1980 GOP platform contained unequivocally pro-life language. Reagan visited Lynchburg, Falwell's home base, in the final weeks of the campaign.[58]

National security once again provided a common tie between all of the groups opposing President Carter's reelection in 1980. Like Evangelical and Fundamentalist Christians, the neoconservatives behind the Coalition for a Democratic Majority had expected Carter to be on their side. He was not. He excluded neoconservatives from his administration. "We got one unbelievably minor job," said Elliott Abrams, who had jumped from Scoop Jackson's office to Daniel Patrick Moynihan's on the New York senator's first day. "It was a special negotiator position. Not for Polynesia. Not Macronesia. But Micronesia." Abrams wasn't exaggerating. Carter's ambassador for Micronesian status negotiations was the former secretary of the Coalition for a Democratic Majority.[59]

The neoconservatives came to oppose Carter's defense plans. They railed against his position on arms control and human rights. They watched in agony as Carter lectured America over its "inordinate fear of Communism," nominated McGovernites to high positions, and zeroed in not on the Soviet Union but on autocratic US allies in Iran and Nicaragua. They lost it when Carter's UN ambassador, Andrew Young, downplayed Cuban military deployments to Africa. Don't "get all paranoid over a few Communists," Young said.[60]

In late 1976 a bipartisan group of anti-Communists had formed the Committee on the Present Danger. They borrowed the name from another nongovernmental group that had supported National Security Council Paper 68, President Harry Truman's secret directive outlining his "containment" strategy toward the Soviet Union, back in 1950. Paul Nitze, the paper's primary author, joined former military leaders such as Admiral Elmo Zumwalt and Generals Matthew Ridgway and Maxwell Taylor in forming the new group. It also included labor activists Bayard Rustin and Jay Lovestone; former government officials William Casey, George Shultz, Dean Rusk, and Ray Cline; neoconservatives Midge Decter, Norman Podhoretz, Nathan Glazer, Jeane Kirkpatrick, and Seymour Martin Lipset; novelists Saul Bellow and James T. Farrell; and politicians John Connally and Ronald Reagan.

The committee took its cues from the work of Albert Wohlstetter, who in an influential 1974 article in *Foreign Policy* suggested that the United States had been regularly underestimating the Soviet nuclear threat. According to Wohlstetter, the Russians were trying to win the arms race, while the Americans actually were not racing at all. As a result, then Central Intelligence Agency director George H. W. Bush commissioned an independent study, called "Team B," to offer an outside assessment of the spy agency's annual estimate of Soviet military capability. Team B included Nitze, Paul Wolfowitz, and Richard Pipes, a Harvard historian of the Russian Revolution. It concluded that the Soviet goal was nuclear dominance and that America was rapidly losing its advantage in strategic weaponry. When its findings were disclosed at the outset of Carter's term, liberals roundly attacked Team B for exaggerating the Communist threat.

As Carter's term unfolded, however, Team B did not seem so far off the mark. In 1979 the government of Nicaragua and then the shah of Iran fell to anti-American revolutionaries. The Soviets invaded Afghanistan. A mob loyal to Ayatollah Ruhollah Khomeini stormed the US embassy in Tehran and seized American diplomats as hostages. The hostage taking infuriated Americans. They became more willing to support an assertive foreign policy. "I'm sick of being stomped on!!" one man told *CBS News*. "We're not going to take it anymore!! America!! America!!" After the Soviet invasion of Afghanistan at the end of that same year, Carter assumed a more aggressive posture. He shelved the SALT II arms-control treaty with the Soviets. He announced a boycott of the 1980 Moscow Summer Olympics. He authorized the Central Intelligence Agency to fund the mujahideen Afghan resistance. And he imposed a grain embargo on the Soviet Union. But Carter's reputation for passivity, ineptness, and equivocation stuck.[61]

Around this time, Jeane Kirkpatrick wrote a long article for *Commentary* blasting Carter's foreign policy. Norman Podhoretz gave it the title "Dictatorships and Double Standards." Kirkpatrick did not mince words. "The failure of the Carter administration's foreign policy is now clear to everyone except its architects," she began. She argued that autocracies could reform into democracies, but Marxist governments could not. The progressive and idealistic rhetoric of the Left lured policymakers in the Carter administration to turn a blind eye toward anti-American revolutionaries while castigating and helping to collapse anti-Communist authoritarian regimes. "Liberal idealism need not be identical with masochism," Kirkpatrick wrote, "and need not be incompatible with defense of freedom and the national interest."[62]

After "Dictatorship and Double Standards" appeared in *Commentary*'s November 1979 issue, Reagan adviser Richard V. Allen passed it along to his boss. Reagan loved it. He called Kirkpatrick and asked for her support. She demurred. But she changed her mind after meeting with President Carter in January 1980. "The White House," wrote Norman Podhoretz, "had arranged the meeting in the expectation that it would assuage our skepticism about the claim—vital to Carter's chances of beating Reagan—that the invasion [of Afghanistan] had brought him around to a point of view on the dangers of Soviet expansionism much the same as ours."[63]

This expectation was not met. The meeting began when Vice President Walter Mondale welcomed those present, including Kirkpatrick, Podhoretz, Midge Decter, Elliott Abrams, and Ben Wattenberg. But Carter was hurried and annoyed. "Carter didn't even understand who we were," Wattenberg complained. "His briefing memo had said that we were interested in human rights. Carter went on about a difficult human rights situation in Ecuador. (Ecuador!)" As the participants left the White House, Kirkpatrick muttered to Midge Decter that she could not vote for Carter. By the spring, she had made up her mind. She endorsed Reagan.[64]

International terrorism, the disastrous failure of the US military operation to rescue the hostages held in Iran, and Iraqi dictator Saddam Hussein's invasion of Iran in 1980, weeks before the US election, contributed to the widespread sense of chaos, fear, and disarray. Norman Podhoretz released a book, *The Present Danger*, highlighting the Soviet military buildup and savaging what he called "the culture of appeasement." Reagan gave it a strong endorsement.

The Republican nominee became the spokesman for national pride. "I would like to be the president who takes the message to the world that there will be no more Taiwans, no more Vietnams—that there will be no more betrayals of friends by the United States," he said. In September 1980 he told the Veterans of Foreign Wars that Vietnam was "a noble cause." Back in 1977, an editorial cartoon in the *Los Angeles Times* had joked that Reagan had been "born again in the waters of the Panama Canal." By the time he ran for president in 1980, he had brought together the New Right, the neoconservatives, the supply-siders, and the religious Right in a broad conservative coalition.[65]

For most Americans, Reagan had none of Goldwater's baggage, asperity, and association with the fringe. "I've always believed that you say the qualifier first," Reagan said in an interview, referring to his attempts to assuage undecided voters that he was not an extremist ideologue. Nor did Reagan possess Carter's feelings of guilt, doubt, and anguish. "We live in the future in America, always have," he said.[66]

In his campaign announcement speech, Reagan proposed an "open border project" that would join the United States, Mexico, and Canada in a free trade zone. He welcomed additional Mexican immigrants. His campaign ads exhorted the viewer, "Let's make America great again." His two main television spots referenced JFK's tax cuts and promoted a sense of common feeling. "Those who have the least will gain the most," one said. "If we put incentives back into society, everyone will gain." Jude Wanniski gleefully told a friend, "Watch Reagan win in November by a landslide—because he is a conservative populist where Goldwater was a conservative elitist."[67]

It pained Reagan that he was unable to include more black voters in his majority. He denounced racial bigotry and made several attempts to reach out to African Americans. None succeeded. Reagan was not personally racist. It is telling that historians have found only a single instance of him making a bigoted remark, in a private conversation, over the course of his ninety-three years. His one major stumble during the 1980 campaign was a visit to the Neshoba County Fair in Philadelphia, Mississippi, where three civil rights activists had been murdered in 1964. Reagan had intended to address the Urban League that day, but a change of schedule found him awkwardly using the incendiary phrase "states' rights" before a low-energy audience. His heart wasn't in it—though his opponents wasted no time accusing him of using a racist trope.

This attack was ineffective. On Election Day, Reagan was carried along by a global conservative tide. Menachem Begin's Likud Party had won in Israel in 1979, as had Margaret Thatcher's Conservative Party in the United Kingdom. Adoring crowds eager to worship God greeted John Paul II, the new Polish, anti-Communist pope, when he visited America that fall. On November 4, 1980, Reagan won forty-four states. He earned eight million more votes than Carter. The Republican Party picked up thirty-four House seats and took control of the Senate for the first time since 1954.

Not six years earlier, in the aftermath of Watergate, conservatism had seemed moribund and the Republican Party irrelevant. The deterioration of America's economy, society, and global stature revived the Right and the GOP. Stagflation, crime, affirmative action, values issues, and assaults on the nation's pride debilitated the Democratic Party. "There was unrest in the country," Reagan later wrote, "and it was spreading across the land like a prairie fire."[68]

And in 1981 the prairie fire reached Washington.

CHAPTER TEN

PRESIDENT REAGAN

R ONALD REAGAN WAS THE MOST POPULAR AND SUCCESSFUL Republican president since Theodore Roosevelt. He was the only president since Ulysses S. Grant to hand his office over to a successor of his own party after serving two full terms. In the space of sixteen years, he had brought the conservative movement from electoral repudiation to the White House. He restored the ethos of "Calvinism" to 1600 Pennsylvania Avenue. Like his conservative predecessor of the 1920s, Reagan cut taxes, lionized the Constitution, and promoted a nonsectarian form of civil religion. Coolidge's portrait hung on a wall in Reagan's Cabinet Room.

Though he harkened back to Coolidge, Reagan nonetheless differed from pre– and anti–New Deal Republicans. Franklin Roosevelt was his role model. He did not attempt to reverse the New Deal—or, in truth, much of the Great Society. Reagan's temperament, rhetoric, and policies made the American Right seem more populist, more forward-looking, and more optimistic than it had been before. "Emerson was right," he told the 1992 Republican National Convention. "We are the country of tomorrow."[1]

Reagan's understanding of human nature differed from that of many conservatives. He believed in the innate goodness of people.

He said that they would choose the right thing if left alone. That was not the typical conservative view of either human nature or human progress. Reagan also had an uncanny ability to shrug off bad news. He refused to dwell on setbacks and defeats. Unlike many experts and politicians, who believed the problems facing America were too complex to be solved, Reagan grasped the key to the situation. He distilled his approach in simple, clarifying language. His strategy for the Cold War was, "We win, they lose."

Not for nothing did some of Reagan's critics deride him as a "right-wing liberal." Reagan's pro-market, pro-democracy politics retained elements of his youthful liberalism. He loved to quote Thomas Paine's phrase that we have it in our power to make the world over again. His speeches mentioned Thomas Jefferson, Andrew Jackson, and FDR more than Dwight Eisenhower and Richard Nixon. "He was constantly probing, fiddling, and experimenting to find a better way to reach his goals," wrote Rowland Evans and Robert D. Novak in *The Reagan Revolution* (1981). This willingness to experiment, create, and draw from the deep well of conservative and neoconservative thought was one reason Daniel Patrick Moynihan could write in the *New York Times* in 1980, "Of a sudden, the GOP has become a party of ideas."[2]

Reagan exhibited courage in sticking with policies that at first seemed unpopular and ineffective. He did not stop Federal Reserve chairman Paul Volcker from squeezing inflation out of the economy through a form of "shock therapy" and the harsh 1981–1982 recession. He knew that the downturn's long-term effects on price stability would benefit consumers, savers, and retirees. He fired the air traffic controllers in 1981 because they violated his principle that public safety officers should not be allowed to strike. He persisted in deploying intermediate-range nuclear missiles in western Europe despite the widespread and vociferous opposition of the nuclear freeze movement. In 1982 the outrage at Reagan's missile decision culminated in one of the largest public demonstrations in US history. Reagan's unwillingness to succumb to the pressure strengthened his hand in future negotiations with the Soviet Union. Eventually it led to the disappearance of both the missiles and the Communist superpower at which they were aimed.

The rise of what historian Angela D. Dillard called "multicultural conservatism" showed that a wide variety of people marched under Reagan's banner. In 1978 a black member of Young Americans for Freedom named Jay Parker had founded the Lincoln Institute for Research and Education in his native Philadelphia. The institute published the *Lincoln Review*, which became a home for black conservative academics scattered throughout the country. Its most prominent contributor was Thomas Sowell. Born in North Carolina in 1930 and raised in New York City, Sowell was the first member of his family to progress beyond the sixth grade. He served in the US Marines before attending Howard University, Harvard, Columbia, and the University of Chicago. Milton Friedman was his PhD adviser.[3]

Affirmative action, Sowell argued, was harming its intended beneficiaries. He studied such programs worldwide and wrote up his revisionist and unpopular findings for the *Public Interest* and *Commentary*. When Sowell moved to the University of California, Los Angeles, he met another black libertarian, economist Walter Williams. The two men engineered nothing less than an intellectual counterrevolution in works such as Sowell's *Black Education: Myths and Tragedies* (1972) and *Race and Politics* (1975) and Williams's *The State Against Blacks* (1982). Along with Robert Woodson, the civil rights activist who had worked with Richard Neuhaus and Peter Berger on *To Empower People*, Parker, Sowell, and Williams argued that federal interventions had done more harm than good for black people and that educational choice, safe streets, and economic freedom promoted racial equality.

A little over a month before Reagan took office, Sowell organized a conference at the Fairmont Hotel in San Francisco on "black alternatives." The conference drew an esteemed crowd, including Reagan adviser Edwin Meese, as well as civil rights leaders not predisposed to Sowell's worldview. Among the attendees was a thirty-two-year-old aide to Republican senator John Danforth of Missouri named Clarence Thomas. A graduate of Holy Cross and Yale Law, where he had embraced black nationalism, Thomas changed his mind on economics and politics after reading Sowell. Unlike his mentor, Thomas ended up working for Reagan, first in the Department of Education and then as head of the Equal Employment Opportunity Commission. Among Thomas's first hires at the commission were two associates of Harry Jaffa's named John Marini and Ken Masugi. Thomas asked them to tutor him in political philosophy.

Conservatives experienced both victories and setbacks under Reagan. By the time he moved into 1600 Pennsylvania Avenue, his energy was often depleted. He was sixty-nine years old—the oldest man to win the presidency prior to 2016. Not long into his term, on March 30, 1981, the would-be assassin John Hinckley seriously wounded Reagan as the president exited the Washington Hilton hotel, leading to emergency surgery and twelve days of recovery in George Washington University Hospital. The attempt on his life and his bouts with cancer slowed him down.

Reagan's management style contributed to a sense of disillusionment among conservatives. His big-picture strategy never wavered, but he also delegated a great amount of authority to his staff. And many of them were not movement conservatives. The person closest to Reagan, his wife Nancy, treated the Right with suspicion. The administration was filled with representatives of the conflict-averse business community. It contained Republican "pragmatists" in the mold of Vice President George H. W. Bush and chief of staff James Baker. As the seemingly imperturbable Reagan looked at the whole canvas, squabbling groups of aides and policymakers struggled to fill in the details. The scene could get messy.

The tussles, regrets, and recriminations began with Reagan's economic program. By incorporating Jack Kemp's proposals into the agenda he presented before Congress early in 1981, Reagan took supply-side economics from the edge of American politics to the center. But few supply-siders held high-ranking positions within the executive branch. And the tax cuts that Congress passed, while large, were delayed, extended over several years, and weakened by increases in the payroll tax.

There was little doubt, however, that Reagan stood for supply-side economics and the free market revival. The 1981 publication of George Gilder's *Wealth and Poverty* exemplified the celebrations of market economics that defined Regan's presidency. Gilder's soaring affirmation of capitalism lionized entrepreneurs and "the spirit of enterprise" (the title of his follow-up). It received Reagan's endorsement and became a best seller. Whereas fellow supply-sider Irving Kristol had offered just two cheers for capitalism in a 1978 essay collection, Gilder gave a hearty three, even four.

In the spring of 1981 Kristol and Gilder debated the strengths and weaknesses of capitalism at a gala of the Intercollegiate Studies Institute in Washington. They were not the only proponents of supply-side economics who held divergent views. The movement contained several warring factions. The main disagreement was over monetary policy: no one could decide if "true" supply-siders backed a gold standard, fixed exchange rates, or a Federal Reserve that sought price stability. Personal feuds and eccentricities also prevented supply-siders from reaching consensus. "There is nothing wrong with supply-side economics," Kristol once wrote, "but there is often something wrong with people attracted to it."[4]

Supply-siders were quick to anathematize perceived heretics. David Stockman, for example, was a twenty-nine-year-old former Harvard divinity student when he wrote an essay for the *Public Interest* in 1975 attacking "the social pork barrel." He was elected to Congress as a Republican from Michigan in 1976, became an ally of Kemp's and the supply-siders, and had just won a third term when President Reagan appointed him director of the Office of Management and Budget (OMB) at the age of thirty-four. Within a year, he had turned against his boss.[5]

It was the most dramatic betrayal of a president since White House counsel John Dean turned on Richard Nixon during the Watergate crisis. In late 1981, in a long interview with journalist William Greider published in the *Atlantic Monthly* under the title "The Education of David Stockman," the young OMB director said that the Kemp-Roth bill was a "trojan horse to bring down the top [tax] rate" and that "Art Laffer sold us a bill of goods." Stockman attacked Reagan from the libertarian right. He accused the former actor of betraying the ideals of small government and larding up the budget with defense spending. Amazingly, Reagan did not fire him. Stockman kept his job until the summer of 1985.[6]

When he left government, Stockman wrote a memoir, *The Triumph of Politics* (1986), describing his disappointment in Reagan for not taking his side in intramural disputes. Stockman was an early conservative apostate. He broke from the movement after it failed to live up to his standards. Like many on the right, he had misread Reagan's victory as a mandate for deep budget cuts rather than as a public endorsement of economic recovery and national pride. Personal gripes aside, many conservatives shared at least some of Stockman's disappointment in the failure of the Reagan administration to defund the bureaucracy—though the Democratic House of Representatives limited what Reagan could achieve.

Conservative views of Reagan's foreign policy were also ambivalent. Reagan was more confrontational with the Soviets during his first term than in his second. He refused to meet with Soviet leaders, joking, "They keep dying on me." In addition to his deployment of Pershing and cruise missiles in Europe and his announcement of the space-based, antiballistic missile Strategic Defense Initiative, which drew from research conducted at the Heritage Foundation,

Reagan massively increased the defense budget. He appointed Jeane Kirkpatrick ambassador to the United Nations where, in the spirit of Daniel Patrick Moynihan, she pressed America's case and defended Israel in the General Assembly.

Other veterans of the Committee on the Present Danger and "Team B" joined the administration as well. Richard Allen became Reagan's national security adviser. William Casey became Central Intelligence Agency director. George Shultz became secretary of state. John Lehman became secretary of the navy. Richard Perle became assistant secretary of defense. Paul Wolfowitz served as assistant secretary of state and ambassador to Indonesia. And Richard Pipes served as a National Security Council director.

In his speech to the British Parliament at Westminster in 1982, Reagan prophesied that the Soviet Union was destined for the "ash heap of history." He called for the establishment of a National Endowment for Democracy to promote human rights and democratic institutions throughout the world. The endowment's first president was Carl Gershman, who had moved from Social Democrats USA to the Reagan administration. The following year, Reagan told the National Association of Evangelicals that the Soviet Union was an "evil empire." Also in 1983, after withdrawing US Marines from Lebanon, Reagan ordered US troops to remove the Marxist-Leninist government of Grenada, a Caribbean ally of Soviet Russia.

This was Reagan's way of pursuing the strategy of psychological and ideological warfare to "roll back" Communist regimes that James Burnham had outlined in his trilogy of books written at the beginning of the Cold War. Reagan acknowledged his debt to Burnham in 1983, when he awarded the Presidential Medal of Freedom, the nation's highest civilian honor, to the retired *National Review* editor, who was still recovering from a stroke. "Throughout the years traveling the mashed-potato circuit I have quoted you widely," Reagan told Burnham, who died four years later. He was not the only Cold Warrior whom Reagan honored.

In 1984 Reagan awarded the Medal of Freedom posthumously to Whittaker Chambers. In 1985 he bestowed it upon Sidney Hook, Paul Nitze, and Albert and Roberta Wohlstetter, acknowledging his debt to the varying strands of anticommunism.[7]

Working from the premises of the "morality in foreign policy" plank in the 1976 GOP platform, Reagan placed a much greater emphasis than past Republican presidents on the promotion of democracy and human rights. He valorized as "freedom fighters" the guerrillas combating Soviet-installed governments around the world. He offered them financial and military assistance. Funds and matériel for anti-Communist insurgents in Afghanistan, Nicaragua, and Angola and for the anti-Communist government of El Salvador became known as the "Reagan Doctrine."

This phrase was coined by a thirty-five-year-old clinical psychiatrist turned journalist named Charles Krauthammer in an April 1985 essay for *Time* magazine. Krauthammer had written speeches for Vice President Walter Mondale during the final year of the Jimmy Carter administration. On the day of Reagan's inauguration, he joined the *New Republic*, a bastion of Scoop Jackson liberal anticommunism. It took him several years to notice the similarities between Reagan's strategy and Burnham's. "There is an echo here of the old 1950s right-wing idea of 'rolling back' communism," Krauthammer wrote of Reagan's aid to anti-Communist rebels. "But with a difference. This is not the reckless—and toothless— call for reclaiming the core Soviet possessions in Eastern Europe, which the Soviets claim for self-defense and, more important, which they are prepared to use the most extreme means to retain. This is a challenge to the peripheral acquisitions of empire."[8]

The Reagan Doctrine was no abstraction. It was the application of Reagan's beliefs to a given set of circumstances: in this case, the global increase in Soviet military and political power since America's withdrawal from Vietnam. Reagan unleashed a multipronged attack on the Soviet system. "Helping the contras, helping

UNITA, helping the Afghans, helping the KPNLF, helping the Ethiopian freedom fighters is not only morally and strategically permissible," Jeane Kirkpatrick told the Conservative Political Action Conference in January 1986. "It is morally and politically—and strategically—*necessary*."[9]

Of course, as Daniel Bell liked to joke, the greatest historian in the world is "Dr. Hind Zeit." Reagan's strategy seems more coherent in the light of the twenty-first century than it did at the time. In fact, conservative sniping at Reagan's foreign policy began early. During his first year, conservatives opposed Reagan's decision to lift the Soviet grain embargo imposed by Carter. They said his response to the imposition of martial law in Poland against the pro-democracy, pro-labor Solidarity movement did not go far enough. "This administration evidently loves commerce more than it loathes communism," George Will wrote in a withering column in January 1982. A few weeks earlier, Norman Podhoretz had taken to the *New York Times* to vent his criticisms at length in an article headlined "The Neoconservative Anguish over Reagan's Foreign Policy."[10]

Social conservatives had more reasons to be disappointed in Reagan than either the supply-siders or the anti-Communists. His support for the Moral Majority was mostly performative. He appointed C. Everett Koop surgeon general and Fundamentalist James Watt as secretary of the interior but ran into trouble with the religious Right when he nominated Sandra Day O'Connor, who had supported an abortion bill while in the Arizona state legislature, for the Supreme Court in 1981. And yet, even as many religious conservatives found themselves excluded from the corridors of power in the Reagan administration, religious neoconservatives began to play an increasingly important part in American intellectual life and policymaking.

George Weigel, a Catholic journalist and just-war theorist who would serve as biographer of Pope John Paul II, reconciled his friends Richard John Neuhaus and Michael Novak in 1981. Together they founded the Institute for Religion and Democracy, with the purpose of fighting the spread of Communist ideas in Latin America. The following year saw the release of Novak's *The Spirit of Democratic Capitalism*, a full-length argument for America's interlocking political, economic, and cultural systems. And in 1983, amid the hysteria surrounding the nuclear freeze movement, William F. Buckley Jr. devoted an entire issue of *National Review* to Novak's rebuttal of a Catholic bishops' letter supporting the "no first use" of nuclear weapons.

Novak and Neuhaus called for a new religious pluralism that would protect the right of believers to practice and speak on behalf of their faiths. They drew from the work of Will Herberg and John Courtney Murray, a Jewish theologian and a Catholic priest who had written so powerfully in defense of pluralism during the Eisenhower era. The myth of a secular society, Neuhaus wrote in *The Naked Public Square* (1984), not only pushed religious discourse and religious people out of public debate but also threatened the American experiment itself.

According to Neuhaus, the secularization and politicization of the mainline Protestant churches had destabilized American cultural and political life. It was a mistake to assume, he continued, that a public square emptied of religion would be devoid of moral certitudes. "If it is not clothed with the 'meanings' borne by religion," he wrote, "new 'meanings' will be imposed by virtue of the ambitions of the modern state." Neuhaus's work reintroduced religious and moral categories into policy debate—and provided an intellectual justification for the involvement of religious traditionalists in national politics.[11]

As his 1984 bid for reelection approached, Reagan amped up his public defense of religion. He published a short book, *Abortion and the Conscience of the Nation*, drawn from an essay in the *Human Life Review* that linked the freedom of self-government to the pro-life cause. He wrote, "There is no cause more important for preserving that freedom than affirming the transcendent right to life of all human beings, the right without which no other rights have any meaning." (As governor of California, Reagan had signed a liberal abortion bill, but he came to regret the decision and adopted the pro-life cause during his 1976 campaign.)[12]

Reagan also enacted the so-called Mexico City policy that banned the use of federal funds for abortions overseas. He campaigned on a constitutional amendment restoring prayer in schools. Like Calvin Coolidge so long before, he said there was a link between religious devotion and American renewal. "The truth is, politics and morality are inseparable," he told a gathering of seventeen thousand at a prayer breakfast in Dallas after accepting renomination.

When Reagan used such language, he drove secular intellectuals and pro-choice activists to fury. At this point, however, the religious Right was not an overwhelming force in the Republican coalition. The GOP was divided over the question of abortion. The twice-married Reagan smarted during his first televised debate with 1984 Democratic nominee Walter Mondale when moderator Fred Barnes asked him why he rarely attended church.

Reagan's words stirred the religious Right, but his actions focused on the economy and national security. And his work paid off. Volcker's painful reduction of the money supply ended inflation. Reagan's new tax rates were tied to the Consumer Price Index to forestall bracket creep. The extra disposable income provided by those tax cuts, combined with Reagan's large defense expenditures, the stable monetary environment, and a pro-business regulatory regime, unleashed a boom. Reagan was returned to office in a landslide: he won forty-nine states and 59 percent of the popular vote.

REAGAN'S PRESIDENCY CHANGED NOT ONLY THE WORLD BUT ALSO the American Right. The locus of conservative life became the

Beltway. Think tanks, journals, wonks, judges, and politicians made up a conservative version of the "Iron Triangle" of lobbyists, bureaucrats, and Congress. The libertarian Cato Institute moved to DC in 1981. In 1983 Reagan himself attended the ribbon cutting for *National Review*'s Washington bureau.[13]

The migration of conservative intellectuals to Washington accelerated during Reagan's second term. It was there in 1985 that Irving Kristol cofounded a foreign affairs magazine, the *National Interest*, with Australian journalist Owen Harries. In 1986 the *American Spectator* sold its Bloomington farmhouse and rented office space in the DC suburb of Arlington, Virginia. And in 1988 Kristol and his wife, historian Gertrude Himmelfarb, left New York City for an apartment in the Watergate. The *Public Interest* came with them.[14]

Washington had a growing number of experts in public policy who constituted a sort of intellectual community. The premier conservative think tank of the Reagan era was the Heritage Foundation. Ed Feulner was a genius at tying together the strands of the American Right. Not only were the New Right and the religious Right well represented among his staff, but traditionalists also could point to Russell Kirk's participation in Heritage events. Neoconservatives could note Midge Decter's appointment to Heritage's board in 1981, and libertarians could boast of Friedrich Hayek's visit to Heritage's Capitol Hill offices in 1982. Feulner introduced Hayek to Reagan in 1983. "You have influenced my thinking on economics," the president told the Austrian Nobel Prize laureate.[15]

Heritage's desire to shape policy had been evident since the 1980 presidential transition. Shortly before Reagan took office, the think tank released a 1,093-page blueprint for conservative governance called *Mandate for Leadership*. Over the years Heritage had mastered what its vice president, Burton Pines, called the "decision-making loop." Its studies found welcome soil in conservative journalism and germinated into Republican policies. In addition to its work on the Strategic Defense Initiative, Heritage scholar Stuart Butler proposed the creation of "enterprise zones" where black and Hispanic entrepreneurs would be freed from regulations and taxes. The idea of enterprise zones began appearing in speeches by Jack Kemp and Reagan. Heritage also published the first major study on welfare reform authored by the thirty-nine-year-old Charles Murray.[16]

After graduating from Harvard in 1965, Murray had spent five years in Thailand, first as a Peace Corps volunteer, then as a social scientist examining rural attitudes toward the central government. When he returned to the states, Murray analyzed domestic social programs at the American Institutes for Research. After a personal crisis led him to quit his job, he accepted a Heritage grant to assess whether welfare benefits had achieved their intended results. His report, "Safety Nets and the Truly Needy," came out in 1982. He wrote an op-ed for the *Wall Street Journal* stating his findings: welfare, he argued, hadn't achieved its goals. Among his readers was Irving Kristol, who arranged for Murray to expand his study into a book.

Murray's *Losing Ground* was published in 1984. It contained graph after graph illustrating how the lives of the poor had taken a turn for the worse *after* the government interventions of the Great Society. But Murray's proposed solutions were so radical as to be utopian: tearing up the affirmative action regime, distributing vouchers so that the poor could purchase their own education and housing, and "scrapping the entire federal welfare and income-support structure for working-aged persons, including [Aid to Families with Dependent Children], Medicaid, Food Stamps, Unemployment Insurance, Worker's Compensation, subsidized housing, disability insurance, and the rest." The Left's reaction to *Losing Ground* was fiercely negative. That was something Murray would have to get used to.[17]

The prominence of the Heritage Foundation in Ronald Reagan's Washington was a contributing factor in the management crisis that engulfed its rival, the American Enterprise Institute (AEI). The institute's staff was depleted because many scholars had departed for jobs in the administration. By 1986, AEI president Bill Baroody Sr. had retired. The think tank was now in the hands of his son, William Baroody Jr., who carried over many of the informal business practices of his father but without the elder Baroody's success in convincing donors that his initiatives were worth supporting.

To build on the findings of Neuhaus and Berger's *To Empower People*, for instance, Baroody Jr. launched a project called "Meeting Human Needs" and backed Michael Novak's 1987 anthology *The New Consensus on Family and Welfare*. But money was beginning to run out. In 1985, when the president of the Olin Foundation, former treasury secretary William Simon, demanded to know what was going on with its grants, AEI began a process of layoffs and cutbacks. Baroody Jr. left the institute on June 26, 1986. The place was in such a shambles that the board of trustees had to decide whether AEI was worth saving and, if so, who should run it. The board decided to keep AEI. It settled on Christopher DeMuth, a forty-year-old economics consultant and former director of Reagan's office of regulation, to be the think tank's president. One of his first moves was naming political scientist and *Public Interest* contributor James Q. Wilson chairman of AEI's council of academic advisers.[18]

Turmoil was constant at the *Washington Times*. The conservative daily newspaper was founded on May 17, 1982, by Reverend Sun Myung Moon, a Korean national who in the mid-1960s had founded the Unification Church. He moved to the United States in 1971. Moon believed that he was the messiah and destined to unify the world under his rule. He first gained attention during the 1970s for vigorously defending Nixon during Watergate. His friends on the American Right tended to gloss over the practices of his church, including mass weddings of total strangers, which led to accusations that Moon led a cult. His friends preferred instead to focus on Moon's devoted anticommunism, his support for Republican politicians and conservative causes, and the variety of groups he set up during the 1980s to advance his beliefs. The *Times* was one of them.

It was controversial from the start. When *Washington Post* reporter Elisabeth Bumiller asked James Whelan, the paper's first publisher and editor, if its existence legitimated the Unification Church, Whelan replied, "Who the hell are you to stand in judgment?" Most of the daily's employees and freelance authors denied that Unification officials interfered with editorial content. In its first year of operation, however, the paper declined to print a negative review of the movie *Inchon*, citing a conflict of interest since Moon had produced the film.[19]

Moon was a gusher of money for the Right. In a 1991 speech, he said that he had spent between $900 million and $1 billion on the newspaper alone. Most Republicans and conservatives had no problem with their new financier. In 1987 *National Review* publisher Bill Rusher, who sat on the *Times*'s advisory board, told the *American Spectator*, "The Unification Church has settled itself into the landscape of Washington as a good influence." Reagan and George H. W. Bush penned tributes to the paper and its founder, who was convicted of tax fraud in 1982 (he served thirteen months in prison before his release in 1985). Much later, in a bizarre ceremony held on Capitol Hill, Moon crowned himself "king" of America. In public, however, only a few conservatives voiced disturbance at the ease with which their peers had cozied up to the "True Father."[20]

Moon was not the only source of financing in Reagan's Washington. The city became more than a site for politics and policy. It became rich. This process had been long in the making. The regulatory explosion that began in the late 1960s contributed to the growth in lawyers and lobbyists as professional associations moved to the capital. Congressional staff multiplied. Reagan made DC exciting—it was the center of a political revolution. And his defense spending drew contractors and consultants to the Beltway. Reagan aides such as Michael Deaver and Don Regan perfected the art of the best-selling Washington tell-all. Then they found gigs in consulting and lobbying. "The irony of his presidency," Fred Barnes wrote of Reagan in 1987, "is that the more he railed against Washington, the more he made the city a magnet."[21]

Reagan's popularity and sunny disposition made it all too easy to assume that the various bands of conservatives were in harmony. But the profusion of money into the nation's capital, the competition for jobs and for influence over policy, and the loosening hold of anticommunism intensified the animus that some traditionalist conservatives felt toward the neoconservatives and supply-siders. The fissure opened in 1981, when Reagan chose his nominee for director of the National Endowment of the Humanities. There were four candidates: Ronald Berman of the University of California, San Diego; Mel Bradford of the University of Dallas; Robert Hollander of Princeton; and William J. Bennett of the National Humanities Center in Chapel Hill, North Carolina.

The conservative senators from North Carolina, Jesse Helms and John East, favored Bradford. Bennett was a 37-year-old registered Democrat who, like other neoconservatives, opposed racial preferences and anti-American trends in academia. He contributed to *Commentary* and enjoyed the support of his friend Michael Joyce, executive vice president of the Olin Foundation, and of Joyce's associate, Irving Kristol.

Bradford was a more accomplished scholar than Bennett, but his appointment was guaranteed to be controversial. He had supported George Wallace. He had penned ferocious attacks on Abraham Lincoln in which he likened the Rail Splitter to twentieth-century totalitarians. Neoconservatives weren't alone in thinking that a Bradford appointment would be a mistake. Ed Feulner and Burton Pines also lobbied the White House personnel office against him. In the end, Reagan nominated Bennett on November 19. Bradford held a grudge: he challenged one of his antagonists to a duel.[22]

Bradford's supporters began to refer to themselves as the "Old Right." They saw the neoconservatives as impostors, as power-hungry opportunists who had no problem with the New Deal or Medicare or war. And in 1986 they launched a counterattack on the neoconservative "interlopers."[23]

The quarterly journal of the Intercollegiate Studies Institute, *Intercollegiate Review*, devoted its spring issue that year to a symposium on the state of conservatism. It was not a celebration. "I believe that it is descriptively accurate to say that most of us who regarded ourselves as 'intellectual conservatives' before 1964 are in a state of demoralization and discouragement at the status of conservatism in 1986," wrote Clyde Wilson, a historian at the University of South Carolina and editor of John Calhoun's papers. "The conservative movement," intoned Russell Kirk, "is enfeebled, intellectually and in backing, at the very hour of its popular ascendancy." Historian Paul Gottfried, then editor of *Continuity: A Journal of History*, wrote that the "Old Right," comprised of the movement's remaining intellectual founders (a vanishing breed), southern conservatives, and "socio-biologists," had no doubt who was responsible for the degradation of conservatism. "Essentially at peace with the welfare state," wrote *Intercollegiate Review* editor Gregory Wolfe, "the neoconservatives continue to speak the language of social science and their policy initiatives often substitute one statist program for another."[24]

The Old Right stepped up its barrage that April at a meeting of the Philadelphia Society, a conservative discussion group established in 1964. Historian Stephen J. Tonsor delivered the opening speech. He claimed that he had no problem with neoconservatives as part of a coalition but was bothered that the neocons were in charge. He likened them to a "town whore" whose religious conversion ended not in the pews but at the pulpit. His speech left many in the audience aghast. When asked by a member of the audience if the Old Right had any room for the ex-Communists who had done so much to shape American conservatism, Tonsor replied, "Would you accept an ex-Nazi?" It came as something of a relief to the participants that none of the other speakers were as disputatious as Tonsor. Even Mel Bradford left his dueling kit at home.[25]

The argument between the Old Right and the neoconservatives was set against the backdrop of rising anti-Semitism. One month before the meeting of the Philadelphia Society, the *Nation* magazine had published its 120th anniversary issue. It contained a scurrilous attack by novelist Gore Vidal on Norman Podhoretz and Midge Decter, whom he accused of constituting an "Israeli Fifth Column Division," lobbying for a foreign power, and spreading the "politics of hate."

In response, Podhoretz launched a letter-writing campaign and called on *Nation* contributors to denounce Vidal. Few did. "*The Nation* once again confirms its reputation as the cesspool of opinion journalism," *National Review* editorialized. But the cesspool was growing, and it did not respect ideological boundaries. Among Vidal's defenders was *National Review* senior editor and Buckley protégé Joseph Sobran, who launched his own assaults on Podhoretz and Decter. So did *Chronicles* magazine, an Old Right monthly published by the Rockford Institute in Illinois.[26]

William F. Buckley Jr. published an editorial in *National Review* criticizing Sobran. It was Buckley's attempt to split the difference. He severed the magazine's connection with Sobran—but on the matter of Jews and Israel alone. He still allowed Sobran to contribute on other topics. This half measure satisfied no one. In the 1950s, Buckley had been adamant that his editors would not appear in anti-Semitic publications. In the 1960s, he had forsworn the conspiracy theories of the John Birch Society. In the 1970s, he had renounced his views on segregation. But here he was making excuses for Sobran. He was delaying the inevitable.

For social conservatives, Reagan's second term was only mildly better than the first. Nancy Reagan expanded her "Just Say No" antidrug campaign. Her husband moved William J. Bennett to the Department of Education and Ed Meese to the Department of Justice. Bennett used his position to attack the education "blob" of bureaucrats and teachers' unions and to argue for character education, high academic standards, and an appreciation of Western civilization. Perhaps his most consequential policy was a regulatory change that made it easier for families to homeschool. Meese, for his part, chaired a commission on pornography and—most importantly—initiated a debate on the role of the judiciary in a democratic society.

It was a debate for which the Right was well prepared. The conservative legal movement had been growing since the 1970s. Back then, Robert Bork had befriended and been influenced by fellow Yale professor Alexander Bickel, a moderate liberal advocate for judicial restraint who drew insights from Edmund Burke and James Madison. Bork also found himself responding to a series of landmark books on rights such as John Rawls's *A Theory of Justice* (1971), Robert Nozick's *Anarchy, State, and Utopia* (1974), and Ronald Dworkin's *Taking Rights Seriously* (1977). These works forced him to examine closely the original understanding of the constitutional structure through which the Founders protected individual rights by dispersing and diffusing power. Around the same time, the national bicentennial resuscitated the political thought of the Founders. People took a renewed interest in how the Declaration and the Constitution came to be written and what their authors intended to say.

This historical turn in conservative legal thought was evident in Bork's 1971 paper "Neutral Principles and Some First Amendment Problems," in which he wrote, "The judge must stick close to the text and the history, and their fair implications, and not construct new rights." Bork was describing the legal theory of constitutional originalism: a judge should interpret the constitutionality of statutes according to the text of the Constitution itself.[27]

A colleague of Bork's, University of Chicago professor Antonin Scalia, carried this principle over to a second theory he called "textualism": a judge, he said, should base decisions not on his or her preferences but on a statute's language. Meanwhile, in the activist realm, conservative lawyers started a number of public interest law firms, such as the Pacific Legal Foundation (1973), the Landmark Legal Foundation (1976), and the Washington Legal Foundation (1977), to represent clients whose individual rights had been violated by government.

With Reagan's reelection, the conservative legal movement took a quantum leap. Meese's public endorsement of originalism was so significant that he provoked Associate Justice William Brennan to offer a public rebuttal. Meese worked with the first generation of originalists, who had joined the Justice Department and White House Counsel's Office out of law school and clerkships. They took a burgeoning legal theory and gave it political energy through judicial appointments and administration policy. Originalism became the basis not only for constitutional interpretation but also professional affiliation. While teaching at the University of Chicago Law School, Scalia had helped to create the Federalist Society, a network of young conservative lawyers.

When Chief Justice Warren Burger retired in 1986, Reagan nominated conservative justice William Rehnquist for chief. And he picked Scalia, who had joined the DC Court of Appeals a few years before, to fill Rehnquist's spot. Scalia's role as the face of legal conservatism was exactly what originalism needed: his happy warrior approach (though more warrior than happy) galvanized the political and intellectual energy surrounding the movement. It also helped, a cynic might note, to connect legal conservatism to what at the time was an important ethnic bloc: Italian Americans. There was a reason the Senate voted 98–0 to confirm Scalia.

On July 1, 1987, Reagan announced that he would nominate Bork, who by then was also on the DC Circuit, to replace retiring justice Lewis Powell. At this point, however, Reagan's power was ebbing. The Democrats had won the Senate the previous year. And shortly after the midterm election, the first disclosures surfaced in the press of an illegal arms-for-hostages arrangement with Iran that had sent money to the anti-Communist contras in Nicaragua. The Iran-Contra scandal came to dominate the final years of the Reagan administration. At its worst point, there was speculation that the president might be impeached. The Democrats were on the prowl.

Within hours of Bork's nomination, Senator Edward Kennedy of Massachusetts denounced Bork on the floor of the Senate. This eminent legal mind became, in the senator's fevered words, the custodian of

a land in which women would be forced into back-alley abortions, blacks would sit at segregated lunch counters, rogue police could break down citizens' doors in midnight raids, schoolchildren could not be taught about evolution, writers and artists would be censored at the whim of government, and the doors of the Federal Courts would be shut on the fingers of millions of citizens for whom the judiciary is often the only protector of the individual rights that are the heart of our democracy.

Bork could not believe what he was hearing. "Not one line of that tirade was true," he thought. He became the target of unrelenting hostility from the Left. Why? Because his confirmation would be another victory for the Right in its campaign to restore judicial restraint and reverse the holding in *Roe v. Wade*.[28]

If Bork joined the Court, the entire edifice of liberal jurisprudence might be jeopardized. As Democratic senators lined up against his nomination, Bork refused to withdraw. He pressed for a full vote in the Senate even after the Judiciary Committee denied him its recommendation. Bork's nomination was defeated 58–42 on October 23. It was a reminder that, despite the successes of conservatism, the movement did not yet have the ability to counteract the combined forces of Democratic legislators and liberal communications media. It was also a reminder that political power mattered.

BETWEEN THE LOSS OF THE SENATE, THE IRAN-CONTRA SCANDAL, Bork's defeat, the stock market crash in October 1987, and Reagan's ongoing arms-control negotiations with the liberalizing general secretary of the Soviet Communist Party, Mikhail Gorbachev, the Right found itself weakened and confused. The rivalry between the Old Right and neoconservatives grew deeper. By 1988, the Old Right had established an institutional base at the Rockford Institute. It had found a cause in the drastic reduction of all forms of immigration into the United States. And with the publication of *The Conservative Movement*, a history coauthored by Paul Gottfried and *Chronicles* editor Thomas Fleming, it adopted a new name: paleoconservatism.

The obvious distinction between the paleoconservatives and the neoconservatives was chronological. Most of the paleoconservatives simply had been conservative for longer than the neoconservatives. But the antagonism went deeper. Their attitudes toward modern America most clearly separated the two strains of conservatism. The paleoconservatives defended the Lost Cause of the South, despised Lincoln, and rejected the natural rights philosophy of the American founding. These lines of thought converged in a revulsion for present-day America, whose increasing ethnic and racial diversity, information- and service-based economy, and global dominance made it a country that the paleoconservatives did not recognize.

Nor were the paleos entirely wrong when they accused the neo-conservatives of caring more about liberal democracy than conservative dogma. Neoconservatives had come to their views through a critical examination of the New Left's anti-American turn in the 1960s and 1970s. "In different historical circumstances, however, in which the challenge came from the opposite flank, it is entirely conceivable that the friends of liberal democracy would make ready to do battle with the right," attorney Dan Himmelfarb wrote in a prophetic review of the Gottfried-Fleming book.[29]

As the Cold War thawed, the threat of nuclear war abated, and anticommunism lost its relevance, Russell Kirk sounded more and more like a member of the isolationist Right to which he had belonged in his youth. The divide between paleos and neos grew in October 1988, when Kirk delivered one of his occasional lectures at the Heritage Foundation. The topic was neoconservatism. "For some persons who are called, or who call themselves, neoconservatives, my approbation is undiminished," he began. Kirk's problems lay elsewhere. The neoconservatives whom Kirk had in mind—implicitly the editor of *Commentary* and his extended family—"have tended regrettably to become a little sect, distrusted and reproached by many leaders of what we may call mainline conservatives, who now and again declare that most of the neoconservatives are seeking place and preferment chiefly."[30]

Then Kirk delivered a line that Charles Lindbergh might have uttered fifty years earlier. Neoconservatives, he said, sometimes "have been rash in their schemes of action, pursuing a fanciful democratic globalism rather than the true national interest of the United States; on such occasions I have tended to side with those moderate Libertarians who set their face against foreign entanglements. And not seldom it has seemed as if some eminent neoconservatives mistook Tel Aviv for the capital of the United States." The slanderous charge of dual loyalty was not mitigated by Kirk's next sentence, in which he acknowledged that neoconservatives had "helped to redeem America's foreign policy from the confusion into which it fell during and after the wars in southeastern Asia."[31]

The fulminations of the paleoconservatives were part of widespread angst on the right. The libertarians at the Cato Institute found little to celebrate in their 1988 volume *Assessing the Reagan Years*. "The Reagan years have involved a rolling referendum on government," wrote George Will. "The results are clear, and they are not what conservatives wanted." Fred Barnes noted the irony that the most popular and successful Reaganites were men and women comfortable with government responsibility and state power. These officials understood that government was not going to grow smaller as a result of budget cutting. The best they could do was hold down spending levels while the economy grew, thereby diminishing government's size relative to gross domestic product. "Since we're going to have big government anyway," Barnes wrote, "it makes sense to have conservative big government. It's not an oxymoron."[32]

Since the 1970s, Irving Kristol had been calling on Republicans to think about how a "conservative welfare state" might function. Kristol suggested that health and life insurance premiums and pension contributions, including additional contributions to Social Security, should be tax deductible. Later on, he added that the child tax credit should be greatly expanded. He wanted to deny welfare benefits to able-bodied men—and to teenage mothers.[33]

George Will took up Kristol's challenge at the outset of the Reagan presidency. When he delivered the Godkin Lecture on the Essentials of Free Government and the Duties of the Citizen at Harvard in 1981, Will criticized the Right for its insufficient attention to the ways in which government shaped individual character. "A conservative doctrine of the welfare state is required if conservatives are even to be included in the contemporary political conversation," he wrote in the book that came out of those lectures, *Statecraft as Soulcraft* (1983). In addition to following Kristol's recommendations, Will's conservative welfare state would provide direct cash benefits to reduce bureaucracy, offer school vouchers to subsidize religious education, and restructure welfare programs to support the two-parent family.[34]

The idea of a conservative welfare state did not take off. As noted by both Kristol and Will, many European welfare states had been built by conservatives wary of social disruption. The American welfare state, however, had been constructed by liberals who wanted to make good on American ideals. This difference in origin helped to explain why American conservatism was anti-statist. Conservatives saw the welfare state not as the guarantor of civil society but as a threat to it.

In America, a conservative restoration arrived not from the top but from the bottom as voters rebelled against liberal governance. The paradox was that the same populist sentiments animating the New Right often dissipated once populists found themselves in power. These sudden reversals prevented populists from contemplating seriously how to use the government against which they rebelled. Finally, the business interests that supported the Right were more concerned with getting government off of their backs than getting government to work for others.

For all these reasons, conservatives during the end of the Reagan era were running up against the limits of politics. They controlled the executive branch but could not roll back the state. During the last two years of Reagan's presidency, they were locked out of both the House and the Senate. And liberals owned the culture.

A deep-seated pessimism resurfaced in conservative thought. The two most popular and controversial conservative books of

1987 shared a bleak view of America's prospects. Tom Wolfe's best-selling novel *The Bonfire of the Vanities* satirized a New York City boiling over with class and racial tensions. And political philosopher Allan Bloom's *The Closing of the American Mind* diagnosed the problems of a generation suffering from incuriosity and flirting with nihilism.

Bloom's surprise best seller had its origins in a 1982 article for *National Review*. Erwin Glikes, a former Columbia University dean who left academia to work for Irving Kristol at Basic Books, had become publisher of the Free Press, where he published George Will and management consultant Michael Porter. He thought Bloom's article could be expanded into a book—but only if Bloom moved his criticisms of rock and roll to the top of the manuscript. Saul Bellow, a friend of and co-instructor with Bloom at the University of Chicago's Committee on Social Thought, wrote the preface. The book sold more than one million copies.[35]

Thirty-six years after Buckley released *God and Man at Yale*, conservatives continued to identify the university as the source of American decline. But Bloom was no ordinary conservative. He was a self-professed liberal Democrat whose favorite philosophers, Plato and Jean-Jacques Rousseau, held a different conception of freedom than the editors of *National Review*. Still, Bloom had learned from his teacher, Leo Strauss, that liberal education acculturated gentlemen in a democracy. His profound, close to four-hundred-page work was Straussianism distilled. (It is interesting to note that Strauss is mentioned just once in the entire book.) Bloom argued that in the 1960s the academy had self-destructed and relativism spread throughout the land. "After the theory of the rights of man was no longer studied or really believed," he lamented, "its practice also suffered."[36]

The contrast between *God and Man at Yale* and *The Closing of the American Mind* is revealing. Buckley's main complaint at the beginning of the 1950s was that the university had failed to educate students in the cultural inheritance of Christianity and in the economics of the free market. Bloom wrote that the university had abandoned the theory of natural rights that informed the American founding. He mentioned neither God nor the market.

Inspired by Willmoore Kendall, Buckley had argued that the university failed to promote religious and political orthodoxy. In the years since *God and Man at Yale,* campuses had indeed succumbed to an orthodoxy—the orthodoxy of relativism and multiculturalism. They were places where some questions were closed and some truths were beyond criticism. In academia, conservatives were perennial rebels and dissenters. But the censoriousness of the campus Left had unintended consequences.

The campus Right became more provocative, more combative, and more irresponsible than it had been in the past. Dinesh D'Souza, for example, had come to the United States as a seventeen-year-old exchange student from India in 1978. One year later, he enrolled at Dartmouth and joined the student newspaper. At the end of his freshman year, the paper's editor, Gregory Fossedal, was fired for supporting Ronald Reagan. So in the fall of 1980, Fossedal started a conservative campus paper called the *Dartmouth Review.* D'Souza followed him there.[37]

The inspiration behind the *Review* was *National Review* senior editor and Dartmouth professor Jeffrey Hart, whose son was a peer of Fossedal and D'Souza's. Hart was a campus fixture, a mentor, a generous and eccentric teacher with an unforgiving sense of humor and a willingness to offend. His sophistication and culture did not prevent him from sometimes taking the low road. One of the first articles of his that D'Souza read was a Swiftian upbraiding of student protesters for being ugly. Hart poked fun at gays, women, and minorities just to watch their reactions. Under his tutelage, the editors of the *Dartmouth Review* became analog precursors of Internet trolls. "We were not above using ad hominem attacks," D'Souza wrote.[38]

Nor were they above crude stereotypes. The *Review* published offensive spoofs written in black dialect. It ran an article about the end of the school term under the headline "Final Solution." It outed members of the gay student association.

These offenses gained the paper attention. But the media were not interested in the arguments or scholarship of the *Review*. They were interested in its coarseness. Before long, D'Souza exemplified the sort of conservative who challenged regnant opinion through provocation. He became a media personality by purposely flouting liberal norms of discourse regarding race. The editors of the *Review* used transgressive means to protest a politically correct campus administration, champion free and open debate, and win notoriety.

Its editors and staff, including a Russian and English major named Laura Ingraham, carried this model of confrontation and polarization into their professional careers. D'Souza joined the Heritage Foundation. He helped promote the idea of a "Third Generation" of conservatives—following the first two generations of Russell Kirk and Paul Weyrich, respectively—that would carry the conservative banner into the twenty-first century. The Third Generation did not follow liberal rules. It was not afraid to be crass or gauche. Ed Feulner once had to apologize to George H. W. Bush when a Third Generation gathering featured a sculpture of the president's head on a platter.[39]

The Third Generation of the Right in the 1980s and the New Left in the 1960s had some similarities. Both groups shared a revolutionary mentality, a combative and confrontational edge, and a willingness to elicit outrage in order to gain publicity for their cause. It may have been no accident that some former radicals associated with the New Left joined the Right during the Reagan years. Most prominent among them was David Horowitz, the former editor of the far-left *Ramparts* magazine and associate of the Black Panthers who voted for Reagan in 1984. In 1987

Horowitz and fellow ex-radical Peter Collier organized a "Second Thoughts" conference in Washington, where they traded war stories and insights with Irving Kristol and Norman Podhoretz. Like earlier ex-leftists who joined and influenced the Right, Horowitz carried with him some of his revolutionary habits of thought and action: polemical skill, a talent for organizing, and a strong grasp of invective.

By the beginning of the 1990s, D'Souza, the Third Generation, and the "Second Thoughts" crowd were ensconced within the conservative network in Washington, DC. D'Souza was a conservative wunderkind who jousted with liberals in print and on television. He worked briefly at the Reagan White House before joining the American Enterprise Institute, where he completed *Illiberal Education* (1991), his analysis of political correctness on college campuses. His book was well timed. It followed not only *The Closing of the American Mind* but also the protests against Stanford's core curriculum in 1988, when civil rights activist and Democratic presidential candidate Jesse Jackson led crowds in chanting, "Hey ho, Western Civ has got to go!"

The furor that surrounded the publication of *Illiberal Education* marked the beginning of a confusing new era in American intellectual and political life: the Soviet Union was on the verge of collapse, but at home the economy was sputtering, and Reaganism was in eclipse. In the coming decades, politics would be less about the distribution of wealth and more about the hierarchy of values. The culture war had begun.

CHAPTER ELEVEN

NEW WORLD ORDER

T HE PERIOD BETWEEN GEORGE H. W. BUSH'S NOVEMBER 1988 election as president and the departure of his Democratic successor, William Jefferson Clinton, in January 2001, saw a consolidation of Ronald Reagan's legacy. It also coincided with the loss of anticommunism as the gravitational force binding the American Right. For at least five decades—since the engaged nationalism of James Burnham, William F. Buckley Jr., Barry Goldwater, and Ronald Reagan had replaced the disengaged nationalism of Charles Lindbergh and Robert Taft—anticommunism had been the one thing that united economic, religious, and national security conservatives. Then it disappeared.

Populism reemerged as the X factor that could make or break GOP presidencies. Lacking an external threat of Soviet communism's magnitude, conservatives turned inward. In the final decade of the twentieth century, conservatives became more southern, more religious, and more nationalistic. They concentrated their energies against domestic liberalism in a protracted electoral war of attrition. An intra-Right civil war broke out between the conservative establishment based in Washington, DC, and New York City and the populist critics of immigration, foreign trade, and foreign interventions. The ensuing struggle shaped the nature of the Right for the next two decades. It culminated in the populist rejection of the establishment in 2016.

Back in 1970, when he ran for the Senate from Texas (and lost), George H. W. Bush had joked that the only way to outflank him from the right was to drop off the face of the earth. The man who prepared to succeed Ronald Reagan was different. He was conservative, for sure, but more in instinct and temperament than in ideology and program. He did not belong to the conservative movement. As a candidate for the GOP nomination in 1980, Bush had tagged Reagan's supply-side tax plan as "voodoo economics." As the incumbent vice president and the presumptive GOP nominee for president in 1988, he wanted to soften the sharp edges of Reaganism, especially after the Iran-Contra scandal and the implosion of the savings and loan industry.[1]

Conservatives had doubts about Bush. In January 1987, during his stint as White House communications director under Reagan, Pat Buchanan had met with friends and advisers at his home in McLean, Virginia. The topic of discussion was whether Buchanan should run for president in 1988. Bush was a loyal and decent person, Buchanan believed, but he was not the right man to advance the conservative cause. And Bush's most likely challenger from the right, Jack Kemp, was not exciting either. Buchanan and Kemp were friends, but they had different approaches to politics. Kemp was a fervent proselytizer for the supply-siders. He believed in a politics of inclusion and consensus. Buchanan held to the politics of division and confrontation that he had learned from Richard Nixon. After mulling the question over for a few days, however, Buchanan decided against a run. Kemp would have his chance.[2]

The 1988 GOP primary was a test of which variety of American conservatism held the most sway with the party base. Kemp's focus, for instance, was primarily economic. The preferred candidate of the national security conservatives, Jeane Kirkpatrick, decided not to run. And social conservatives were drawn to the televangelist Pat Robertson, who delivered an impressive second-place finish, behind Kansas senator Bob Dole, in the Iowa caucuses.

The Buffalo congressman launched his campaign on April 6, 1987. It did not go well. He could not translate his passion for tax cuts into public support. His campaign also exhibited the differences between conventional opinion inside the Beltway and the sentiments of the rest of America. Kemp's smarts and polish may have appealed to the political press, but they failed to impress Republican primary voters. Kemp lacked stature. No member of the House had gone straight to 1600 Pennsylvania Avenue since James Garfield in 1880. Nor did Kemp's missionary quest to broaden GOP ranks by including Hispanic and black voters capture the imaginations of white Republicans. He ran his campaign with a harmful mix of detachment and micromanagement. And GOP voters did not consider him "next in line" for the nomination.

Kemp's foibles illustrated the strengths and vulnerabilities of the Reagan legacy. The fortieth president had moved his party to the right to such an extent that most of his potential successors, including Vice President Bush and Senate minority leader Bob Dole, offered at least rhetorical support for the conservative agenda. Still, no candidate appealed to the full spectrum of economic, national security, and social conservatives.

The overall political appeal of Reaganism faded. Stagflation was a thing of the past. Religious conservatives had reestablished a presence in the public square. The welfare state had revealed itself to be pretty much impregnable. Taxes could be cut and services trimmed, but the ongoing demand for benefits seemed to confirm Reagan's joke that the closest thing to immortality in this world is a government program. And the Soviet Union had been defanged. In the spring of 1988 Reagan visited Moscow, where he spread the gospel of freedom and signed (over conservative objections) an arms-control treaty reducing nuclear stockpiles.

The American economy had been transformed. Employment grew in the service sector and fell in manufacturing. International competition eroded the bargaining power of workers and inundated the market with low-cost imports. The party system was breaking down too. Voters left the two major parties and declared themselves "independents." And the culture was changing: education levels rose, upwardly mobile "Yuppies" had liberal social attitudes and a lot of discretionary income, and discussions and depictions of sex and violence on television became more explicit.

In the end, Bush's identification with Reagan, the weakness of the Democratic nominee, Massachusetts governor Michael Dukakis, and an effective series of hot-button television ads designed by Nixon media consultant Roger Ailes and Republican strategist Lee Atwater brought the incumbent party a third-term victory for the first time since Franklin Roosevelt. Bush won forty states and 53 percent of the vote. The controversial manner of his campaign, which slammed Dukakis for weakness on crime and an unwillingness to ban flag burning, anticipated the electoral power of cultural issues in the post–Cold War era. That was just one of the ways the late 1980s and early 1990s served as a transition from Reaganism to values politics and the "Third Generation" of conservative leadership.

The Bush administration had few close ties to the conservative movement. Bush had chosen a conservative freshman senator, Dan Quayle of Indiana, as his running mate. And Quayle selected William Kristol, Irving Kristol's thirty-six-year-old son (and this writer's father-in-law) for vice presidential chief of staff. Bush also put Kemp in charge of the Department of Housing and Urban Development. William J. Bennett led a newly established Office of National Drug Control Policy. Bush's most consequential choice, however, may have been Dick Cheney, by then the House minority whip, for secretary of defense.

Bush had wanted John Tower of Texas for the job. But the Senate refused to confirm one of its own members after stories of Tower's personal indiscretions leaked to the press. The elevation of Cheney opened a leadership vacancy in the House GOP. Newt Gingrich, his replacement as whip, won the contest by a single vote.

Gingrich had spent the 1980s perfecting an aggressive, combative politics that put institutional tradition and niceties aside in his quest to win a Republican House majority. Once elected as whip, he launched a public relations and ethics campaign against House Speaker Jim Wright for a shady book deal. Wright resigned— becoming the first Democratic speaker Gingrich would topple.

Gingrich also clashed with Bush. The president had pledged at the 1988 Republican convention that he would not raise taxes. Within months of assuming the presidency, however, Bush knew that he would have to do so. "I cannot break my 'Read My Lips' pledge," he wrote in his diary on April 2, 1989. "I would be totally destroyed if I did." He was right. Bush held off for a year. In the fall of 1990, he agreed to the congressional Democrats' budget offer and reversed his campaign pledge. The decision infuriated Gingrich and the conservatives. "For many Democrats," wrote George Will, "Heaven on Earth is watching George Bush eat his words to the sound of snickering from a cynical public that never thought he meant them." The *Wall Street Journal* editorial board argued that the move contributed to the growing disaffection of the electorate and its alienation from both parties. "With his approval rating plummeting," warned the editors of *National Review*, Bush "risks becoming the Republican Jimmy Carter."[3]

Then foreign affairs interfered. When a thirty-six-year-old State Department official named Francis Fukuyama published an essay in the summer 1989 issue of the *National Interest*, asking if the West had reached the "end of History," the Berlin Wall was a few months away from coming down. A student of Allan

Bloom's, Fukuyama had been influenced by the work of Bloom's friend Alexander Kojève, the French philosopher whose lectures on G. W. F. Hegel had reintroduced the theoretical framework of the Hegelian dialectic into European thought. History, in this understanding, was the unfolding story of the state's recognition of man's freedom. Fukuyama argued that liberal democracy was "the endpoint of mankind's ideological evolution." It was the "final form of human government." Western victory in the Cold War would give rise to the "common marketization" of the world. No ideology, he said, had the capacity to threaten the dominance of liberal democracy.

Fukuyama had delivered the original version of his essay at a University of Chicago lecture organized by Bloom. He expanded his thesis into a book published by Erwin Glikes and the Free Press in 1992. By that time, however, Fukuyama was somewhat less triumphalist. He mulled over the conditions of life in democracies under no serious threat. Perhaps, he ruminated, material plenty and personal freedom would not be enough to satiate voters' appetites. "For are there not reservoirs of idealism," he asked, "that cannot be exhausted—indeed, that are not even touched—if one becomes a developer like Donald Trump, or a mountain climber like Reinhold Messner, or a politician like George Bush?"[4]

Fukuyama's article was a global sensation. It arrived at the exact moment when America was beginning to figure out what its role in the world might be after the defeat of Soviet communism. It was also the subject of heated debate. One of Fukuyama's former Harvard professors, political scientist Samuel P. Huntington, was among the many thinkers who deeply disagreed with it. A lifelong Democrat who had served in the Carter administration, Huntington seriously doubted that the world was destined to embrace liberal democracy. He noticed that Fukuyama was rather insouciant about China. "Maybe China will be different from all the other major powers and not attempt to expand its influence and control as it industrializes," Huntington wrote in the fall 1989 issue of the *National Interest*. "But how can one be confident that it will pursue this deviant course?" For Huntington, the end of the Cold War did not mean the end of History. It meant the revival of ethnic, national, and religious conflict, enacted primarily between "civilizations" based on ancient cultural practices.[5]

The Fukuyama-Huntington debate was not just another quarrel in a little magazine. It was an attempt to direct US foreign policy for decades to come. What exactly would the post–Cold War world look like? A second debate, also conducted in the pages of the *National Interest*, centered on the role the United States should play in this brave new post-Soviet world. The boldest contribution was from Charles Krauthammer. In the winter 1989 issue he called for nothing less than "universal dominion." "After having doubly defeated totalitarianism," he wrote, "America's purpose should be to steer the world away from its coming multipolar future toward a qualitatively new outcome—a unipolar world whose center is a confederated West." Krauthammer conceded that his goal might be unachievable. Still, he wrote, the aim was worth pursuing. Years later, in a conversation with this writer, Krauthammer wryly noted that he may have been a little carried away.[6]

Pat Buchanan was Krauthammer's opposite. As early as 1984, he had been calling for "a new nationalism" and "a belief again in America First, if not forsaking all others, at least *before* all others." The end of the Cold War gave him the opportunity to restore the foreign policy tradition of Lindbergh and Taft. The title of Buchanan's *National Interest* essay said it all: "America First—and Second, and Third." Buchanan argued that if the Red Army withdrew from central Europe, Germany reunified, and Russia abandoned Marxism, then America should remove its troops from Europe. As Russia's inner empire disintegrated, America should practice diplomacy rather than war. US troops, he went on, should also return from South Korea and Japan. Like Fukuyama, Buchanan dismissed Communist China as a potential adversary. "It will not survive the decade."[7]

The decision point for American foreign policy arrived on August 2, 1990. That was the day Iraq's tanks rolled into neighboring Kuwait. Krauthammer explained the significance of the event in "The Unipolar Moment," a lecture delivered in the fall of 1990 and reprinted in the winter 1990/1991 issue of *Foreign Affairs*. The waning of American power, Krauthammer said, would come from internal rather than external causes. Global peace depended on public willingness to sustain unipolarity. The sort of neo-isolationism espoused by Buchanan sapped the confidence of Americans in the international order only they could maintain.

Even a foreign policy "realist," Krauthammer said, should recognize the importance of preventing Iraqi dictator Saddam Hussein from monopolizing Gulf oil. Nor was it possible, as Jeane Kirkpatrick had suggested in her contribution to the *National Interest* symposium, for the United States to become once again "a normal country in a normal time." America was not a normal country. It was too powerful. And there is no such thing as a normal time. Krauthammer, like James Burnham and Norman Podhoretz, argued that the fate of the world depended on American self-confidence.[8]

These views took hold in the most influential parts of the conservative movement. The editors of the *Wall Street Journal* said that the "optimum" scenario included US forces not merely ejecting the Iraqi army from Kuwait but also overthrowing Saddam and installing "a MacArthur regency" in his place. The editors of *National Review* backed Operation Desert Shield, which deployed US troops to Saudi Arabia in order to deter Saddam from further expansion, and then, in January 1991, Operation Desert Storm, which evicted Iraqi forces from Kuwait.[9]

On January 29, 1991, as American bombers pounded Saddam Hussein's Republican Guard, President Bush addressed a joint session of Congress. Sounding like Woodrow Wilson, he told the assembled lawmakers that the war against Iraq was about more than oil or retribution. The issue was not Kuwait. "It is a big idea: a new world order, where diverse nations are drawn together in common cause to achieve the universal aspirations of mankind."[10]

The Gulf War ended Iraq's occupation of Kuwait. But it did not end Saddam's regime. He continued to rule from Baghdad. And the war between paleoconservatives and neoconservatives was not settled either. In the run-up to the American intervention, Joe Sobran, the *National Review* writer whom William F. Buckley Jr. had chided for his anti-Israel and anti-neoconservative views, dissented from *National Review*'s editorial line. Patrick Buchanan had said on television that the only people backing intervention were the Israeli Foreign Ministry and "its Amen corner in the United States." Buchanan had also written an offensive column contrasting the Jewish surnames of some prominent war supporters with hypothetical Anglo- and Afro-American surnames of the boys who would fight it.

Nor did Buchanan let up after the cease-fire. In May 1991 he authored two columns attacking the neoconservatives. In the first, he wrote, "Before true conservatives can ever take back the country, they are going to have to take back their movement." In the second, he identified the true enemy as the "ex-liberals, socialists, and Trotskyists who signed on in the name of anticommunism and now control our foundations and set the limits of permissible dissent." Through his opposition to the war, Buchanan met and befriended Sobran, as well as New Right theorist Sam Francis, a contributor to the paleo *Chronicles* who was then working for the *Washington Times*. By the end of the first Iraq War, Buchanan was not just another paleocon. He was their leader.[11]

In the July 1991 issue of the *American Spectator*, a thirty-year-old, Canadian-born *Wall Street Journal* editorial page staffer named David Frum attempted to write Buchanan out of the conservative movement. According to Frum, the victory of paleoconservatism would be the end of conservatism as a movement acceptable to the American mainstream and credible to the American elite. All the work that *National Review* and Ronald Reagan had done to make conservatism respectable was in jeopardy. Buckley had repudiated the Birchers—after a fashion. Now he needed to repudiate Buchanan.

Republicans caught a frightening glimpse of the dark side the previous year, when a former grand dragon of the Ku Klux Klan, David Duke, ran as a Republican in Louisiana for the US Senate. A political opportunist and publicity hound, for his latest trick Duke had won a seat in the state senate and was using it to broaden his national profile. Duke called himself a conservative Republican. He pretended to disassociate himself from his racist and anti-Semitic activities while hinting, correctly, that he hadn't changed. And yet, even with most of the national and state GOP disavowing him and endorsing his opponent, Duke managed to capture 44 percent of the vote in his loss to Democrat J. Bennett Johnson.

BY THE END OF 1991, THE PRESIDENT'S TRIUMPH IN THE GULF War had faded. The recession from July 1990 to March 1991 had drained support for Bush's economic agenda. With the Soviet Union circling the drain, voters concentrated their attention on home. In one poll during the summer of 1991, just 21 percent approved of Bush's domestic policy.

Any favorability Bush had gained from his masterful handling of the attempted coup in August against Soviet president Mikhail Gorbachev was no more. Conservatives had no love for Bush's 1990 Supreme Court nominee David Souter or for his signing of an updated Civil Rights Act in 1991 (conservatives said the bill enshrined racial quotas). That year's battle over the nomination of Clarence Thomas to replace Thurgood Marshall on the

Supreme Court was a success—but only after a grueling fight over law professor Anita Hill's accusations that Thomas had sexually harassed her.[12]

On December 10, Buchanan announced his challenge against Bush. At the same time, Buckley devoted an entire issue of *National Review* to his essay "In Search of Anti-Semitism," an evaluation of the charges of anti-Semitism against Buchanan and Sobran. Buckley concluded that he could defend neither man. Sobran was gradually cut from the magazine, but Buchanan was not. On the contrary, on the eve of the February 1992 New Hampshire primary, *National Review*, now edited by British journalist John O'Sullivan, offered a "strategic" endorsement of Buchanan's candidacy.[13]

Buchanan's campaign became the rallying point for the paleo-conservative Right. If Jack Kemp's 1988 campaign had pointed to a Republican future where economics took priority and the party made strenuous efforts to increase its support among minorities, Buchanan's 1992 bid pointed in the opposite direction. Buchanan's GOP was a party of nationalists and populists that stressed the issues of culture, identity, and faith. At a March 1992 meeting of the John Randolph Club, founded the year prior, Austrian economist and critic of movement conservatism Murray Rothbard joined forces with Russell Kirk to support the Buchanan insurgency:

The proper strategy for the Right-wing must be what we can call "Right-wing populism": exciting, dynamic, tough, and confrontational, rousing, and inspiring not only the exploited masses, but the often shell-shocked Right-wing intellectual cadre as well. And in this era where the intellectual and media elites are establishment liberal-conservatives, all in a deep sense one variety or another of social democrat, all bitterly hostile to a genuine Right, we need a dynamic, charismatic leader who has the ability to short-circuit the media elites, and to reach and rouse the masses directly.[14]

Buchanan was not that man. He was unable to get more than 38 percent of the vote in New Hampshire. But the world seemed determined to wrest itself free of George H. W. Bush. In February, Texas billionaire H. Ross Perot entered the presidential race as an independent, focusing on the budget deficit and opposing the Reaganite vision of a North American Free Trade Agreement. Then, in the spring, South Central Los Angeles was consumed by six days of rioting over the acquittal of police officers who had been videotaped beating a black man named Rodney King. Bush had to send in the National Guard. More than sixty people were killed. Property damage topped $1 billion.

When Buchanan addressed the Republican National Convention in Houston that August, he offered Bush his endorsement. He told the audience, "There is a religious war going on in this country. It is a cultural war, as critical to the kind of nation we shall be as was the Cold War itself, for this war is for the soul of America." He spoke of "the troopers of the 18th Cavalry who had come to save the city of Los Angeles." They had stared down the mob through "force, rooted in justice, and backed by moral courage." Republicans needed to emulate the young soldiers in LA. "We must take back our cities, and take back our culture, and take back our country."[15]

The initial reaction to Buchanan's address was positive. Bush called to congratulate him. But the sweet reviews quickly turned sour. News outlets reported that Reagan had qualms about Buchanan's speech. Barry Goldwater, whose grandson was gay, made no secret of his disgust at the changing nature of the Right.[16]

In the absence of the looming Soviet bear, the anti-statist impulse in American conservatism atrophied. The emphasis was ever more on social and cultural topics that divided Republicans just as much as Democrats. The strength of Buchanan and Perot also revealed discontent among conservative ranks with the results of Reagan's policies of free trade, high immigration, and democracy promotion. The voters who agreed with Buchanan and Perot's rejection of the status quo abandoned George H. W. Bush. The man who won in a landslide four years earlier received only 37 percent of the vote. Bill Clinton, the forty-six-year-old governor of Arkansas, was on his way to the White House.

Conservatives took some comfort in the knowledge that Bush and Perot's combined 56 percent of the vote was much greater than Clinton's 43 percent. They took this fact as evidence that the presidential electorate continued to lean right. They assumed that Clinton would be a one-term president. Then Clinton, who campaigned as a "New Democrat" willing to break with his party on crime, welfare, and affirmative action, began his administration by reinforcing his left flank. And the ensuing backlash made conservatives think that Congress might be up for grabs as well.

BY 1993, REAGAN'S TRUE SUCCESSOR HAD REVEALED ITSELF. IT was not a single political figure. It was the conservative institutional and media superstructure that had taken on gigantic dimensions during twelve years of Republican presidents. This network of think tanks, foundations, special interest groups, activists, columnists, magazines, and newspapers, such as the *Wall Street Journal* editorial pages, the *Washington Times*, and *Investor's Business Daily*, had grown beyond reckoning. Decades earlier, Buckley had complained of the "Apparatus" that broadcast the Left's ideas. Now the Right had one of its own.

Conservatism was larger than one individual. And it continued to expand. The Reagan years saw the birth of contentious chat shows on cable TV and in syndication, such as *Crossfire*, *The McLaughlin Group*, *Inside Washington*, and *The Capital Gang*. Regulatory and technological changes made it possible for conservative talk radio hosts to reach national audiences. The repeal of the fairness doctrine in 1987 liberated network affiliates to air controversial political opinions without balance—and without government scrutiny. The AM band opened up to talk shows. Toll-free calling technology allowed the host to interact with a nationwide audience. In 1988, with the syndication of *The Rush Limbaugh Show* across the country, talk radio became the primary means of conservative communication. It was the circulatory system of the conservative movement. And its heart was a college dropout from Cape Girardeau, Missouri.

Rush Limbaugh changed the nature of broadcasting—and plenty of other things as well. Before he went national, conservative talk radio had been local, niche, and predominantly Christian. Limbaugh was the first to capitalize on the prospect of syndication. He made the most of this economy of scale while contributing his own stylistic innovations. He treated politics not only as a competition of ideas but also as a contest between liberal elites and the American public. He added the irreverent and scandalous humor and cultural commentary of the great DJs. He introduced catchphrases still in circulation: "dittohead," "drive-by media," "feminazi," "talent on loan from God." And he became immensely popular. His monthly audiences grew to tens of millions of listeners. He did more than create the conservative talk radio industry: he also helped start the boom in conservative publishing and conservative television programming. His syndicated *The Rush Limbaugh Show* ran on television for four years. It was produced by Roger Ailes.

Limbaugh's importance to the conservative movement cannot be overstated. In 1992 a visibly nervous Limbaugh appeared on *Firing Line* alongside his hero, William F. Buckley Jr., whose presence symbolized the transference of ideological leadership from the magazine editor to the bombastic talk show host. Not long after the 1992 election, Reagan himself called Limbaugh "the Number One voice for conservatism in our country." In 1993 *National Review* deemed Limbaugh head of the opposition to Bill Clinton. Limbaugh, said William J. Bennett, "is doing to the culture what Ronald Reagan did to the political movement."[17]

Radio and television privileged volubility, volume, agitation, emotion, and exhortation. Radio was also interactive in a way that newspapers and magazines were not. On-air personalities became much more famous than professional scribblers. One's presence on television indicated one's status in the conservative movement— the more often you appeared, the more often you were recognized, the more important you became. Radio, television, and celebrity-driven conservative book publishing were profitable, unlike small magazines, journals, and newsletters. Success in talk radio or on television did not just elevate your profile. It made you rich. Limbaugh's politics were the same as the conservative movement's, but his vocal stylings and radio sketches were also typical of outlandish radio hosts. He was there not merely to pontificate. He was there to entertain, enliven, educate, and enrage.

This self-sustaining conservative network generated massive profits for its best-known faces. So vast had the conservative galaxy become that one could make a career without ever being employed by a liberal. Young conservatives started off as reporters or production assistants at a newspaper, magazine, radio show, or television network. Then they moved to the Hill as speechwriters or legislative assistants. Then they took a turn at a consulting shop or as corporate speechwriters. Then perhaps they advised a donor, or managed a campaign, or someday ran for office themselves. At any point in this journey, their connections, ingenuity, and good luck might make them fantastically rich. Then they would pour their resources back into conservative foundations, networks, and institutions. Opportunities for advancement and enrichment were everywhere.

Especially during the Clinton years. The new president energized his conservative opposition. Addressing the twenty-fifth anniversary dinner of the *American Spectator* shortly after the 1992 election, journalist P. J. O'Rourke joked, "Ladies and gentlemen, we have game in our sights. Clinton may be a disaster for the rest of the nation, but he is meat on our table."[18]

Indeed, some conservatives developed an obsession with Clinton. They raged at his ability to escape the consequences of immoral behavior. Guests at the *Spectator*'s dinner noticed that editor Bob Tyrrell wore a pin that he said had been awarded by the Arkansas National Guard. The magazine had investigated Arkansas state troopers' allegations that Clinton had indulged in various extramarital affairs during his time in office as governor. But its stories about Clinton, and especially his wife Hillary, often escaped factuality and loosed the surly bonds of plausibility.[19]

Conservative publications, authors, and politicians insinuated that Clinton had been involved in drug trafficking. They said that his friend and aide Vincent Foster hadn't committed suicide but was murdered. Clinton's actual misdeeds, from infidelity to the bizarre land deal known as Whitewater—not to mention his willingness to throw the truth aside when politically convenient—only made conservatives angrier. They viewed Clinton as the personification of immorality. He was a walking, talking symbol of the worst excesses of the 1960s. They contrasted his persona with an American public that they said was eager for moral renewal despite the depredations of the liberal elite.

"The dominant media culture in this country does not believe in the things that the vast majority of the people do believe in," Limbaugh said during his appearance on *Firing Line*, "and even go so far as to impugn and make fun of those things." What things? Limbaugh mentioned religious belief and "virtue and character being important things in leadership." In the spring of 1993, the editorialists at the *Wall Street Journal* wrote that intellectuals and politicians—namely, Bill Clinton—more or less could get by without authoritative standards of behavior. "But for a lot of other people it hasn't been such an easy life to sustain," the *Journal* continued. "These weaker or more vulnerable people, who in different ways must try to live along life's margins, are among the reasons

that a society erects rules. They're guardrails." And without guardrails, people drove off the side of the road.[20]

In 1993 Bill Bennett's *The Book of Virtues*, a collection of fables
and stories with moral lessons intended to be read to children, was
a massive hit. There was speculation that Bennett, who had joined
forces with Jack Kemp and Jeane Kirkpatrick at an organization
they called Empower America, might run for president. (He did
not.) With the Soviet Union gone, the Right focused its atten-
tions on what William Kristol called the "politics of liberty" and
the "sociology of virtue." The end of the Cold War, wrote Irving
Kristol, coincided with the beginning of "the real cold war." It
would be waged against the "liberal ethos" of "political and social
collectivism on the one hand, and moral anarchy on the other" that
had "ruthlessly corrupted" "sector after sector of American life."[21]

Charles Murray, a fellow at the American Enterprise Institute
(AEI) since 1990, warned in the fall of 1993 of "the emergence of a
white underclass." The number of births to unmarried white mothers was approaching the level that had prompted Daniel Patrick
Moynihan to write *The Negro Family: A Case for National Action*
back in 1965. What's more, Murray wrote, these births were geo-
graphically concentrated. They were not to mothers in inner cities.
They were to women who lived in pockets of exurban and rural
America. And this rise in single motherhood, Murray went on,
would contribute to American decline. "My proposition," Murray
wrote, "is that illegitimacy is the single most important social problem of our time—more important than crime, drugs, poverty, illit-
eracy, welfare, or homelessness because it drives everything else."[22]

By the 1990s, most conservatives said that they adhered to the
principle of color blindness. They believed that stable families,
self-reliance, drive, and moral character determined individual
success or failure. But, as had happened so often before, the Right
found it impossible to discuss families, culture, crime, educational

and financial attainment, and personal agency without tripping over the color line. Murray's next book, *The Bell Curve*, cowritten with Harvard psychologist Richard J. Herrnstein and released by the Free Press in 1994, examined the relationship between intelligence and social status. The authors warned of the social stratification that would result from marriage based on educational attainment. This new upper class, they said, would be isolated from and resented by the rest of the country.

This prescient message was completely overshadowed, however, by the contents of the book's thirteenth chapter. Titled "Ethnic Differences in Cognitive Ability," it dealt with the divergence in scores on mental tests between blacks and whites. Murray and Herrnstein wrote that the relationship between genetics and IQ is unknown. They said that the environment could play a part in cognitive ability. "It seems highly likely to us that both genes and the environment have something to do with racial differences," they wrote. "What might the mix be? We are resolutely agnostic on that issue; as far as we can determine, the evidence does not yet justify an estimate." They reminded readers that there was no reason for someone to treat another person differently on account of either race or intelligence.[23]

Even so, their connection of race and IQ was incendiary. Murray knew what he was getting into. When he offered his colleagues at the American Enterprise Institute a preview of the book, Irving Kristol tried to dissuade him from publishing Chapter 13. Murray plowed ahead anyway. Kristol said, "Well, Charles, we'll defend you—up to a point." Herrnstein's death prior to publication did not make Murray's job any easier. Nor did it help that, as journalist Charles Lane reported in the *New York Review of Books*, among the hundreds of sources referenced in *The Bell Curve* was an anthropological journal founded by white supremacists. AEI's president and trustees stood by Murray as he was denounced as a racist.[24]

The most thoughtful reactions to *The Bell Curve* came from the small group of black conservatives. In the *American Spectator*, Thomas Sowell wrote, "Contrary to much hysteria in the media, this is not a book about race, nor is it trying to prove that blacks are capable only of being hewers of wood and drawers of water." But Sowell also noted that some of Herrnstein and Murray's claims were either inaccurate or open to dispute. And he pointed out that correlation does not equal causation. After all, females of one ethnicity often outperform their male co-ethnics, as do the heavier of identical twins with different birth weights. A host of variables, not just intelligence, affect the aptitudes and capacities of human beings.[25]

To even discuss race and IQ seemed irrelevant and gratuitous to Glenn Loury, a black economist then at Harvard who had written critically of both the civil rights establishment and affirmative action in the *Public Interest* and *Commentary*. "Whatever the merits of their science, Herrnstein and Murray are in a moral and political cul-de-sac," he wrote in *National Review*. "I see no reason for serious people to join them there."[26]

Loury's reaction to Dinesh D'Souza's *The End of Racism*, published the following year, was more outraged. D'Souza's follow-up to *Illiberal Education* was a five-hundred-page attack on political correctness. He also defended Murray and Herrnstein. But *The End of Racism* resembled a *Dartmouth Review* provocation more than D'Souza's previous books. An outrageous statement could be found on almost every page. "If America as a nation owes blacks as a group reparations for slavery," D'Souza wrote, "what do blacks as a group owe America for the abolition of slavery?" This sort of sentence was the author's way of tossing credibility aside for showmanship. Loury severed his ties with AEI, where D'Souza remained a fellow. In the *New York Times*, Robert Woodson announced that he also was ending his two-decade relationship with the think tank. Conservative intellectuals had alienated some of their most important allies. It was an error all too typical of conservative race relations.[27]

This argument over race occurred during a period of Republican revival. In 1993 the GOP won the governorships of Virginia and New Jersey and, for the first time in a generation, the mayoralty of New York City. Republicans swept the 1994 midterm elections, winning fifty-four House seats, eight Senate seats, and ten governorships. On January 4, 1995, Newt Gingrich became the first Republican speaker of the House in forty years.

His path to the speaker's chair wove through the landscape of post-Reagan conservatism. Early on, Gingrich had decided that he wanted to wake up the somnolent Republican House minority. In September 1980 he arranged for Reagan and George H. W. Bush to join him and two hundred GOP congressmen on the Capitol steps to unveil a "contract with the American people." In 1983 he founded the Conservative Opportunity Society and in 1985 he wrote a book, *Window of Opportunity*, outlining his "blueprint for the future."

It was telling that *Window of Opportunity* was published by TOR, a science fiction house. Building on the ideas of management guru Peter Drucker and futurists Alvin and Heidi Toffler, Gingrich argued that America was on the verge of a "Third Wave" of economic and social organization. Technological breakthroughs would revolutionize American life. "Gingrich understood and argued that the Republican Party could not simply be against," said Minnesota congressman and Gingrich ally Vin Weber. "They had to replace what existed with something new."[28]

The "opportunity society" would incentivize personal responsibility and risk taking by reorganizing government bureaucracies along principles of private-sector efficiency. Inspired by science fiction writer Jerry Pournelle, who had outlined a program of space exploration in his book *A Step Farther Out* (1979), Gingrich explained that information technology would render the welfare state unnecessary. Gingrich had a gift for framing issues, identifying goals, and attacking the opposition. He possessed an amazing ability to organize congressional candidates. He marched under a populist banner. And he accused the entrenched Democratic majority of self-dealing and corruption.

The 1994 Republican victories raised expectations among conservatives that a new majority had arrived. American politics had realigned. Republicans and conservatives were the new governing class. "The American people now have a Republican Party that is future-oriented, rather than 'conservative' in the older stick-in-the-mud meaning of the term," wrote Irving Kristol. The Republican takeover of Congress vindicated Kristol's idea that, to succeed in the real world of Washington bureaucracy and the welfare state, conservatives required a forward-looking agenda.[29]

The personal and professional networks that Kristol had done so much to build supplied the personnel for Gingrich's revolution. As he celebrated his seventy-fifth birthday, Kristol could look back with satisfaction at the alterations he had made to the conservative movement. The rising generation of conservative activists and journalists turned to him for guidance. The signs of this generational transition were widespread. In 1990 William F. Buckley Jr. had stepped down as editor of *National Review*. Both Richard Nixon and Russell Kirk died in 1994. That was the year Reagan announced he suffered from Alzheimer's disease and said farewell to public life. In 1995 Norman Podhoretz retired as editor of *Commentary*.

In September 1995 Bill Kristol and John Podhoretz—Norman Podhoretz's journalist son—joined with Fred Barnes to launch the *Weekly Standard*. It was a Beltway-centric conservative magazine with the goal of influencing the direction of the Republican majority. (This writer worked there from 2003 to 2011.) Australian press mogul Rupert Murdoch funded the *Standard* as part of his News Corporation media empire. The target audience was the several

317

hundred "VIPs" who received hand-delivered copies of the magazine on Sunday mornings, less than forty-eight hours after it had gone to press.

The border between *National Review* conservatism and neoconservatism evaporated within the pages of the *Weekly Standard*. In one early issue, Buckley wrote a favorable review of Irving Kristol's *Neoconservatism: The Autobiography of an Idea*. In 1995, in the thirtieth anniversary issue of the *Public Interest*, Irving Kristol wrote, "The merger of neoconservatism and traditional conservatism, under way since the election of Ronald Reagan, is largely complete." And in January 1996 Norman Podhoretz delivered a "eulogy" for neoconservatism at AEI.[30]

The Right had great hopes for the Republican congressional majority. But it had forgotten the law of unintended consequences. Newt Gingrich made several mistakes that arrested the momentum of the GOP takeover of Congress, also known as the "Republican Revolution." In a turnabout from his 1980s crusade against Jim Wright, the Democrats launched an ethics investigation into Gingrich's lucrative book deal with one of Rupert Murdoch's companies. Gingrich was less interested in the mechanics of passing legislation than in finding and expounding on his next big concept. He faced constant bickering and challenges to his authority from his lieutenants. And he could not figure out President Clinton. Indeed, Clinton ended up having more of an impact on conservatism during the 1990s than Gingrich did.

Clinton outmaneuvered Gingrich during budget negotiations in the fall of 1995. The result was two government shutdowns for which Republicans took the blame. The backlash spooked the Republican leadership into avoiding further confrontations with the president. And the president was happy to oblige. He moved into Republican territory. He promoted school uniforms and parental controls on television sets as ways to cope with cultural decay.

It was Clinton who made Reagan's dream of a North American free trade zone a reality. It was Clinton who signed into law the greatest conservative domestic reform of the twentieth century, the Personal Responsibility and Work Opportunity Reconciliation Act of 1996, the "welfare reform" that abolished Aid to Families with Dependent Children, shifted welfare responsibilities to the states, enforced time limits for relief, and required welfare recipients to hold jobs. This achievement, building on the work of Moynihan, Murray, Nathan Glazer, the Heritage Foundation's Robert Rector, and others, led to fewer welfare cases and less poverty. And it was Clinton who agreed to a balanced budget, including a cut in the capital gains tax, in 1997.

During Clinton's tenure in office, conservatives, for all of their hatred of the president, achieved some of their most significant policy successes. Under Mayor Rudolph Giuliani, New York City implemented theories of policing that had been worked out in conservative publications and think tanks such as the Manhattan Institute. James Q. Wilson's studies of crime reinforced the necessity of public order. Wilson highlighted the benefits of community policing—an approach that put cops on the beat as familiar characters in a neighborhood—to reduce tensions in high-crime locations. Giuliani's reforms ushered in a rapid reduction of crime in America's largest city. Soon they were replicated nationwide. On economics, crime, and welfare, the Clinton presidency offered plenty for conservatives to like. They never forgave him for it.

Clinton's new strategy not only helped him win a second term in 1996 but also forced Republicans into a so-called triangulation of their own. The GOP continually had to reposition itself vis-à-vis Clinton. These zigzags had the effect of intensifying strains within the conservative coalition. The *Weekly Standard*, for example, was three months old when it backed Clinton's deployment of peacekeepers to Bosnia during the ethnosectarian wars that broke up the former Communist republic of Yugoslavia. Many of its initial subscribers, furious that a conservative publication would support a Democratic president on any issue, asked for a refund.

The magazine became known for its maximalist vision of American foreign policy. This stance put William Kristol and his frequent coauthor, diplomatic historian Robert Kagan, at odds not only with paleoconservatives such as Buchanan but also with an earlier set of neoconservatives. Irving Kristol had criticized the North Atlantic Treaty Organization, believed that post-Communist Russia should be recognized as a great power, and argued for a foreign policy of unilateral nationalism that had an expansive view of the national interest while avoiding any large-scale diplomatic or military commitments. Jeane Kirkpatrick drew a distinction between friendly autocrats and intransigent totalitarians and thought that a modest foreign policy was appropriate for the post–Cold War world. Neither Irving Kristol nor Kirkpatrick believed in democracy promotion as the central task of diplomacy. Charles Krauthammer, for his part, opposed humanitarian intervention as a waste of resources. Superpowers, he liked to say, don't do windows.

Kristol and Kagan published their manifesto in the July/August 1996 issue of *Foreign Affairs*. In tones reminiscent of Walter Lippmann at the dawn of the Progressive Era, they warned of foreign policy drift and aimlessness. They called for a "neo-Reaganite foreign policy." The Reaganism that they wished to rehabilitate was that of the 1970s, of the Reagan who challenged an incumbent president of his own party on the basis of moral ideals—not of the Reagan who, after the bombing of a marine barracks in Lebanon in 1983, adopted the "Weinberger Doctrine," named after Secretary of Defense Caspar Weinberger, of limiting deployment of US forces only to situations where a "vital national interest" was at stake.

According to Kristol and Kagan, Americans failed to appreciate the virtues of the American-led international order. The real danger to this order, they wrote, was not external but internal. They called for an enlarged defense budget, increased interaction between civilians and the military, and the global promotion of American principles of freedom and democracy. The way to deal with rogue regimes, they said in a revised and expanded version of the essay for their edited collection *Present Dangers* (2000), was "not a continuing effort to bribe them into adhering to international arms control agreements, but an effort to bring about the demise of the regimes themselves." One year after their *Foreign Affairs* article, Kristol and Kagan formed the Project for a New American Century (PNAC), a small think tank (its staff never grew beyond five people). PNAC compiled reports on US defense programs and organized letters urging the president to adopt a more assertive foreign policy and to remove Saddam Hussein from power in Iraq.[31]

Patrick Buchanan haunted Kristol and Kagan's neo-Reaganite dream. His second attempt at the presidency in 1996 made him even less popular among Republican and conservative elites. For the editors of the *Standard*, Buchanan not only represented a neo-isolationist populist insurgency but also threw into relief the brittleness, fragility, and cowardice of the Republican establishment. There was no doubt that Buchanan connected with large numbers of grassroots conservatives and GOP voters. That Republican leaders sought to handle him with kid gloves, even as they warily negotiated with Clinton, signified a malaise within conservatism.

For *Weekly Standard* senior editor David Brooks, conservatives had become ensnarled in anti-statism and populism. They needed a larger vision of national purpose. They needed fresh and imaginative leadership. Brooks called for "a return to national greatness" in the spring of 1997. A week later, William Kristol wrote, "What's needed is an insurrection—one, two, many insurrections—from within the ranks of the GOP." Together, Brooks and Kristol penned an op-ed for the *Wall Street Journal*, arguing, "What is missing from today's conservatism is the appeal to American greatness."[32]

This idea was not widely held. The conservative movement was less interested in its own shortcomings than in Bill and Hillary Clinton's. Much of the Right saw the federal government as a terrifying and oppressive force. These conservatives pointed to the 1992 shootout between US Marshals, FBI agents, and the family of Randy Weaver, a survivalist living in Ruby Ridge, Idaho, whose wife and fourteen-year-old son were killed in the exchange. These conservatives cited the overreach of the Bureau of Alcohol, Tobacco, Firearms, and Explosives in its raid against the followers of religious sectarian David Koresh in Waco, Texas, in 1993, resulting in the deaths of seventy-six people, including some two dozen children. These conservatives saw American culture as a toxic mix of immorality and willfulness and protested against sex and violence in music, television, and film.

The title of Robert Bork's *Slouching Towards Gomorrah* (1996) best captured these feelings of disgust. Bork himself responded to Brooks and Kristol's argument for national greatness in the *Wall Street Journal*. Monuments, military spending, and democracy promotion, he wrote, were not the answer to the problems of either the conservative movement or the country. The fight was not abroad. It was here. "We must do nothing less," Bork concluded, "than refight the battles we lost in the 1960s—battles over educational curricula, the content of popular culture, the feminization of the military, the understanding of the family, the proper spheres of reason and emotion, and much more." How these battles might be won, Bork never fully explained.[33]

If the "Me Generation" of the 1960s had a mascot, it was Bill Clinton. His dishonesty over his affair with the twenty-two-year-old White House intern Monica Lewinsky drove conservatives into a frenzy. In August 1998, when Clinton admitted that he had lied in denying a relationship with Lewinsky, conservatives called for his impeachment. "Every time Bill Clinton appears in public to perform the work that only a president can, he represents a walking, brutal rebuke to the spirit of our constitutional order," wrote *Standard* editorialist David Tell.[34]

Only a few on the right, while disapproving of Clinton's behavior, did not think it merited removal from office. One was *Standard* senior writer Christopher Caldwell. For Caldwell, the Lewinsky scandal was a way for conservatives and Republicans to avoid confronting the fractures within their coalition. The GOP's dogged pursuit of Clinton over the Lewinsky lie, Caldwell believed, was a consequence of religious conservatives from the South capturing the Republican Party. "Monica Lewinsky became a substitute for anti-Communism," he wrote in the *Atlantic Monthly*.[35]

Surprise Republican losses in 1998 worsened the pang. Democrats won five House seats—it was the first time since 1934 that the president's party picked up seats in a midterm election. (Even so, Republicans kept the majority in both the House and Senate.) An embarrassed Gingrich resigned from Congress. But the GOP did not waver from impeaching Clinton. In December 1998, during the House floor debate over impeachment, Gingrich's designated replacement, Robert Livingston, also resigned after disclosing his own extramarital affair. On December 19 the House impeached Clinton for perjury and obstruction of justice. But the election returns had secured Clinton's future. No one expected the Senate to convict him.

And sure enough, the Senate acquitted Clinton on February 12, 1999. Many conservatives were ready to throw up their hands. "I no longer believe that there is a moral majority," Paul Weyrich wrote after the acquittal. Weyrich concluded that conservatives had no choice but to divorce themselves from the institutions corrupted by "cultural Marxism." The failure was not only the GOP's. It was also the conservative movement's. Political success had not translated into cultural change. The Right had lost the culture war.

It had failed to remoralize society—perhaps, Weyrich implied, because the society was past saving. Weyrich told his supporters to homeschool their children, pull the plug on the television, boycott Disney, and build up an alternative Christian popular culture.[36]

And yet, if the Republican Party and the conservative movement were flailing, the network of conservative media outlets was thriving. The world might not have known about Monica Lewinsky, for example, without the assistance of Matt Drudge—a twenty-eight-year-old Internet journalist whose *Drudge Report* morphed from a Hollywood tip sheet into a powerhouse driver of web traffic and a media pacesetter.

The impeachment controversy was also a boon to the Fox News Channel that Rupert Murdoch launched in 1996. Fox News was a televised version of the conservative *New York Post*, which Murdoch had owned since 1976. Its programming was patriotic, tabloid, and populist. The station's chief executive was Roger Ailes, who established its addictive mix of breaking news, brash talk, and leggy blondes. The network rivaled and eventually surpassed Rush Limbaugh in its ability to set the agenda for Republicans. Its personalities and frequent guests became household names. The Lewinsky scandal created a demand for conservative women to flog the president on cable. It made stars of Monica Crowley, Laura Ingraham, Kellyanne Fitzpatrick (later Conway), and Ann Coulter.

If conservatism's future was uncertain by the beginning of the 2000 election, it did seem as though the paleoconservatives would not have a large part in it. In 1997 William F. Buckley Jr. removed John O'Sullivan as editor of *National Review* and replaced him with Rich Lowry, the magazine's thirty-year-old Washington correspondent. O'Sullivan had become increasingly interested in questions of national identity. He was friendly to Buchanan. He hosted in his pages immigration restrictionists such as Peter Brimelow, a Canadian-born journalist and author of the anti-immigration manifesto *Alien Nation* (1995), and Steve Sailer, a former marketing specialist turned freelance writer who coined the term "human biodiversity" to describe racial differences. While the magazine did not abandon immigration restrictionism under Lowry, its foreign policy was often on the same side as the *Weekly Standard*'s.

When many Republican politicians and conservative movement elites supported Clinton's humanitarian intervention to protect the Muslim population of Kosovo from attacks by the government of Serbia, Buchanan was disgusted. The promise of federal campaign funds for third parties attracted him. He left the GOP in October 1999. Neoconservatives were ecstatic. "Pat Jumps Ship," read the cover line of the *Weekly Standard*. "A successful demagogue needs the ferocity of a lion and the cunning of a fox," William Kristol editorialized. "Thankfully, Pat Buchanan doesn't quite measure up." That issue's "Parody" column mocked one of Buchanan's opponents for the Reform Party nomination: "Donald Trump Inaugurated," read the gag.[37]

CHAPTER TWELVE

THE FREEDOM AGENDA

A
S GOVERNOR OF TEXAS FROM 1995 TO 2000, GEORGE W. Bush was neither a neoconservative nor a populist. In 1999, when he launched his campaign for the nation's highest office, Bush made it clear that he did not intend to be a foreign policy president. He shared the instincts of the GOP establishment and opposed what he called the "three -isms" of nativism, protectionism, and isolationism. He backed intervention in the Balkans, an increase in the defense budget, and a commitment to multilateral institutions.

By the time he defeated Arizona senator John McCain for the 2000 Republican nomination, Bush had adopted a tone of foreign policy realism that resembled his father's. He told the Republican convention in Philadelphia, "When America uses force in the world, the cause must be just, the goal must be clear, and the victory must be overwhelming." On the campaign trail, Bush said that he was against "nation-building." In a televised debate with his opponent, Vice President Al Gore, he called for a "humble" foreign policy.[1]

Such modesty cut against the crusading internationalism of the *Weekly Standard*. In a September 2000 editorial, David Brooks and William Kristol, who both had supported McCain in the primary, wrote, "The Bush campaign has thus far bungled the foreign policy issue by displaying the sort of ambivalence about American power that used to mark Democratic campaigns." Robert Kagan, who also had supported McCain, wrote in the *Washington Post*, "On the biggest issue where they don't agree, American intervention abroad, Gore is probably more right than they [the Bush team] are." A couple of weeks before the election, Bill Kristol observed that "despite Gore's manifest flaws, Bush has not closed the sale." And on Fox News Channel, on the eve of the election, Kristol predicted a Gore victory. The Bush team was not pleased.[2]

Nor did the election result improve its mood. Republicans held on to a narrow congressional majority, but the White House came down to Florida, whose votes in the Electoral College would decide whether Bush or Gore became the forty-third president. The problem was that the results in Florida were disputed. The certified results declared that Bush had won the state. But Gore, who had won the national popular vote, challenged the outcome in select counties, where his lawyers said that a confusing ballot design had misled voters into supporting Pat Buchanan. When the ensuing recount plunged the country into a constitutional limbo, the *Weekly Standard* joined with other conservative institutions and rallied behind Bush.[3]

For over a month, the machinations in Florida riveted the country. Campaign officials resorted to the courts to determine the winner of the state and thus of the presidency. For conservatives, the Florida recount was nothing less than an attempt by Gore and the Democrat-appointed judges on the Florida Supreme Court to override an election. In the end, Bush appealed to the US Supreme Court to stop the recount. And on December 12, a 5–4 majority ruled in *Bush v. Gore* that the state certification of Bush as the winner in Florida would stand. Gore conceded the next day.[4]

What happened in Florida set the tone for the next several decades of American politics. Bush's victory was significant not only because of the consequential decisions he made as president. It mattered because the election results had revealed a closely divided nation whose opposing factions viewed each other as not just mistaken but illegitimate. Bush became president without winning the popular vote—the first time that had happened since 1888. The election also introduced the terms "Red America" (Republican) and "Blue America" (Democratic) into the political vocabulary, heightening the sense of national division and alienation. The echoes of 2000 continue to reverberate.

At first, Bush's presidency focused on bringing his form of conservatism to bear on domestic issues. By the late 1990s, the intellectual tradition that Peter Berger and Richard John Neuhaus inaugurated with *To Empower People* had become something of a movement. Historian Gertrude Himmelfarb had laid the foundations for the revival of civil society through her extensive research into the intellectual, social, and moral culture of the Victorian era. In 1990 journalist Marvin Olasky had written *The Tragedy of American Compassion*, a detailed examination of how impersonal bureaucracies crowd out personal charities. Three years later, Myron Magnet, editor of the Manhattan Institute's *City Journal*, cataloged the moral and cultural toll of the 1960s in *The Dream and the Nightmare*. In October 1995 Senator Dan Coats of Indiana launched the Project for American Renewal, a package of nineteen pieces of legislation devoted to revitalizing civil society. Through tax credits, vouchers, grants, and matched spending, Coats hoped to reduce divorce and abortion and to promote adoption and single-sex education.

The Coats legislation did not get far. But its spirit lived on in the work of the senator's chief speechwriter, Michael Gerson. Born in 1964 and a graduate of Wheaton College who had worked for former Richard Nixon aide turned Evangelical activist Charles

Colson, Gerson believed that religious values motivated social justice movements from abolition to civil rights to antiabortion. He had little regard for libertarianism. He thought conservatives were too dismissive of the legacies of slavery and segregation. For Gerson, conservatism was compatible with political idealism. His version of the Social Gospel had conservative ends in mind. But it still believed in progress—and in state action.

After a brief stint in journalism during Bill Clinton's second term, Gerson encountered then Texas governor George W. Bush, who shared his views and admired his writing. In April 1999 Bush asked Gerson to join his nascent presidential campaign as chief speechwriter and policy adviser. Gerson agreed. On his way to Austin to work for Bush, he jotted down two objectives for the days ahead: "the recovery of American rhetoric" and "giving Republicans a message of social justice."[5]

He met his goals. George W. Bush's speeches were of unusually high quality. And they conveyed a coherent worldview whose "social justice" component came to be known as "compassionate conservatism." This was conservatism in service not of limiting the state but of comforting the weak and welcoming the stranger. Unlike Newt Gingrich, Bush sought to expand government involvement in the education sector. He supported an immigration reform that would legalize the status of illegal immigrants. He wanted to expand Medicare to include a prescription-drug benefit. As Bush told Dan Balz of the *Washington Post* in the spring of 1999, "There is a role for government. But there is also a role for institutions that are value-laden, value-oriented, and that exist all across America."[6]

Compassionate conservatism entailed a wide-ranging agenda. Bush proposed a faith-based initiative that would have provided resources to churches and other religious nongovernmental organizations. He wanted to expand programs to subsidize homeownership among minorities. He wanted to increase foreign aid massively to address HIV/AIDS in Africa. Compassionate conservatism was no marketing scheme. It was a fleshed-out philosophy of government activism in the service of moral ideals.

But it was also not very conservative—insofar as conservatism's primary domestic concern since 1932 had been limiting the federal government. Compassionate conservatism recognized the success of Bill Clinton in portraying the Republicans as enemies of education, Medicare, and the environment. It was an attempt to take back the moral high ground from the Democrats (there was no need to take it back from Clinton). For Bush and Gerson, "ideals" were similar to the "transcendental moral order" in which previous generations of conservatives had believed. Whereas those conservatives understood this moral order to place limits on state action, Bush and Gerson's ideals made state action compulsory. As Bush once put it, "We have a responsibility that when somebody hurts, government has got to move."[7]

Congress passed Bush's tax cut plan, which sent rebates to Americans. He worked with Ted Kennedy on an education bill that required states to test student achievement and measure school performance. He urged Congress to add a prescription-drug entitlement to Medicare that incentivized competition and expanded health savings accounts. And he treated seriously the bioethical debates over human cloning and stem cell research. The relationship between science, government, and religion seemed poised to become the dominant theme of the Bush presidency. In a time of peace and plenty, questions of human nature and its susceptibility to technological manipulation came to the fore. These questions also raised the larger topic of human dignity. Bush was intrigued.

On August 9, 2001, Bush devoted his first nationally televised address to the subject of federal funding for stem cells. Later in the year, he empaneled a presidential commission on bioethics. Its eighteen members were drawn from the fields of science, law, philosophy, theology, and journalism. The commission's chairman was University of Chicago bioethicist and philosopher Leon Kass. A legendary instructor on the university's Committee on Social Thought, Kass had been born to Yiddish-speaking parents in the South Side of Chicago in 1939. He had graduated from the University of Chicago with a medical degree and then obtained a PhD in biochemistry from Harvard. He had registered voters in Mississippi in 1965. The next year, Kass began thinking seriously about the intersection of science, philosophy, and ethics. His first contribution to the *Public Interest* appeared in 1972. By 1974, he was coteaching with his wife Amy at St. John's College in Annapolis and then at the University of Chicago.

Drawing on deep resources of humanistic, religious, and political wisdom, Kass led his commissioners in a kind of seminar devoted to the permanent questions of human existence. The direct outcome of this work was several major publications on human cloning, biotechnology, and human dignity. But the commission also inspired a journal, the *New Atlantis* (2003), published by the Ethics and Public Policy Center and edited by Eric Cohen. Its contributors explored the interaction of technological innovation and human nature.

In the summer of 2001 the conservative movement and the Republican Party may well have seemed headed toward a theologically minded politics of domestic reform. No successor had replaced the Soviet Union as a global threat demanding the world's attention. The 1990s had seen a series of small engagements overseas often based on the principle of humanitarian intervention. Bush's foreign policy would be unilateralist but uninterested in foreign deployments. He withdrew from the Kyoto climate protocol because he believed that its restrictions on greenhouse gas emissions would harm the US economy while allowing other emitters off the hook. He took America out of the 1972 Anti-Ballistic Missile Treaty because its cosigner, the Soviet Union, no longer existed and because it restricted the development of land-based missile-defense technology.

Bush's administration was populated with eminences from the Republican foreign policy establishment. Vice President Dick Cheney had served as George H. W. Bush's defense secretary and Gerald Ford's chief of staff. Secretary of State Colin Powell had been chairman of the joint chiefs under Bush senior. Secretary of Defense Donald Rumsfeld had been Ford's chief of staff and defense secretary and Richard Nixon's ambassador to the North Atlantic Treaty Organization (NATO). These men were cautious, circumspect, and suspicious of ideology in foreign affairs.

The *Weekly Standard* did not approve. In the spring of 2001, a US reconnaissance plane collided with a Chinese interceptor jet that had been closely tailing it over international waters. The American plane, which carried a crew of twenty-four, was forced to make an emergency landing on China's Hainan Island. The People's Liberation Army detained the Americans for ten days as the Bush administration negotiated their release. The crew was freed after Secretary of State Powell hand-delivered a letter to a Chinese official saying the United States was "very sorry" for what had happened. Kagan and Kristol called this response a "national humiliation."

Nor did the second George Bush take action against Saddam Hussein during the first months of his administration. And when Bush's first defense budget request came in too low for the *Standard*, Kristol and Kagan began their editorial this way: "Here's some unsolicited advice for two old friends, Donald Rumsfeld and Paul Wolfowitz: Resign." It would not be the last time Kristol urged them to do so.[8]

ON THE BRIGHT, CLOUDLESS MORNING OF SEPTEMBER 11, 2001, al-Qaeda terrorists hijacked four airliners and rammed them into the World Trade Center, the Pentagon, and a field in Shanksville, Pennsylvania. More than three thousand people were killed. Bush, like the rest of his countrymen, was outraged. "They were going to pay," he later recalled.[9]

There was a snap consensus, especially on the right, that the American response needed to go beyond law enforcement. "War was long ago declared on us," wrote Charles Krauthammer. "Until we declare war in return, we will have thousands of more innocent victims." George Will said that the attacks marked the end of America's "holiday from history." The *Standard* published a cover that read, "America at War."[10]

Conservatives also drew a line from al-Qaeda leader Osama bin Laden to Saddam Hussein. Some speculated that Iraqi intelligence may have been involved in the attack. Others, such as Vice President Cheney, publicized a story that hijacker Mohammed Atta had met with an Iraqi agent in Prague in the run-up to 9/11. *Weekly Standard* staff writer Stephen F. Hayes did not go that far, but he did write prolifically about the connections between al-Qaeda terrorists and Iraqi intelligence assets. Beginning with the magazine's first post-9/11 issue, the editorial line held that the war on terror Bush had declared would not be successful until Saddam was removed from power. *National Review* and the *Wall Street Journal* editorial board, along with hosts on Fox News and talk radio, said the same thing.

For a time, it seemed as if Islamic terrorism and the ideology of radical Islamism might replace communism as the unifying enemy of the American Right. Conservative hawks had no problem thinking so. For Norman Podhoretz, Bush's "war on terror" was actually "World War IV"—next in line after James Burnham's "Third World War" against Soviet communism. Religious conservatives deplored the persecution of Christians in Muslim countries and the terrorist atrocities against Israel. They looked with suspicion on Islam itself.

Economic conservatives, however, blanched at the expense of George W. Bush's war on terror and the new bureaucracies, such as the Department of Homeland Security, that it required. The divide between libertarians and conservatives over the war's cost—and over Bush's policies of domestic surveillance and the detention, rendition, and interrogation of prisoners captured overseas—was a preview of further discontent and division.

On October 7, 2001, President Bush launched Operation Enduring Freedom, the military campaign to remove the Taliban militia from power in Afghanistan, where they were sheltering Osama bin Laden and al-Qaeda. Bush began to make the case for removing Saddam Hussein in 2002. His State of the Union address that year warned of an "axis of evil" between rogue states armed with weapons of mass destruction and terrorist organizations that could use such weapons against unsuspecting populations. In June, he told graduates of West Point, "Our security will require all Americans to be forward-looking and resolute, to be ready for preemptive action when necessary to defend our liberty and to defend our lives." In September, he told the UN General Assembly, "The United States supports political and economic liberty in a unified Iraq." If Saddam refused to comply with UN resolutions calling on him to disarm, Bush went on, "a regime that [had] lost its legitimacy [would] also lose its power." In the official national security strategy released that month, National Security Adviser Condoleezza Rice wrote, "We reject the condescending view that freedom will not grow in the soil of the Middle East—or that Muslims do not share in the desire to be free."[11]

The unity with which the world had greeted America's initial response to the 9/11 attacks disappeared. Unlike in Afghanistan, war against Saddam Hussein would not involve NATO. Neither the French nor German governments wanted to overthrow Saddam. Nor did Rice's mentor, Brent Scowcroft, a Kissinger protégé who had served as national security adviser under George H. W. Bush. Similar opposition came from James Webb, the marine Vietnam veteran turned novelist who had been secretary of the navy under Ronald Reagan.

Webb was an interesting case. He descended from, and saw himself as a spokesman for, Scotch-Irish "Jacksonian" culture (the label was historian Walter Russell Mead's). Jacksonians were the Appalachian and southern populists who filled up the ranks of America's armed forces. They supported an antielitist, nationalist politics that defended gun rights, military valor, territorial integrity, the privileges of citizenship, and middle-class entitlements. While the Jacksonians, like a majority of the US Congress and American people, initially backed the overthrow of Saddam, Webb's widely discussed op-ed in the September 4, 2002, *Washington Post* suggested that their support might not last. "The issue before us," wrote Webb, "is not simply whether the United States should end the regime of Saddam Hussein, but whether we as a nation are prepared to physically occupy territory in the Middle East for the next 30 to 50 years." Patience for an extended and bloody occupation of Iraq would wear thin.[12]

The paleoconservatives, of course, had no interest in resuscitating the engaged nationalism of the Cold War under the auspices of the war on terror. They steadfastly opposed Bush as he made the case for war against Saddam Hussein. In October 2002 Pat Buchanan launched a new magazine, the *American Conservative*. In the lead feature, titled "Why I Am No Longer a Conservative," New Right guru Kevin Phillips sounded like a Southern Agrarian as he bemoaned the "financialization" of the economy, the loss of manufacturing jobs, the privileging of investment income over labor income, pork barrel corruption and bailouts, and the looming invasion of Iraq. As US forces began marching toward Baghdad, Buchanan wrote a cover story whose title asked, "Whose War?" He offered the same answer he had a decade prior, during the previous war with Saddam. Rather than attack the most famous and important leaders of the "War Party," all of whom were gentiles, he impugned the Jewish intellectuals who backed the invasion. He said that these neoconservatives put Israel's interests ahead of

America's. He called them a "cabal." He accused them of colluding with a foreign power. He might as well have been quoting the *Protocols of the Elders of Zion.*[13]

Operation Iraqi Freedom began on March 20, 2003. Around this time, David Frum, who had spent a year writing speeches for President Bush before publishing a memoir, *The Right Man*, in 2003, also repeated an argument he had made in the 1990s. The moment had arrived, Frum wrote, to expel the paleoconservatives from the conservative movement. "The paleoconservatives have chosen—and the rest of us must choose too," he wrote in "Unpatriotic Conservatives," his controversial piece for *National Review*. "In a time of danger, they have turned their backs on their country. Now we turn our backs on them."[14]

Frum went after more than the usual suspects. He also named Robert Novak, a veteran conservative columnist and prominent voice on cable news. Though a harsh critic of Israel's policies toward the Palestinians and an opponent of the Iraq wars, this army veteran and long-standing conservative—who had reviewed *The Right Man* savagely in Buchanan's magazine—could not plausibly be described as unpatriotic. William F. Buckley Jr. sent a private email to Novak saying that he continued to admire him, but a public apology sought by *National Review* board member Neal Freeman never materialized. Instead the magazine published a symposium on the Frum piece. The episode saddened Novak. It led to a break not only with *National Review* but also with some of his longtime friends. He was the first conservative the Iraq War would sever from his movement and his party. There would be many others.

The war became much harder to defend after both US forces and a UN commission failed to find the weapons of mass destruction on which the Bush administration had based its case for Saddam's removal. Francis Fukuyama, for example, had signed a 1998 Project for a New American Century letter that advised President Clinton to adopt a strategy aimed "above all, at the removal of Saddam Hussein's regime from power." By 2004, however, as American troops were fighting Sunni and Shiite insurgents and al-Qaeda in Iraq, Fukuyama announced his opposition to the policy he had advocated six years earlier. A Charles Krauthammer lecture at the American Enterprise Institute (AEI) triggered him.[15]

Krauthammer had defended a foreign policy of "democratic realism" against the opposing schools of Pat Buchanan's isolationism, Brent Scowcroft's realism, and Bob Kagan and Bill Kristol's "democratic globalism." Krauthammer's defense of the war on terror and the invasion of Iraq did not persuade Fukuyama, who believed that Krauthammer downplayed the violence, chaos, and terrorism of the post-Saddam insurgency. For Fukuyama, neither al-Qaeda nor Saddam presented an existential threat to the United States. Nor did he understand how self-described neoconservatives could express such confidence in the ability of the United States to transform a nation such as Iraq into "a Western-style democracy." Earlier neoconservatives, Fukuyama pointed out, had warned Americans of the unintended consequences of idealistic government action, and Iraqi culture presented peculiar obstacles to democracy. Nor was the American record of nation-building reassuring. Fukuyama renounced his association with neoconservatism and with the Republican Party.[16]

His recoil was not unusual. In April 2004 David Brooks acknowledged in one of his *New York Times* columns about the war, "I never thought it would be this bad." In May, George Will began walking away from his (rather halfhearted) support for the invasion. "This administration needs a dose of conservatism without the prefix," he wrote. The next month, in an interview announcing his retirement from *National Review*'s board, the seventy-eight-year-old Buckley told David D. Kirkpatrick of the *New York Times*, "If I knew then what I know now about what kind of situation we would be in, I would have opposed the war."[17]

By Election Day 2004, there was little doubt that Iraq was a liability for Bush and the GOP. But the memory of 9/11 still loomed large in the public imagination. Nor was Iraq so bad as to doom Bush. On the contrary, he faced a particularly maladroit opponent. Massachusetts senator John Kerry had originally voted to authorize the war and proposed no major changes in its conduct, but he opposed a major foreign aid bill to fund Iraq's reconstruction and then memorably said, "I actually did vote for the $87 billion before I voted against it."

Even so, Bush's reelection was a close call. He defeated Kerry 51 to 48 percent in the popular vote, but his victory hinged on his 110,000-vote margin in Ohio. The winds of polarization had been rising since the end of the Cold War and the 1992 election. They had not abated.

AS CONDITIONS IN IRAQ GREW WORSE, BUSH BECAME MORE COM- mitted to democracy as the cure for the toxic condition of the Arab world. An avid reader, he found himself agreeing with the former Soviet dissident turned Israeli political figure Natan Sharansky, whose *The Case for Democracy* (2004) distinguished between "free societies," where dissent flourished, and "fear societies," where unpopular opinions risked imprisonment and death. Sharansky linked the previous crusade against communism to the contemporary struggle against Islamism. Bush invited Sharansky to the White House. He decided that his second inaugural would make the case for freedom over fear. The speech that resulted was a model of American rhetoric. It was also the epitome of Bush's idealism.

"We are led, by events and common sense, to one conclusion," Bush said after being sworn in for a second term on January 20, 2005. "The survival of liberty in our land increasingly depends on the success of liberty in other lands." In an allusion to the "Truman Doctrine" speech of 1947, Bush said, "So it is the policy of the United States to seek and support the growth of democratic movements and institutions in every nation and culture, with the ultimate goal of ending tyranny in our world."

This open-ended goal overshadowed the many subtleties of the text. Bush said that ending tyranny was "not primarily the task of arms." He acknowledged that this "great objective" is "the concentrated work of generations." Victory was not inevitable, he went on. But "we have confidence because freedom is the permanent hope of mankind, the hunger in dark places, the longing of the soul."

Not everyone was so confident. Bush's opponents on both the antiwar Left and the paleoconservative Right criticized the address for its audacity, its lack of details, and its omission of Iraq. This speech differed, however, in the circumspection with which some of the opinion writers within the Republican establishment greeted it. "It left me with a bad feeling, and reluctant dislike," former Reagan speechwriter Peggy Noonan wrote in her *Wall Street Journal* column. To Noonan, Bush was more than idealistic. He was utopian.[18]

Still, Bush appeared to be on stable political ground through the summer of 2005. The prospects for the so-called Freedom Agenda looked good despite the insurgencies in Iraq and Afghanistan. Elliott Abrams, then serving on the staff of the National Security Council, described 2005 as the "high-water mark" for democracy promotion. Bush spent much of the first half of that year in a failed attempt to cajole Congress into writing Social Security reform legislation that included personal accounts. By the time he left for his August vacation in Crawford, Texas, the president had scored some minor victories on free trade, bankruptcy reform, and the nomination of John Roberts to the Supreme Court. (Bush had nominated Roberts to replace the retiring associate justice Sandra Day O'Connor, but in September, after the death of Chief Justice William Rehnquist, Bush renominated him for the top position on the Court.) Bush's approval rating hovered at slightly under 50 percent in the Gallup poll.[19]

Then Bush's stay in Texas was interrupted. First, Cindy Shee-han, the mother of a soldier killed in Iraq, kept a vigil outside the president's ranch that attracted media coverage. Then Hurricane Katrina hit the Gulf Coast while Bush was on his way back to Washington. The image of Bush staring at the damage in New Orleans from the window of Air Force One was the beginning of his transformation into a political pariah. From that point forward, the blows to his reputation never ceased.

Bush's pledge to spend billions rebuilding New Orleans in-furiated House conservatives, including Mike Pence of Indiana, chairman of the conservative Republican Study Committee. A series of mistaken decisions and terrible events further marred Bush's image and sullied his relationship with the Right: the nom-ination of White House lawyer and Bush family friend Harriet Miers to replace Justice Sandra Day O'Connor; a botched effort to sell some US ports to a company based in Dubai; Vice President Cheney's accidental shooting of a friend on a hunting trip. (The friend survived.)

Above all, immigration divided Bush from the populist grass roots. Bush famously had told a voter during the 2000 campaign that family values did not stop at the Rio Grande. But for many on the right, they did. Nor was Bush punctilious about border en-forcement before or after 9/11. The war on terror did not cause him to abandon his goal of regularizing the status of Mexican nation-als residing illegally in the United States. He tried twice during his second term, working with John McCain and liberal icon Ted Kennedy, to pass comprehensive immigration reform. Resentment toward such policies grew whenever Bush ascribed his opponents' views to nativism or bigotry.

The conservative base of the GOP was disturbed by the in-creasing numbers of illegal immigrants from Mexico. As early as 2003, the classicist and military historian Victor Davis Hanson wrote that illegal immigration had turned his home state into

"Mexifornia." The following year, Samuel P. Huntington published his final book: *Who Are We?*

For Huntington, it was an open question. He argued that the rise of a global financial and cultural elite untethered to national identity and the influx of low-skilled Hispanic immigrants threatened to destroy America's Anglo-Protestant cultural base and undermine the American creed. The borders, common language, and shared history essential to US nationhood were at risk of erasure.[20]

The threat of jihadist terrorism and the rising number of foreign-born residents in Western societies made the question of national identity unavoidable. Huntington's thesis was similar to one that British philosopher Roger Scruton had advanced in his 2002 book *The West and the Rest*. Scruton argued that the political, economic, and social disruptions that followed this diminution of national sovereignty had perverse effects, including Islamic terrorism. The object, Scruton thought, was to "constrain the process of globalization" and "reinforce the nation-state, which has brought the great benefits that distinguish the West from the rest, including the benefits of personal government, citizenship under a territorial jurisdiction, and government answerable to the people."[21]

This was music to Pat Buchanan's ears. He understood the vulnerability in Bush's argument for immigration amnesty: Bush's program tended to downplay the prerogatives of American citizens in order to extend the benefits of freedom to non-Americans at home and abroad. "It's a paleo moment in America," Fred Barnes wrote in the winter of 2006. He asked Buchanan what his message would be if he were to run for president once more. "Secure the borders, stop exporting jobs, and bring the troops home," Buchanan said. He spoke a decade too soon.[22]

Bush's second term was only a few months old when conservative intellectuals began to think about the policy agenda that future Republican candidates ought to embrace. Their first attempt was "The Party of Sam's Club," an essay in the *Weekly Standard* in September 2005 by two twenty-five-year-old journalists, Ross Douthat and Reihan Salam. "Putting Families First," by twenty-nine-year-old former White House aide Yuval Levin, was published the next year. In April 2006, *National Review* senior editor Ramesh Ponnuru called for expanding the child tax credit to improve the lives of working parents. In 2007 David Frum published *Comeback*, arguing that the GOP needed to formulate realistic health care policies and embrace environmental conservation. In 2008 Douthat and Salam released *Grand New Party*, where they fleshed out their proposals for consumer-directed health care, family-friendly tax reform, and wage subsidies. And in 2009 Levin started *National Affairs*, a successor to the *Public Interest*, which had closed its doors four years earlier.

These writers, along with Bush aides Michael Gerson and Peter Wehner, were the core of what would become known as reform conservatism. Nicknamed "Reformocons," they believed that the GOP domestic agenda had been formulated in the 1970s and 1980s as a response to the crises of that era: inflation, bracket creep, stagflation, crime, welfare dependency. That agenda, the Reformocons continued, had solved these problems by lowering taxes, changing policing strategies and incarcerating criminals, and introducing work requirements into social programs. But Republicans had not kept pace with the times. They were either ignoring or failing to respond to the mounting challenges of the early twenty-first century. Reformocons wanted to apply conservative principles to contemporary realities.

Reformocons understood that the realignment of white voters without college degrees toward the GOP presented a political opportunity the party had not fully seized. Reformocons wanted to persuade GOP policymakers that changing their approach to the welfare state would advance their cause as well as their careers. Like earlier conservatives, the Reformocons pitched their arguments to elites. Their audience was mainly other intellectuals and policy wonks. They had trouble finding a political champion who, like Jack Kemp in the 1970s, could introduce their ideas into the highest level of public debate. They believed that having an elite spokesperson for working-class families would redirect the energy of the party's populist wing toward productive ends. No such figure appeared.

Republicans once had been the party of WASP blue bloods in New England and of farmers and Elks Clubbers in the Midwest. Republicans once had been connected, wealthy, and well schooled. Republicans once had led Democrats among college-educated white voters—the class of voter to which most conservative intellectuals belong—by eleven points. And yet, over the course of the post–Cold War era, Democrats had closed the gap. In the Republican Party, white voters who had not graduated from college were replacing the whites who had.

In 1992, 50 percent of white voters with a high school degree or less identified as a Democrat. That was nine points higher than the percentage identifying as a Republican. By 2016, the Republicans enjoyed the support of this cohort, and by an incredible number: 59 to 33 percent. This shift in levels of educational attainment was guaranteed to make the GOP a more populist party. Whites without college degrees had been integral to GOP majorities since the "hard hats" who backed Nixon, but these voters were growing in size and importance within the party (even as their numbers in the overall population diminished). And they neither belonged to the conservative intellectual movement nor felt represented in Washington, DC.

In truth, no one was feeling particularly well represented in Washington. The policy architecture of the war on terror had started to buckle. Bush's plans to try captured terrorist suspects in military commissions in Guantánamo Bay were foiled and delayed. More and more people came to view as torture, and Congress forbade, the "enhanced interrogation techniques," such as waterboarding, that had been used on high-value terrorists in the aftermath of 9/11. In late 2005 the *New York Times* revealed the existence of the Terrorist Surveillance Program, which collected information, without a warrant, on phone calls by foreigners originating in or routed through the United States. The sensationalist news coverage, as well as the legal morass, that accompanied every revelation of Bush's secret counterterrorism efforts divided America—and the conservative movement.

Bush's refusal to send more troops to Iraq risked the breakup of that country and America's defeat at the hands of Sunni insurgents, Shiite militias, and al-Qaeda terrorists. The bombing of the al-Askari shrine in Samarra on February 22, 2006, initiated a terrible bloodletting along ethnosectarian lines in Iraq and marked the onset of civil war. American casualties rose. Bush's poll numbers fell.

The Republican congressional majority was demoralized and practically resigned to defeat. The scandals associated with the crooked lobbyist Jack Abramoff, a onetime chairman of the College Republican National Committee who cheated his Indigenous gaming clients of millions of dollars in fees, were further evidence that the GOP Congress had turned out to be just as self-seeking and corrupt as its Democratic predecessor. By the 2006 midterm elections, the Bush White House was in disarray. Republicans lost control of Congress after twelve years in power. Democrats won thirty-one seats in the House and five in the Senate. Bush called it a "thumpin'."[23]

Bush also announced that he had accepted the resignation of Secretary of Defense Donald Rumsfeld, who had come to embody the administration's failed war strategy. The incoming Democratic majority, led by House Speaker Nancy Pelosi, wanted America to announce a timeline for withdrawal from Iraq. Bush refused. But he did say that he would listen to a commission on Iraq whose chairmen, James Baker and Lee Hamilton, represented the foreign policy establishment opposed to his ideas. Conventional wisdom in Washington assumed that the Baker-Hamilton Commission would provide Bush cover to sound the retreat.

The president went in another direction. In January 2007 he named General David Petraeus, author of the army's counterinsurgency manual, commander of US forces in Iraq. He deployed another five combat brigades (some twenty thousand troops). The so-called Iraq surge was the most consequential example of an idea originating within the conservative movement becoming reality. The war plan was designed by retired four-star army general Jack Keane and Frederick W. Kagan, Robert Kagan's brother and a military historian at AEI. Fred Kagan called for the additional troops to pursue a counterinsurgency strategy, with the aim of establishing security for the Iraqi people and turning communities against the insurgents, militias, and terrorists. The plan was floated in the pages of the *Weekly Standard*. General Keane and Bill Kristol promoted it on television.

The surge recognized that Iraqi security was intertwined with both Iraqi democracy and the possibility of a peaceful American withdrawal. It was based on the idea that Iraq was integral to the war on terror. In an April briefing, Petraeus said, "Iraq is, in fact, the central front of al Qaeda's global campaign and we devote considerable resources to the fight against al Qaeda Iraq."[24]

Casualties spiked in the spring and summer of 2007 as US forces rooted out the enemy. Then violence in Iraq fell precipitously. By the time Petraeus and US ambassador to Iraq Ryan Crocker testified before Congress in September 2007, the strategy had acquired momentum. Iraq was stabilizing.

But the Bush administration was not. It was caught between a Congress controlled by Democrats and grassroots opposition from populists. Compassionate conservatism had been abandoned, democracy promotion neglected, Social Security privatization and immigration reform defeated. Conservative critics derided Bush as an apostate whose social conservatism barely hid the fact that he was a big-spending liberal interventionist. Exhausted by war, depleted by a loss of key personnel, and dogged by Pelosi and Senate Democratic majority leader Harry Reid, Bush's second-term administration—with the notable exception of the surge—came up short.

The hits kept coming. In the spring of 2007, Jeane Kirkpatrick's posthumous study of post–Cold War foreign policy (she had died the previous December), *Making War to Keep Peace*, was published. The book garnered publicity for the neocon grande dame's admission that, while publicly supportive of Bush's right to invade Iraq, she privately opposed the war and believed that the administration's failure to account for postwar stabilization "helped to create the chaos that [had] overtaken the country." Kirkpatrick belonged to an earlier generation of neoconservatives who privileged order and deterrence over liberation and preemption. Her reprimand from the grave illustrated how far the Right's foreign policy had drifted from its Cold War moorings.[25]

When the 2008 presidential cycle began, John McCain campaigned for president on the success of the surge. He attacked former Massachusetts governor Mitt Romney's lukewarm support for the shift in strategy, and he won the New Hampshire primary and, eventually, the Republican nomination. But McCain was no one's idea of a conservative favorite. "It's entirely possible I will go the distance without saying I support a candidate," Rush Limbaugh told the *New York Times* in February 2008. Only when the *Times* published a lengthy piece insinuating a relationship between McCain and a lobbyist did Limbaugh rally to the defense of the Arizona senator.[26]

McCain's primary victory was an exception. Overall, the politics of Iraq no longer favored advocates of the invasion. A neophyte senator from Illinois named Barack Obama based his claim to the Democratic nomination on his criticism of the Iraq War, which he had opposed since 2002. Within the Republican Party, the gad-fly presidential candidacy of seventy-three-year-old antiwar GOP congressman Ron Paul of Texas revealed that a significant number of Republicans, especially young ones, were veering away from anything having to do with George W. Bush. "Paul represents a different Republican Party from the one that Iraq, deficits, and corruption have soured the country on," Christopher Caldwell explained in the *New York Times Magazine*. Paul was an early hit on social media. Clips of his interviews and debate performances went viral, in particular an exchange with former New York City mayor Rudy Giuliani over the causes of Osama bin Laden's war on the West. Paul became the emblem of dissent, fear, and protest for voters disaffected with the political process and the conservative establishment.[27]

The racist and anti-Semitic language that had been published in Paul's newsletters during the 1980s did not turn off his committed supporters. Paul was less sophisticated and literary than Pat Buchanan and more interested in constitutionalism and monetary policy than in manufacturing and trade. But both men opposed the "globalism" of a "neoconservative" foreign policy that sought to maintain Pax Americana. "Ron Paul's an old friend of mine and I like him, admire his consistency and his political courage," Buchanan told one interviewer. They were birds of a feather.[28]

Caldwell noticed that many of the people attending Paul rallies and meetups had connections to the John Birch Society. The anti-Communist group that Buckley had anathematized decades earlier was finding its way back into conservative politics. This was one of the many unanticipated results of the Iraq War. Its duration and cost exceeded the patience of the American public and much of the conservative and Republican grass roots. It catalyzed a revolt against the conservative and Republican establishment. Compassionate conservatism and the Freedom Agenda were not the only casualties of the war in Iraq. The barriers that had long insulated conservative elites from the dark side of their movement fell too.

The clash between technocrats of both parties and populists of the nationalist Right defined the post-Bush era. The suave, literary, Harvard-educated, unflappable Obama's opposite was Alaska governor Sarah Palin, who joined the McCain ticket on August 29, 2008, to uproarious applause from conservatives. Palin was a pro-life mother of five. Her oldest son served in the army, and her youngest child had Down's syndrome. She had battled with the GOP establishment in Juneau during her brief tenure as governor. And with her Pentecostal religion, folksy manner, and complicated educational and family history, she had more in common with many Republican (and Democratic) voters than with either Democratic or Republican elites.

But Palin was also unpolished and untested. Her resume was thin. She spoke from the gut, in tones and syntax unfamiliar to Washington. She often misstated the facts or gave confusing and substance-free answers to off-the-cuff-questions. Her combination of media stardom and antielitism made her an electric figure for the descendants of the New Right. But her lack of experience, unfamiliarity with the details of domestic and foreign policy at the federal level, and chaotic personal life worried both Democratic and Republican elites.

This anxiety often turned into unremitting hostility—which only reaffirmed her conservative movement support. The attacks on Palin caused many conservatives, including this writer, to rally to her defense and to the defense of the non-college-educated Republicans she represented. Palin also had a male counterpart in the person of Joe Wurzelbacher, a plumber in Toledo, Ohio, whose encounter with Obama on the street in early October 2008 dramatized incipient working-class resistance to liberal wealth redistribution. But it was Palin's placement on the national ticket that signified the arrival of populism at the highest levels of Republican politics and opened the door to presidential contenders from outside the system. Ironically, John McCain, a dyed-in the-wool member of the establishment, put her there. Palin's defenders in the conservative intellectual movement hoped that she would temper her populism with a respect for the establishment and its views of how politics ought to be conducted. What we missed—and what Palin understood—was that the establishment and its rules were on their way out the door.

The long-standing urge of street-corner conservatives and the New Right to oppose whatever the political class had to offer manifested itself in September 2008. The Great Recession triggered a global financial crisis weeks before Election Day. The bailouts necessary to rescue the global financial system erased whatever credibility elites had in the eyes of the populist Right. Most conservative lawmakers were not willing to reward bankers and automakers for the bad bets they had made during the housing bubble—even at the risk of economic calamity. As a result, the first version of the Troubled Assets Relief Program fell in the House of Representatives. Only after the stock market plunged did enough Republicans back the initiative for it to become law.

As the wars in Iraq and Afghanistan continued, the worst recession since the Great Depression took hold, and the election loomed, Republicans had two ways to express disgust with the tenure of George W. Bush. They could follow Bush's former secretary of state, Colin Powell, and endorse Barack Obama. Or they could rebel against the GOP "establishment" that had brought the country to this impasse. Most grassroots conservatives opted for the latter course.

John McCain went down to defeat. And President Bush's vision of an idealistic Republican Party went with him.

CHAPTER THIRTEEN

THE CRISIS OF THE
TWENTY-FIRST CENTURY

ERALDED AS A TRANSFORMATIONAL PRESIDENT WHO would enact a second New Deal, Barack Obama ended up the midwife of an antielitist, isolationist politics of national populism. By the time he arrived in Washington, DC, for his inauguration in January 2009, the Republican Party had been shattered, and the conservative movement was uncertain of its future. The intellectuals and leaders who had guided conservatism for decades were disappearing. Robert Bartley had died in 2003, Ronald Reagan in 2004, Milton Friedman in 2006, William F. Buckley Jr. in 2008, and Richard John Neuhaus and Irving Kristol in 2009.

Obama represented a young, multiracial generation that had witnessed the failures of social and religious conservatism to oust Bill Clinton, of national security conservatism to stabilize Iraq and Afghanistan, and of economic conservatism to prevent the Great Recession and global financial crisis. Obama spoke of a "postpartisan" awakening. He promised a restoration of etiquette and good feeling in Washington.

One week before taking the oath of office, Obama visited the home of George Will, where he had dinner with a group of

conservative journalists, including Bill Kristol, Charles Krauthammer, and David Brooks. The talk radio Right, meanwhile, viewed
the incoming president's overtures to conservative elites with suspicion. "This was inside-the-Beltway conservative pundits," Rush
Limbaugh told his audience, "and it was obvious to me Obama's
objective here is to sway what I call establishment punditry."[1]

Among the consequences of Obama's presidency was a widening gulf between Limbaugh's audience and "establishment
punditry." Obama framed his agenda as a restructuring of the
American political economy that would put the country on a "new
foundation" of equitable growth. It was an expansion of government that was sure to cross conservatives who worried about the
reach of the state. As the first black president, who had been raised
in Indonesia and Hawaii before attending Occidental College and
Columbia University, Obama was the target of conspiracy theories
and racism. All of the kooky things some inhabitants of the Right
had said about Bill Clinton were said about Obama too, in email
chain letters and elsewhere. But the fantasies about Obama also
carried with them the fear of foreign invasion: the conspiracists
said that he had been born in Kenya, that he was a Muslim, and
that he was a Communist.

In fact, Obama was nothing more than a conventional academic
liberal. He hewed closely to the beliefs and tastes of upscale, metro-
politan academics throughout the country. Like earlier Democratic
presidents, including John F. Kennedy, Obama used the extreme
Right as a foil for himself and a cudgel against congressional Republicans. He told audiences that the Republican Party was in the
grip of a "fever" of antielitism and antigovernment sentiment and
that the fever would break as he became more successful. But the
"fever" did not break. It swelled.

During the Obama years, images of decline, irreparable trans-
formations, unbridgeable divides, and fascistic liberals filled the
minds of conservatives. Every faction of the Right treated the

Obama presidency as an inflection point. America's fate would be decided one way or the other. It was said that Obama's victory presaged America's slide into European social democracy and global irrelevance. Obama's stated desire to reverse the Reagan revolution flamed conservative fears. Charles Krauthammer argued that Obama undermined the "moral foundation of American dominance."[2]

To "inside-the-Beltway" conservative analysts such as Krauthammer, Obama's foreign and domestic policies worked synergistically to undermine America's superpower status and bring an end to unipolarity. Obama's foreign policy of retrenchment opened space for challengers to fill. Obama's expansion of the welfare state crowded out funds for national defense. Nor was the potential cost limited to the United States. Foreign policy thinker Robert Kagan moved away from both neoconservatism and the *Weekly Standard* during the Obama years and adopted the label "liberal interventionist." Still, Kagan warned, Obama's policies threatened the "liberal world order" that America had sustained since 1945.[3]

LESS THAN A MONTH AFTER OBAMA'S INAUGURATION, THE GRASS-roots rebels who had marched against George W. Bush's immigration proposals and lobbied GOP congressmen to oppose the bank bailout were fighting the new president's tax, spending, environment, and health care plans. On February 19, 2009, the CNBC personality Rick Santelli delivered an on-air rant. His target was the expansion of the bailout and Obama's $1 trillion economic stimulus package. Santelli called for concerned Americans to hold a "tea party" like the patriots of the American founding.

The Tea Party was noteworthy for its hostility to both the Democratic and the Republican parties. When it turned to electoral politics, the Tea Party backed antiestablishment candidates, with a mixed record in general elections. That was because the Tea Party brought out both optimistic, forward-looking, mainstream supply-siders and pessimistic, anti-institutional, conspiracy-minded extremists. The "Birther" demand to see Obama's birth certificate attested to the prevalence of conspiracy theories in American life. The Tea Party's media spokesman, Fox host Glenn Beck, had an apocalyptic worldview in which the fate of the republic was one bad election away. References to shadowy groups and global bankers filled his monologues. He scribbled on a chalkboard.

"Establishment" pundits tended to gloss over the more exaggerated aspects of the Tea Party. They focused instead on its potential to ground the populist Right in the text and structure of the Constitution. George Will, for example, called the Tea Party "the most welcome political development since the Goldwater insurgency in 1964." Charles Krauthammer urged Republicans to adopt "a reformed, self-regulating conservatism that bases its call for minimalist government—for reining in the willfulness of presidents and legislatures—in the words and meaning of the Constitution." David Brooks wrote in the *New York Times*, "Personally, I'm not a fan of this movement," but "I can certainly see its potential to shape the coming decade."[4]

There was more to the Tea Party than constitutionalism, however. It was a manifestation of America's "folk libertarianism": a widespread oppositional attitude toward authority of all stripes. It was also anti–illegal immigration. When Congressman Joe Wilson screamed, "You lie!" at Obama during an address to a joint session of Congress in September 2009, he was referring to the possible eligibility of illegal immigrants for health coverage. Many members of the Tea Party were religious conservatives who opposed funding in the Affordable Care Act national health bill, aka "Obamacare," for insurance plans that covered abortion. They heard in Sarah Palin's invocation of "death panels" a warning against medical rationing and government-subsidized euthanasia.

The few remaining pro-life Democrats opposed the pro-choice elements of Obamacare until the last holdout, Bart Stupak, gave in. That guaranteed the health care bill's passage in the spring of 2010 (and doomed Stupak's reelection). Liberals mocked the apocryphal Tea Party protester who held a sign saying, "Keep your government hands off my Medicare." They did not understand that the Tea Party had no problem with universal entitlements in principle. Rather, it opposed redistribution: shifting tax dollars from middle-class entitlements to the nonworking poor.

In foreign policy, the Tea Party was noninterventionist and unilateralist. Kentucky senator Rand Paul was his father's son in politics. Utah senator Mike Lee and Texas senator Ted Cruz were suspicious of overseas entanglements. That did not mean the Tea Party was soft on terrorism, however. Far from it: its members viewed jihadism as a civilizational conflict with radical Islam. The Tea Party took its cues not from Francis Fukuyama but from Samuel P. Huntington. In 2011 the Tea Party rallied against a proposed mosque at Ground Zero, the site of the World Trade Center attacks, in New York City. The more extreme Tea Partiers, meanwhile, became convinced that the Muslim Brotherhood was engaged in a conspiracy to introduce Islamic sharia law into the United States.

The conservative grass roots wanted to thwart Obama's perceived radicalism by any means. The nation was split between a ruling class and a country class, wrote international relations professor Angelo Codevilla in a best-selling 2010 book, *The Ruling Class*, which carried a foreword by Rush Limbaugh. Codevilla did not conceive of this division in partisan terms. "As it was before, and has been after Ronald Reagan," he wrote, "the Republican Party has zero claim to the Country Class's trust because it does not live to represent the Country Class." The constitutionalism of the Tea Party was not so much about what the Constitution said. It was about the willingness of Obama—and the judges and bureaucrats who shared his worldview—to recognize the document's guarantee of popular sovereignty.[5]

The challenge for the GOP was finding a way to harness the populist energy of the Tea Party while integrating it into a party agenda that could appeal to the suburban voters who had fled George W. Bush's wars and burst housing bubble. The party settled on a critique of the cost of Obama's programs and the lack of rapid job growth. Republicans said that embracing Obama's vision would put the country on a path to insolvency. And they found the ideal spokesman for the cause of budget restraint: Wisconsin Republican House member Paul Ryan.

Hailing from Janesville, Wisconsin, Ryan had scaled the conservative superstructure. He went from an internship with Congressman Bob Kasten, to working for Jack Kemp and Bill Bennett at Empower America, to winning a congressional election in 1998 at age twenty-eight. As ranking member of the Budget Committee in 2008, Ryan had released the "Path to Prosperity," an entitlement and tax reform that would have changed Medicare into a defined-contribution plan, introduced personal savings accounts into Social Security, and block-granted Medicaid to the states.

In 2010, in an anti-Obama wave election, Republicans won back the House of Representatives. Now Budget Committee chairman, Ryan reintroduced his bill. Rechristened "The Roadmap to America's Future," Ryan's revised proposal dropped the Social Security provisions and retained the current entitlement structure for everyone over the age of fifty-five. Boyish, earnest, and in command of detail, Ryan became the Republican spokesman. He overshadowed House Speaker John Boehner. The GOP House adopted the Roadmap in an April 2011 vote. Mitt Romney would choose Ryan as his vice presidential nominee the following year.

When the Romney-Ryan ticket went down to defeat in 2012, many Republican and conservative elites interpreted the loss as a reason to moderate the party. Immigration reform was a necessity. The GOP "autopsy" released in the spring of 2013 counseled Republicans to support the legalization of illegal immigrants and to move away from strong stances on abortion and same-sex marriage. "There's no need for radical change," wrote Krauthammer. "The other party thinks it owns the demographic future—counter that in one stroke by fixing the Latino problem." Michael Gerson and Peter Wehner made the same case in a *Commentary* essay. "Most voters already favor less punitive immigration policies than the ones angrily advocated by clenched-fist Republicans unwilling to acknowledge that immigrating—risking uncertainty for personal and family betterment—is an entrepreneurial act," wrote George Will.[6]

In 2013 former Florida governor Jeb Bush, son of one president and brother of another, coauthored *Immigration Wars* with lawyer (and now Arizona Supreme Court justice) Clint Bolick. They proposed a version of the compromise immigration reform that George W. Bush had twice failed to convince Congress to pass and that Florida senator Marco Rubio would soon fail to get across the finish line in the Senate. Bush and Bolick drew a connection between the tough views on immigration Romney adopted during the primary and his general election loss. They warned that Texas, Florida, and Arizona might go the way of California if Republicans did not adopt their preferred strategy. They argued that immigration hurt Romney, but they did not discuss its relation to John McCain's loss in 2008. The Arizona senator had been the main advocate for the second-term Bush plan. It seemed to do him no good in 2008.

The conservative grassroots, talk radio, and activist network argued that Romney had failed because he was a creature of the party establishment. After all, during his four years as governor of Massachusetts from 2003 to 2007, he had been the architect of the law that became the model for Obamacare. In the final weeks of the 2012 election, moreover, Romney had failed to stand up to the bias of debate moderator Candy Crowley of CNN when she erroneously and improperly took Obama's side during an exchange over the president's response to the terrorist attack on the US consulate in Benghazi, Libya. Romney hadn't been combative enough. He had focused on the economy, which was sluggish but growing, to the exclusion of social issues. He represented the executive suite rather than the laborers without college degrees who swung elections.

Steve Sailer, a contributor to paleoconservative journals, put forward an alternative to the Jeb Bush–RNC autopsy strategy of outreach to minority groups and young people. Sailer called his approach "in-reach." Because Republicans drew primarily from white voters, especially married white voters with families, Sailer reasoned that the party should seek to boost turnout among its core constituency rather than fritter away political capital on minority groups whose objections to the GOP were in all likelihood insurmountable. Sailer's thesis found empirical support when election analyst Sean Trende examined the "missing white voters" in the 2012 election. "The increased share in the minority vote as a percent of the total vote is not the result of a large increase in minorities in the numerator, it is a function of many fewer whites in the denominator," wrote Trende. The drop-off had been greatest in the rural areas of rust belt states like Ohio.[7]

The dueling autopsies—outreach versus in-reach—fueled the distrust and loathing between the conservative "establishment" and the talk radio Right. The rise of social media during the first decades of the twenty-first century exacerbated this divide. Celebrities, provocateurs, presidential aspirants, and established media personalities had the largest Facebook and Twitter accounts, but technology altered the forms of communication to such a degree that no one editor or journal had the ability to establish the definitive conservative position. Any man, woman, or child with a WordPress or Facebook or Twitter or Periscope or YouTube account could advocate for a cause, support a candidate, voice an argument, and share a story, no matter how politically incorrect or outright racist or loony the words uttered might be. An alternative viewpoint was always one click of the keyboard away.

Social media tore down the walls that separated the credentialed from the fringe. The very terms "credentialed" and "fringe" became fraught in a world where opinions were accessed directly and where there was no third-party validation. Social media undermined the authority of elites to rule from above in every country, in every industry, in every sphere of human activity. Conservative intellectual elites were not immune from this development. The boundaries of "permissible dissent" that Pat Buchanan had complained about were washed away in an unending digital flood.

Wild accusations zipped across the Internet at light speed. The "Birther" smear was just a start. In 2010 Dinesh D'Souza had released *The Roots of Obama's Rage*, arguing that the president was motivated by his Kenyan father's anticolonial Marxism. Newt Gingrich provided a cover blurb. Then D'Souza adapted the book into a high-grossing 2012 movie, *2016: Obama's America*. Obama's anti-Western ideology, D'Souza said, inspired the president consciously to undermine America's economic and national security.[8]

The loudest antiestablishment voice was Breitbart.com. Its founder, Andrew Breitbart, had apprenticed under Matt Drudge. Breitbart believed politics was downstream from culture and that conservatives and liberals were in a political-cultural war. There could be only one victor. Breitbart pioneered the use of new media to advance conservative politics. His high point came when he received explicit photos of Anthony Weiner, the New York congressman married to Hillary Clinton's closest aide. This exclusive resulted in Weiner's resignation—and in vindication of the Breitbart model.

When Breitbart died suddenly in 2012, his company fell into the hands of his friend and collaborator Stephen K. Bannon. Bannon was a fifty-nine-year-old navy veteran who had worked at Goldman Sachs before investing in Biosphere 2, an earth science research facility in the Arizona desert. He also produced conservative documentaries. Bannon believed that the United States was on the cusp of a revolution. He subscribed to a cyclical theory of history in which a cataclysm that begins with every third generation is resolved in a "fourth turning." The global financial crisis, Bannon thought, was the nemesis of the third generation after World War II.[9]

Bannon had supported Reagan. But he turned against George W. Bush when the wars in Iraq and Afghanistan dragged on, the southern border remained open, and the Republican president bailed out Wall Street. In an interview with documentarian Errol Morris for the film *American Dharma* (2018), Bannon recalled his disgust upon seeing that the uniform his daughter wore to her graduation from West Point had been made in Vietnam.

Bannon believed that the elites who congregated each year in Davos, Switzerland, to discuss the future of global capitalism and the "rules-based international order" were reenacting David Halberstam's tale of Vietnam-era folly, *The Best and the Brightest* (1972). He was convinced that American businessmen and politicians turned a blind eye to the rising threat of China out of greed and willful ignorance. He reconfigured *Breitbart* into an antiestablishment assault vehicle.

The site hit Republicans and Democrats alike for weakness on immigration, willingness to offshore American jobs, and acquiescence in "endless wars" in the Middle East. Bannon was ready to abandon the label "conservative" altogether. He preferred "nation-state populism" or "national populism" as a description of his views. He told one interviewer that *Breitbart* was a "platform" for the "alt-right," an amorphous anti-Semitic and racialist online movement that defined itself in opposition to the "Conservatism Inc." of the Beltway.[10]

Conservatives grew especially angry when Chief Justice John Roberts, a Bush appointee, voted in 2012 to uphold the constitutionality of the Obamacare requirement that individuals purchase health insurance. And yet Roberts's vote, and the reaction to it, signaled how much America's legal culture had moved toward the right. As the number of legal conservatives on the Court increased, the grounds of legal debate shifted. The decades-old argument between originalism and so-called living constitutionalism turned into a contest between competing understandings of originalism.

Having seen what the Earl Warren Court did with judicial power, Antonin Scalia and Robert Bork advocated an ethic of judicial restraint and deference to legislatures. Over time, however, conservative judges focused more and more on restraining legislatures through the courts by invalidating some laws as unconstitutional. Originalism was both a "shield" against judicial overreach and a "sword" to be used against acts of Congress. In *United States v. Lopez* (1995), for example, the Supreme Court knocked down the Gun Free School Zones Act of 1990 for exceeding congressional authority.

Justice Clarence Thomas was a critical figure in this debate. His interest in natural law and his willingness to recognize rights not mentioned specifically in the text of the Constitution were amplified by the increasingly influential movement of legal scholars who called for "judicial engagement"—whereby judges ruled against unconstitutional statutes—rather than "judicial restraint." Foremost among these legal minds was Randy Barnett, author of *The Structure of Liberty* (1998). Barnett was a convincing advocate for his position. George Will, for instance, had defended Bork's judicial restraint in the 1980s but embraced Barnett's judicial engagement in the 2010s, even writing the foreword for his *Our Republican Constitution* (2016).

By 2012, judicial engagement had achieved mainstream credibility. "The chickens of the conservative commitment to judicial restraint had thus come home to roost," Barnett said of Roberts's decision in favor of Obamacare. Of course, some might wonder how "judicial restraint" describes a single justice rewriting a statute to preserve the individual mandate as a "tax" rather than a regulation, especially given that the Court's leading originalist, Antonin Scalia, condemned Roberts's move in scathing prose.[11]

The restrainers worried that judges would view themselves as not only readers but makers of law. That is, in effect, what happened in 2015, when Justice Anthony Kennedy cast the deciding vote in *Obergefell v. Hodges* and established a constitutional right to same-sex marriage. His decision nullified bans on gay marriage in thirty-one states. Social conservatives were apoplectic at Kennedy's judicial usurpation.[12]

Ironically, two center-right authors, Andrew Sullivan and Jonathan Rauch, had done the most to popularize the idea of gay marriage as a fundamentally conservative act—as a bourgeois commitment to an institution, the family, that conservatives prized. Or as David Brooks put it in a 2003 *New York Times* column in support of same-sex marriage, "The conservative course is not to banish gay people from making such commitments. It is to expect that they make such commitments." But gay rights never had much appeal for movement conservatives, despite arguments for fair treatment of homosexuals in *National Review* beginning in 1974. (It's worth noting that some of these articles were written pseudonymously to protect the authors' identities—a sign of just how far gays had to go to avoid vilification.) Though gays were well represented in conservative and Republican circles, most of the movement opposed same-sex marriage on constitutional as well as moral grounds. That mismatch resulted in embarrassment whenever a conservative who opposed gay rights in public was revealed to have engaged in homosexual activity in private.[13]

Nor did it help conservatives when their spokesmen engaged in deliberately provocative rhetoric. One of Buckley's worst moments, for instance, was his suggestion in the *New York Times* in 1986 that "everyone detected with AIDS should be tattooed in the upper forearm, to protect common-needle users, and on the buttocks, to prevent the victimization of other homosexuals." Ultimately, opposition to gay rights did little to increase conservatism's appeal among young Americans, who backed same-sex marriage and prided themselves on their values of tolerance and inclusion.[14]

Sullivan, a popular blogger whose self-professed conservatism did not preclude him from supporting Obama, felt that the Right's stance on gays demonstrated its subordination to the religious Right. He espoused a Burkean conservatism of adaptation to changing circumstances. "A conservative in government expects such changes in society as time goes by," he wrote in *The Conservative Soul* (2006). "His job is to accommodate them to existing institutions." But the Right no longer widely practiced this sort of institutionalism. By Obama's second term, the populist American Right was less interested in preserving institutions than in tearing them down.[15]

OBAMA'S TOTAL WITHDRAWAL OF US TROOPS FROM IRAQ IN 2011 and his failure to enforce the red lines he drew against Syrian dictator Bashar al-Assad in 2013 established the ground for both the rise of the Islamic State of Iraq and Syria and the 2014–2015 European refugee crisis. Rising terrorism against Europeans and Americans galvanized Republican opinion in a national populist direction. Tea Party legislators devoted years to investigating the Obama administration's response to the attack in Benghazi in 2012. The administration's worries about Islamophobic backlash infuriated conservatives even more. The refugee crisis, made worse when German chancellor Angela Merkel welcomed more than a million asylum seekers into her country, empowered the nationalist Right in Europe. And it reinforced calls for border protection in the United States.

Immigration continued to separate Republican elites from the conservative grass roots. In 2013 Obama's call for an immigration amnesty had attracted some GOP officials, most prominently Florida senator Marco Rubio. But the plan failed amid an upsurge of antagonism helped along by *Breitbart*, Alabama senator Jeff Sessions, and Sessions's chief aide, a thirty-year-old speechwriter named Stephen Miller.

Miller was a California native drawn into the world of talk radio by black conservative host Larry Elder. Inspired by National Rifle Association (NRA) chairman Wayne LaPierre's *Guns, Crime, and Freedom* (1994), Miller tormented his affluent Santa Monica high school with conservative hijinks. As an undergraduate at Duke, he defended the members of his university's lacrosse team who had been unjustly accused of rape. A brief turn working for Tea Party congresswoman Michelle Bachmann led to the position with Sessions. Miller came to believe that immigration was the master issue of American politics: it involved questions of citizenship, patriotism, welfare, crime, and terrorism.

In 2014, as Muslim migrants from Africa and the Middle East moved toward Europe, the number of unaccompanied minors from Central America on America's southern border also began to rise. The Obama administration scrambled to address the growing humanitarian crisis, caused in part by the expectation that the president would legalize undocumented immigrants unilaterally at some point in his second term. That was, after all, exactly what Obama did in November 2014 for the undocumented parents of US citizens and legal residents, despite having just lost the Senate to the Republicans in the midterm election and saying multiple times that he lacked such authority.

Obama relied heavily on executive orders and bureaucratic decrees to enact his agenda. Many of these decisions split Republicans and contributed to mounting conservative feelings of helplessness over the loss of popular sovereignty. The trend began as early as 2011, when the Department of Education informed universities receiving public funds (i.e., practically all of them) that they should interpret Title IX regulations in such a way as to end due process for students accused of sexual assault on campus. In 2012 the Department of Health and Human Services mandated that insurance plans in the Obamacare exchanges pay for contraceptives and abortifacients. In 2015 the Environmental Protection Agency designated the coal industry for destruction with its Clean Power Plan and asserted authority to regulate huge swaths of private property with its Waters of the United States rule. In 2016 the Department of Education issued another ruling advising school systems to allow students who identified as transgender to use the bathrooms of their choice.[16]

These administrative dictates made many conservatives question the efficacy of controlling Congress. The legislative body seemed unable to prevent the Obama agenda in any fashion. This apparent inability of the GOP to check the Democratic president soured the grass roots on the party establishment. Talk radio hosts went from decrying Republican impotence to suggesting party elites actually were in cahoots with Obama. "The GOP brand was in such lousy shape because Republicans would suit up for one team and end up playing for another," wrote Laura Ingraham.[17]

To make matters worse, Obama's unpopular mix of aloof yet imperious governance accompanied a multidimensional social crisis. In 2012, in the title of his best-selling book, Charles Murray warned that America was *Coming Apart*. At the top of society, a self-perpetuating elite lived inside a bubble of affluent neighborhoods in postal codes Murray called "Super-Zips," while mass suffering played out below. Most Americans, Murray pointed out, did not enjoy the benefits of intact families, vibrant communities, and church membership. Be they known as James Burnham's "managerial elite," Robert Reich's "symbolic analysts" (from his 1991 book *Work of Nations*), the "cognitive elite" that Murray and Richard Herrnstein described in *The Bell Curve*, Christopher Lasch's "elites" (*Revolt of the Elites*, 1996), David Brooks's "Bobos"

(*Bobos in Paradise*, 2000), or Richard Florida's "creative class" (*The Rise of the Creative Class*, 2002), the Americans whose status was grounded in undergraduate and postgraduate educations and assortative mating were far removed from the rest of the country.[18]

Murray was not an optimist. Only a religious revival, he wrote, similar to the growth of Methodism in Victorian England, could restore social capital and repair the social fabric. Murray's colleague at the American Enterprise Institute, demographer Nicholas Eberstadt, cataloged the decline of work among males in their prime years. These men were dropping out of the workforce and, to a great degree, society as well. The welfare state sustained them. Through expanded Medicaid and disability programs, they came into contact with opiates. The addiction levels were staggering. Opioid and heroin abuse caused a spike in deaths, in some years killing as many Americans as had died in Vietnam. In a paper released in December 2015, Anne Case and Angus Deaton revealed that death rates among non-Hispanic whites experienced a "marked increase" between 1999 and 2013.[19]

All of this happened under the noses of most conservative and Republican elites. They lived in the wealthy Virginia and Maryland counties surrounding Washington, DC. They enjoyed life in the Super-Zips. They were not only center-right individuals adrift in a sea of blue. They also were separated from growing numbers of their own political party by background, education, income, and lifestyle.

In its attitudes and priorities, the white working class was closer to Kevin Phillips and Pat Buchanan than to Milton Friedman and William F. Buckley Jr. The issues that most deeply affected it— trade, illegal immigration, and drug addiction—were not at the top of the conservative intellectuals' to-do list. A major document of conservative reformers, the 2014 report *Room to Grow*, mentioned free trade twice, both times positively; it mentioned immigration and drug addiction not at all. The *Weekly Standard* did not reference the opioid addiction crisis until the late summer of 2016. These omissions happened not because conservative intellectuals were negligent but because such issues did not penetrate the bubble until the 2016 presidential campaign began.[20]

The "next-in-line" candidate that year was Jeb Bush. He announced his presidential campaign on June 15, 2015. The next day, Donald Trump rode down the escalator of his eponymous Manhattan tower and declared himself a candidate as well. The dark horse had arrived, bragging about his wealth and television ratings, declaring the American dream dead, and promising to build a wall to keep out illegal immigrants and "make America great again." The thrice-married Trump had changed his voter registration three times as well: from Republican to Reform Party, from Reform to Democrat, and, in 2009, from Democrat to Republican. He had no affiliation with the Republican Party establishment and no pull with conservative pundits. "It is simply childish to trust this contemptible parody of a father figure," wrote Michael Gerson in the *Washington Post*. George Will said that he deserved to lose fifty states. Krauthammer called him a "rodeo clown."[21]

Rush Limbaugh disagreed. The day Trump announced, he told his audience, "All of this, I'm telling you, is going to resonate with people. And here's something else to watch: The more the media hates this and makes fun of it and laughs, the more support Trump's going to get." And sure enough, within about a month, Trump had surpassed Bush in the national poll averages and become the frontrunner. He maintained that status throughout the primary— except for a few days in the beginning of November 2015 when another outsider, Dr. Ben Carson, briefly took the lead.[22]

Donald Trump was a showboat and celebrity, a self-promoter and controversialist. He was silly and mocking, a caricature of a caricature. Antiestablishment conservatives found him refreshing. Not one iota of Trump was politically correct. He played by no rules of civility. He genuflected to no one. He despised the media with the same intensity as the conservative grass roots. He challenged the conventional wisdom of both party establishments. He declared that illegal immigration and trade with China carried great costs. He directed his foreign policy not toward Eurasia so much as toward America's southern border. He followed Pat Buchanan in decrying outsourcing, foreign trade agreements, immigration, and the Iraq War.

That Trump chose illegal immigration as his main issue made him all the more polarizing, visceral, contentious, and spiteful. Immigration restriction had replaced Social Security as the "third rail" of American politics. Trump decided not only to touch the third rail but to hug it. It made him electric. Republicans, Democrats, journalists, corporations, entertainment and sports figures, and even the Pope felt it necessary to define themselves against him. Their flaunting of their moral superiority only made Trump more attractive to voters alienated from the political process. Rush Limbaugh read aloud a 1996 essay by New Right guru Sam Francis to explain Trump's appeal. "Angelo Codevilla in that original piece he did on the ruling class versus the country class, he predicted this as well," Limbaugh said.[23]

After terrorist attacks in Paris, France, and San Bernardino, California, in the fall of 2015, Trump announced his support for a ban on Muslim entry into the United States. The speed with which prominent Republicans and conservatives condemned his proposal revealed that the future of the GOP depended on the identity of the party's 2016 nominee. Nominating Trump would alter the character of the GOP in a fundamental way: just as Barry Goldwater had given conservatives a foothold in the GOP after decades of exile, just as George McGovern's nomination had caused liberal anti-Communist and Catholic working-class voters to leave the Democratic coalition, just as Ronald Reagan's nomination had confirmed the GOP's identity as a conservative, pro-life party, a Trump nomination would recalibrate American politics along the axis of national identity. Trump masterfully exploited these divisions within the conservative movement and the GOP as he accelerated the party's move toward national populism. He drew huge crowds to his tentpole rallies. He set the agenda. He made all the headlines.

As Trump moved closer to the GOP presidential nomination, it became clear that large parts of the conservative movement had different institutional priorities than many Republican voters. The most striking example of this disintermediation between intellectuals and voters was the "Against Trump" issue that *National Review* published on the eve of the 2016 Iowa Caucuses. Following Buckley's example, the editors sought to consign the star of *Celebrity Apprentice* to the dustbin of conservative pretenders. They brought together some of the biggest names on the right. "Trump is a philosophically unmoored political opportunist who would trash the broad conservative ideological consensus within the GOP in favor of a free-floating populism with strong-man overtones," said an unsigned editorial. "If Donald Trump wins the Republican nomination, there will once again be no opposition to an ever-expanding government," wrote Glenn Beck. "I think this is a Republican campaign that would have appalled Buckley, Goldwater, and Reagan," wrote the vice president of the Cato Institute. "A shoot-from-the-hip, belligerent show-off is the last thing we need or can afford," wrote Thomas Sowell. Among the contributors who warned conservatives and Republicans about embracing Trump's candidacy were the editors of *First Things* and *National Affairs*, Brent Bozell III, two former attorneys general, and the presidents of the Club for Growth and the Ethics and Religious Liberty Commission of the Southern Baptist Convention. *National Review* editor Rich Lowry unveiled the symposium in an interview on Fox News Channel with anchor Megyn Kelly.[24]

None of it mattered. Not only was this advice ultimately disregarded and Trump nominated and elected president, but the editors

of *National Review* found themselves the subjects of vitriolic criticism, ad hominem insults, and harassment on social media. They
were flayed as the actual traitors to the Right. Some donors to
the magazine were furious. Readers canceled subscriptions. What
might have been a laudable stand for principle inadvertently revealed both the ineffectuality of opinion journalism and the widening gulf between conservative intellectuals and the movement
they sought to lead. Donald Trump did not need *National Review*.
He had Twitter. And talk radio. And, increasingly, the Fox News
Channel itself.

Trump arrived at a time of dissociation—of unbundling, fracture, disaggregation, and dispersal. The disconnectedness was not
only social and cultural. It was also political—a separation of the
citizenry from the government founded in their name. Trump was
dismissed as "not a real conservative" because of his past positions
on abortion and guns and because of his current positions on entitlements, trade, and war. In truth he worked hard to forge alliances
with key constituencies within the conservative movement and Republican coalition. Since 2011, he had been unabashedly pro-life.
He was the NRA's dream candidate. He brought on supply-siders
Lawrence Kudlow and Steve Moore. He stirred the crowd at the
American Israel Public Affairs Committee and castigated Obama's
2015 nuclear deal with Iran. After Justice Scalia died suddenly in
early 2016, Trump worked with the Federalist Society to unveil a
list of potential Supreme Court nominees.

Trump's strongest supporters within the conservative movement came from the network of institutions, spokesmen, and
causes that the New Right established during the 1970s. Trump
deployed New Right symbols. His antagonism toward the establishment was obvious. The single-issue groups for gun rights, for
the right to life, and for the right to work were all behind him. So
was the American Conservative Union. Phyllis Schlafly was one
of his most committed supporters before her death in 2016. Pat

Buchanan cheered him on. Jerry Falwell Jr. endorsed him. Richard Viguerie said, "Donald Trump will be helping to advance the conservative movement." John Wayne's daughter endorsed Trump. Clint Eastwood expressed tepid support.[25]

Trump did well where George Wallace had done well. He flourished in places with whites without college degrees, in the South, and in ethnic blue-collar enclaves such as Staten Island. In Orange County, California, Trump took 77 percent of the Republican primary vote. Just north of Orange County sit the Claremont Colleges, where Harry Jaffa taught until his death in 2015. At the pro-Trump Claremont Institute and in its publication, the *Claremont Review of Books*, a Manichean understanding of politics and an apocalyptic vision of the nation's future took hold. For decades, the American Right had defended the spirit of institutions such as the academy, the Congress, the presidency, the market, the church, and even the press from liberals and radicals. Now large sectors of the Right were giving up on those institutions as hopelessly corrupt.

Now the dividing line was between those who thought that the result in 2016 would determine the nation's continued existence and those who thought that it was just another election. "Those most likely to be receptive of Trump," wrote Claremont Institute senior fellow John Marini, who had tutored Justice Clarence Thomas in political philosophy years before, "are those who believe America is in the midst of a great crisis in terms of its economy, its chaotic civil society, its political corruption, and the inability to defend any kind of tradition—or way of life derived from that tradition—because of the transformation of its culture by the intellectual elites." For Claremont senior fellow Angelo Codevilla, the nation might continue under Democratic nominee Hillary Clinton, but the republic itself had long since expired.

A third Claremont figure, former George W. Bush official Michael Anton, wrote under a pseudonym that "2016 is the Flight 93 election: charge the cockpit or you die. You may die anyway."

Conservatism had failed to stop America's descent, Anton wrote. Conservative intellectuals were more interested in preserving their status and wealth than in saving the nation. The republic was dying because of immigration. "The election of 2016 is a test—in my view, the final test—of whether there is any *virtù* left in what used to be the core of the American nation." Rush Limbaugh read the entire piece on the air.[26]

Noticeably absent in all of these essays was empirical evidence. Notably absent in all of these essays was sympathy for contemporary America, and reasons it might be worth defending, and charity for "Blue" America. Such qualifications did not count for much in a media environment shaped by Facebook, Twitter, talk radio, and cable television. The large and diverse conservative movement simply could not handle the compound stresses of war, immigration, and populism. The opinions of Donald Trump the person became hard to disentangle from assessments of his program. Fights over his rhetoric, behavior, and symbols, such as the border wall (decades after the fall of a different wall), morphed into struggles over his economic and foreign policies, then changed back again. It was easy to score points by associating one's opponents with either Trump's most radical supporters or his most vociferous detractors. Alt-right trolls, libertarians, Reformocons, Never Trumpers, Claremonsters, traditionalist Catholics, paleos, a few remaining neos, and other varieties of conservatives competed for attention online.

Conspiracies flourished. Civil discourse became a relic. Reputations were bruised, jobs were lost, alliances sundered, friendships ended, and conservatism ruptured. Bill Kristol, for example, had endorsed David Horowitz's collection of essays, *The Politics of Bad Faith* (1998), but when Kristol began lobbying individuals to launch an anti-Trump Republican or independent campaign, Horowitz attacked him on *Breitbart* as a "renegade Jew." Kristol shrugged it off. "That's something new," he said. And it was new.

The anti-Semitism directed at Trump critics such as Kristol and former *Breitbart* contributor Ben Shapiro had an intensity and force that was as novel as it was frightening.[27]

Trump's luck was incredible. First he defeated the Republican establishment in the primary. Then, in the general election, he faced Hillary Clinton, who was just as establishmentarian as Jeb Bush and even more polarizing and disliked. Trump was the most unpopular major party nominee in history, but Hillary Clinton was number two. She played into Trump's hands, demeaning his supporters and catering to the wishes of her Democratic base rather than those of independent swing voters.[28]

And she paid for it. By 2:30 a.m. on the morning after Election Day, the Republican nominee had won enough states to be declared the winner. The GOP ticket racked up 304 Electoral College votes to Clinton's 227, even as it lost the popular vote, 46 to 48 percent. And on January 20, 2017, Donald J. Trump became the forty-fifth president of the United States.

CHAPTER FOURTEEN

THE VIRAL PRESIDENT

D ONALD TRUMP WAS THE LATEST MANIFESTATION OF A
recurring antiestablishment spirit in America. He was a
populist like Andrew Jackson, William Jennings Bryan, Huey
Long, Father Charles Coughlin, Joseph McCarthy, George Wallace, Ross Perot, Pat Buchanan, and Sarah Palin. He represented
a rejection of the way in which America had been run since the
turn of the century. The Republican Party and conservative establishment were too weak to contain him. If he had lost to Hillary
Clinton, the antiestablishment national populists might have been
thwarted. Their opposite numbers in the GOP might have been
strengthened. Instead, Trump won.

By becoming president, he altered the direction not only of the
country but of the American Right. Trump's inaugural address,
with its description of "American carnage," was a wake-up call
for Republicans who thought he might become more conventional
when he moved into the White House. Leaving the ceremony,
George W. Bush was heard saying that Trump's speech was "some
weird s—t."[1]

Things might have made more sense to Bush if he had studied the
two thinkers with the most insight into the Trump phenomenon:

375

Michael Goldhaber and Martin Gurri. Both men came up with conceptual frameworks to understand media and politics in the Trump era long before the man himself ran for president. Goldhaber, a scientist, was the first to propose the idea of an "attention economy" in an article for *Wired* magazine in 1997. The Internet, Goldhaber argued, created a star system whose winners had the imagination and gall to hijack our time and concentration. Gurri, a former analyst for the Central Intelligence Agency, noticed in 2010 that social media enabled a "revolt of the public" against existing structures of authority. Be it the kleptocratic Egyptian regime of Hosni Mubarak, social order in Ferguson, Missouri, or the 2016 campaign trail, Facebook, Twitter, SMS, Instagram, YouTube, and the rest allowed noncredentialed information to go viral, enrage millions, and inspire and organize mobs.[2]

With his Twitter account, mass rallies, background in television, and shamelessness, Donald Trump was the perfect accelerant for the trends Goldhaber and Gurri pinpointed. But was he more than a mere social media phenomenon? And what did he say about the nature of the American Right? The rise of Donald Trump, Brexit, and nation-state populism throughout the world certainly suggested that something had changed in global politics. The trouble was that no one was able to say definitively what it was.

BEGINNING IN 2016, INTELLECTUALS WHO FAVORED TRUMP searched for a new touchstone for conservative thought and politics. Broadly speaking, they adopted the banner of national populism. They believed that the nation-state was the core unit of geopolitics. They thought that national sovereignty and independence were more important than global flows of capital, labor, and commodities. They reacted, in different ways, to perceived failures, whether of William F. Buckley Jr.'s conservatism, George W. Bush's presidency, or the inability of the conservative movement to stop same-sex marriage and the growth of the administrative state.

They turned away from libertarian arguments and economistic thinking. They followed the trail Patrick Buchanan had blazed two decades earlier. "The ideas made it, but I didn't," said the seventy-eight-year-old paleoconservative, who had lost his cable contract in 2012 but still churned out a syndicated column twice a week.[3]

The writers and thinkers on the margins of the GOP—the Claremont gang, paleoconservatives, social traditionalists, and antiestablishment national populists—felt that Trump's victory favored their side. Such vindication may have been a mirage. Trump failed to win a popular vote majority—he captured a smaller percentage of the vote than Mitt Romney had in 2012. His Electoral College win rested on seventy-seven thousand voters spread across three states. And for all his personal excesses and haphazard policy-making, Trump stuck rather closely to the Republican agenda of tax cuts, defense spending, and conservative judicial appointments. He rarely broke faith with either the New Right interest groups he had wooed during the campaign or with his core supporters, who would continue to defend him, he once said, even if he shot someone in the middle of Fifth Avenue. Trump fans stuck with him as he was dogged by accusations that he had colluded with Russia to win the election—a strange reversal of the post-Vietnam order in which Democrats were now anti-Russia hard-liners and Trump conservatives were doves.

Trump's presidency emboldened the forces within the conservative movement that had long sought to expel the neoconservatives and libertarians. On February 21, 2017, a reception was held at the Harvard Club in New York to mark the beginning of a new conservative journal. *American Affairs* and its thirty-year-old founder, Julius Krein, opposed "neoliberalism," the set of public beliefs and practices that, since the Ronald Reagan era, had privileged the market over the state and the individual over the community. For Krein and his deputy editor, University of Dallas political scientist Gladden Pappin, the neoliberal regime had weakened America vis-à-vis China by hollowing out the nation's industrial base and promoting self-seeking individualism. The result was the social crisis from which Trump emerged.

The editors of *American Affairs* supported universal government-provided health insurance, government-directed industrial policy and research and development, and a debt-financed cash benefit for parents with children that, at the present fertility rate, would consume 6.5 percent of gross domestic product (GDP). (At the time of writing, defense spending is 3 percent of GDP.) Much as liberals had spent decades problematizing conservatism, the contributors to *American Affairs* began to treat "liberalism" as a problematic ideology—and not just liberalism as incarnated in the agenda of the Democratic Party. Every issue of *American Affairs* diagnosed and sought to combat liberalism itself: the political philosophy of individual rights and consensual government developed by Thomas Hobbes, John Locke, Montesquieu, and the American Founders.[4]

Because its origins were so closely related to Trump's candidacy and to Trump's own criticisms of the Republican establishment, there was some reason to expect that *American Affairs* might play the same role in defining and guiding the intellectual direction of Trump's presidency that *National Review*, the *Public Interest*, and *Commentary* had played for Reagan's and that the *Weekly Standard* had for George W. Bush's. The presence at the magazine's debut of the Silicon Valley investor Peter Thiel fed into this presupposition.

The son of German immigrants to the United States who arrived in Cleveland when he was one year old, Thiel had founded the conservative *Stanford Review* while an undergraduate in Palo Alto and worked in law before entering finance. Founding CEO of PayPal, a director of Facebook, and a friend of entrepreneur Elon Musk, Thiel was a contrarian thinker drawn to unconventional views. He donated to Trump, became the first out gay man to address a Republican convention in sixteen years, and joined the president's tech council at the outset of the administration. Thiel's biggest fear was economic and technological stagnation. He contrasted the benefits of technological innovation with the neutral or regressive effects of economic globalization. He also shared with the editors of *American Affairs* a skepticism of liberal democracy and worried that freedom and democracy were no longer compatible.[5]

President Trump was less interested in the contents of *American Affairs* than in tax cuts, Obamacare repeal, and who had been mean to him on television that morning. There was no distinguishing between "Trumpism" and Trump. His rejection of politics as usual included the "decision-making loop" through which ideas traveled from the conservative superstructure to the legislative and executive branches of government. All that mattered to Trump was the last thing you said about him. His impulses replaced the daily schedules and routine processes of earlier White Houses. And his personal behavior put *American Affairs* in a bind.

Any influence that the journal might have had eroded further in the summer of 2017, after Trump's tin-eared and self-indulgent response to the death of a counterprotester at an alt-right rally in Charlottesville, Virginia. Krein disavowed his support of the president. In the pages of the *New York Times*, he wrote, "Mr. Trump has betrayed the foundations of our common citizenship." Rather than becoming the quarterly journal of Trumpism, *American Affairs* turned into something rather different: the quarterly journal of postliberalism.[6]

Four thinkers led the postliberal turn within conservative intellectual circles: *First Things* editor R. R. Reno and Israeli political philosopher Yoram Hazony (who were both on the *American Affairs* board of advisers), political philosopher Patrick Deneen, and Harvard Law School professor Adrian Vermeule. Reno had become editor of *First Things* in 2011. A former professor of theology at Creighton University, he was born an Episcopalian but converted to Roman Catholicism in 2004. Under his direction, *First Things* began moving away from the religious neoconservatism of Richard John Neuhaus, Michael Novak, and George Weigel and assumed a more adversarial posture toward the modern world. Reno's 2016 book *Resurrecting the Idea of a Christian Society* warned of a dissolving middle class and an unstable polity. As he put it in the *New York Times*, Trump succeeded "because over the last two decades our political elites, themselves almost entirely white, have decided, for different reasons, that the white middle class has no role to play in the multicultural, globalized future they envision, a future that they believe they will run."[7]

This sort of sweeping generalization had become common in conservative talk. Reno interpreted Trump's victory as the repudiation of Ronald Reagan's philosophy of government. The new politics, he said, would concern itself with the debate between globalism and national solidarity. The defense of the individual that characterized the politics of Reagan and Buckley was no longer relevant. Nor were the intellects who had shaped Reno's own publication. In the fall of 2017 Reno attacked Novak, who had died earlier in the year. Reno denied that he and *First Things* were anticapitalist. "I count myself on Madison and Hamilton's side," he wrote. And Trump's.[8]

Born in Israel, Yoram Hazony attended Princeton, where he cofounded the conservative *Princeton Tory*. He studied political philosophy at Rutgers, home to the legendary communitarian Wilson Carey McWilliams, and received his PhD in 1993. In 2016 he turned his attention to nationalism. The idea of cultural units called nations was not something to fear, Hazony said. Nations were a conservative force. In Hazony's telling, nationalism and imperialism were opposites, and liberalism was an imperial ideology. It erased national attachments in favor of universal principles of reason.

Patrick Deneen also held a negative view of liberalism. He understood liberal political thought as the engine of both radical individualism and state control—neither of which he liked. Like Hazony, Deneen saw liberalism as an abstract theory unattuned to the empirical realities of human life. Also like Hazony, Deneen wrote that most American conservatives were not really conservative. They were classical liberals.

Hazony and Deneen differed on the question of America. For Hazony, the United States retained preliberal elements and institutions, such as the family, religious feeling, and national pride. It could be rehabilitated. But Deneen, echoing arguments Brent Bozell had made in *Triumph* magazine decades earlier, saw the United States as the paragon of liberalism. It had to be refounded. Liberalism was acidic. It ate away at family, community, and faith. That was "why liberalism failed"—the title of Deneen's 2018 book.[9]

Adrian Vermeule also denied that there was any possibility of going back to an earlier, more modest liberalism. He argued that since originalism—the idea that judges should interpret laws with reference to the text of the Constitution—"has now outlived its utility," the Right should embrace a "common good constitutionalism" whose object is "certainly not to maximize individual authority or to minimize the abuse of power (an incoherent goal in any event), but instead to ensure that the ruler has the power needed to rule well." Yet the use of coercive power to engineer "more authentic desires" separated progressive liberalism from its classical antecedents. Perhaps the postliberals had more in common with their opponents than they were willing to admit.[10]

Vermeule espoused "integralism." This Catholic teaching held that economic, political, and religious life should work together in furtherance of the common good. Integralism found a receptive audience among a rising generation of young traditional Catholics who came of age during a time of institutional and social disruption. These Millennial and Zoomer Catholics looked upon the religious neoconservative thinkers as obsolete—the church child-abuse scandal, the Iraq War, the judicial recognition of same-sex marriage, and the dislocations of the early twenty-first century had delegitimized them. The prevalence of social media allowed these critics of the religious neoconservatives to find each other online at websites such as "The Josias," founded by a Cistercian monk in his early thirties named Pater Edmund Waldstein. Like Brent Bozell in the 1960s, integralists denied that they were theocrats. But it could be difficult to tell.

Postliberal thought was out of step with American politics. That was why postliberals and integralists looked to European national populists for models. In some precincts on the right, Trump, Brexit, and Muslim immigration contributed to a reevaluation of strongmen. Some conservatives praised the Law and Justice Party in Poland, Prime Minister Viktor Orbán of Hungary, and Deputy Prime Minister Matteo Salvini of Italy. They shared social conservatism, opposition to the European Union, and tough enforcement of borders. In a February 2017 talk sponsored by the Claremont-influenced Hillsdale College, Christopher Caldwell said that Vladimir Putin was an iconic figure in the global drive for national sovereignty. Putin held the same allure for the national populist Right that Ché Guevara had held for the Cold War Left. No wonder President Trump was a fan of the Russian autocrat.

For Trump's conservative opponents, this move away from liberalism redefined the political landscape. Liberal democracy required defense against authoritarianism. "One of the historic tasks of American conservatism has in fact been to preserve and strengthen American liberal democracy," wrote William Kristol in the *Weekly Standard*. Syndicated columnist Jonah Goldberg wrote that human nature was leading Americans away from institutions and practices that had enriched them for centuries. To David Frum, Trump was an autocrat manqué whose restless pushing of democratic norms caused grave damage to America. Charles Krauthammer saw the democratic world in a process of retraction. For Krauthammer, Trump was pulling Americans toward authoritarianism by presenting an image of strength counterposed against weak-kneed bureaucrats, professors, and officials.[11]

To a large degree, the debate over "liberalism" was confined to intellectual elites who were trying to make sense of the Trump phenomenon in theory while it was occurring in practice. One of the few pieces of evidence that postliberal thought had filtered to the conservative grass roots was a positive change in Republican attitudes toward Putin as measured by opinion polls. Still, the "postliberal" trend was nevertheless important because it revealed both the revulsion of religious conservatives at the direction of American society and the willingness of the rising generation of conservative intellectuals to abandon the ideas of political and economic freedom that had been so important to the movement since its beginnings. By the end of Trump's second year in office, most conservatives and Republicans rejected the idea that Trump represented a threat to their freedom. On the contrary, Trump enjoyed great popularity among both party regulars and self-identified conservatives. "Trump, with all his vices, has the necessary virtues and strength to fight the fight that needs to be fought," Norman Podhoretz told the *Claremont Review of Books* in 2019. "And if he doesn't win in 2020, I would despair of the future."[12]

The party and movement reoriented themselves around Donald Trump's personality, his irritations, his obsessions, and his inclinations. Not just talk radio and Fox were behind Trump. Newer outlets such as Newsmax, Sinclair Broadcasting, and One America News were even more devoted to him. The White House shut out think tanks that opposed Trump. The Conservative Political Action Conference, or CPAC, became, in the words of Trump counselor Kellyanne Conway, "TPAC."[13]

This reversal of intellectual currents manifested itself physically. Republican politicians who crossed Trump retired. The anti-Trump conservatives known as Never Trumpers left the GOP. Others died of natural causes. Fox's most famous Trump-critical pundit, Charles Krauthammer, succumbed to cancer in June 2018. Trump's high-profile Republican antagonist, John McCain, died that August. And in December 2018, Philip Anschutz, who had owned the *Weekly Standard* since buying it from Rupert Murdoch in 2009, closed down the magazine after it became the intellectual platform of "Never Trump" conservatism.

The writings of Sohrab Ahmari illustrated this metamorphosis. Born in 1985 in Iran, Ahmari immigrated with his mother to the United States when he was a teenager. His disgust at the injustices of the Iranian government during the Green Revolution of 2009 led him to begin writing opinion pieces while a student at Northeastern Law School. He decided against a career in law and joined the editorial page of the *Wall Street Journal*. The *Journal* sent him to London, where he converted to Catholicism in December 2016. The following year he joined the staff of *Commentary*, where he lamented the turn toward illiberalism in an October 2017 cover story that earned a rebuke from R. R. Reno.[14]

A little over a year later, when he became op-ed editor of the *New York Post*, Ahmari left both *Commentary* and liberalism behind. The word "liberty" faded from his vocabulary. He referred to "autonomy" instead. He attacked Trump critic Max Boot, a columnist for the *Washington Post* with whom Ahmari once had shared many foreign policy positions. In the spring of 2019, incensed by a Facebook advertisement for a "Drag Queen story hour" at a San Francisco library, he went on a Twitter rant against conservative bystanders in the "cultural civil war."

Ahmari singled out *National Review* staff member David French, an Evangelical Christian, First Amendment attorney, and Iraq War veteran who had flirted with launching an independent candidacy against Trump three years earlier. French was a prolific writer who castigated religious conservatives for overlooking Trump's character defects. Ahmari charged "conservative liberals like French" with abandoning the culture war because of their "great horror of the state, of traditional authority and the use of the public power to advance the common good, including in the realm of public morality." These conservative liberals were decent and civil opponents of progressive liberalism, but, according to Ahmari, "civility and decency are secondary values." His aim was "defeating the enemy and enjoying the spoils in the form of a public square re-ordered to the common good and ultimately the Highest Good."[15]

This statement of what might be called "integralism lite" mystified French. In a replay of long-ago debates over the relationship of freedom and virtue between *National Review*'s Frank Meyer and Brent Bozell, French said that Ahmari mistakenly had applied the metaphor of civilizational war to his own country, with baleful consequences. The situation was nowhere as dire as Ahmari portrayed it to be. After all, classical liberal principles of cross-examination, empiricism, due process, and the presumption of innocence had saved the 2018 nomination of Brett Kavanaugh to the Supreme Court after the appeals court judge had been accused, on the basis of no evidence, of sexual indiscretions as a teenager. "There is no political 'emergency' that justifies abandoning classical liberalism," French wrote. "And there will never be a temporal emergency that justifies rejecting the eternal truth."[16]

In a subsequent piece, Ahmari tried to add more substance to his vision of the common good. "The new American right doesn't ask: How would this or that development promote or impede individual autonomy?" he wrote. "Rather, it asks whether or not a new development allows man to participate in common goods proper to family, polity, and the religious community." As for specifics, Ahmari urged the Right to "tame Big Tech and tax well-endowed elite universities, to reenact Sunday trading bans, guarantee paid family leave, shield children from LGBT indoctrination, and so forth." That "so forth" covered a lot of ground.[17]

Support for Trump really held this newer Right together. Fox News host Tucker Carlson was among the few members of the Washington A-list to see Trump's appeal early on. Carlson had taken over Fox's 8 p.m. hour in April 2017, when sexual harassment accusations forced cable host Bill O'Reilly out of a job. (Roger Ailes, who had been fired from his position as head of Fox for similar reasons in 2016, died in May 2017.) Carlson became the most prominent expositor of national populism. "Left and right are no longer meaningful categories in America," he wrote in *Ship of Fools* (2018). "The rift is between those who benefit from the status quo, and those who don't." But the status quo was not so bad for Carlson. He directed much of his ire at Wall Street firms and so-called market fundamentalists, even as President Trump tweeted enthusiastically about the latest stock market highs.[18]

Where conservatives in the 1990s had emphasized character and moral education, conservatives in the Trump era were pounding the table about economics—and about how globalization had supposedly resulted in job loss and social fragmentation. Oren Cass, for example, was a former management consultant at Bain & Company and policy adviser to Mitt Romney who had become a critic of Wall Street and a supporter of industrial policy. At the root of America's troubles, Cass said, was the degradation of the American worker. Economic "piety"—an overemphasis on growing and redistributing GDP—blinded policymakers to the structures buttressing social health and stability.

Cass was not so different from the Reformocons who wanted to update conservative policy for contemporary circumstances. Nor were the postliberals so different from early neoconservatives who recognized the limits of capitalism and the necessity of some form of welfare state. But Reformocons and the early neoconservatives still believed in a free society. And the Trumpified Right had far greater confidence in the ability of the state to coordinate activity and attain its desired outcomes. The basis of this faith was unclear.

The national populisms of Europe did not map easily onto the Jacksonian impulse of Middle America. Nor could they substitute for it. America had been founded as a refuge for men and women fleeing the unity of church, state, and society. The anti-statist bent of "folk libertarianism" was unique to the United States. The Jacksonians, moreover, were the descendants of Scotch-Irish Protestants. The postliberals tended to be Roman Catholics. And Donald Trump was no integralist. He was the beneficiary of a revolt against the political leadership of both parties. For most Republicans, a vote for Trump had not been a rejection of Lockean liberalism. It had been a rebuke of Hillary Clinton.

The rise of postliberal thought was one way that Trump catalyzed long-standing debates within American conservatism. Another was Trump's resuscitation of the argument over the shape of the post–Cold War world. Back in the 1990s, Samuel P. Huntington and Pat Buchanan had been on one side and Francis Fukuyama and Charles Krauthammer on the other. Trump called the match, at least for the moment, in favor of Huntington and Buchanan. He effectively recycled Charles Lindbergh's America First ideology for the twenty-first century. He combined the aviator's disengaged nationalism with his own support for Israel and willingness to use economic coercion vis-à-vis allies like Canada, Mexico, and the European Union and adversaries like Iran, Venezuela, and China. If George W. Bush had looked to the future, seeing compassionate conservatism as an improvement on earlier Republican domestic policies and the war on terror and the Freedom Agenda as the next iteration of crusading anticommunism, Donald Trump looked to the past. His American Right resembled conservatism before the Cold War.

As Charles Kesler, editor of the *Claremont Review of Books*, first observed, Trump's foreign policy, protectionism, and immigration restrictionism recalled the presidencies not of Bush and Reagan but of Warren Harding and Calvin Coolidge. Like the

GOP presidents of the 1920s, Trump based the success of his presidency on broadly shared prosperity. Unlike the 1920s Republicans, however, Trump was a populist demagogue. But here, too, Trump was no alien invader of American conservatism. In his marriage of the policy views of Coolidge with the rabble-rousing of McCarthy, Donald Trump was the return of a repressed memory.[19]

BY HIS FOURTH YEAR IN OFFICE, WHEN HE DELIVERED HIS annual State of the Union address to a joint session of Congress on February 4, 2020, Trump was in a celebratory mood. The unemployment rate was the lowest it had been in half a century. Female and minority unemployment were at record lows. Incomes were rising. The poverty rate was falling. The previous summer, Trump had presided over an agreement with Mexico to hold asylum seekers from Central America on the southern side of the border while their claims were processed. Illegal crossings fell.

One month before Trump's speech, after Iranian-backed militias launched a series of rocket attacks against US installations in Iraq, Trump ordered the killing of General Qassim Soleimani, who ran the Quds Force within Iran's Islamic Revolutionary Guard Corps. Iran's response was meager. Trump also had personal reasons to be happy. Back in 2019, special counsel Robert Mueller, whom the Justice Department appointed to investigate whether Trump had engaged in a conspiracy with Russia to affect the 2016 presidential election, had been unable to charge him with obstruction of justice. (Mueller said that department policy prohibited him from doing so, but independent counsel Ken Starr nonetheless had informed Congress in 1998 that Bill Clinton, in his view, had committed perjury and obstruction.)

Then, in December 2019, the House had voted to impeach Trump for abuse of power and obstruction of Congress over his implied threat to withhold foreign aid to Ukraine unless its government opened a corruption investigation into the son of former vice president Joe Biden. But Trump, as he spoke in the House, knew that the next day the Senate would vote to acquit him. While several of his campaign associates faced jail time, Trump remained untouched. He used the investigations into his conduct and relationship with Russia as evidence that the establishment was out to get him.

Trump's reelection campaign was off to a strong start—and not only because voters, however much they disliked him personally, continued to give the president good marks on the economy. Trump's chances were high because the opposition party seemed determined to nominate an unelectable challenger. The day before the State of the Union, socialist Vermont senator Bernie Sanders had won the Iowa Democratic Party caucus. A week later, Sanders won the New Hampshire primary. And on February 22, he won the Nevada caucus.

Sanders's early wins highlighted the Democrats' lurch to the left. The most prominent members of the Democratic House majority were the far-left radicals who comprised "the Squad." Its leader, Representative Alexandria Ocasio-Cortez of New York, commanded a huge following on social media. Many of the Democratic presidential candidates embraced socialistic policies such as the government-expanding Green New Deal, the abolition of private health insurance as part of Medicare for All, the decriminalization of border crossings, and a universal basic income or federal jobs guarantee. The party coupled these far-reaching economic plans with pledges to expand civil rights and affirmative action programs. Trump understood that his best shot at reelection was public anxiety over the progressive agenda. "We will never let socialism destroy American health care," Trump told Congress.[20]

The State of the Union celebrated the populist ethos that brought Trump to power. In the gallery was Rush Limbaugh, who had recently disclosed he was suffering from stage 4 lung cancer. Trump announced that he was awarding Limbaugh the

Presidential Medal of Freedom—live on primetime television. The talk radio host was overwhelmed. Limbaugh had become devoted to this most unlikely president.

The two men had much in common. They both built media brands on their reputations for blunt and controversial speech. They both flouted the rules of political correctness. They both held expert opinion in disdain. They both personified the brash, irreverent, uncouth, confrontational, and demotic style that was dominant on the right.

As much as Trump's conduct and behavior divided the country, his policies and accomplishments unified conservatives and the Republican Party. He faced no primary challenger. Only one Republican senator, Mitt Romney of Utah, voted to convict him of the House's charges. The endless parade of controversies over Trump's insulting tweets and off-the-cuff remarks had become just another part of the political landscape. It was background noise that many people simply ignored. For conservatives and Republicans, the constant argument over what Trump did or did not do, what he did or did not say, was either nonsense invented by a hostile media or the annoying but bearable cost of restricting immigration, cracking down on China, exerting maximum pressure on Iran, confirming originalist judges, promoting job creation, and resisting socialism and identity politics.

Trump changed his party. He changed the conservative movement. The party no longer openly discussed giving illegal aliens a pathway to US citizenship. The party no longer championed multilateral trade deals. The party no longer brought up Social Security and Medicare. The party no longer defended the Iraq War. These shifts may or may not have been correct as a matter of principle. They may or may not have been in the GOP's long-term interest. But they could not be denied.

And Trump changed the Democratic Party. Antipathy for him pushed it to the left. At the same time, in defiance of Trump's antielitism and contempt, the party became more closely tied to the national security and intelligence establishment, to the tech giants in Silicon Valley, and to the national print and television media. Progressives became less interested in the fortunes of the working class, especially the white working class, than in advancing the interests of what French political economist Thomas Piketty called the "Brahmin Left." Its base was affluent, upwardly mobile professionals in the cities and inner suburbs.

For all their determination to transform America into a social democracy, the Democrats accepted some of Trump's alterations to US political economy. They remained circumspect about major trade agreements. Nor were they about to reverse Trump's move of the US embassy in Israel to Jerusalem, or his recognition of Israeli sovereignty over the Golan Heights, or the Abraham Accords he superintended between Israel, the United Arab Emirates, and Bahrain in the fall of 2020. Many Democrats also recognized that China was at best a strategic competitor and at worst a geopolitical adversary.

By the time Trump delivered his 2020 State of the Union address, the first cases of the COVID-19 coronavirus had been confirmed in the United States. Originating in Wuhan, China, the virus transformed global economics, politics, and society. As case numbers mounted in February, Trump downplayed the seriousness of what would soon be declared a pandemic. He said he did not want to sow panic and jeopardize the economy. He barred certain forms of travel to and from China. He visited the headquarters of the Centers for Disease Control and Prevention in Atlanta. He also continued to hold campaign rallies and complained about media coverage of the virus.

It soon became clear that the coronavirus would be a disaster of historic proportions. A flight to safety occurred in both economics and politics. Just when Sanders appeared unstoppable, Representative James Clyburn of South Carolina, the highest-ranking African American in Congress, endorsed former vice president

Biden, whose third campaign for president seemed on the verge of failure. Biden had been leading Trump in general election polls for months. Democrats believed him to be the most electable candidate. His defeat might hand reelection to Trump. But Clyburn came through: Biden won the South Carolina primary in a landslide. The party consolidated behind him. The candidates with profiles most like Biden's dropped out. Their supporters turned to Biden on Super Tuesday, March 3, when he took ten states to Sanders's four. Biden was well on his way to the nomination.

On March 11 Trump gave a prime-time speech on COVID from the Oval Office. He expanded restrictions on travel to include Europe. Two days later, in an appearance in the Rose Garden, he declared a national emergency. His medical advisers urged Americans to remain in their homes. States issued lockdown orders restricting economic activity. Debt markets froze. For a brief moment, Trump looked to be taking seriously the twin problems of contagion and economic contraction. His approval rating began to rise. It reached a high of 47 percent in the *RealClearPolitics* average on April 1. That put him in the zone for reelection, according to *Washington Post* columnist Henry Olsen.[21]

Then things went downhill for both Trump and the United States. Coronavirus case numbers and fatalities rose sharply. The toll of lockdowns and school closures began to mount. The Trump boom disappeared. Unemployment skyrocketed. Congress and the Federal Reserve flooded the economy with fiscal and monetary stimulus. Trump's nightly press conferences turned into petty and awkward confrontations between the president and the media he loathed.

Meanwhile Biden went into seclusion in his Delaware home. His absence from the campaign trail and Trump's reduced campaign schedule severely limited the incumbent's ability to define his challenger. Biden was simply "not Trump"—and the polls said that would be enough.

In late May, a shocking video of a Minneapolis police officer killing George Floyd, an unarmed black man, went viral on the Internet. A wave of protests over racial injustice swept the nation. Many turned violent. Vandals toppled statues of Confederate generals, of Christopher Columbus, even of Frederick Douglass.

Crime skyrocketed in cities where police pulled back enforcement over fears of backlash. In Seattle a hip-hop artist and club promoter became the spokesman for a group of anarchists who established a six-block "autonomous zone." In Portland the masked and violent protesters known as antifa coordinated attacks against federal property and nightly clashes with local police and federal security officers that lasted for months. The Squad and progressive opinion leaders called on government to "defund the police." For some, that meant abolishing police departments and prisons altogether.

On June 1, in the midst of the upheaval, police chaotically dispersed the crowd of protesters at Lafayette Square across the street from the White House before Trump walked to St. John's Church. He stood outside in silence holding a Bible. For Trump's fans, the moment displayed bravery and resolve. For his detractors, it was a bizarre and meaningless stunt. Any unity the threat of coronavirus had brought to American life was gone. America was just as divided over Trump as it had been since 2016.

The virus ended the economic boom. And though international politics seemed frozen in place, civil tranquility vanished. The one-two punch of coronavirus shutdowns and the collapse of the rule of law in many cities devastated American self-confidence. Trump, echoing Richard Nixon, called for a restoration of law and order.

By the time the party conventions began in August, the distance between Democrats and Republicans, progressives and conservatives, appeared insuperable. The Democratic convention was a virtual, somber, almost mournful affair. Barack Obama said that democracy might not survive a second Trump term. Bernie

Sanders crowed over the concessions he had won in the party platform. Jill Biden spoke from an empty school, even though her husband's financial supporters in the teachers' unions were the main reason that schools remained closed. Kamala Harris, Biden's vice presidential nominee, introduced herself to the public as a child of immigrants, proud graduate of Howard University, and loving stepmom. Biden himself spoke of grief and healing. He put himself forward as the antidote to Trump.

The Trump convention was boisterous. Parts of it were held live outdoors, with crowds. Immigrants and black Americans celebrated the American dream and economic empowerment. One night Trump greeted first-line health care workers in the White House—on live video. The next night he held a naturalization ceremony. Nicholas Sandmann—the Kentucky high school student who had settled libel suits against major media organizations, including CNN, after they portrayed him as a racist during that year's March for Life—spoke against political correctness and donned a red MAGA cap. Trump framed the election as a referendum on the American idea. It was a choice between freedom and socialism, national pride and shame.

The successful GOP convention reset the presidential race. In late September, Trump nominated his third Supreme Court justice, Amy Coney Barrett, a protegee of Antonin Scalia, to replace the deceased Ruth Bader Ginsburg. Barrett's investiture solidified a conservative majority on the Court for the first time in a century. Her qualifications were remarkable. Her presence was sensational. The September 26 announcement ceremony, held outdoors in the Rose Garden, was a joyous occasion—the pinnacle of the conservative legal movement. Trump invited Barrett's seven children to join him onstage. His approval rating began climbing. It was back to 45 percent. Reelection was still a possibility.

What came next should have been no surprise. Several of the participants in the White House event for Barrett came down with

COVID. And the first presidential debate on September 29 was a national embarrassment. It was an hour and a half of interruptions, shouting, and crosstalk between the candidates and moderator. It seldom made sense.

Trump was Biden's opposite in his attitude toward the virus. He resisted the use of masks, traveled widely, and took few precautionary measures in the White House. By the end of debate week, he announced that he had been diagnosed with coronavirus. He was transported to Walter Reed National Military Medical Center, where doctors could better monitor his condition. The administration did a poor job of informing the public about the president's health. Then Trump took a limo ride around the Walter Reed campus while he was sick just to wave to supporters. When he returned to the White House on October 5, he dramatically unmasked himself while standing on the balcony. These cavalier acts erased whatever momentum had been building for the incumbent in the polls.

Trump's diagnosis led to the cancelation of the second presidential debate, denying him another chance to portray Biden as a creature of Washington whose agenda was far more left-wing than the American electorate knew or desired. But the third debate was better for the president: he held his own, he did not interrupt, and he goaded Biden into repeating the Democratic wish to "transition" the economy from fossil fuels. Then Trump resumed his nonstop, whirlwind campaign schedule of 2016. He crisscrossed the nation, boasting of his achievements and lambasting the progressive agenda. But it was too late for Trump to change the minds of voters who had already cast ballots. Because of the coronavirus, states had liberalized mail-in and early voting, and millions of Americans had voted before Trump's last-minute comeback. The exit polls suggested that Trump won late deciders. But late deciders matter less when most ballots are cast early.

Biden won the Electoral College by a vote of 306 to 232. He took the popular vote by 51 to 47 percent. Trump lost reelection because he failed to expand the coalition that put him in office. The combination of his policies and his antics repelled independents and college-educated voters in the suburbs. But his loss was not the definitive repudiation of conservatism and the GOP that Republicans had feared it would be.

Indeed, the election was much closer than the polls had suggested. Trump drew more votes than he had four years before and, despite charges of racism, improved his numbers among minorities. His coattails in defeat were longer than Biden's in victory. The GOP gained House seats. Partisan control of state legislatures and governor's mansions hardly changed, with Republicans picking up the governorship of Montana.

The election showed that the alliance between the conservative movement and national populism remained potent—if not quite powerful enough to win majorities. Trump had exposed many of the assumptions of conservatism circa 2014 as false. He had regrounded the GOP upon a base of white working-class and rural voters who were antielitist, suspicious of government, doubtful about America's overseas commitments, and fearful of globalization. He convinced this base to view the federal government as a vast and corrupt engine of special privileges and redistribution on the bases of identity, partisan affiliation, and personal connections. He moved the culture war away from sex and toward US history and patriotic symbols such as flags, holidays, language, and statuary.

Trump established incontrovertible facts on the ground. He moved embassies, cut off funds for the Palestinians, confronted China, killed terrorists, repurposed monies to build the border wall, and eliminated regulatory obstacles to the development and distribution of a coronavirus vaccine. He showed that the experts and consultants were often wrong. And he revealed that many American institutions—from the press to polling to social media to "woke" corporations whose campaigns for social justice did not extend to oppression in China—were often hypocritical, dishonest, and self-interested.

Abrasive, touchy, combative, and unable to refrain from responding to criticism, Trump ignored conventional wisdom and enacted policies conservatives had desired for decades. The Trump method of bluster, ambiguity, threat, and parry created a sense of ongoing crisis. It alienated critics, strained overseas alliances, and exhausted the patience of the electorate. Populism identified real problems and acted as a check on unaccountable elites, but it was also susceptible to demagoguery, scapegoating, and conspiracy theories.

These weaknesses were on display in the election's aftermath. Trump refused to concede. He and his legal team said that political machines in Democratic cities had used corrupt mail-in balloting to guarantee Biden a win. This was false. Trump lost because of the vote not in the cities but in the suburbs. There was no precedent for his behavior. He wanted the Supreme Court to throw out the results in Georgia, Pennsylvania, Arizona, and Wisconsin and hand him a second term.

Trump and his lawyers said that there was massive evidence for their claims. They had none. The press (including news anchors on the Fox News Channel), judges nationwide, and his own attorney general could not verify the existence of fraud sufficient to swing an election. Trump lost case after case in court. The swing states certified their results, the presidential transition began, and the Electoral College met on December 14 to pronounce Biden the winner. In the meantime, the president pressed on with his claim of a stolen election.

This decision had terrible consequences. It didn't just undermine the legitimacy of the American political system. Belief in the conspiracy theory that systemic fraud had denied Trump a second term turned the GOP on itself. In the run-up to runoffs in Georgia that decided two Senate seats, some pro-Trump lawyers urged voters not to participate. Trump himself targeted the Georgia

Republican state leadership. He campaigned unenthusiastically for the GOP Senate candidates—who both lost. Control of the Senate passed to the Democrats. In the space of four years, Republicans had gone from running the White House, the House of Representatives, and the Senate to losing all three.

Yet Trump's fight to overturn the election increased his stature within the GOP. His strategy was far more successful politically than legally. Contributions poured into his political action committee, which doubled as his legal defense fund. He laid the groundwork for another run for the presidency in 2024. He swore that he would avenge the "stolen" election of 2020. Republican officials were forced to choose between congratulating Biden or sticking with Trump. Most went with Trump.

Postelection surveys of Republicans showed that party regulars had not abandoned their leader. In one poll, a majority of Republicans and Republican leaners said that Trump should remain a leading voice in the GOP. A majority also supported Trump's renomination in 2024. But the numbers were not necessarily insurmountable for other presidential aspirants. About a third of respondents said they preferred someone new. That number might rise should Trump's postelection strategy prove harmful in the 2022 midterms. But there was no appetite for a pre-Trump Republican Party. Just 16 percent wanted new leaders who resembled George W. Bush and Mitt Romney.[22]

Trump supporters really wanted to fight the "deep state," RINOs (Republicans in name only), and the Squad. They said that the game was rigged against them and that only Trump had the audacity to throw out the rule book. This devotion to an antiestablishment politics of confrontation had limits, however. When Trump ran for reelection, he found himself unable to articulate a second-term agenda. For the first time since 1856, the Republican Party did not issue a platform. Delegates to the Republican National Convention rereleased the 2016 document, with a brief prefatory note. It pledged to "enthusiastically support the President's America-first agenda." As if there were any doubt.

Trump had several opportunities to end his election challenge and concede defeat. He never took them. To the contrary, he amped up his rhetoric. He summoned his followers to Washington, DC, on January 6, 2021, the day Congress met in joint session to certify the Electoral College vote. He tweeted on December 19, "Be there, will be wild!"[23]

When January 6 arrived, Trump waited until noon to address the large crowd that had gathered on the Ellipse. He spent his talk denouncing his own vice president, Mike Pence, for failing to stop the certification of Biden's victory—something Pence had no power to do. Trump told his supporters that through "strength" they would "take back" their country. And then a considerable segment of the audience began to march toward the Capitol building.

The protesters knocked over barriers, assaulted Capitol Police officers, scaled walls, bashed windows, forced open doors, and despoiled public property. These were acts of violence, of vandalism, and of desecration of the people's house. The men and women who breached the House and Senate chambers were doing it for Trump. They carried just as many Trump flags as American (or Confederate) ones. They were not chanting, "Make America great again!" as he fueled their anger during his speech at the Ellipse. They were crying, "Fight for Trump!" They stood not for an idea or even a country but for one man.

What the rioters expected was unclear. There was no way that majorities in the House and Senate would send the election "back to the states" after they trashed the offices of the people's representatives. There was no way that they could prevent the inauguration of the duly elected president and allow Donald Trump to remain in office. Trump did not declare martial law in the recalcitrant states or nationwide. Such hopes were as wild and disturbing as the conspiracy theories that gave rise to them.

Perhaps the vandals did not really want anything. Maybe they just wanted to "fight." Maybe they just enjoyed the chaos. The word for that is nihilism—but the American conservative movement and the Republican Party had stood against nihilistic lawbreaking since the cultural revolution of the 1960s. Every bad habit of the Right was on display in the Capitol riot that left five dead, $30 million in damage, close to three hundred arrested, and Capitol Hill an armed camp.[24]

Signs had accumulated for over a decade that racists and anti-Semites were joining conservative institutions at an alarming rate. By the end of the Bush era, the Moon family had sacked the editor and managing editor of the *Washington Times* for neo-Confederate sympathies and racist ideology. (New Right theorist Sam Francis had been fired as a columnist for the same reason in 1995.) A leader of the white nationalist alt-right served as an assistant editor at the *American Conservative* for several months during 2007 until he was fired for extremism. Another contributor to the *American Conservative* lost his job as an aide to Kentucky senator Rand Paul when a conservative website (edited by this writer) discovered that he had made offensive statements routinely while working as a disc jockey known as "the Southern Avenger."[25]

The conservative *Daily Caller* website dropped a contributor after reporters unearthed his pseudonymous writing for racist publications. In 2019 the Charlemagne Institute, a conservative think tank in Minnesota, cast off one of its employees after his racist and anti-Semitic writing was publicized online. In July 2020 Tucker Carlson's lead writer quit Fox News Channel after his own bigoted and misogynist writing came to light. In the January 6, 2021, battle of Capitol Hill, with its Confederate paraphernalia and men in Viking costume, all of the unreason and hatred that had been silently growing in the body of the Right burst into the open.[26]

Trump's reckless and destructive behavior guaranteed that he would be remembered as the first president to be impeached twice in a single term. (The second impeachment was also bipartisan: ten House Republicans and seven Senate Republicans voted to convict Trump on the charge of incitement of insurrection.) Historians would record that the signal event of Trump's presidency was his refusal to admit he lost the 2020 election. He had stood by as his supporters invaded the US Capitol and interfered in the operation of constitutional government. Trump divided the country between Americans loyal to him and Americans loyal to the rule of law.

If Trump had followed the example of his predecessors and conceded power graciously and peacefully, he would have been remembered as a disruptive but consequential populist leader who, before the coronavirus pandemic, presided over an economic boom, reoriented America's opinion of China, removed terrorist leaders from the battlefield, revamped the space program, secured an originalist majority on the US Supreme Court, and authorized Operation Warp Speed to produce a COVID-19 vaccine in record time. Instead, when historians write about the Trump era, they will do so through the lens of January 6. They will focus on Trump's tortured relationship with the alt-right, on his atrocious handling of the deadly Charlottesville protest in 2017, on the rise in political violence during his tenure in office, and on his encouragement of malevolent conspiracy theories.

Trump joined the ranks of American villains from John C. Calhoun to Andrew Johnson, from Joseph McCarthy to George Wallace. On the evening of January 6, the *Wall Street Journal* editorial board called on him to resign before the end of his term. "There is no doubt that Donald Trump has committed an impeachable offense," wrote the editors of *National Review*. "I'd like to see January 6 burned into the American mind as firmly as 9/11," George Will told *This Week with George Stephanopoulos*.[27]

Yet substantial elements of the American Right, including many GOP officials, accommodated Trump in his antidemocratic act. A month before the riot, dozens of conservative leaders signed a letter calling on state legislatures in Pennsylvania, Wisconsin, Michigan, Georgia, Arizona, and Nevada—states that Biden won—to appoint pro-Trump slates of electors. One hundred twenty-one congressmen and six senators voted to object to Biden's certification *after* the attack on the Capitol.[28]

But they did not succeed in overturning the 2020 election. On the cold morning of January 20, 2021, Joe Biden swore an oath to preserve, protect, and defend the Constitution as the forty-sixth president of the United States of America. In the middle of a plague, in a country exhausted by war and economic calamity, he promised a return to normalcy.

The moment was eerily similar to Warren Harding's inauguration one century earlier—but the two parties had been reversed. Now the Democrats, in the person of Biden, stood for the accepted way of doing things. And the Republicans, in the person of Trump, resembled the outsider populists led by William Jennings Bryan.

In the space of one hundred years, despite setbacks and internal battles, the American Right had come of age, gained the trust of its fellow countrymen, changed the world, and then, after decades of confusion, joined forces with a man it did not trust but eventually came to adore. That man departed Washington with the Republican Party out of power, conservatism in disarray, and the Right in the same hole it had dug with Charles Lindbergh, Joe McCarthy, the John Birch Society, George Wallace, and Pat Buchanan. Not only was the Right unable to get out of the hole; it did not want to.

CONCLUSION

An American Conservatism

I N FEBRUARY 2021 THE FBI INDICTED L. BRENT BOZELL IV FOR crimes committed during the Capitol riot. The significance of Bozell's presence in the rabble that broke into the Senate chamber was not lost on the media. "Mr. Bozell's father is a high-profile right-wing activist known for infusing his politics with Christian values," the *New York Times* mentioned in its write-up of the arrest. And Bozell's grandfather, L. Brent Bozell Jr., had been William F. Buckley Jr.'s debate partner, Joseph McCarthy's and Barry Goldwater's ghostwriter, the founder of *Triumph*, and organizer of the first antiabortion protest in the United States.[1]

Liberal critics traced the arc of the American Right from Bozell Jr.'s anticommunism, to Bozell III's institution building, to Bozell IV's lawbreaking in the name of Donald Trump. "The floundering conservative movement, as it bids adieu to Rush Limbaugh, seems also to be seeing the last of the Bozell dynasty," wrote Timothy Noah of the *New Republic*. Limbaugh had died on February 17, 2021.[2]

If one looked at the American Right only as a post–World War II phenomenon, one would be forced to conclude that by the spring of 2021 the movement Bozell Jr. had helped Buckley and Goldwater launch had reached an impasse. The Republican Party, while maintaining its strength in state capitals, was frozen out of power in Washington, DC. The National Rifle Association declared bankruptcy after it found itself under investigation for corruption by the attorney general of New York. Jerry Falwell Jr., one of Donald Trump's most devoted supporters, resigned as president of Liberty University after salacious images and stories appeared on social media.

Facebook and Twitter banned Trump for his role in the January 6 attack on the Capitol. Living on the grounds of his private clubs in Florida and New Jersey, he sent out tweet-like press releases often several times a day, relitigating his election loss and insulting the Republicans who had voted to impeach him for incitement. One of those Republicans, House conference chair Liz Cheney, daughter of former vice president Dick Cheney, was removed from her post for continuing to use her platform to combat Trump. GOP leaders hoped that by ignoring the former president, they could unite their party around opposition to President Joe Biden. They must have forgotten that they had tried the same strategy in 2015, when they blithely assumed that Trump would fade as the first caucuses and primaries came into view. Trump hadn't faded then. Nor was there reason to assume that he would do so now.

The tension between populism and elitism that persisted throughout the history of the American Right between the years 1920 and 2020 was not going anywhere. At the beginning of the Biden presidency, the populists had the upper hand. In 1993 Irving Kristol had written in the *Wall Street Journal* that the "three pillars" of conservatism were "religion, nationalism, and economic growth." Some thirty years later, a fourth pillar had been raised beneath the conservative roof: populism.[3]

The Right was unabashedly opposed to liberal elites, skeptical of credentialed experts, and hostile to the established voices of print and cable media. Kristol himself had undertaken a reevaluation of populism over the duration of his career: In the 1970s he fretted over populism's tendency to devolve into lawless revolt, conspiracy theory, and scapegoating of vulnerable minorities. By the mid-1980s, however, he saw the activism of the populist New Right as "an effort to bring our governing elites to their senses." The events on January 6, 2021, took place more than a decade after Kristol's death but confirmed his initial reservations.[4]

The character of President Ronald Reagan may have affected Kristol's rosy assessment of populism. The fortieth president injected the populist rebellion of the late 1970s with his peculiar qualities of optimism, sunniness, humor, and unflappability. Just as watching the captive nations of Eastern Europe throw off the shackles of communism and adopt democracy had distorted expectations of what might follow the 2001 invasion of Afghanistan, the 2003 invasion of Iraq, and the 2011 Arab Spring, the rosy afterglow of Reagan's presidency warped conservative intellectuals' perceptions of post–Cold War conservative populism. Always looking out for the next Reagan, conservative thinkers were too quick to ignore or discount or assume victory over national populism when it manifested itself in the candidacies of Patrick Buchanan, Ron Paul, Sarah Palin, and Donald Trump. Reagan's unique personality and the extraordinary success of his presidency obscured the larger history of the American Right of which he was just one part.

When one examines the Right in the full light of the pre-Reagan experience and conservatism as it developed over the last century, one recognizes that its defeats and setbacks have been temporary. There has always been an American Right to resist or counteract liberalism's idealistic programs of reform and radicalism's utopian desires for repudiation and revolution. And there is good reason to assume there always will be. The question then becomes what form that Right will take and whence it will originate.

At the beginning of this history, the American Right, like the Right in Europe, stood largely for the preservation of the status quo. Unlike in Europe, however, where the Right aligned with the institutions of monarchy, aristocracy, established church, and ethnicity, the American Right in the first third of the twentieth century defended free enterprise, foreign policy restraint, US patriotism, and nonsectarian (though Protestant-tinged) civil religion. When the Great Depression upended the established order, however, Franklin Delano Roosevelt created a new bureaucratic structure of government that inspired in the American Right neither allegiance nor affection. The partisans of strict constitutionalism and nonintervention in economics and foreign affairs were driven from power and influence. The rise of fascism and communism in Europe and militarism and imperialism in Japan worsened their position. The opponents of American intervention in World War II found themselves discredited by Charles Lindbergh's anti-Semitism and Japan's surprise attack on Pearl Harbor. By the end of World War II, the Right was a minority tendency not only in intellectual and cultural circles but also in the Republican Party and the country at large.

The threat of Soviet power and the potential for nuclear war revived the Right. The conflict between the United States and the Soviet Union shaped practically every aspect of world politics between 1947 and 1989. Even before the onset of the Cold War, however, opposition to the Soviet Union and to the spread of communism and socialism unified conservatives. William F. Buckley Jr. referred to anticommunism as the "harnessing bias" of the movement. This bias informed conservative calls for political-ideological warfare against Moscow, for the rollback of Soviet dominion, for a buildup of conventional and nuclear forces, for aid to anti-Communist authoritarian regimes, for an end to détente and "coexistence," and for a reassertion of national pride and willpower.

Every variety of American conservative had a reason to oppose communism and to work with others to arrest its advance. Economic conservatives and libertarians knew that communism did not work and that Communist societies crushed economic freedom. Traditionalist and religious conservatives viewed communism as an atheistic heresy that blighted the heritage of Western civilization and endangered the future of Christianity. Ex-Communists had experienced communism as a totalizing ideology that would not stop spreading until the revolution was either completed or defeated.

The postwar conservative movement succeeded in reclaiming its place in the Republican Party. The Goldwater nomination ended in a landslide victory for Lyndon Johnson, but it also reestablished the GOP's conservative brand. It guaranteed conservatives a spot in the party's organizational structure. Not all subsequent Republican nominees belonged to the conservative movement (far from it). But each one included conservatives in his coalition. The GOP became the instrument through which the conservative movement reoriented the nation's foreign, economic, social, and judicial policies. Of these realms of activity, foreign policy was by far the most important.

Anticommunism contributed to the Right's advance in the 1960s and 1970s. America's defeat in Vietnam broke the confidence of many Cold War liberals. It split FDR's Democratic Party into pieces: liberal Democrats in the North, conservative Democrats in the South, and working-class ethnic voters nationwide. Many of the left-liberals became anti-anti-Communists, and they briefly took over the Democratic Party beginning with George McGovern's victory in the 1972 presidential primary. Other anti-Communist liberals broke with liberalism or with the Democratic Party itself. They became neoconservatives. The most famous of these was Reagan, who, like many ex-Democrats, did not entirely abandon his belief in a hopeful future.

The "hard hats" who rebelled against the Left's defeatism abroad and quotas, inflationary economics, and tolerance of crime at home swelled the potential audience for conservative ideas. The religious conservatives who awakened from a fifty-year slumber in the 1970s to campaign for Reagan under the auspices of the Moral Majority also placed national security and anticommunism, along with support for Israel (itself a Cold War chess piece), at the top of their priorities. When Ronald Reagan became president in 1981, he pursued a multifaceted strategy against the Soviets that resembled what he had been reading in conservative journals for decades. In the aftermath of Vietnam, conservatism provided the intellectual and political support for a strategy of renewed containment and confrontation that accelerated the Soviet Union's demise.

By the end of 1991, the Soviet Union was gone. The end of communism also meant the end of conservative unity. The Right never settled on a strategy for the post–Cold War world. For a time, the democratic triumphalism of Francis Fukuyama and the universal hegemony of Charles Krauthammer were dominant. In this brief period, which coincided with the presidency of the "New Democrat" Bill Clinton, the agenda worked out by conservative intellectuals, operating within a thick network of magazines and institutions, was put into practice. The expansion of political freedom in both formerly Communist countries and pro-American authoritarian regimes that followed the death of communism coincided with and drew energy from a global turn toward free markets. Tax and poverty rates fell. Private- and public-sector unions diminished. Consumer goods became cheaper. Stagflation was no longer an issue. Immigration was higher. And the world economy was more integrated because of the work of conservative and libertarian economists such as Friedrich Hayek, Milton Friedman, George Stigler, James Buchanan, and Robert Mundell.

Crime rates plunged when cities adopted the strategies advocated by James Q. Wilson. In 1996 the Republican Congress and President Bill Clinton agreed to a welfare reform that made assistance temporary and linked benefits to employment. The Personal Opportunity and Work Responsibility Act was the most dramatic blow against the welfare state in half a century. It was the culmination of a long-running argument between the Right and the Left over individual agency and the demoralization that accompanies dependency.

Meanwhile, the conservative legal movement permeated the federal judiciary and the legal academy. And the institutional superstructure that conservatives had built up over the decades—from foundations to journals to think tanks to professional associations to activist groups—guaranteed that the Right's viewpoint would be heard.

After the terrorist attacks of September 11, 2001, President George W. Bush adopted the foreign policy that William Kristol and Robert Kagan had sketched out in the pages of *Foreign Affairs* and the *Weekly Standard*. Seen as the follow-up to the Cold War, the war on terror was another long, twilight struggle against a totalitarian enemy. This time, however, the United States faced no great power opposition. It could intervene earlier and more often, act preemptively, and pursue regime change against states harboring terrorists and thought to be developing weapons of mass destruction. The war on terror and support for unborn life, wrote *First Things* editor Joseph Bottum in the summer of 2005, could be the double helix of a "new fusionism" for the conservative movement. Bush's reelection in 2004 seemed to validate the idea that national security conservatives and religious conservatives formed the backbone of what Republican strategist Karl Rove called a "durable" majority.[5]

The durable majority lasted until 2006. In truth, the war on terror was not as powerful a framework as anticommunism. For one thing, terrorism was a tactic, not an ideology or nation-state or empire, so the war's aims, adversaries, and end state were nebulous. For another, fighting for democracy in the Middle East was not the same as preserving the nation's very existence against Soviet missiles, tanks, submarines, and bombers. Reagan's descendants also forgot that, for all of his rhetorical firepower, for all of his spending on defense, for all of his tough negotiating positions, he committed US forces abroad only twice—once in Lebanon, which ended in tragedy and withdrawal, and again, more successfully, in Grenada. Instead he relied on aid to proxy forces and on punitive missile strikes when Libyan leader Muammar Qaddaffi or Iran's Ayatollah Ruhollah Khomeini crossed his red lines.

Meanwhile, the disengaged nationalism of Charles Lindbergh and Robert Taft lived on in the personages of Patrick Buchanan and Ron Paul. As the American occupation of Iraq grew more violent, discontent bubbled to the surface of the American Right. That distaste for Bush and his variety of conservatism and for the conservative think tanks, journals, and politicians espousing it erupted in grassroots opposition to Bush's immigration bills and in support for Paul's antiwar presidential campaigns in 2008 and 2012.

The dissent grew in magnitude during the Great Recession that began in 2007 and the global financial crisis of 2008, taking the form of the anti–bank bailout, anti–big government Tea Party, which directed its animus as much at "establishment" Republicans as at Barack Obama Democrats. This antielitism took over the GOP with the nomination of Donald Trump and his unexpected victory in the 2016 election. Trump represented a return to the beliefs and practices of 1920s and 1930s Republicanism coupled with the religious populism of a William Jennings Bryan. He disestablished the postwar conservatism of Buckley and Goldwater, of Irving Kristol and Ronald Reagan, of William Kristol and George W. Bush.

Though their policies may have shared the same spirit, there were serious differences between Calvin Coolidge and Donald Trump. Coolidge was a model of reticence and comportment. Trump was not. Coolidge stood for the "American" way of doing things and presided over a "normal" government in a "normal" time. Trump stood outside the system, even during the years in which he was president. He and his supporters were not preserving the status quo. They were challenging it. They rebelled against expert opinion, "political correctness," media narratives, and the ways of the Washington "swamp." Coolidge was distinctly American in philosophy and outlook. Trump resembled national populist leaders in Europe, in the Middle East, in South America, and in Russia. In all these places, opposition to immigration and global trade, religious traditionalism, and charismatic strongmen defined the Right.

What began in the twentieth century as an elite-driven defense of the classical liberal principles enshrined in the Declaration of Independence and Constitution of the United States ended up, in the first quarter of the twenty-first century, as a furious reaction against elites of all stripes. Many on the right embraced a cult of personality and illiberal tropes. The danger was that the alienation from and antagonism toward American culture and society expressed by many on the right could turn into a general opposition to the constitutional order. That temptation had been present in the writings of the Agrarians, in the demagogy of Tom Watson, Huey Long, and Father Charles Coughlin, in the conspiracies of Joseph McCarthy, in the racism of George Wallace, in the radicalism of *Triumph*, in the sour moments of the paleoconservatives, in the cultural despair of the religious Right, and in the rancid anti-Semitism of the alt-right. But it was cabined off. It was contained. That would not be the case forever—as Trump and January 6, 2021, had shown.

TO SOME, THIS HISTORY WILL LOOK LIKE A CHRONICLE OF INCO-
herence and failure. But there really is such a thing as American conservatism, even if its record is not unblemished. Over the
course of the past century, conservatism has risen up to defend
the essential moderation of the American political system against
liberal excess. Conservatism has been there to save liberalism from
weakness, woolly-headedness, and radicalism. "I think today that
the principal task of conservatism is to save liberalism from the
liberals," political philosopher Harvey Mansfield once said. "They
misinterpret their own doctrine; pervert it and render it dangerous
to freedom and peace alike."[6]

This task is unending. If you had asked an American in the late
1970s what problems the country faced, he or she would have mentioned inflation, crime, and national dishonor. Conservatives were
able to trace these challenges back to liberal economic, social, and
foreign policies, and they offered plausible ways of solving them.
In some ways, the problems America faces today are also the result
of too much liberalism—an out-of-control egalitarianism, an unwillingness to maintain public order, a culture that silences politically incorrect views. The question—and it is an open question—is
whether there is a viable conservatism to resist these trends.

The conservative movement, in its present disagreeable and
hesitant condition, must forge a new consensus, based on the
particularly American idea of individual liberty exercised within
a constitutional order, that addresses the challenges of our time.
Conservatives need to ask the following: How can we address the
problems everybody sees, while trying to keep the concerns unique
to us from overwhelming our society?

The likely answer probably will incorporate the modifications
to conservative policy positions that Donald Trump forced upon
the movement—a belief in secure borders and national sovereignty,
an emphasis on the condition of working people without college
degrees, a tough stance toward China, and a reluctance toward

humanitarian intervention abroad. But a conservatism anchored to Trump the man will face insurmountable obstacles in attaining policy coherence, government competence, and intellectual credibility.

Untangling the Republican Party and conservative movement from Donald Trump won't be easy. It will require Republican officials to follow the lead of conservative jurists who acknowledged the reality of Joe Biden's victory. It will require a delicate recalibration of the relationship between party elites and the grassroots populism that fuels the Trump phenomenon. It will require a depersonalization of the Right, with leaders focusing less on individual candidates and more on the principles that have guided the movement for more than half a century: anti-statism, constitutionalism, patriotism, and antisocialism. It will require a willingness to look ahead to the next election rather than dwelling on 2020. And it will require leaders who can set the agenda, define the alternatives, and model appropriate standards of behavior. The alternative would be a national populist GOP dominated by a single man whom not only educated elites but also a majority of the American people view with contempt.

It is worth considering whether the elite-driven strategy that for decades provided structure and stability to the conservative movement is possible in the America of the twenty-first century. It may turn out to be the case, as political analyst Jonah Goldberg has suggested, that the intellectual conservatism of tomorrow will have the same attenuated relationship to politics as H. L. Mencken and Albert Jay Nock's conservatism had in their day. Or the future may look more like the present at the time of writing, as parents organize spontaneously at the grassroots level to reject (and in some cases ban) what they see as politically correct and anti-American school curricula. If social media platforms now serve as the public square, then the future may hold more contentious debates over vaccinations and over independent "audits" to find voter fraud where none exists.[7]

So long as Democrats can point to Donald Trump, independents and college-educated white voters will avoid association with the Republican Party and conservatism. At the same time, following the example of mayoral candidate Eric Adams in New York, Democrats may appropriate issues, such as law and order, once associated with Republicans. Indeed, the rise of liberal critics of "woke" racial-equity politics may portend a new center—potentially a new neoconservatism—based in the classical liberal principles of individual freedom, personal responsibility, equal opportunity, merit-based achievement, and color blindness.

Still, the problem with predictions is that they tend to be wrong. However the future unfolds, conservatives must return to the wisdom of their best minds and advocates. "The proper question for conservatives: What do you seek to conserve?" George Will wrote in *The Conservative Sensibility* (2019). "The proper answer is concise but deceptively simple: We seek to conserve the American Founding." Or as Bill Buckley said in 1970, "I see it as the continuing challenge of *National Review* to argue the advantages to every one of the rediscovery of America, the amiability of its people, the flexibility of its institutions, of the great latitude that is still left to the individual, the delights of spontaneity, and, above all, the need for superordinating the private vision over the public vision." Buckley's challenge to *National Review* is also the challenge to today's conservatives and Republicans.[8]

This "rediscovery of America" must center on America's founding documents, for there would be no American conservatism without the American founding. The Constitution and its twenty-seven amendments anchor conservatives eager to preserve and extend the blessings of liberty that are the birthright of every American. The Constitution grounds conservatives in a uniquely American tradition of political thought that balances individual rights and popular sovereignty through the separation of powers and federalism. The Constitution not only protects human freedom but also creates the space for the deeper satisfactions of family, religion, community, and voluntary association. "A free society certainly needs permanent means of restricting the powers of government, no matter what the particular objective of the moment may be," wrote Friedrich Hayek. "And the Constitution which the new American nation was to give itself was definitely meant not merely as a regulation of the derivation of power but as a constitution of liberty, a constitution that would protect the individual against all arbitrary coercion."[9]

One cannot be an American patriot without reverence for the nation's enabling documents. One cannot be an American conservative without regard for the American tradition of liberty those charters inaugurated. "Conservatives may of course draw from foreign sources—I yield to no one in the admiration due to Edmund Burke, a great friend of America—but they should be read with a view to possibilities in America," Harvey Mansfield said. "America cannot abandon the great principles of liberalism, above all the principle of self-government and, with it, the constitutional means for achieving and preserving it."[10]

Nor can conservatives abandon America. The preservation of the American idea of liberty and the familial, communal, religious, and political institutions that incarnate and sustain it—that is what makes American conservatism distinctly American. The Right betrays itself when it forgets this truth.

Why? Because the job of a conservative is to remember.

AFTERWORD

The Trump Era

"A N OLD MAN IN A HURRY" WAS HOW LORD RANDOLPH CHUR-
chill described then British prime minister William Gladstone in 1886. Gladstone was seventy-six at the time. On January
20, 2021, the seventy-eight-year-old President Joe Biden made it
clear in his inaugural address that he, too, was in a rush.[1]

Biden had described himself during the presidential campaign
as a "bridge" to "an entire generation of leaders." One of his advisers had called him a "transition figure." Yet Biden's self-description
as an interim leader diminished neither his ego nor his aspirations.[2]

His first speech as president set out his priorities. His rather
abstract and platitudinous words nevertheless signaled that his administration would lean left, and that he would attempt to reverse
the legacy of his predecessor.

Indeed, Donald Trump shaped the entirety of Biden's presidency. As he had since 2015, Trump continued to dominate the
culture and politics of his era unlike any figure since Theodore
Roosevelt. No matter how much the public came to disapprove
of Biden's policies and job performance, in the 2022 midterm

elections it blanched at the prospect of restoring full control of Washington to Trump and the Make America Great Again (MAGA) Republicans. Despite the narrow GOP takeover of the House of Representatives, the Right ended Biden's first two years as president much as it began them: divided, querulous, and unable to convince independent and suburban voters that it was prepared to govern.

The Left was not in great shape either. Biden came to office with an anti-mandate: his slim majorities in Congress, including a tied Senate and the smallest Democratic House majority in nearly a century, signaled that the public was more interested in removing Trump from office than it was in handing power to the Progressive wing of the Democratic Party.

Biden pledged to unite the country, but he had a funny under-standing of unity. To him, national unity required the nation to rally behind the latest Democratic Party initiative. Biden's defini-tion of unity was contested, to say the least. Consequently, Amer-ica was no more unified at the midpoint of Biden's term than it was at the beginning.[3]

This ongoing stalemate was not inevitable. It was the result of choices made by Biden on one hand and Republican leaders and primary voters on the other. Biden decided to govern from the Left. The GOP fell in line behind Trump and MAGA. And inde-pendent voters, suburbanites, parents of school-age children, and so-called normie Americans were caught in between.

"WE'LL GIVE HIM THE BENEFIT OF THE DOUBT, WHICH IS WHAT every new American President deserves," wrote the editorial board of the *Wall Street Journal* in a charitable reading of Biden's inau-gural address. Before long, however, Biden confirmed the wor-ries of the *Journal* and other conservatives. He wasted no time in repudiating Trump's immigration and energy initiatives. And he prepared the ground for trillions in additional domestic spending.[4]

Biden signed seventeen executive orders upon becoming president. He halted construction on the southern border wall. He lifted restrictions on migration and travel from thirteen countries linked to national security threats. He relaxed interior immigration enforcement and restored legal protections to certain classes of illegal immigrants. He rolled back the "Remain in Mexico" policy, whereby applicants for asylum in the United States had to wait elsewhere until their claims were decided. And he terminated "safe third country" agreements that required asylum seekers to apply for protection in the first new country they entered.

Biden also canceled the Keystone XL pipeline between the United States and Canada. He stopped oil and gas exploration in the Arctic National Wildlife Refuge. He forbade drilling in large parts of Utah. One week after taking office, he stopped issuing new oil and gas leases on public property. "Any doubt that the Biden administration plans to slowly regulate fossil fuels out of existence vanished this week," the *Journal*'s editors wrote in disappointment.[5]

Nor was it just conservatives who were skeptical of Biden's new direction. Lawrence Summers, a former economic adviser to presidents Bill Clinton and Barack Obama, suggested in a February *Washington Post* op-ed that Biden's $1.9 trillion coronavirus stimulus package—the American Rescue Plan Act—was a recipe for inflation. The White House rebuked him. "It's just flat-out wrong that our team is, quote, 'dismissive' of inflationary risks," said Council of Economic Advisers member Jared Bernstein. On March 10, 2021, the Democratic Congress passed the American Rescue Plan on a party-line vote.[6]

If Biden acted heedlessly, it was not only because he felt that he had a short time to make big change. It was also because he carried a chip on his shoulder. Biden had spent eight years as vice president to Barack Obama, who often ignored or disputed his advice. Now, close to half a century after he first entered the US Senate, Biden was on a mission to prove that he was more than a garrulous and somewhat comic DC fixture whose past was a reminder of life's contingency and tragic nature.[7]

The press welcomed Biden's attempt at sweeping change. After the passage of the American Rescue Plan, *New York Times* columnist David Brooks wrote a piece with the headline, "Joe Biden Is a Transformational President." Two weeks later, in a report on a meeting between Biden and a group of historians, Mike Allen of Axios wrote that "Biden's presidency has already been transformative."[8]

Whether the transformation would be for good or ill was left unsaid.

The initial fallout from Biden's decisions was unpleasant. In March 2021, Secretary of Homeland Security Alejandro Mayorkas told Congress that the southern border faced its largest increase in illegal border crossings in two decades. That turned out to be a massive underestimate. Over the next year, record numbers of illegal immigrants—some four million in all—would cross the border into Arizona and Texas. The cartels and coyotes who arranged for migrants to voyage northward used the same routes to traffic illegal narcotics responsible for the deaths of more than one hundred thousand Americans per year.[9]

Around the time that the border was becoming more of an aspiration than a reality, consumer prices began to rise. Lawrence Summers's warning proved true: the economic recovery, supply chain issues, and the Biden administration's injection of monetary and fiscal stimulus generated inflation. The increase in the price level, combined with Biden's restrictions on oil and gas development and a lack of refining capacity, resulted in a gasoline price surge. At first, Biden and his lieutenants said that inflation would be temporary. They were wrong.

Biden did not abandon his spending and energy policies, however. The combined cost of his proposed American Jobs Plan and American Families Plan was upward of $4 trillion. To put downward pressure on the price of gasoline, he released stockpiles from the Strategic Petroleum Reserve (SPR) and lobbied Saudi Arabia to produce more oil. He also worked to revive the Joint Comprehensive Plan of Action (JCPOA), the nuclear deal with Iran that would permit the Islamic theocracy to contribute more barrels of oil to the global market.

As spring turned into the summer of 2021, Biden's disappointments began to mount. His opening bid of $4 trillion in domestic spending was whittled down. A bipartisan infrastructure package of $1.2 trillion, including $550 billion in "new" funds, passed the Senate in August 2021 and the House that November.

Yet the remaining trillions of Biden's Build Back Better agenda remained stuck in negotiations among the White House, Senate majority leader Charles Schumer (D-NY), and Senator Joe Manchin (D-WV). The West Virginia Democrat, whose state voted for Donald Trump in 2020 by a thirty-nine-point margin, would not accede to a spending splurge amid high inflation. His fellow Democrats were furious at Manchin's opposition both to Build Back Better and to abolishing the filibuster requirement of sixty votes to end legislative debate.

Biden may have been so fixated on transforming America that he forgot about the coronavirus pandemic. His jab-first strategy emphasizing vaccinations seemed to be producing results during his first six months in office. By the Fourth of July, he was ready to declare America's independence from the virus. "We all know powerful variants have emerged, like the Delta variant," he told an Independence Day gathering at the White House. "But the best defense against these variants is to get vaccinated."[10]

That was not quite true. Vaccination may have reduced the severity of infection, but its effect on viral spread was much less apparent. Not long after Biden's remarks, case numbers attributable to the Delta variant began to rise. Later in the year, with the arrival of the Omicron variant, recorded cases spiked to the highest level of the pandemic. The persistence of COVID-19 left many Americans in an uncomfortable gray zone of vaccine requirements, mask-wearing, remote work and school, desolate city centers, and social isolation.[11]

Biden's popularity began to wane. On April 29, 2021, the hundredth day of his presidency, his approval rating according to the FiveThirtyEight poll average was 54 percent. By August 7, the two hundredth day, that number had slid to 50 percent.[12]

It was about to get worse. Biden inherited from Trump an agreement between the United States and the Taliban, the Islamic militia and ally of al-Qaeda fighting the US-backed government in Afghanistan. The deal stipulated that American forces would leave Afghanistan under two conditions: if the Taliban participated in intra-Afghan peace negotiations, and if it pledged not to use the territory under its control for terrorist activities.

When Biden became president, about thirty-five hundred troops were left in the war-torn land whose democratic government US soldiers had protected for almost twenty years. According to the Trump agreement, the last US soldier was due to leave Afghanistan by May 2021. On April 4, however, Biden delayed the withdrawal of remaining US forces until that September 11.

Many observers scratched their heads at the odd symbolism of timing the US departure to coincide with the anniversary of the terrorist attacks against America that precipitated the war on terrorism. The Taliban, for its part, declared that the United States had violated the Trump-brokered peace deal. The Islamic holy warriors escalated their campaign to reconquer Afghanistan by force.

Biden pressed on. Smarting from the public reaction to his September 11 deadline, he announced on July 8 that America would be out of Afghanistan by August 31. By the end of July, US Central Command stated that the withdrawal was 95 percent complete. America fell back, the Afghan Army disintegrated, and the Taliban advanced. It captured its first provincial capital on August

6. A week later, the Taliban controlled the cities of Kandahar and Herat. On August 15, Taliban forces entered the Afghan capital of Kabul. All hell broke loose.[13]

Afghanistan's president fled the country. American citizens, permanent residents, and former translators for US military personnel, along with civilians from NATO allies and partners, scrambled to leave before the Taliban had a chance to consolidate power. Amid the chaos, Biden defended his timeline for withdrawal. He ordered troops to Afghanistan to assist in the evacuation—more than had been there when he took office. The Taliban controlled safe passage to the Kabul International Airport, where American forces scrambled to help as many people as they could flee oppression. On August 26, Islamic State terrorists detonated an explosive at the airport. More than 150 Afghans died. Thirteen US servicemen were killed. They were the first US casualties in Afghanistan in more than a year.

Biden was dumbfounded. But he would not deviate from his commitment to American retreat. The US retaliated with drone strikes that missed their target and killed civilians, including children—proving that Biden's vaunted "over-the-horizon" counterterrorism capability was not quite as good as he said it was.

Afghanistan sank back into the medieval swamp of Taliban rule. A crestfallen America completed its withdrawal on August 30. That day, for the first time in his presidency, more Americans disapproved of Joe Biden than approved of him. He has not recovered.

REPUBLICANS AND CONSERVATIVES BENEFITED FROM BIDEN'S troubles. They spoke relentlessly of the problems at the southern border, blamed inflation on excessive federal spending, criticized Biden's energy policies for high gas prices, and exploded in furor at the debacle in Afghanistan. But the party and movement had problems of their own.

The main challenge was figuring out what to do about Donald Trump. According to the Gallup poll, Trump left office with a 34 percent approval rating, the lowest figure of his presidency. Sixty-two percent of Americans disapproved of him. Social media giants such as Facebook and Twitter banned Trump from their platforms. Ten House Republicans voted to impeach him for the events of January 6, 2021. Seven GOP senators voted to convict.

Yet Trump remained the undisputed leader of the Republican Party. More than half of the House GOP conference voted to challenge the 2020 election results *after* the riot at the Capitol. Eight Republican senators did the same. Millions of Republicans and conservatives still believed that Trump had been unfairly maligned throughout his presidency and was never given a fair chance to drain the Washington swamp. Millions of Republicans and conservatives still believed that Trump was the only thing standing in the way of national dissolution.

The conservative media ecosystem, including talk radio and the Fox News Channel, elevated Trump defenders and minimized Trump critics. Prominent conservatives opposed Trump's second impeachment as frivolous and ill-considered. "Few people in Congress are actually thinking calmly or rationally right now," said Fox News contributor Mollie Hemingway.[14]

Republican leaders approached the former president in different ways. Mitch McConnell, the GOP Senate leader from Kentucky, ignored Trump as best he could. Kevin McCarthy, the top Republican in the House, prioritized party unity and sought to keep Trump within the GOP. That choice would bring significant changes to the party over the next two years.

McCarthy, born in 1966, was a former Hill staffer from Bakersfield, California. He was neither an ideologue nor a wonk, but a classic politico whose chief interest was the mechanics of majority building. Surveying the post-2020 landscape and perceiving the rapidity with which Republicans and conservatives rallied behind

Trump after January 6, McCarthy concluded that excluding the former president from the GOP was not possible given the size and intensity of the president's devoted following.

On January 28, 2021, McCarthy visited Trump in Florida. After the meeting, Trump's political action committee released a photo of the two men smiling in the great room at the Mar-a-Lago estate. The image represented Trump's staying power despite his exile from social media, and despite his decision to keep a somewhat lower public profile for the time being. The optics of McCarthy's trip, in which the Republican leader took the initiative and traveled to Florida for Trump's blessing, reinforced Trump's stature within the GOP.

A third Republican leader, House conference chair Liz Cheney of Wyoming, rejected both avoidance of Trump and association with him. She opted for confrontation. "There has never been a greater betrayal by a president of the United States of his office and his oath to the Constitution," she said in a statement released after her vote to impeach Trump. Cheney never looked back. She had no desire to move on to other subjects. She kept up her indictment of Trump over the objections of her House colleagues.[15]

Cheney was a pro-life, pro–Second Amendment, pro-defense, tax-cutting movement conservative with a 76 percent lifetime rating from the American Conservative Union (ACU). She had supported Trump for president in both 2016 and 2020. Yet her hostility toward Trump after January 6 made her an uncomfortable fit in the modern Republican Party. One of Trump's most devoted supporters, Representative Matt Gaetz of Florida, held a rally in Cheyenne in late January 2021 to call for a primary challenge against her.[16]

Early the next month, Cheney survived an attempt to expel her from the House leadership. She did not trim her sails. A few weeks after the challenge, McCarthy became piqued when Cheney publicly and adamantly disagreed with his assessment that Trump had a place in the Republican Party. She also insisted that Congress establish a commission to report on the reasons behind, and lessons to be drawn from, the events of January 6. As most Republicans shifted their focus to combating the Democratic majority, Cheney became a single-issue politician. The issue was stopping Trump.[17]

By May 2021, Cheney's place in leadership had become untenable. An unapologetic Cheney was removed as chair of the House Republican Conference by voice vote. McCarthy then endorsed Rep. Elise Stefanik of New York to replace her. Stefanik, whose lifetime rating from the ACU was 48 percent, won the post on May 14.[18]

Infighting over the third-ranking position in the House Republican leadership is not generally considered a national issue. The Cheney saga drew considerable attention not only for the congresswoman's anti-Trump stance, but also because it was a proxy for the larger fight over the meaning of January 6. House Speaker Nancy Pelosi (D-CA), for example, agreed with Cheney that a commission should examine Trump's activities between November 2020 and January 2021. Pelosi further understood that such an investigation would pay political dividends for her party. McCarthy and McConnell knew that the converse was also true: the more the country dwelled on Trump's behavior in the runup to January 6, the less likely it would be to swing Republican.

On May 18, McCarthy said he opposed the proposal for an independent commission that had been worked out between House Homeland Security Committee chairman Bennie Thompson (D-MS) and ranking member John Katko (R-NY). Both Thompson and Katko had voted for Trump's second impeachment. Their bill passed the House the next day on a 252–175 vote, with the support of thirty-five Republicans. Two weeks later, McConnell came out against the bill. Senate Republicans used the filibuster to block it.[19]

Conservative elites agreed with McCarthy and McConnell that the Thompson-Katko commission would have given too much authority to its Democratic chairman. These conservative elites pointed out that the work of the commission would have over-lapped with other ongoing inquiries, and that a fair panel would have also addressed other instances of political violence. "It's a shame to say it," wrote the editors of the *Wall Street Journal*, "but there isn't enough shared trust in Washington these days to pull off a bipartisan inquiry on so polarized a subject."[20]

Pelosi went ahead anyway. On June 30 the House passed a resolution establishing a select committee on January 6. This new arrangement granted even more power to the Democrats than the earlier Thompson-Katko deal. Liz Cheney and Adam Kinzinger of Illinois, who also voted for Trump's second impeachment, were the two Republicans who voted for the resolution. The next day, Pelosi appointed eight members, including Cheney, to the new committee.[21]

A few weeks later, McCarthy named five members to the committee. Pelosi did not approve. She told McCarthy that she would not allow two of his picks—Jim Jordan of Ohio and Jim Banks of Indiana—to join the body because of their efforts to challenge the 2020 election result. McCarthy responded by saying he wouldn't appoint anyone until Pelosi guaranteed acceptance of his selections. The chances of a truly bipartisan commission vanished.[22]

The Pelosi-appointed Cheney and Kinzinger were the only Republicans on what became known as the January 6 Committee. Their presence served Pelosi's ends. She had corralled Republicans into serving as Trump's blocking tackles. That was where she wanted them. "Her real goal," wrote the *Wall Street Journal* editorial board, "is to keep January 6 alive in the public mind to use against Republicans to maintain control of the House in 2022. Democrats also hope the committee will divide Republicans." Their hopes of GOP disharmony would be fulfilled.[23]

NOT EVERYTHING WAS AS TORTUOUS AS THE INQUIRY INTO January 6 for Republicans and conservatives. Beyond the fallout from 2020 and internal disagreements over Trump, the GOP and conservative movement stood united against the Biden Democrats. Conservatives welcomed new allies into their coalition. As always, the Right benefited from the Left's overreach.

Many figures on the populist right envisioned a future wherein the GOP became the party of industrial laborers and union workers. On election night 2020, Senator Josh Hawley (R-MO) tweeted, "We are a working-class party now." A week later, Senator Marco Rubio (R-FL) said, "The future of the party is based on a multi-ethnic, multiracial, working-class coalition."[24]

When Trump addressed the Conservative Political Action Conference (CPAC) in February 2021, he told the crowd, "The future of the Republican Party is a party that defends the social, economic, and cultural interests and values of working American families of every race, color, and creed." The following month, Rep. Jim Banks, chair of the conservative Republican Study Committee, issued a six-page memo outlining how "House Republicans can broaden our electorate, increase voter turnout, and take back the House by enthusiastically rebranding and reorienting as the Party of the Working Class."[25]

Some of these claims were overstated. The GOP was still the party of white married Christians. The populists were correct to note the rising numbers within Republican ranks of white voters with college degrees, Hispanic voters, and Black men. Yet class consciousness did not bring these groups of voters together. Hostility toward an aggressive and extreme cultural liberalism did. "Trumpism is an anti-leftist, anti-elitist cultural stance," wrote Ryan Streeter of the American Enterprise Institute. "It is not a policy agenda."[26]

The populist right fashioned itself in opposition not only to expert opinion and bureaucratic authority but also to the cultural tropes associated with what was known as "wokism." The Black Lives Matter and Defund the Police movement, the push to define

Hispanic Americans as "Latinx," advocacy of Critical Race Theory (CRT), and the "gender ideology" of LGBT rights—these were major concerns of the conservative street. Americans of every race and ethnicity rejected this left-wing ideology that treated Biblical ideas of sex, gender, and marriage with contempt and looked upon America as corrupted from within and incapable of redemption.

Christopher Rufo, an activist, journalist, and documentarian, became the face of the anti-woke backlash. His intrepid reporting and frequent appearances on *Tucker Carlson Tonight* on the Fox News Channel highlighted the degree to which public schools, government agencies, and even corporate boardrooms had become sites of left-wing indoctrination. Parents were furious at the behavior of teachers' unions and school officials who had kept kids out of classrooms for as long as possible during the pandemic. Now they were coming face to face with what some of their children were being taught. And they were horrified. "When they see what is happening," Rufo said in a speech at Hillsdale College, "Americans are naturally outraged that critical race theory promotes three ideas—race essentialism, collective guilt, and neo-segregation—which violate the basic principles of equality and justice."[27]

Not every voter had heard of CRT. Yet every parent of young children had dealt with school closures, remote learning, and draconian testing and quarantine policies. The intellectual and moral bankruptcy of the public schools became an important issue in the 2021 off-year elections.

Glenn Youngkin, a former Carlyle Group executive, allied himself with parental advocacy organizations opposed to "woke" school boards in the Virginia suburbs of Washington, DC. Youngkin won the Republican nomination for governor of Virginia and emphasized parental rights in education and reviving the commonwealth's inflation-plagued economy. Youngkin faced Democrat Terry McAuliffe, a former governor looking to reclaim his old job.

Education was the decisive issue in the campaign. McAuliffe allied himself with the teachers' unions that had slow-walked re-opening schools during the pandemic. One of his loudest surrogates on the campaign trail was American Federation of Teachers president Randi Weingarten. In an act of political malpractice, McAuliffe said during a debate with Youngkin that he did not believe parents should be telling teachers what to teach. His comment became fodder for Youngkin's attack ads.

McAuliffe attempted to paint Youngkin as a MAGA extremist. He found it hard to do so. Though Trump endorsed Youngkin in the Republican primary, he did not campaign in person for Youngkin during the general election. Nor did Youngkin talk much at all about Trump's signature issue of illegal immigration. What's more, Youngkin did not come across as a pitchfork populist. His personal demeanor and positive, optimistic attitude insulated him from attack.

On Election Day 2021, there was a twelve-point swing among Virginia voters toward Republicans since 2020 and an eleven-point swing since the last governor's race in 2017. Youngkin won by three points, becoming the first Republican governor of Virginia in almost a decade.

Anger at the educational, economic, public safety, and pandemic policies of liberal Democrats was not limited to the Old Dominion. In New Jersey, Republican gubernatorial candidate Jack Ciattarelli closed an eight-point gap in the polls to lose narrowly to Democratic incumbent Phil Murphy. An unknown truck driver unseated the veteran Democratic president of the New Jersey state senate. Local offices in Nassau County on Long Island flipped to the GOP. For the culture warriors of the anti-woke Right, the lessons of 2021 were obvious. "Glenn Youngkin made critical race theory the closing argument to his campaign and dominated in blue Virginia," Rufo tweeted. "We are building the most sophisticated political movement in America—and we have just begun."[28]

Rufo, born in 1984, was something of an intermediary between established conservative institutions and the group of dissidents from movement conservatism known as the New Right. He was a senior fellow at the Manhattan Institute, the storied New York City think tank that had played an important role in Rudolph Giuliani's and Michael Bloomberg's successful mayoralties in the 1990s and 2000s. But he also was a key figure in "national conservatism," the dominant faction on the New Right that sought to recast conservatism in a more culturally traditionalist and religious mold.

Perhaps the best way to understand national conservatives or "natcons" and the New Right to which they belonged was to revisit the work of political scientist James W. Ceaser. In a paper delivered at the 2010 meeting of the American Political Science Association, Ceaser had written of conservatism's "four heads and common heart." The common heart was antipathy toward modern liberalism, aka Progressivism. That heart sustained conservatism's four heads: traditionalism, neoconservatism, libertarianism, and the religious right.[29]

For national conservatives, two heads were better than four (or one). According to the leaders of national conservatism, such as Israeli political philosopher Yoram Hazony, for too long the Right had privileged neoconservatism's universal principles of freedom and libertarianism's reliance on markets over traditional culture and Biblical revelation. The national conservatives believed that Donald Trump provided the Right an opportunity to adjust to the social and cultural realities of the twenty-first century.

National conservatives, and the New Right more generally, rejected neoconservatism and libertarianism. In their many books, articles, Twitter threads, and conferences, they argued that Ceaser's "four heads" model of conservatism had calcified into a "dead consensus" that had conserved nothing. They wanted to use state power to constrain left-wing institutions. They sought to rectify political economy to the advantage of working-class male wage earners. And they called for an "America First" foreign policy of retrenchment and restraint.[30]

National conservatism and the New Right drew much of their following from young people attracted to the controversial ideas that circulate on social media. The movement's leaders, however, were older conservatives who had spent years working in three precincts of the Right: the religious right; Patrick Buchanan's antiwar, traditionalist paleoconservatism as exemplified in the pages of *The American Conservative* and *Chronicles*; and political philosopher Harry Jaffa's Claremont Institute.

The presence of Jaffa's cohort in this mix was puzzling. No one had been a greater advocate of universal standards of morality or a greater opponent of paleoconservatism than Jaffa, the great scholar of Abraham Lincoln who had died in 2015. Still, Jaffa had been a lifelong critic of the Republican establishment whose worldview was tinged with apocalypticism and whose rhetoric, especially against his fellow conservatives, was often overheated. His students had carried these traits even further.

Since the 2000s, Jaffa's followers had made common cause with paleoconservatives on immigration restriction, foreign nonintervention, and support for Trump and MAGA. Writers and thinkers associated with the Claremont Institute pronounced the American republic dead, convinced themselves that America was engaged in a "cold civil war," and raised the possibility of secession. Claremont legal scholar John Eastman persuaded Trump that Vice President Mike Pence could sustain congressional challenges to the Electoral College vote. He set in motion the scheme to keep Trump in office and spoke at the Stop the Steal rally that preceded the violence at the Capitol on January 6, 2021.

This alliance between paleoconservatism and Claremont was neither anticipated nor widely acclaimed. Jaffa's son, Philip, accused the Claremont Institute of betraying his father's legacy. In a comment to a blog published in 2022, he recalled that "My father's exact words, which he repeated over and over, were: 'They did not wait to bury the teaching with the teacher. What they are trying to do is put a top hat on Jefferson Davis and call him Abraham Lincoln.'"[31]

Christopher Rufo, who had been a Claremont Institute Lincoln Fellow in 2017, was emblematic of the New Right's embrace of the culture war. (This writer was a Lincoln Fellow in 2011.) Rufo was a recognized critic of the Walt Disney Company's Diversity, Equity, and Inclusion policies even before the company became embroiled in a fight with Florida's Republican governor Ron DeSantis.[32]

In the spring of 2022, when the Florida legislature passed the Parental Rights in Education law barring public school teachers from discussing sexual orientation and gender identity from kindergarten through third grade, Disney employees staged walkouts and demanded that the company take a stand against the legislation. On the day DeSantis signed the bill into law, a spokesman for Disney issued a statement reading, "Florida's HB 1557, also known as the 'Don't Say Gay' bill, should never have passed and should never have been signed into law. Our goal as a company is for this law to be repealed by the legislature or struck down in the courts, and we remain committed to supporting the national and state organizations working to achieve that."[33]

DeSantis sensed a political opportunity. He knew that when voters were told the details of the education law, they supported it. Just as Ronald Reagan gained popularity as governor by taking a stand against campus radicals in the University of California system, DeSantis put himself on the side of the public against a "woke" corporate giant. "This state is governed by the interests of the people of the state of Florida," DeSantis said. "It is not based on the demands of California corporate executives." He moved for the Florida legislature to rescind the tax and regulatory concessions that had been granted to Disney in 1967 when it started construction on Walt Disney World Resort. Within weeks, he signed into law a bill revoking Disney's special privileges.[34]

Libertarians and other free market conservatives worried that DeSantis's retaliation set a bad precedent against corporate speech. Yet many on the Right also believed that DeSantis's withdrawal of economic privileges was not a breach of conservative principle but an attack on cronyism. Moreover, DeSantis understood that aggressive cultural liberalism could be deterred only by hitting back. "We will never win if we play by the rules set by the elites who are undermining our country," Rufo said in an after-action report on the Disney fight. The correct strategy was to "lay siege to our institutions" by mobilizing public support against them, by decentralizing concentrations of power, and by building alternatives.[35]

The New Right may have agreed on the importance of culture and the political talents of Ron DeSantis, but as the movement gained in prominence fractures within it began to appear. For instance, the "postliberal" Catholics who sought a deeper integration of church and state distanced themselves from the national conservatives. Journalist and author Sohrab Ahmari departed the *New York Post* to launch the online journal *Compact* with fellow Catholic journalist Matthew Schmitz and Marxist writer Edwin Aponte.

Compact was a self-described "radical American journal" intended to "challenge the overclass that controls government, culture, and capital." While the editors of *Compact* published some national conservatives, leading Catholic integralists such as Ahmari, Patrick Deneen, and Adrian Vermeule did not appear at the national conservatism conference in 2022.[36]

Foreign policy also became a subject of contention within the New Right. The "America First" national conservatives found themselves in a somewhat awkward position when Russian dictator Vladimir Putin invaded Ukraine on February 24, 2022. Self-professed advocates of national borders and sovereignty had little choice but to condemn Russia's unprovoked violation of Ukrainian independence. "Russia's latest war has been analyzed in terms of spheres of influence, the return of great-power competition, dictatorship versus democracy," said Christopher R. DeMuth, chairman of the Edmund Burke Foundation, at the opening of a national conservatism conference in Europe one month after the war began. "But the heart of the matter is the integrity of the nation."[37]

That was not how Ahmari saw it. He helped to organize an open letter demanding that the Biden administration negotiate a "humanitarian ceasefire, as a prelude to good-faith negotiations toward a permanent peace that takes into account Ukraine's right to self-determination and Russia's legitimate security needs." Signatories included Christopher Rufo; Patrick Deneen; Helen Andrews, the editor in chief of *The American Conservative*; and Ryan Williams, president of the Claremont Institute. Their chief worries were that American policy had backed Russia into a corner where it had no choice but to invade, and that American assistance to Ukraine would result in an escalatory spiral and potential nuclear exchange.[38]

Neither DeMuth's nor Hazony's name was attached to the letter. Their reluctance to join *Compact* put them in the mainstream of opinion on the Right. Most Republican officials and most Republican voters blamed the war on Putin's aggression, viewed Ukrainian president Volodymyr Zelensky as a heroic champion of freedom, and supported both military aid to Ukraine and Swedish and Finnish accession to NATO. Most conservative intellectuals did too. "Ukrainians are fighting for freedom and self-rule," wrote the editors of *National Review*. "They have won glory. Glory to Ukraine." When the ninety-nine-year-old Henry Kissinger floated the outlines of a peace deal, public outrage forced him to backtrack. "At no point did I say that Ukraine should give up any territory," he told *Der Spiegel*. "I said the logical dividing line for a ceasefire is the status quo ante."[39]

New Right skepticism toward involvement in the Russo-Ukraine war grew over the course of 2022. The movement's spokesmen aligned with their Hungarian hero, Prime Minister Viktor Orbán, who also called for a ceasefire and said that Donald Trump was just the person to negotiate it. Tucker Carlson denounced Zelensky regularly on air. Christopher Caldwell of the *Claremont Review of Books* said in a speech, "The U.S. is not just supporting Ukraine. It is fighting a war in Ukraine's name." Kevin Roberts, president of the Heritage Foundation, led his organization in opposing the $40 billion in economic and military assistance that Congress authorized for Ukraine in May.[40]

The New Right took on the appearance of the New Left. Both persuasions said that Russia was misunderstood. Both were antiwar—except in the culture. Both were suspicious of and hostile to capitalism. Both were part of an international movement. And both tended toward heated rhetoric and ad hominem attack.

The New Right, however, reversed the New Left's idea that the personal is political. For the New Right, the political was personal. If you disagreed with its ends and means, you were, in the words of Harry Jaffa biographer Glenn Ellmers, "a zombie and a human rodent who wants a shadow-life of timid conformity."[41]

The New Right, like the New Left, was radically alienated from the United States of America. According to Ellmers, "Most people living in the United States today—certainly more than half—are not Americans in any meaningful sense of the term." In a since-deleted Tweet, Sohrab Ahmari wrote, "I'm at peace with a Chinese-led 21st century. Late-liberal America is too dumb and decadent to last as a superpower." At an Intercollegiate Studies Institute (ISI) panel discussion in the summer of 2021, *American Affairs* editor Julius Krein said, perhaps half-kiddingly, that he would love to move to the People's Republic of China. The topic of the Philadelphia Society's 2022 annual meeting was, "Can American institutions still be conserved?" One participant, Claremont's Michael Anton, admonished conservatives for not taking seriously the right of revolution against tyrannical government.[42]

The national conservative "statement of principles" released in the summer of 2021 was an eloquent declaration of traditionalist and religious concerns and priorities. Yet it contained no reference to the Declaration of Independence. It raised the possibility of a moratorium on all immigration into the United States. And it cast serious doubts on the American political traditions of federalism and separation of church and state, proclaiming that the majority religion of a given country "should be honored by the state and other institutions both public and private." At a New Right conference in Steubenville, Ohio, in October 2021, Catholic political scientist Mary Imparato of Belmont Abbey College recalled a youthful desire to see a statue of Mary, mother of Jesus, replace the Statue of Freedom atop the US Capitol.[43]

Back in the 1960s, the New Left's main target was the liberal establishment and liberal elites. For the New Left, the Right was hopeless, almost irrelevant. Liberals were the real enemy. Sociologist Robert Nisbet, a well-known conservative, noticed that the radicals on campus at the University of California–Riverside in the 1960s did not attack him. In fact, many of the far-left students had read his books and agreed with them.

The New Right exhibited the same strange type of respect for left-wing thinkers—from political theorist Wilson Carey McWilliams and historian Christopher Lasch to postmodern philosophers Michel Foucault and Slavoj Žižek—that the New Left once bestowed on right-wing communitarians like Nisbet and Libertarian anti-anticommunists like Murray Rothbard.

The New Right was willing to drop its association with conservatism entirely. Neither *American Affairs* nor *Compact* identified as conservative. Mollie Hemingway, who became the editor in chief of *The Federalist* in the winter of 2022, quoted Patrick Buchanan in her acceptance address at the 2021 Bradley Foundation Prize awards dinner and said, "All of a sudden, the conservative project is not a conservative one, so much as a counterrevolutionary one." In

September 2021, attorney Bruce Abramson wrote a piece for Real-ClearPolitics with the title, "The Conservative Temperament Is Dooming America." A year later, John Daniel Davidson, a senior editor at *The Federalist*, wrote a piece headlined, "We Need to Stop Calling Ourselves Conservatives."[44]

People are free to call themselves what they choose. But the New Right did not want to separate itself from the conservative movement. It wanted to take it over. In addition to building its own counterinstitutions, the New Right challenged the Republican and conservative establishment. Conservative strongholds behaved just as liberal institutions had done when faced with the New Left generations ago: they bent to the will of this insurgent force. A glance at the programming of both ISI and the Philadelphia Society revealed that they were headed in a New Right direction. The Conservative Political Action Conference, organized by journalist and activist M. Stanton Evans in 1974, became a Trump roadshow.

Tucker Carlson's program on Fox News Channel was a ratings giant. Heritage president Roberts told the 2022 national conservatism conference, "I come not to invite Natcons to join our movement, but to acknowledge that Heritage is part of yours." In the autumn of 2022, when former congresswoman Tulsi Gabbard announced that she was leaving the Democratic Party, Roberts welcomed this ideological liberal, best known for her harsh criticism of US treatment of Syria and Russia, to the ranks of Heritage's "third way" foreign policy.[45]

The New Right, allied with Trump, made its presence felt in the Republican Party. As the GOP selected its nominees for the 2022 midterm elections, Trump made sure to campaign against Republicans who had voted to impeach him. In other races, Trump and the New Right backed candidates who participated in the "Stop the Steal" efforts after the 2020 election and opposed continued aid to Ukraine.

Of the ten House Republicans who voted to impeach Trump, four retired. Another four, including Liz Cheney, lost primaries. Only two remained as of November 2022. Of the seven Senate Republicans who voted to convict Trump, three retired. Another, Lisa Murkowski of Alaska, won reelection in a three-way race. Mitt Romney of Utah, Susan Collins of Maine, and Bill Cassidy of Louisiana would not face voters until either 2024 or 2026.[46]

Cheney was Trump's top target. He endorsed her primary opponent, an attorney (and former Cheney supporter) named Harriet Hageman, early in September 2021. Several months later, in the winter of 2022, Kevin McCarthy endorsed Hageman as well. Cheney raised plenty of money, most of it from outside Wyoming, but her hopes to retain the seat rested on the unlikely possibility that the MAGA forces would split the vote and allow Democrats and independents to give her a plurality. From her position as ranking member of the Select Committee on January 6, Cheney orchestrated a series of public hearings, beginning in the spring of 2022, laying out Trump's attempt to remain in office. The first hearing, held in June, drew an audience of at least twenty million people.[47]

They probably were not Republican primary voters. By Wyoming's August 16 primary, Trump's dominance of the party was unquestioned. Hageman crushed Cheney, 66 percent to 29 percent.[48]

The split in the conservative intellectual movement was apparent the next month. Cheney and Hageman gave dueling Constitution Day speeches at, respectively, the American Enterprise Institute and Heritage Foundation in Washington, DC. "We are to this day living through the impact of a president who has abandoned his oath," Cheney said. Across town, Hageman denounced the recent FBI search of Trump's Mar-a-Lago property and seizure of classified materials he had taken from the White House.[49]

Trump endorsed more than two hundred GOP candidates. Most were incumbents all but certain to win. But Trump's endorsement counted for a lot. Representative Madison Cawthorn of North Carolina, beset by personal scandal, was the lone Trump-endorsed incumbent to lose a primary. All of Trump's Senate endorsees won their primaries. Trump fared less well against incumbent Republican governors such as Brian Kemp of Georgia, but overall 91 percent of Trump's endorsees won their party's nomination. According to one analysis, more than three hundred Republican candidates for House, Senate, and high state office had cast doubt on or outright denied the legitimacy of Biden's election.[50]

As had been happening since the dawn of the Trump era on June 16, 2015, the GOP was being remade in the image of the former president. Trump fans and New Right intellectuals looked at the primary returns and President Biden's continued unpopularity and saw a "red wave" of Republican victories building offshore. "Mitch McConnell may question 'candidate quality,' but the Republican Party's embrace of apparently high-risk candidates is a sign of confidence, not weakness," wrote Daniel McCarthy, editor of *Modern Age*, in a guest essay for the *New York Times*. "The party's voters feel strongly enough about the populist, pro-Trump positioning that they have supported those candidates over more experienced and less controversial candidates." McCarthy's piece was headlined, "Republicans Are Doubling Down on Trumpism. It's Going to Work."[51]

Not exactly.

The fundamentals of the 2022 election favored the GOP. The out-party typically does well in midterms. Biden's approval rating was below 50 percent. Inflation and supply shortages convinced most Americans that the economy was in a recession. Republicans led Democrats on the congressional generic ballot for most of 2022. The public furor that greeted the Supreme Court's June 24 reversal of *Roe v. Wade* seemed to dissipate over time.

In late July, though, Democrats began to gain. On July 27, seventeen Republicans voted to pass the CHIPS Act, subsidizing US semiconductors for reasons of national security. Hours later, Chuck Schumer announced that he had reached a deal with Joe Manchin on a climate, health care, and tax bill called the Inflation Reduction Act. Senate Republicans had been outmaneuvered. "Looks to me like we got rinky-doo'd," said GOP senator John Kennedy of Louisiana. "That's a Louisiana word for 'screwed.'"[52]

Then, on August 2, voters in Kansas rejected an effort to overturn a state court's ruling that the Sunflower State constitution guaranteed a right to abortion. Similar referenda allowing state legislatures to regulate abortion had passed in West Virginia, Alabama, Tennessee, and Louisiana. This was the first such initiative put to the ballot since the demise of *Roe v. Wade*. Kansas voted for Donald Trump by fifteen points in 2020. It voted to maintain a state right to abortion by eighteen points in 2022.[53]

The reversal of *Roe* was a triumph for the pro-life cause. It culminated the conservative legal movement's multigenerational effort to appoint judges who interpreted law based on the original meaning of the US Constitution. Yet the ruling also mobilized an important Democratic constituency: voters, especially women, with high levels of educational attainment. On August 23, Democrat Pat Ryan defeated Republican Marc Molinaro in a closely watched congressional special election in New York. It was the latest in a string of special elections where Democrats performed above expectations. Ryan staked his campaign on preserving abortion rights. Molinaro focused on inflation. Voters had a clear-cut choice between the two parties' messages. Abortion won. "After *Dobbs*, and with Mr. Trump back at the center of public debate, Democrats have a chance to overcome President Biden's low popularity," wrote the editors of the *Wall Street Journal*. "GOP candidates have been warned."[54]

Republicans shrugged off the warning. They changed the subject. They launched a barrage of ads attacking Democrats on crime. The tactic appeared to work. Senator Ron Johnson, a Republican incumbent from Wisconsin, pulled ahead of his Democratic challenger. Mehmet Oz, the Trump-endorsed candidate for Senate from Pennsylvania, gained ground against his opponent. The rise in violent crime since 2019 became a top concern of voters. This shift in public opinion helped candidates such as Republican congressman Lee Zeldin, who was running to replace Democrat Kathy Hochul as governor of New York. Zeldin surged in the polls after Hochul dismissed his argument about public safety as reckless fearmongering.[55]

Republicans and conservatives, always doubtful of public opinion surveys, convinced themselves that a tied poll meant the Republican candidate would end up winning. Most Democrats went into Election Day thinking that Republicans would take both chambers of Congress and flip governors' mansions to the GOP. That did not happen.

Republican gains were lackluster. Republicans won the national House vote, but they took control of the House by the slimmest of margins. At best, Republicans would simply hold their current fifty seats in the Senate. And governors' races were a wash: Republicans won Nevada, and Democrats won Arizona.

Conservatives were disappointed. "We have Joe Biden, who is the least popular president since Harry Truman, since presidential polling happened, and there wasn't a red wave," said former presidential speechwriter and *Washington Post* columnist Marc Thiessen on Fox News Channel during election night. "That is a searing indictment of the Republican Party."[56]

Trump's high-profile endorsements did not fare well. The only nonincumbent Senate candidate he endorsed who went on to win was J. D. Vance of Ohio—and Vance ran well behind incumbent Republican governor Mike DeWine, who won reelection by twenty-five points. The only nonincumbent gubernatorial candidate Trump endorsed who went on to win was Joe Lombardo of Nevada. None of his secretary of state picks won. Philip Wallach of the American Enterprise Institute calculated that in the 114 most competitive House districts, Trump-endorsed candidates underperformed expectations by an average of five points. Indeed, Republicans took the House largely on the coattails of Lee Zeldin's strong (but ultimately unsuccessful) performance in New York and Ron DeSantis's million-vote reelection victory in Florida.[57]

Since Donald Trump became president, Republicans had lost independent voters and suburban voters and, consequently, the House, the White House, and the Senate. And yet GOP success at the state level showed what was possible when Trump was not the decisive factor in voters' minds. DeSantis's twenty-point victory garnered the most national attention, but he was far from alone in offering a popular model of conservative governance. From Mike DeWine, Chris Sununu of New Hampshire, Greg Abbott of Texas, and Brian Kemp of Georgia to the departing Charlie Baker of Massachusetts and Larry Hogan of Maryland, Republican governors broadened the party's appeal by meeting voters where they lived—seizing the commonsense mainstream and addressing public concerns calmly and effectively and often without the sort of backlash Trump inspired.

Retiring governor Doug Ducey of Arizona signed the most expansive school choice bill ever. Youngkin's win in 2021, Kemp's reelection after standing up to Trump in 2020, and the almost ten-point swing toward DeSantis in Florida from 2018 to 2022 showed that a different version of the GOP was waiting in the wings. This party would be able to rise above the self-imposed limits of Donald Trump's coalition without giving much up.

Moving beyond Trump did not require Republicans to repudiate his agenda, or to insult or condescend to his voters. Republican governors run the gamut from abortion-rights moderates to antiabortion MAGA culture warriors. What made figures such as Kemp, Youngkin, and DeSantis unique was their ability to exploit the weaknesses of the cultural Left without frightening the center of the electorate.

Donald Trump was not going anywhere. One week after the election, on November 15, he announced his third campaign for the presidency. He entered the primary race as the frontrunner for the nomination of a party he had transformed. Whatever the future might bring, it would be folly to dismiss the former president. The Trump era was not about to end any time soon.

ED FEULNER, WHO COFOUNDED THE HERITAGE FOUNDATION IN 1973 and served as its president from 1977 to 2013, used to issue periodic reports on the state of conservatism. Conservatism, in Feulner's view, may have been sectarian. It may have faced setbacks. But the future always remained bright for a movement dedicated to constitutionalism, limited government, the rule of law, and a strong national defense.

As 2022 came to an end, the Republican Party was beleaguered yet powerful. It had won control of the House for the second time in thirty years, guaranteeing divided government in Washington through 2024. Conservatives had made sweeping changes to the judiciary. They had overturned *Roe v. Wade*, reasserted the individual right to keep and bear arms, reined in freewheeling executive agencies, and stood on the precipice of eliminating racial preferences in college admissions. In Florida, DeSantis had the potential to succeed Trump as a leader who could unify the party and win a national election.

Running alongside these political gains and constitutional victories, however, was a stream of intellectual doubt and sectarian division. To speak of the conservative movement in 2022 was to describe a philosophical tendency in a condition of fracture and flux. It was hard to tell who belonged on the Right and who did not. Membership in the Trump coalition depended most of all on one's posture toward the former president. The term "RINO" had been drained of all meaning. RINOs used to be liberal or moderate Republicans who deviated from conservative positions on taxes, life, or guns. More recently, "RINO" was used simply to describe a critic of Trump or MAGA.

Trump, populism, and the New Right had retailored the fabric of conservatism. Some of their alterations were necessary. The New Right had legitimate gripes against the corrupted state of American institutions. It was right to stand athwart the radicalism of cultural gatekeepers. Populism always will be part of conservatism. And conservatives have made arguments for a more selective immigration policy, strategic decoupling from China, policies that benefit wage earners without college degrees, parental involvement in education, and treating the major tech platforms as common carriers. All these ends are in harmony with the American constitutional order.

And it is the constitutional order that American conservatives are meant to defend. A constitutional order founded on the principle of human freedom and dignity. A constitutional order of enumerated powers, individual rights, and religious freedom. An order designed to "decide the important question, whether societies of men are really capable or not of establishing good government from reflection and choice, or whether they are forever destined to depend for their political constitutions on accident and force." An order in which the deliberate sense of the people is channeled through representative institutions into positive law meant to "form a more perfect Union, establish Justice, ensure domestic Tranquility, provide for the common defense, promote the general welfare, and secure the blessings of liberty to ourselves and our posterity." An order informed by "a standard maxim for free society" that is "constantly spreading and deepening its influence and augmenting the happiness and value of life to all people of all colors everywhere."[58]

Times change. People change. Movements change. The Left changes. But human nature does not. Nor do the timeless truths of the American Founding. American conservatism exists to remind the world of these facts, and to apply those truths prudentially and moderately to the problems of the moment. If some on the New Right no longer want to call themselves conservative, if they no longer want to be part of the tradition of liberty, then conservatives must let them go. And when the Right recommits itself to constitutional democracy and the American idea of liberty under law, the state of conservatism will be strong.

—November 18, 2022

ACKNOWLEDGMENTS

THIS BOOK HAS BEEN LONG IN THE MAKING—AND I ACCUMU-lated many debts while making it. My thanks first go to Roger Hertog, without whose inspiration, guidance, and support this book would not exist. Robert Doar and Yuval Levin brought me on as a fellow at the American Enterprise Institute (AEI), allowing me to commit to paper all the stray thoughts on conservatism I'd been accumulating for some time. I am also grateful to Michael Goldfarb and Eliana Johnson at the *Washington Free Beacon*, who gave me the freedom to pursue my idiosyncratic interests.

Glen Hartley and Lynn Chu have helped me navigate the publishing world since 2005. Lara Heimert at Basic Books cared deeply about this project and offered excellent advice. Cheryl Miller, Neal Kozodoy, Eric Cohen, John Podhoretz, and Andrew Ferguson read the first draft of the manuscript and provided helpful feedback. Robert Asahina's suggestions on the second draft were invaluable, and Roger Labrie performed essential work on the third. Sam Goldman, Peter Berkowitz, Jerry Muller, Adam White, Ramesh Ponnuru, and Nicole Penn participated in an instructive reading group at AEI. Vic Matus proofread the final copy. Tal Fortgang and J. R. Roach provided research assistance. And I owe Bill and Susan Kristol more than I can repay.

It may not take a village to raise a child, but it does take a family to write a book. This text belongs as much to my parents, my wife, and my children as it does to me. Not any errors, of course. Those are mine alone.

NOTES

INTRODUCTION: 1150 SEVENTEENTH STREET

1. John Micklethwait and Adrian Wooldridge, *The Right Nation: Conservative Power in America* (New York: Penguin Press, 2004).

2. Adam Nagourney, "President, Why Not? Says Man at the Top," *New York Times*, September 25, 1999, B1.

3. Mark Preston and Adam Silverleib, "Trump Endorses Romney," CNN, February 3, 2012, http://www.cnn.com/2012/02/02/politics/campaign-wrap/index.html.

4. George H. Nash, *The Conservative Intellectual Movement in America Since 1945* (Wilmington, DE: ISI Books, 2006); Patrick Allitt, *The Conservatives: Ideas and Personalities Throughout American History* (New Haven, CT: Yale University Press, 2009).

CHAPTER ONE: NORMALCY AND ITS DISCONTENTS

1. Bradley C. S. Watson, *Living Constitution, Dying Faith: Progressivism and the New Science of Jurisprudence* (Wilmington, DE: ISI Books, 2009), 105.

2. Christopher Caldwell, "Schoolmaster to the World," *Claremont Review of Books* 14, no. 1 (winter 2013/2014): 22.

3. A. Scott Berg, *Wilson* (New York: G. P. Putnam's Sons, 2013), 323.

4. Walter A. McDougall, *The Tragedy of U.S. Foreign Policy* (New Haven, CT: Yale University Press, 2016), 149, 152.

5. Berg, *Wilson*, 437.

6. Bill Kauffman, *America First! Its History, Culture, and Politics* (Amherst, NY: Prometheus Books, 2016), 40, 50–51.

7. Gregory L. Schneider, *The Conservative Century: From Reaction to Revolution* (Lanham, MD: Rowman & Littlefield, 2009), 6.

8. Steven Shapin, "Man with a Plan: Herbert Spencer's Theory of Everything," *New Yorker*, August 6, 2007, 75–79.

9. Allan J. Lichtman, *White Protestant Nation: The Rise of the American Conservative Movement* (New York: Atlantic Monthly Press, 2008), 47.

10. As early as 1914, Henry Campbell Black, a former president of Bucknell College, established the National Association for Constitutional Government to resist the centralization of power in the federal government, the use of such power to effect changes in society, the expanding role of the president, and efforts to reform the judiciary. For twelve years the center published a journal, the *Constitutional Review*, whose editors and contributors insisted that public veneration of the Constitution was the way to stable and munificent government.

11. Calvin Coolidge, "Speech on the 150th Anniversary of the Declaration of Independence," Teaching American History, July 5, 1926, https://teachingamericanhistory.org/library/document/speech-on -the-occasion-of-the-one-hundred-and-fiftieth-anniversary-of-the -declaration-of-independence.

12. Lichtman, *White Protestant Nation*, 42; Paul Johnson, *Modern Times: The World from the Twenties to the Nineties* (New York: Harper Perennial Modern Classics, 2001), 204.

13. "10,000 Klansmen Burn Cross at Oceanside," *New York Times*, July 26, 1925, 66.

14. Frederic D. Schwarz, "The Klan on Parade," *American Heritage*, July/August 2000, https://www.americanheritage.com/klan-parade.

15. Lichtman, *White Protestant Nation*, 44; Seymour Martin Lipset and Earl Raab, *The Politics of Unreason: Right-Wing Extremism in America, 1790–1970* (New York: Harper & Row, 1970), 135; Lipset and Raab, *Politics of Unreason*, 111; Amity Shlaes, *Coolidge* (New York: Harper, 2013), 274.

16. Johnson, *Modern Times*, 204; Calvin Coolidge, "Toleration and Liberalism: Speech Before the American Legion Convention," Coolidge

Foundation, October 6, 1925, https://coolidgefoundation.org/resources /speeches-as-president-1923-1929-4.

17. Jonathan Bean, ed., *Race and Liberty in America: The Essential Reader* (Lexington: University Press of Kentucky, 2009), 139, 150.

18. Bean, *Race and Liberty in America*, 149.

19. Michael Cromartie, *Religious Conservatives in American Politics, 1980–2000: An Assessment*, Witherspoon Fellowship Lectures (Washington, DC: Family Research Council, 2001), transcript in author's possession.

20. J. Gresham Machen, *Christianity and Liberalism* (New York: Macmillan, 1923), 146.

21. Jeffrey P. Moran, *The Scopes Trial: A Brief History with Documents* (Boston: Bedford/St. Martin's/Macmillan Learning, 2021), 162.

22. H. L. Mencken, *A Mencken Chrestomathy* (New York: Vintage, 1982), 145–148.

23. Murray N. Rothbard, *The Betrayal of the American Right* (Auburn, AL: Ludwig von Mises Institute, 2007), 19; Albert Jay Nock, *Cogitations from Albert Jay Nock*, ed. Robert M. Thornton (Irvington-on-Hudson, NY: Nockian Society, 1970), 43.

24. Shlaes, *Coolidge*, 362.

25. David Greenberg, "Calvin Coolidge: Domestic Affairs," University of Virginia Miller Center, https://millercenter.org/president/coolidge /domestic-affairs.

26. Calvin Coolidge, "State of the Union, 1928," American History: From Revolution to Reconstruction and Beyond, December 4, 1928, http://www.let.rug.nl/usa/presidents/calvin-coolidge/state-of-the-union -1928.php.

CHAPTER TWO: THE REVOLUTION OF 1932

1. Seymour Martin Lipset and Earl Raab, *The Politics of Unreason: Right-Wing Extremism in America, 1790–1970* (New York: Harper & Row, 1970), 150.

2. David M. Kennedy, *Freedom from Fear: The American People in Depression and War, 1929–1945* (New York: Oxford University Press, 1999), 92.

3. David Kennedy, "F.D.R., Budget Hawk," *New York Times*, July 29, 2011, https://www.nytimes.com/roomfordebate/2011/07/20/presidents -and-their-debts-fdr-to-bush/fdr-budget-hawk.

4. Franklin Delano Roosevelt, "Radio Address from Albany, New York: The 'Forgotten Man' Speech," April 7, 1932, American Presidency Project, https://www.presidency.ucsb.edu/documents/radio-address -from-albany-new-york-the-forgotten-man-speech.

5. Franklin Delano Roosevelt, "Document: Commonwealth Club Address," September 23, 1932, Teaching American History, https:// teachingamericanhistory.org/library/document/commonwealth-club -address.

6. Eric F. Goldman, *Rendezvous with Destiny: A History of Modern American Reform* (New York: Vintage Books, 1977), 324.

7. Lipset and Raab, *Politics of Unreason*, 200; Garland S. Tucker III, *Conservative Heroes: Fourteen Leaders Who Shaped America, from Jefferson to Reagan* (Wilmington, DE: ISI Books, 2015), 147.

8. Allan J. Lichtman, *White Protestant Nation: The Rise of the American Conservative Movement* (New York: Atlantic Monthly Press, 2008), 58.

9. Herbert Hoover, *American Individualism* (Stanford, CA: Hoover Institution Press, 2016), xxviii.

10. Albert Jay Nock, "Isaiah's Job," in *Did You Ever See a Dream Walking? American Conservative Thought in the Twentieth Century*, ed. William F. Buckley Jr. (Indianapolis: Bobbs Merrill, 1970), 512.

11. Garet Garrett, "The Revolution Was," Mises Institute, January 26, 2008, https://mises.org/library/revolution-was; Justin Raimondo, *Reclaiming the American Right: The Lost Legacy of the Conservative Movement* (Wilmington, DE: ISI Books, 2008), 189; Murray N. Rothbard, *The Betrayal of the American Right* (Auburn, AL: Ludwig von Mises Institute, 2007), 51.

12. Twelve Southerners, *I'll Take My Stand: The South and the Agrarian Tradition* (Baton Rouge: Louisiana State University Press, 1977), xxxviii.

13. Seward Collins, "Editorial Notes," *American Review* (April 1933): 122.

14. C. Vann Woodward, *Tom Watson: Agrarian Rebel* (New York: Macmillan Company, 1938).

15. Henry C. Simons, *A Positive Program for Laissez Faire: Some Proposals for a Liberal Economic Policy* (Chicago: University of Chicago Press, 1934), 2.

16. Mark Skousen, *Vienna and Chicago, Friends or Foes? A Tale of Two Schools of Free-Market Economics* (Washington, DC: Regnery, 2005), 5–8.

17. Ludwig von Mises, *Notes and Recollections: With the Historical Setting of the Austrian School of Economics* (Indianapolis: Liberty Fund, 2013), 106–107, 108.

18. Ronald L. Trowbridge, ed., *In the First Place: 20 Years of the Most Consequential Ideas from Hillsdale College's Monthly Journal Imprimis* (Hillsdale, MI: Hillsdale College Press, 1992), 69; Lanny Ebenstein, *Chicagonomics: The Evolution of Chicago Free Market Economics* (New York: St. Martin's Press, 2015), 209.

19. Lipset and Raab, *Politics of Unreason*, 160–162.

20. "William Dudley Pelley, 75, Dies," *New York Times*, July 2, 1965, 27.

21. Alan Brinkley, *Voices of Protest: Huey Long, Father Coughlin, and the Great Depression* (New York: Vintage, 1983).

22. Kennedy, *Freedom from Fear*, 236.

23. Huey P. Long, *Every Man a King: The Autobiography of Huey P. Long* (New York: Da Capo Press, 1996).

24. Arthur M. Schlesinger Jr. and John S. Bowman, eds., *The Almanac of American History* (New York: Putnam, 1983), 472; Henry Ford, "Alfred M. Landon," *New York Times*, October 18, 1936, 94.

25. Damon Root, *Overruled: The Long War for the Control of the U.S. Supreme Court* (New York: Palgrave Macmillan, 2014), 71.

26. "Gannett Censures Roosevelt Speech," *New York Times*, September 20, 1937, 16.

27. Tucker, *Conservative Heroes*, 125.

28. Charles Murray, *By the People: Rebuilding Liberty Without Permission* (New York: Crown Forum, 2015), 16.

29. Tucker, *Conservative Heroes*, 130–131.

30. Lichtman, *White Protestant Nation*, 104.

31. Russell Kirk and James McClellan, *The Political Principles of Robert A. Taft* (New York: Fleet Press, 1967), 13, 17; James T. Patterson, *Mr. Republican: A Biography of Robert A. Taft* (Boston: Houghton Mifflin, 1972), 176.

32. Ronald Radosh, *Prophets on the Right: Profiles of Conservative Critics of American Globalism* (New York: Simon & Schuster, 1975), 120.

33. Kirk and McClellan, *The Political Principles of Robert A. Taft*, 167; Patterson, *Mr. Republican*, 196.

34. Radosh, *Prophets on the Right*, 132; Patterson, *Mr. Republican*, 217, 247.

35. Patterson, *Mr. Republican*, 215; Radosh, *Prophets on the Right*, 130.

36. Patterson, *Mr. Republican*, 242; John B. Judis, *William F. Buckley, Jr., Patron Saint of the Conservatives* (New York: Simon & Schuster, 1988), 18.

37. A. Scott Berg, *Lindbergh* (New York: G. P. Putnam's, 1998), 411.

38. Berg, *Lindbergh*, 415.

39. Berg, *Lindbergh*, 418.

40. Berg, *Lindbergh*, 428; Rothbard, *Betrayal of the American Right*, 45n10.

41. Berg, *Lindbergh*, 431–432.

CHAPTER THREE: FROM WORLD WAR
TO COLD WAR

1. David M. Kennedy, *Freedom from Fear: The American People in Depression and War, 1929–1945* (New York: Oxford University Press, 1999), 782; Russell Kirk and James McClellan, *The Political Principles of Robert A. Taft* (New York: Fleet Press, 1967), 43.

2. Kennedy, *Freedom from Fear*, 751.

3. Jonathan Bean, ed., *Race and Liberty in America: The Essential Reader* (Lexington: University Press of Kentucky, 2009), 174–177.

4. Albert Jay Nock, *Memoirs of a Superfluous Man* (New York: Harper & Brothers, 1943), 239.

5. Bradley J. Birzer, *Russell Kirk: American Conservative* (Lexington: University Press of Kentucky, 2015), 72; George H. Nash, *The Conservative Intellectual Movement in America Since 1945* (Wilmington, DE: ISI Books, 2006), 18.

6. Friedrich A. von Hayek, *Hayek on Hayek: An Autobiographical Dialogue*, ed. Stephen Kresge and Leif Wenar (Chicago: University of Chicago Press, 1994), 97; Friedrich A. von Hayek, *Studies in Philosophy, Politics, and Economics* (New York: Simon & Schuster Clarion Books, 1969), 216–217.

7. Friedrich A. von Hayek, *The Road to Serfdom* (London: Routledge & K. Paul, 1979), 26, 44.

8. Hayek, *Road to Serfdom*, 28–29.

9. Barbara Wootton, *Freedom Under Planning* (Chapel Hill: University of North Carolina Press, 1945); Herman Finer, *Road to Reaction* (Boston: Little, Brown, 1945); Hayek, *Road to Serfdom*, 13.

10. Henry Hazlitt, "An Economist's View of Planning," *New York Times*, September 24, 1944; Brian Doherty, *Radicals for Capitalism: A*

Freewheeling History of the Modern American Libertarian Movement (New York: PublicAffairs, 2007), 91–92.

11. Hayek, *Hayek on Hayek*, 104–105.

12. Steel, *Walter Lippmann and the American Century*, 368.

13. Daniel Stedman Jones, *Masters of the Universe: Hayek, Friedman, and the Birth of Neoliberal Politics* (Princeton, NJ: Princeton University Press, 2012), 353n51.

14. Hayek, *Studies in Philosophy, Politics, and Economics*, 149.

15. "Statement of Aims," Mont Pelerin Society, April 8, 1947, https://www.montpelerin.org/statement-of-aims; Eamonn Butler, "A Short History of the Mont Pelerin Society," Buried Truth, accessed October 3, 2021, https://buriedtruth.com/files/Mont_Pelerin_Society-History_of_MPS-2014.pdf.

16. Hayek, *Studies in Philosophy, Politics, and Economics*, 178–179.

17. Hayek, *Studies in Philosophy, Politics, and Economics*, 194.

18. James T. Patterson, *Mr. Republican: A Biography of Robert A. Taft* (Boston: Houghton Mifflin, 1972).

19. George Novack, "The Road We Have Traveled: Five Decades of Building the Revolutionary Party in the United States, 1919–1969," *Socialist Action*, August 15, 1969, https://www.marxists.org/history/etol/document/swp-us/idb/swp-1966-69/v27n11-aug-1969-db.pdf.

20. James Burnham, *The Machiavellians, Defenders of Freedom* (Washington, DC: Regnery, 1963), xx.

21. James Burnham, *The Managerial Revolution: What Is Happening in the World* (Westport, CT: Greenwood Press, 1941), 148.

22. James Burnham, "To See the World and Man," *Chronicles of Culture*, April 1984, 4; Burnham, *The Machiavellians*, 110.

23. James Burnham, *The Struggle for the World* (New York: John Day Co., 1947), 160; Burnham, *Managerial Revolution*, 36.

24. Hedda Hopper, "Mr. Reagan Airs His Views," *Chicago Tribune*, May 18, 1947, 1, G7.

25. Hopper, "Mr. Reagan Airs His Views."

26. Ralph de Toledano and Victor Lasky, *Seeds of Treason: The True Story of the Hiss-Chambers Tragedy* (New York: Funk & Wagnalls, 1950), 4.

27. Whittaker Chambers, *Witness* (New York: Random House, 1952), 16.

28. Richard M. Nixon, *Six Crises* (New York: Pocket Books, 1962), 55.

29. Nixon, *Six Crises*, 67.

30. Nash, *Conservative Intellectual Movement in America*, 151–152; John Earl Haynes and Harvey Klehr, *Venona: Decoding Soviet Espionage in America* (New Haven, CT: Yale University Press, 2000).

31. Chambers, *Witness*, 9.

32. 96 *Congressional Record* S7725 (May 25, 1950); Joseph McCarthy, "Enemies from Within," Texas Liberal Arts, February 20, 1950, https://liberalarts.utexas.edu/coretexts/_files/resources/texts/1950%20McCarthy%20Enemies.pdf.

33. Richard Gid Powers, *Not Without Honor: The History of American Anticommunism* (New York: Free Press, 1995), 239.

34. Seymour Martin Lipset and Earl Raab, *The Politics of Unreason: Right-Wing Extremism in America, 1790–1970* (New York: Harper & Row, 1970), 219; Allan J. Lichtman, *White Protestant Nation: The Rise of the American Conservative Movement* (New York: Atlantic Monthly Press, 2008), 176.

35. Margaret Chase Smith, "Declaration of Conscience," US Senate, June 1, 1950, https://www.senate.gov/artandhistory/history/resources/pdf/SmithDeclaration.pdf.

36. Douglas MacArthur, "Farewell Address to Congress," American Rhetoric, April 19, 1951, https://www.americanrhetoric.com/speeches/douglasmacarthurfarewelladdress.htm.

37. Lipset and Raab, *Politics of Unreason*, 222.

38. Joseph McCarthy, "The History of George Catlett Marshall," Fordham University, June 14, 1951, https://sourcebooks.fordham.edu/mod/1951mccarthy-marshall.asp.

39. "The Faith of the *Freeman*," *The Freeman*, October 2, 1950, 5; Morrie Ryskind, "For Joe McCarthy," *The Freeman*, September 8, 1952, 832.

40. Ronald Radosh, *Prophets on the Right: Profiles of Conservative Critics of American Globalism* (New York: Simon & Schuster, 1975), 151; Patterson, *Mr. Republican*, 503.

41. Patterson, *Mr. Republican*, 530.

42. Lichtman, *White Protestant Nation*, 181.

43. Lichtman, *White Protestant Nation*, 180.

44. W. H. Lawrence, "Taft Fights to Stop Eisenhower with Coalition in Ballot Today; Platform Wins Without Clash," *New York Times*, July 11, 1952, 1.

45. Alonzo L. Hamby, *Liberalism and Its Challengers: From F.D.R. to Bush* (New York: Oxford University Press, 1992), 114.

46. Nixon, *Six Crises*, 82.

47. Patterson, *Mr. Republican*, 563.

CHAPTER FOUR: IKE, MCCARTHY,
AND THE NEW CONSERVATISM

1. Alden Whitman, "Reinhold Niebuhr Is Dead; Protestant Theologian, 78," *New York Times*, June 2, 1971, 1, 45.

2. Richard M. Weaver, *The Southern Tradition at Bay: A History of Postbellum Thought* (Washington, DC: Regnery Gateway, 2021), xx.

3. Richard M. Weaver, "Lee the Philosopher," *George Review* 2, no. 3 (fall 1948): 301.

4. Peter Viereck, *Conservatism Revisited: The Revolt Against Revolt* (New York: Scribner's Sons, 1949), 28.

5. Whittaker Chambers, *Witness* (New York: Random House, 1952), 17.

6. Russell Kirk, *Confessions of a Bohemian Tory: Episodes and Reflections of a Vagrant Career* (New York: Fleet Publishing Corporation, 1963), 27.

7. Bruce Frohnen, Jeremy Beer, and Jeffrey O. Nelson, eds., *American Conservatism: An Encyclopedia* (Wilmington, DE: ISI Books, 2006), 472.

8. Frohnen, Beer, and Nelson, *American Conservatism*, 472.

9. Frank S. Meyer, "Collectivism Rebaptized," *The Freeman* 5, no. 13 (July 1955): 560.

10. Rick Perlstein, *Before the Storm: Barry Goldwater and the Unmaking of the American Consensus* (New York: Hill and Wang, 2001), 74.

11. John B. Judis, *William F. Buckley, Jr., Patron Saint of the Conservatives* (New York: Simon & Schuster, 1988), 46.

12. Judis, *William F. Buckley Jr.*, 53, 57.

13. William F. Buckley Jr. to Henry Regnery, September 25, 1954, Buckley Papers, Yale University Library, New Haven, CT; William F. Buckley Jr., *Miles Gone By: A Literary Autobiography* (Washington, DC: Regnery, 2005), 36.

14. Buckley, *Miles Gone By*, 286.

15. Judis, *William F. Buckley Jr.*, 80.

16. William F. Buckley Jr., *God and Man at Yale: The Superstitions of Academic Freedom* (Chicago: Regnery, 1951), unpaginated foreword; Jon

Meacham, "'Miles Gone By': Bill and God's Excellent Adventure," *New York Times*, October 17, 2004, section 7, 28.

17. Henry Regnery, *Memoirs of a Dissident Publisher* (Chicago: Regnery Books, 1985), 168.

18. Regnery, *Memoirs of a Dissident Publisher*, 168; McGeorge Bundy, "The Attack on Yale," *Atlantic Monthly*, November 1951, https://www.theatlantic.com/magazine/archive/1951/11/the-attack-on-yale/306724.

19. Fred I. Greenstein, *The Hidden-Hand Presidency* (New York: Basic Books, 1982), 175, 209; see also David A. Nichols, *Ike and McCarthy: Dwight Eisenhower's Secret Campaign Against Joseph McCarthy* (New York: Simon & Schuster, 2017).

20. James Burnham, "A Letter of Resignation," *Partisan Review* (December 1953): 716–717.

21. Michael Warner, "Origins of the Congress for Cultural Freedom, 1949–1950," CIA, https://www.cia.gov/static/4b453cae3b528c19248e6a4cf4a65616/origins-congress-cultural-freedom.pdf.

22. Russell Kirk, "Conformity and Legislative Committees," *Confluence*, September 3, 1954.

23. Richard Milhous Nixon, *RN: The Memoirs of Richard Nixon* (New York: Grosset & Dunlap, 1978), 144; Whittaker Chambers, *Odyssey of a Friend: Whittaker Chambers' Letters to William F. Buckley, Jr., 1954–1961*, ed. William F. Buckley Jr. (New York: Putnam, 1969), 47, 52.

24. Jeffrey Hart, *The Making of the American Conservative Mind: National Review and Its Times* (Wilmington, DE: ISI Books, 2005), 86.

25. Nixon, *RN*, 149.

26. Richard Nixon, *Richard Nixon: Speeches, Writings, Documents*, ed. Rick Perlstein (Princeton, NJ: Princeton University Press, 2008), 85–86.

27. William R. Conklin, "McCarthy Seeking to Push Inquiries: Would Turn to Other Cases if Army Dispute Is Delayed by Hunt for Counsel," *New York Times*, March 31, 1954, 16; Richard Brookhiser, *Right Time, Right Place: Coming of Age with William F. Buckley Jr. and the Conservative Movement* (New York: Basic Books, 2009), 15.

28. William F. Buckley Jr. and L. Brent Bozell, *McCarthy and His Enemies: The Record and Its Meaning* (Chicago: H. Regnery Co, 1954), 323–324.

29. Allan J. Lichtman, *White Protestant Nation: The Rise of the American Conservative Movement* (New York: Atlantic Monthly Press, 2008), 191.

30. "G.O.P. Unit Hears Buckley Address: Talk Defending McCarthy Follows a Clash Among Clubwomen of Party," *New York Times*, April 27, 1954, 33.

31. Lichtman, *White Protestant Nation*, 191.

32. Russell Porter, "2,000 Honor Cohn at a Dinner Here: McCarthy Is Chief Speaker—Plaques Are Presented to Former Inquiry Counsel," *New York Times*, July 29, 1954, 9.

33. "Censure Report Criticized: Findings on Senator McCarthy Held No Basis for Proceedings," *New York Times*, November 16, 1954.

34. James Burnham, "The Third World War," *National Review*, June 1, 1957, 518.

35. William F. Buckley Jr., "Roy Cohn's Book," *National Review*, September 10, 1968, 925.

CHAPTER FIVE: A MOVEMENT GROWS

1. William F. Buckley Jr. to chairman of *Yale Daily News*, November 26, 1951, Buckley Papers, Yale University Library, New Haven, CT.

2. George H. Nash, *The Conservative Intellectual Movement in America Since 1945* (Wilmington, DE: ISI Books, 2006), 211.

3. Nash, *Conservative Intellectual Movement in America*, 41.

4. Sidney Blumenthal, *The Rise of the Counter-establishment: From Conservative Ideology to Political Power* (New York: Harper & Row, 1986), 25.

5. William F. Buckley Jr., "*National Review*: Statement of Intentions," in *Conservatism in America Since 1930: A Reader*, ed. Gregory L. Schneider (New York: New York University Press, 2003), 198; Allan J. Lichtman, *White Protestant Nation: The Rise of the American Conservative Movement* (New York: Atlantic Monthly Press, 2008), 210.

6. Blumenthal, *Rise of the Counter-establishment*, 26.

7. Whittaker Chambers, *Odyssey of a Friend: Whittaker Chambers' Letters to William F. Buckley, Jr., 1954–1961*, ed. William F. Buckley Jr. (New York: Putnam, 1969), 79.

8. Russell Kirk, *The Sword of Imagination: Memoirs of a Half-Century of Literary Conflict* (Grand Rapids, MI: William B. Eerdmans Publishing Company, 1995), 53.

9. William F. Buckley Jr., "Publisher's Statement," *National Review*, November 19, 1955, 5.

10. Buckley, "Publisher's Statement," 5.

11. Willmoore Kendall, "The Liberal Line," *National Review*, November 19, 1955, 8; John B. Judis, *William F. Buckley, Jr., Patron Saint of the Conservatives* (New York: Simon & Schuster, 1988), 135.

12. Lionel Trilling, *The Liberal Imagination: Essays on Literature and Society* (New York: New York Review of Books, 2008), xv.

13. Samuel P. Huntington, "Conservatism as an Ideology," *American Political Science Review* 51, no. 2 (1957): 472; see also Nash, *Conservative Intellectual Movement in America*, 208.

14. William F. Buckley Jr., *Up from Liberalism* (New York: Bantam Books, 1968), 53.

15. Frank S. Meyer, ed., *What Is Conservatism?* (New York: Holt, Rinehart and Winston, 1964), 237; Lichtman, *White Protestant Nation*, 222.

16. Judis, *William F. Buckley Jr.*, 174.

17. Ayn Rand, *Letters of Ayn Rand*, ed. Michael S. Berliner (New York: Dutton, 1995), 14.

18. "Playboy Interview: Ayn Rand," *Playboy*, March 1964, 35, 39–40.

19. Whittaker Chambers, "Big Sister Is Watching You," *National Review*, December 28, 1957, 594–596.

20. William F. Buckley Jr., *A Torch Kept Lit: Great Lives of the Twentieth Century* (New York: Crown Forum, 2016); Rand, *Letters of Ayn Rand*, 571.

21. Russell Kirk, "The Seventh Congress of Freedom," *National Review*, May 3, 1958, 418.

22. Kirk, *The Sword of Imagination*, 198.

23. Friedrich A. von Hayek, *The Essence of Hayek*, ed. Chiaki Nishiyama and Kurt R. Leube (Stanford, CA: Hoover Institution Press, 1984), 281, 283.

24. Hayek, *Essence of Hayek*, 282–283.

25. Hayek, *Essence of Hayek*, 293.

26. Henry Regnery, *Memoirs of a Dissident Publisher* (Chicago: Regnery Books, 1985), 159; Russell Kirk, *Imaginative Conservatism: The Letters of Russell Kirk*, ed. James E. Person Jr. (Lexington: University Press of Kentucky, 2018), 98.

27. Lichtman, *White Protestant Nation*, 187.

28. Clarence Manion, *Let's Face It!* (South Bend, IN: Manion Forum, 1956), viii.

29. Lee Edwards, *Just Right: A Life in Pursuit of Liberty* (Wilmington, DE: ISI Books, 2017), 12.

30. Judis, *William F. Buckley Jr.*, 145.

31. Buckley, *Up from Liberalism*, 84.

32. David A. Nichols, *A Matter of Justice: Eisenhower and the Beginning of the Civil Rights Revolution* (New York: Simon & Schuster, 2007).

33. Richard M. Weaver, *In Defense of Tradition: Collected Shorter Writings of Richard M. Weaver, 1929–1963*, ed. Ted J. Smith (Indianapolis: Liberty Fund, 2000), 717–718.

34. William P. Hustwit, *James J. Kilpatrick: Salesman for Segregation* (Chapel Hill: University of North Carolina Press, 2013), 74; Buckley, *Up from Liberalism*, 36–37.

35. Lichtman, *White Protestant Nation*, 227; George Samuel Schuyler, *Black and Conservative: The Autobiography of George S. Schuyler* (New Rochelle, NY: Arlington House, 1966), 337.

36. Lichtman, *White Protestant Nation*, 227.

37. Leo Strauss, *Jewish Philosophy and the Crisis of Modernity: Essays and Lectures in Modern Jewish Thought*, ed. Kenneth Hart Green. SUNY Series in the Jewish Writings of Strauss (Albany: State University of New York Press, 1997), 461.

38. Leo Strauss, *An Introduction to Political Philosophy*, ed. Hilail Gildin (Detroit, MI: Wayne State University Press, 1989), 81.

39. Leo Strauss, *Liberalism Ancient and Modern* (Chicago: University of Chicago Press, 1995), ix.

40. Harry V. Jaffa, *Crisis of the Strauss Divided: Essays on Leo Strauss and Straussianism, East and West* (Lanham, MD: Rowman & Littlefield, 2012), 8.

41. Harry V. Jaffa, *The Rediscovery of America: Essays by Harry V. Jaffa on the New Birth of Politics*, ed. Edward J. Erler and Ken Masugi (Lanham, MD: Rowman & Littlefield, 2019), 298; Jaffa, *Crisis of the Strauss Divided*, 9.

42. Walter Berns, *Freedom, Virtue, and the First Amendment* (New York: Greenwood Press, 1969), 226.

43. Harry V. Jaffa, *Crisis of the House Divided: An Interpretation of the Issues in the Lincoln-Douglas Debates* (Chicago: University of Chicago Press, 2009), 375.

44. Walter Berns, review of *A Program for Conservatives*, by Russell Kirk, *Journal of Politics* 17, no. 4 (1955): 683–686; Willmoore Kendall, *The Conservative Affirmation in America* (Chicago: Gateway Editions, 1985), 252.

45. John A. Murley and John Alvis, *Willmoore Kendall: Maverick of American Conservatives* (Lanham, MD: Lexington Books, 2002), 192.

46. L. Brent Bozell, "The 1958 Elections: Coroner's Report," *National Review*, November 22, 1958, 333–336.

47. Lichtman, *White Protestant Nation*, 219; Buckley, *Up from Liberalism*, xvii.

48. Rick Perlstein, *Before the Storm: Barry Goldwater and the Unmaking of the American Consensus* (New York: Hill and Wang, 2001), 15.

49. James C. Roberts, ed., *The Best of Human Events: Fifty Years of Conservative Thought and Action* (Lafayette, LA: Huntington House, 1995), 254.

50. Daniel Kelly, *Living on Fire: The Life of L. Brent Bozell Jr.* (Wilmington, DE: ISI Books, 2014), 50–51.

51. Barry M. Goldwater, *The Conscience of a Conservative* (New York: Macfadden Books, 1960), 7.

52. Goldwater, *The Conscience of a Conservative*, 12.

53. Goldwater, *The Conscience of a Conservative*, 23–25.

54. Kelly, *Living on Fire*, 54.

55. Perlstein, *Before the Storm*, 76, 85.

56. Richard M. Nixon, *RN: The Memoirs of Richard Nixon* (New York: Grosset & Dunlap, 1978), 216.

57. Edwards, *Just Right*, 21.

58. William F. Buckley Jr., *Let Us Talk of Many Things: The Collected Speeches* (Roseville, CA: Forum, 2000), 38.

CHAPTER SIX: NEW FRONTIERS

1. Richard M. Nixon, *RN: The Memoirs of Richard Nixon* (New York: Grosset & Dunlap, 1978), 225–226.

2. James Piereson, *Camelot and the Cultural Revolution: How the Assassination of John F. Kennedy Shattered American Liberalism* (New York: Encounter Books, 2013), 31.

3. William F. Buckley Jr., *Rumbles Left and Right* (New York: Macfadden Books, 1964), 65–68.

4. Whittaker Chambers, *Odyssey of a Friend: Whittaker Chambers' Letters to William F. Buckley, Jr., 1954–1961*, ed. William F. Buckley Jr. (New York: Putnam, 1969), 273, 280.

5. Frank S. Meyer, *In Defense of Freedom and Related Essays* (Indianapolis: Liberty Fund, 1996), 35.

6. Frank S. Meyer, *In Defense of Freedom: A Conservative Credo* (Chicago: Regnery, 1962), 136–137.

7. Ralph Raico, ed., *New Individualist Review* (Indianapolis: Liberty Fund, 1981), 86.

8. Raico, *New Individualist Review*, 86.

9. Raico, *New Individualist Review*, 87.

10. George W. Carey, ed., *Freedom and Virtue: The Conservative/Libertarian Debate* (Wilmington, DE: ISI Books, 2004), 16–17.

11. Daniel Kelly, *Living on Fire: The Life of L. Brent Bozell Jr.* (Wilmington, DE: ISI Books, 2014), 67.

12. L. Brent Bozell, *Mustard Seeds: A Conservative Becomes a Catholic* (Front Royal, VA: Christendom Press, 2001), 20.

13. Bozell, *Mustard Seeds*, 24.

14. Russell Kirk, "An Ideologue of Liberty," *Sewanee Review* 72, no. 2 (1964): 349–350; Richard M. Weaver, *In Defense of Tradition: Collected Shorter Writings of Richard M. Weaver, 1929–1963*, ed. Ted J. Smith (Indianapolis: Liberty Fund, 2000), 482.

15. Frank S. Meyer, ed., *What Is Conservatism?* (New York: Holt, Rinehart and Winston, 1964), 241–242.

16. Rick Perlstein, *Before the Storm: Barry Goldwater and the Unmaking of the American Consensus* (New York: Hill and Wang, 2001), 153.

17. William A. Rusher, *The Rise of the Right* (New York: National Review, 1993), 84; Meyer, *What Is Conservatism?*, 237.

18. Seymour Martin Lipset and Earl Raab, *The Politics of Unreason: Right-Wing Extremism in America, 1790–1970* (New York: Harper & Row, 1970), 254–255.

19. Lipset and Raab, *Politics of Unreason*, 254; Gerald Schomp, *Birchism Was My Business: A Fascinating Inside Story of Modern American Right-Wing Extremism by a Former Full-Time, Paid, Professional Superpatriot* (New York: Macmillan, 1970), 73; Allan J. Lichtman, *White Protestant Nation: The Rise of the American Conservative Movement* (New York: Atlantic Monthly Press, 2008), 239.

20. Lichtman, *White Protestant Nation*, 236.

21. Elizabeth Macdonald, "The Kennedys and the IRS," *Wall Street Journal*, January 28, 1997, https://www.wsj.com/articles/SB85441628 6412470000.

22. Robert D. Novak, *The Agony of the G.O.P. 1964* (New York: Macmillan, 1965), 25–28.

23. David B. Frisk, *If Not Us, Who? William Rusher, National Review, and the Conservative Movement* (Wilmington, DE: ISI Books, 2012), 157.

24. Marvin Liebman, *Coming Out Conservative: An Autobiography* (San Francisco, CA: Chronicle Books, 1992), 160.

25. Rusher, *The Rise of the Right*, 85.

26. William F. Buckley Jr., "Goldwater, the John Birch Society, and Me," *Wall Street Journal*, February 27, 2008, https://www.wsj.com/articles/SB120413132440097025.

27. William F. Buckley Jr., "Goldwater, the John Birch Society, and Me," *Commentary*, March 2008, https://www.commentarymagazine.com/articles/william-buckley-jr/goldwater-the-john-birch-society-and-me.

28. Perlstein, *Before the Storm*, 156, 200.

29. Daniel Bell, ed., *The Radical Right: The New American Right* (New York: Doubleday, 1963), 86.

30. Pierson, *Camelot and the Cultural Revolution*, 89; Perlstein, *Before the Storm*, 248.

31. Lee Edwards, *Just Right: A Life in Pursuit of Liberty* (Wilmington, DE: ISI Books, 2017), 49.

32. Edwards, *Just Right*, 50.

33. Ronald Radosh, "Phyllis Schlafly, 'Mrs. America,' Was a Secret Member of the John Birch Society," *Daily Beast*, April 20, 2020, https://www.thedailybeast.com/phyllis-schlafly-mrs-america-was-a-secret-member-of-the-john-birch-society.

34. Phyllis Schlafly, *A Choice, Not an Echo* (Washington, DC: Regnery Publishing, 2014), 26.

35. Edwards, *Just Right*, 78.

36. Perlstein, *Before the Storm*, 255.

37. Milton Friedman, *Bright Promises, Dismal Performance: An Economist's Protest* (New York: Harcourt Brace Jovanovich, 1983), 19.

38. Milton Friedman, *Capitalism and Freedom* (Chicago: University of Chicago Press, 2002), xiv.

39. Milton Friedman, "The Goldwater View of Economics," *New York Times Magazine*, October 11, 1964, 37, 133–137.

40. Perlstein, *Before the Storm*, 337; Frank S. Meyer, "What Next for Conservatism," *National Review*, December 1, 1964, 1057; see also Richard Hofstadter, *Anti-intellectualism in American Life* (New York: Alfred A. Knopf, 1963).

41. Perlstein, *Before the Storm*, 333.

42. Perlstein, *Before the Storm*, 350.

43. Barry M. Goldwater, "The Republican National Convention Acceptance Address," in *Conservatism in America Since 1930: A Reader*, ed. Gregory L. Schneider (New York: New York University Press, 2003), 240.

44. Edwards, *Just Right*, 101; William Safire, ed., *Lend Me Your Ears: Great Speeches in History* (New York: W. W. Norton & Company, 1997), 899; Nixon, *RN*, 260.

45. Lee Edwards, *Goldwater: The Man Who Made a Revolution* (Washington, DC: Regnery, 1995), 236; Perlstein, *Before the Storm*, 364.

46. Robert H. Bork, "Civil Rights—a Challenge," *New Republic*, September 14, 1963, 21–24.

47. William F. Buckley Jr., *Let Us Talk of Many Things: The Collected Speeches* (Roseville, CA: Forum, 2000), 76, 82; Lichtman, *White Protestant Nation*, 242.

48. Ronald Reagan, *An American Life: The Autobiography* (New York: Simon & Schuster, 2011), 137–139.

49. Matthew Dallek, *The Right Moment: Ronald Reagan's First Victory and the Decisive Turning Point in American Politics* (New York: Free Press, 2000), 67.

50. Ronald Reagan, "A Time for Choosing," American Rhetoric, October 27, 1964, https://www.americanrhetoric.com/speeches/ronald reaganatimeforchoosing.htm.

51. Edwards, *Goldwater*, 336.

52. Charles Murray, "Notes and Asides," *National Review*, May 9, 1986, 21.

53. Louis Filler, ed., *Dictionary of American Conservatism* (New York: Philosophical Library, 1987), 83.

54. Donald Janson, "Rightists Buoyed by the Election," *New York Times*, November 23, 1964, 1, 42.

CHAPTER SEVEN: THE GREAT DISRUPTION

1. James T. Patterson, *Freedom Is Not Enough: The Moynihan Report and America's Struggle over Black Family Life—from LBJ to Obama* (New York: Basic Books, 2010), ix.

2. Charles de Gaulle, "De Gaulle's Warning to Kennedy: An 'Endless Entanglement' in Vietnam," *New York Times*, March 15, 1972, 47; Hans J. Morgenthau, "Vietnam—Another Korea?," *Commentary*, May 1962,

https://www.commentarymagazine.com/articles/hans-morgenthau/vietnam-another-korea.

3. Doris Kearns Goodwin, *Lyndon Johnson and the American Dream* (New York: A Thomas Dunne Book for St. Martin's Griffin, 2019), 253.

4. James T. Patterson, *Grand Expectations: The United States, 1945–1974* (New York: Oxford University Press, 1996), 672.

5. Patterson, *Freedom Is Not Enough*, xiii.

6. William F. Buckley Jr., *The Unmaking of a Mayor* (New York: Viking Press, 1966), 355.

7. John B. Judis, *William F. Buckley, Jr., Patron Saint of the Conservatives* (New York: Simon & Schuster, 1988), 237.

8. Rick Perlstein, *Nixonland: The Rise of a President and the Fracturing of America* (New York: Scribner, 2008), 65; Buckley, *Unmaking of a Mayor*, 101–102.

9. Judis, *William F. Buckley Jr.*, 240–241.

10. Buckley, *Unmaking of a Mayor*, 352.

11. Sidney Blumenthal, *The Rise of the Counter-establishment: From Conservative Ideology to Political Power* (New York: Harper & Row, 1986), 29.

12. Seymour Martin Lipset and Earl Raab, *The Politics of Unreason: Right-Wing Extremism in America, 1790–1970* (New York: Harper & Row, 1970), 270.

13. William F. Buckley Jr., *Rumbles Left and Right* (New York: Macfadden Books, 1964), 103.

14. Ronald Reagan, *An American Life: The Autobiography* (New York: Simon & Schuster, 2011), 24; Patrick J. Buchanan, *Nixon's White House Wars: The Battles That Made and Broke a President and Divided America Forever* (New York: Crown Forum, 2017), 394.

15. Reagan, *An American Life*, 20, 22.

16. Robert D. Novak, *The Prince of Darkness: 50 Years Reporting in Washington* (New York: Crown Forum, 2007), 367.

17. Lawrence E. Davies, "Reagan Assesses Political Future," *New York Times*, July 25, 1965, 52.

18. Perlstein, *Nixonland*, 115.

19. Perlstein, *Nixonland*, 83.

20. Matthew Dallek, *The Right Moment: Ronald Reagan's First Victory and the Decisive Turning Point in American Politics* (New York: Free Press, 2000), 188.

21. Dallek, *Right Moment*, 235.

22. Perlstein, *Nixonland*, 165.

23. Ronald Reagan, *The Creative Society: Some Comments on Problems Facing America* (New York: Devin-Adair Company, 1968), 2.

24. Reagan, *Creative Society*, 2.

25. Allan J. Lichtman, *White Protestant Nation: The Rise of the American Conservative Movement* (New York: Atlantic Monthly Press, 2008), 249.

26. Lipset and Raab, *Politics of Unreason*, 352.

27. Judis, *William F. Buckley Jr.*, 283; Russell Kirk, *Imaginative Conservatism: The Letters of Russell Kirk*, ed. James E. Person Jr. (Lexington: University Press of Kentucky, 2018), 191; Frank S. Meyer, "The Populism of George Wallace," *National Review*, May 16, 1967, 527.

28. James Jackson Kilpatrick, "What Makes Wallace Run?," *National Review*, April 18, 1967, 400–409; Jeffrey Hart, "The New Aesthetics of Politics," *National Review*, October 8, 1968, 1009.

29. J. J. Heizer, "To the Editor," *National Review*, May 2, 1967, 448; R. J. Whitter, "To the Editor," *National Review*, May 2, 1967, 448.

30. Lichtman, *White Protestant Nation*, 278; Lipset and Raab, *Politics of Unreason*, 350.

31. Michael T. Kaufman, "Stokely Carmichael, Rights Leader Who Coined 'Black Power,' Dies at 57," *New York Times*, November 16, 1998, B10.

32. Perlstein, *Nixonland*, 238.

33. Patterson, *Grand Expectations*, 680.

34. Margot Adler, "1968 Columbia Protests Still Stir Passion," NPR, April 23, 2008, https://www.npr.org/templates/story/story.php?storyId=89884026; Joseph Dorman, *Arguing the World: The New York Intellectuals in Their Own Words* (New York: Free Press, 2000), 154.

35. William F. Buckley Jr., *The Governor Listeth: A Book of Inspired Political Revelations* (New York: Putnam, 1971), 388; Frederick D. Wilhelmsen, *Seeds of Anarchy: A Study of Campus Revolution* (Dallas, TX: Argus Academic Press, 1969), 25, 33.

36. Frederick F. Siegel, *Troubled Journey: From Pearl Harbor to Ronald Reagan* (New York: Hill and Wang, 1984), 196.

37. James Burnham, *Suicide of the West: An Essay on the Meaning and Destiny of Liberalism* (New York: Encounter Books, 2014), 346; James Burnham, "The New Left and the Right," *National Review*, July 16, 1968, 690.

38. Irving Kristol, "The Education, So to Speak, of a Neoconservative, or Why American Conservatism Is Exceptional," Contemporary Thinkers,

October 15, 2001, https://contemporarythinkers.org/irving-kristol/essay/the-education-so-to-speak-of-a-neoconservative-or-why-american-conservatism-is-exceptional.

39. Daniel Bell, *The End of Ideology: On the Exhaustion of Political Ideas in the Fifties* (Cambridge, MA: Harvard University Press, 2001); "President Names 14 to Automation Unit," *New York Times*, November 15, 1964, 64; Kristol, "Education, So to Speak, of a Neoconservative."

40. Judis, *William F. Buckley Jr.*, 279.

41. Patrick J. Buchanan, *Right from the Beginning* (Washington, DC: Regnery Gateway, 1990), 14.

42. Patrick J. Buchanan, *The Greatest Comeback: How Richard Nixon Rose from Defeat to Create the New Majority* (New York: Crown Forum, 2014), 38.

43. Richard M. Nixon, "What Has Happened to America?," *Reader's Digest*, October 1967, 49–54; Buchanan, *Greatest Comeback*, 255.

44. Buchanan, *Greatest Comeback*, 247–248.

45. Judis, *William F. Buckley Jr.*, 280.

46. Buckley, *Governor Listeth*, 65.

47. Barry Goldwater, "Don't Waste a Vote on Wallace," *National Review*, October 22, 1968, 1060.

CHAPTER EIGHT: NIXON'S CONSERVATIVES

1. Russell Kirk, *Imaginative Conservatism: The Letters of Russell Kirk*, ed. James E. Person Jr. (Lexington: University Press of Kentucky, 2018), 168, 173.

2. Jonathan Aitken, *Nixon: A Life* (Washington, DC: Regnery, 1994), 336.

3. James T. Patterson, *Freedom Is Not Enough: The Moynihan Report and America's Struggle over Black Family Life—from LBJ to Obama* (New York: Basic Books, 2010), 50.

4. Daniel Patrick Moynihan, *Coping: Essays on the Practice of Government* (New York: Random House, 1973), 188; Daniel Patrick Moynihan, *Maximum Feasible Misunderstanding: Community Action in the War on Poverty* (New York: Free Press, 1969), 191; Stephen Hess, *The Professor and the President: Daniel Patrick Moynihan in the Nixon White House* (Washington, DC: Brookings Institution Press, 2015), 71.

5. Kevin P. Phillips, *The Emerging Republican Majority* (Princeton, NJ: Princeton University Press, 2015), 1.

6. Richard M. Scammon and Ben J. Wattenberg, *The Real Majority* (New York: Coward-McCann, 1970), 20, 46.

7. William F. Gavin, "Confessions of a Street-Corner Conservative," *National Review*, December 3, 1971, 1345–1347.

8. Jerome M. Rosow, "The Problem of the Blue-Collar Worker," ERIC, 1970, https://eric.ed.gov/?id=ED045810.

9. Richard Nixon, *Richard Nixon: Speeches, Writings, Documents*, ed. Rick Perlstein (Princeton, NJ: Princeton University Press, 2008), 164.

10. Daniel Patrick Moynihan, *The Politics of a Guaranteed Income: The Nixon Administration and the Family Assistance Plan* (New York: Vintage Books, 1973), 4–5.

11. Milton Friedman and Rose D. Friedman, *Two Lucky People: Memoirs* (Chicago: University of Chicago Press, 1998), 382.

12. Patrick J. Buchanan, *Nixon's White House Wars: The Battles That Made and Broke a President and Divided America Forever* (New York: Crown Forum, 2017), 66–67.

13. Buchanan, *Nixon's White House Wars*, 70.

14. John R. Coyne, *The Impudent Snobs: Agnew vs. the Intellectual Establishment* (New Rochelle, NY: Arlington House, 1972), 267; Richard M. Nixon, *RN: The Memoirs of Richard Nixon* (New York: Grosset & Dunlap, 1978), 412.

15. Buchanan, *Nixon's White House Wars*, 101.

16. Buchanan, *Nixon's White House Wars*, 103.

17. Rick Perlstein, *Nixonland: The Rise of a President and the Fracturing of America* (New York: Scribner, 2008), 376; Walter Berns, *Democracy and the Constitution* (Washington, DC: AEI Press, 2006), 172; Allan Bloom, *The Closing of the American Mind: How Higher Education Has Failed Democracy and Impoverished the Souls of Today's Students* (New York: Simon & Schuster, 2012), 313.

18. Dwight Macdonald, "On the Horizon: Scrambled Eggheads on the Right," *Commentary*, April 1956, https://www.commentary.org/articles/dwight-macdonald/on-the-horizon-scrambled-eggheads-on-the-right; William F. Buckley Jr., *The Governor Listeth: A Book of Inspired Political Revelations* (New York: Putnam, 1971), 150.

19. Jerome Tuccille, *Radical Libertarianism: A Right Wing Alternative* (New York: Perennial Library, 1970), 127–129.

20. Daniel Kelly, *Living on Fire: The Life of L. Brent Bozell Jr.* (Wilmington, DE: ISI Books, 2014), 137; L. Brent Bozell, *Mustard Seeds: A*

Conservative Becomes a Catholic (Front Royal, VA: Christendom Press, 2001), 78, 86.

21. Bozell, *Mustard Seeds*, 132.

22. "Is Conservatism Dead?," *National Review*, April 8, 1969, 317–318.

23. Buckley, *Governor Listeth*, 156.

24. Perlstein, *Nixonland*, 475; Robert H. Bork, *Slouching Towards Gomorrah: Modern Liberalism and American Decline* (New York: Harper Perennial, 2003), 42.

25. Perlstein, *Nixonland*, 498.

26. Joseph Dorman, *Arguing the World: The New York Intellectuals in Their Own Words* (New York: Free Press, 2000), 155.

27. Daniel Bell, "Revolution of Rising Entitlements," *Fortune* (April 1975): 98.

28. Norman Podhoretz, "Critics and Crusaders on Neoconservatism," *Society* 26, no. 2 (February 1, 1989): 6–7.

29. Thomas L. Jeffers, *Norman Podhoretz: A Biography* (New York: Cambridge University Press, 2010), 125.

30. Norman Podhoretz, *Breaking Ranks: A Political Memoir* (New York: Harper & Row, 1979), 334.

31. "Come On In, the Water's Fine," *National Review*, March 9, 1971, 249–250; Nathan Glazer, "Seeking the Tap Root," *National Review*, August 18, 1972, 903–904; John P. Roche, "A Diagnosis of the Anti-Spiro Jitters by a Former Chairman of the ADA," *National Review*, August 25, 1970, 878.

32. Nathan Glazer, *Remembering the Answers: Essays on the American Student Revolt* (New York: Basic Books, 1970), 3; Jeffers, *Norman Podhoretz*, 147.

33. Niall Ferguson, *Kissinger: 1923–1968: The Idealist* (New York: Penguin, 2015), 82.

34. William F. Buckley Jr., *The Reagan I Knew* (New York: Basic Books, 2008), 52–53.

35. Buchanan, *Nixon's White House Wars*, 228, 231; Friedman and Friedman, *Two Lucky People*, 383–384.

36. Patrick J. Buchanan, *Advising Nixon: The White House Memos of Patrick J. Buchanan*, ed. Lori Cox Han (Lawrence: University Press of Kansas, 2019), 134, 139.

37. John B. Judis, *William F. Buckley, Jr., Patron Saint of the Conservatives* (New York: Simon & Schuster, 1988), 338.

38. William F. Buckley Jr., *Execution Eve, and Other Contemporary Ballads* (New York: Putnam, 1975), 37.

39. "Banfield Quits Harvard, Takes Position at Penn," *Harvard Crimson*, December 2, 1971, https://www.thecrimson.com/article/1971/12/2/banfield-quits-harvard-takes-position-at.

40. Edward E. Scharff, *Worldly Power: The Making of the Wall Street Journal* (New York: Beaufort Books, 1986), 240–245.

41. Irving Kristol, "The Two Welfare States," *Wall Street Journal*, October 19, 2000.

42. Dorman, *Arguing the World*, 167.

43. Dorman, *Arguing the World*, 168; James Burnham, "The Welfare Non-issue," *National Review*, March 11, 1969, 222.

44. Robert D. Novak, *The Prince of Darkness: 50 Years Reporting in Washington* (New York: Crown Forum, 2007), 224–226.

45. Buchanan, *Advising Nixon*, 259.

46. Midge Decter, *An Old Wife's Tale: My Seven Decades in Love and War* (New York: ReganBooks, 2001), 105.

47. Decter, *An Old Wife's Tale*, 123–124.

48. Buckley, *Execution Eve, and Other Contemporary Ballads*, 99; Buchanan, *Nixon's White House Wars*, 307.

49. William F. Buckley Jr., "On the Right," *National Review*, February 2, 1973, 131.

50. "Watergate as Power Struggle," *National Review Bulletin*, June 29, 1973, B89; Irving Kristol, "The Nightmare of Watergate," *Wall Street Journal*, May 17, 1973, 20; Irving Kristol, "What Comes Next, After Watergate?," *Wall Street Journal*, June 14, 1973, 16; Russell Kirk, *The Sword of Imagination: Memoirs of a Half-Century of Literary Conflict* (Grand Rapids, MI: William B. Eerdmans Publishing Company, 1995), 335–336.

51. George F. Will, *The Pursuit of Happiness and Other Sobering Thoughts* (New York: Harper & Row, 1978), 47.

52. Morrie Ryskind, "For Joe McCarthy," *The Freeman*, September 8, 1952, 94; Kiron Skinner, Martin Anderson, and Annelise Anderson, *Reagan: A Life in Letters* (New York: Viking Press, 2003), 777; Rick Perlstein, *The Invisible Bridge: The Fall of Nixon and the Rise of Reagan* (New York: Simon & Schuster, 2014), 192.

53. Judis, *William F. Buckley Jr.*, 354–355; Robert Alan Goldberg, *Barry Goldwater* (New Haven, CT: Yale University Press, 1997), 280.

54. Judis, *William F. Buckley Jr.*, 357; James L. Buckley, "Why Richard Nixon Should Resign the Presidency," *National Review*, April 12, 1974, 413–415.

55. William F. Buckley Jr., "On the Right," *National Review*, August 30, 1974, 996–997; "The Nation United," *Wall Street Journal*, August 7, 1974, 10; Goldberg, *Barry Goldwater*, 282.

56. Henry Kissinger, *Years of Upheaval* (New York: Little, Brown, and Company, 1982), 1212.

CHAPTER NINE: THE PRAIRIE FIRE

1. Rick Perlstein, *Reaganland: America's Right Turn, 1976–1980* (New York: Simon & Schuster, 2020), 46.

2. Patrick J. Buchanan, *Conservative Votes, Liberal Victories: Why the Right Has Failed* (New York: Quadrangle/New York Times Co., 1975), 169; Kevin Phillips, *Mediacracy: American Parties and Politics in the Communications Age* (Garden City, NY: Doubleday & Company, Inc., 1975), 228; William A. Rusher, *The Making of the New Majority Party* (Mission, KS: Sheed & Ward, 1975).

3. Myra MacPherson, "The New Right Brigade," *Washington Post*, August 10, 1980, https://www.washingtonpost.com/archive/lifestyle/1980/08/10/the-new-right-brigade/24c8ed98-3af7-4385-9c0e-f973bea20612.

4. Perlstein, *Reaganland*, 782.

5. "Who Is a Liberal? What Is a Conservative?," *Commentary*, September 1976, 88.

6. *The 14th Amendment and School Busing: Hearings Before the Subcommittee on the Constitution of the Committee on the Judiciary, United States Senate, Ninety-Seventh Congress, First Session, on the 14th Amendment and School Busing, May 14 and June 3, 1981* (Washington, DC: US Government Printing Office, 1982), 319.

7. Richard M. Nixon, *From the President: Richard Nixon's Secret Files*, ed. Bruce Oudes (New York: Harper & Row, 1989), 564.

8. Richard A. Viguerie, *The New Right: We're Ready to Lead* (Falls Church, VA: Viguerie Company, 1980), 55–60.

9. Robert Whitaker, ed., *The New Right Papers* (New York: St. Martin's Press, 1982), x.

10. Daniel Patrick Moynihan with Suzanne Weaver, *A Dangerous Place* (New York: Berkley Books, 1980), 37.

11. Kathleen Teltsch, "Moynihan Calls on U.S. to 'Start Raising Hell' in U.N.," *New York Times*, February 26, 1975, https://www.nytimes.com/1975/02/26/archives/moynihan-calls-on-us-to-start-raising-hell-in-un.html.

12. Daniel Patrick Moynihan, "The United States in Opposition," *Commentary*, March 1975, https://www.commentary.org/articles/daniel-moynihan/the-united-states-in-opposition.

13. Norman Podhoretz, "Making the World Safe for Communism," *Commentary*, April 1976, https://www.commentarymagazine.com/articles/norman-podhoretz/making-the-world-safe-for-communism.

14. Nathan Glazer, "American Values and American Foreign Policy," *Commentary*, July 1976, https://www.commentarymagazine.com/articles/nathan-glazer-2/american-values-american-foreign-policy.

15. Henry Kissinger, *Years of Renewal* (New York: Simon & Schuster, 1999), 25.

16. Daniel Patrick Moynihan, *Counting Our Blessings: Reflections on the Future of America* (New York: Atlantic Monthly Press, 1980), 55.

17. Moynihan with Weaver, *A Dangerous Place*, 79; Alexander Solzhenitsyn, *Warning to the West* (New York: Farrar, Straus & Giroux, 1976), 27, 42–50.

18. William F. Buckley Jr., *A Hymnal: The Controversial Arts* (New York: G. P. Putnam's Sons, 1978), 51; Donald Rumsfeld, *Known and Unknown: A Memoir* (New York: Sentinel, 2011), 181; Kissinger, *Years of Renewal*, 651–652, 1071.

19. Elliott Abrams, *Realism and Democracy: American Foreign Policy After the Arab Spring* (New York: Cambridge University Press, 2017), 17; Moynihan with Weaver, *A Dangerous Place*, 220.

20. "Man of the Year," *National Review*, January 23, 1976, 20–21.

21. Moynihan with Weaver, *A Dangerous Place*, 304–305.

22. Moynihan with Weaver, *A Dangerous Place*, 319.

23. Ronald Reagan, *A Time for Choosing: The Speeches of Ronald Reagan, 1961–1982* (Chicago: Regnery Gateway, 1983), 166, 169–170.

24. Craig Shirley, *Reagan's Revolution: The Untold Story of the Campaign That Started It All* (Nashville, TN: Nelson Current, 2005), xvi.

25. Shirley, *Reagan's Revolution*, xvii.

26. Michael Martin, "Jimmy Carter: Proud Son," *Tell Me More*, NPR, May 1, 2008, https://www.npr.org/templates/story/story.php?storyId=90093960.

27. George F. Will, "A Last Look," *National Review*, January 23, 1976, 26.

28. *William J. Baroody, Sr: Recipient of the 1980 Boyer Award* (Washington, DC: American Enterprise Institute for Public Policy Research, 1981), https://www.aei.org/wp-content/uploads/2016/03/BoyerLectures 04.pdf?x91208.

29. Irving Kristol, "The President's Bicentennial Speeches," June 7, 1976, Box 2, Folder "Bicentennial Speeches (1)," Ron Nessen Papers at the Gerald R. Ford Presidential Library, https://www.fordlibrary museum.gov/library/document/0204/1511691.pdf.

30. Michael Novak, *Three in One: Essays on Democratic Capitalism, 1976–2000*, ed. Edward W. Younkins (Lanham, MD: Rowman & Littlefield, 2001), 274.

31. Randy Boyagoda, *Richard John Neuhaus: A Life in the Public Square* (New York: Crown Publishing Group, 2015), 194.

32. Novak, *Three in One*, 325; Michael Novak, *On Cultivating Liberty: Reflections on Moral Ecology*, ed. Brian C. Anderson (Lanham, MD: Rowman & Littlefield, 1999), 278.

33. Boyagoda, *Richard John Neuhaus*, 130.

34. Boyagoda, *Richard John Neuhaus*, 174.

35. Peter L. Berger and Richard John Neuhaus, eds., *Against the World for the World: The Hartford Appeal and the Future of American Religion* (New York: Seabury Press, 1976), vii; Peter L. Berger, *Adventures of an Accidental Sociologist: How to Explain the World Without Becoming a Bore* (Amherst, NY: Prometheus Books, 2011), 131–133.

36. Berger and Neuhaus, *Against the World for the World*, 161.

37. Novak, *Three in One*, 3–5.

38. Berger, *Adventures of an Accidental Sociologist*, 142–149.

39. Peter L. Berger and Richard John Neuhaus, *To Empower People: The Role of Mediating Structures in Public Policy*, ed. Michael Novak (Washington, DC: American Enterprise Institute for Public Policy Research, 1996), 2.

40. Berger and Neuhaus, *To Empower People*, 4.

41. Rumsfeld, *Known and Unknown*, 183.

42. Jude Wanniski, *The Way the World Works* (Washington, DC: Regnery Publishing, 1998), 6.

43. Wanniski, *The Way the World Works*, 359.

44. Irving Kristol, "The Meaning of Proposition 13," *Wall Street Journal*, June 28, 1978; inscribed copy of Jack Kemp, *An American Renais-*

sance: A Strategy for the 1980's (New York: Berkley, 1981), in author's possession.

45. Kemp, *American Renaissance*, 67, 81–82, 139.

46. Kemp, *American Renaissance*, 19; Jack Kemp, *The American Idea: Ending Limits to Growth* (Washington, DC: American Studies Center, 1984), 15.

47. Milton Friedman, "A Friedman Doctrine: The Social Responsibility of Business Is to Increase Its Profits," *New York Times*, September 13, 1970, https://www.nytimes.com/1970/09/13/archives/a-friedman -doctrine-the-social-responsibility-of-business-is-to.html; Milton Friedman, "Inflation: Causes and Consequences," 1963, Collected Works of Milton Friedman Project records, Hoover Institution Library and Archives, https://miltonfriedman.hoover.org/objects/57545/inflation-causes -and-consequences; Lewis F. Powell Jr., "The Memo," Washington & Lee University School of Law Scholarly Commons, August 23, 1971, https://scholarlycommons.law.wlu.edu/powellmemo/1; Robert H. Bork, *The Anti-trust Paradox* (New York: Free Press, 1978); James M. Buchanan and Gordon Tullock, *The Calculus of Consent: Logical Foundations of Constitutional Democracy* (Ann Arbor: University of Michigan Press, 1962); Mancur Olson, *The Logic of Collective Action: Public Goods and the Theory of Groups* (Cambridge, MA: Harvard University Press, 1965).

48. Reagan, *A Time for Choosing*, 187–189.

49. Glenn Fowler, "Buckley Shifts Marijuana Stand," *New York Times*, November 29, 1972, 27, https://www.nytimes.com/1972/11/29/archives /buckley-shifts-marijuana-stand-conservative-editor-says-use-should .html; William F. Buckley Jr., "A Voice from Philistia," *National Review*, August 15, 1975, 900.

50. Charles R. Kesler, "A Special Meaning of the Declaration of Independence: A Tribute to Harry V. Jaffa," *National Review*, July 6, 1979, 850–859.

51. Richard Brookhiser, *Right Time, Right Place: Coming of Age with William F. Buckley Jr. and the Conservative Movement* (New York: Basic Books, 2009), 76.

52. Nathan Glazer, "Fundamentalists: A Defensive Offensive," in *Piety and Politics: Evangelicals and Fundamentalists Confront the World*, ed. Richard John Neuhaus and Michael Cromartie (Washington, DC: Ethics and Public Policy Center, 1987), 254–255.

53. Carol Felsenthal, *The Sweetheart of the Silent Majority: The Biography of Phyllis Schlafly* (New York: Doubleday, 1981), 253.

54. Phyllis Schlafly, *Feminist Fantasies* (Dallas, TX: Spence Publishing Company, 2003), 93; Felsenthal, *Sweetheart of the Silent Majority*, 254.

55. Glazer, "Fundamentalists," 248.

56. Novak, *Three in One*, 118.

57. Judy Klemesrud, "Equal Rights Plan and Abortion Are Opposed by 15,000 at Rally," *New York Times*, November 20, 1977, 32, https://www.nytimes.com/1977/11/20/archives/equal-rights-plan-and-abortion-are-opposed-by-15000-at-rally-like-a.html.

58. Dinesh D'Souza, *Falwell, Before the Millennium: A Critical Biography* (Chicago: Regnery Gateway, 1984), 117, 120–121.

59. Sidney Blumenthal, *The Rise of the Counter-establishment: From Conservative Ideology to Political Power* (New York: Harper & Row, 1986), 128.

60. Perlstein, *Reaganland*, 65.

61. Perlstein, *Reaganland*, 643.

62. Jeane J. Kirkpatrick, *Dictatorships and Double Standards: Rationalism and Reason in Politics* (New York: Simon & Schuster, 1982), 23, 52.

63. Norman Podhoretz, *Why Are Jews Liberals?* (New York: Doubleday, 2009), 183.

64. Ben J. Wattenberg, *Fighting Words: A Tale of How Liberals Created Neo-conservatism* (New York: St. Martin's Press, 2008), 166; Peter Collier, *Political Woman: The Big Little Life of Jeane Kirkpatrick* (New York: Encounter Books, 2012), 108–110.

65. Perlstein, *Reaganland*, 145, 721, 838.

66. Rick Perlstein, *The Invisible Bridge: The Fall of Nixon and the Rise of Reagan* (New York: Simon & Schuster, 2014), 556; Perlstein, *Reaganland*, 223.

67. Perlstein, *Reaganland*, 730–731.

68. Ronald Reagan, *An American Life: The Autobiography* (New York: Simon & Schuster, 2011), 154.

CHAPTER TEN: PRESIDENT REAGAN

1. Ronald Reagan, *The Last Best Hope: The Greatest Speeches of Ronald Reagan* (West Palm Beach, FL: Humanix Books, 2016), 249.

2. Rowland Evans and Robert D. Novak, *The Reagan Revolution* (New York: Dutton, 1981), 9; Daniel Patrick Moynihan, *Miles to Go: A Personal History of Social Policy* (Cambridge, MA: Harvard University Press, 1996), 10.

3. Angela D. Dillard, *Guess Who's Coming to Dinner Now? Multicultural Conservatism in America* (New York: New York University Press, 2001); Lee Edwards, "The Founding Father of the Black Conservative Movement," Intercollegiate Studies Institute, December 3, 2019, https://isi.org /intercollegiate-review/founding-father-black-conservative-movement; "Thomas Sowell," Contemporary Thinkers, https://contemporarythinkers .org/thomas-sowell/biography.

4. Joseph Sobran, "Capitalism and Ecstasy," *National Review*, July 10, 1981, 791–793; Irving Kristol, *Neoconservatism: The Autobiography of an Idea* (New York: Free Press, 1995), 36.

5. David A. Stockman, "The Social Pork Barrel," *Public Interest* 39 (spring 1975): 3–30.

6. William Greider, "The Education of David Stockman," *The Atlantic*, December 1981, https://www.theatlantic.com/magazine/archive /1981/12/the-education-of-david-stockman/305760.

7. Ronald Reagan, "Remarks at the Presentation Ceremony for the Presidential Medal of Freedom," Ronald Reagan Presidential Library and Museum, February 23, 1983, https://www.reaganlibrary.gov/research /speeches/22383c.

8. Charles Krauthammer, *Cutting Edges: Making Sense of the Eighties* (New York: Random House, 1985), 182.

9. Jeane J. Kirkpatrick, *Legitimacy and Force*, vol. 1: *Political and Moral Dimensions* (New Brunswick, NJ: Transaction Books, 1987), 445.

10. George F. Will, *The Morning After: American Successes and Excesses, 1981–1986* (New York: Collier Books, 1986), 316; Norman Podhoretz, "The Neo-conservative Anguish over President Reagan's Foreign Policy," *New York Times*, May 2, 1982, Section 6, 30, https://www.nytimes .com/1982/05/02/magazine/the-neo-conservative-anguish-over-reagan -s-foreign-policy.html.

11. Richard John Neuhaus, *The Naked Public Square: Religion and Democracy in America* (Grand Rapids, MI: W. B. Eerdmans Publishing Company, 1984), vii.

12. Ronald Reagan, *Abortion and the Conscience of the Nation* (Nashville, TN: Thomas Nelson, 1984), 38; "Reagan Affirms Anti-abortion Stand," *New York Times*, February 8, 1976, 44.

13. Ronald Reagan, "Remarks at a Reception Honoring the National Review," American Presidency Project, February 21, 1983, http://www .presidency.ucsb.edu/ws/index.php?pid=40951.

14. Irving Kristol, "Why I Left," *New Republic*, April 11, 1988.

15. Lee Edwards, *The Power of Ideas: The Heritage Foundation at 25 Years* (Ottawa, IL: Jameson Books, 1997), 66; "A Nobel Winner Assesses Reagan," *New York Times*, December 1, 1982, 92; Lee Edwards, *Leading the Way: The Story of Ed Feulner and the Heritage Foundation* (New York: Crown Forum, 2013), 160.

16. Sidney Blumenthal, *The Rise of the Counter-establishment: From Conservative Ideology to Political Power* (New York: Harper & Row, 1986), 49.

17. Charles Murray, *Losing Ground* (New York: Basic Books, 1984), 227–228.

18. Steven M. Teles and Jessica A. Gover, "The American Enterprise Institute's Near-Death Experience: An SNF Agora Case Study," SNF Agora Institute at Johns Hopkins, December 2020, https://snfagora.jhu.edu/wp-content/uploads/2021/01/SNF-Agora-Case-Study_AEI-1.pdf.

19. Elisabeth Bumiller, "The Nation's Capital Gets a New Daily Newspaper," *Washington Post*, May 17, 1982, C1; Lee Edwards, *Our Times: The Washington Times, 1982–2002* (Washington, DC: Regnery, 2002), 174; Lois Romano, "Review Is Killed," *Washington Post*, September 18, 2002, https://www.washingtonpost.com/archive/lifestyle/1982/09/18/review-is-killed/1a499be1-0dd1-460b-896e-14f0a232b84d.

20. Sun Myung Moon, "Our Mission During the Time of World Transition," Unification Home Page, December 23, 1991, https://www.unification.net/1991/911223.html; Arnold H. Lubasch, "Rev. Moon Is Convicted of Income-Tax Fraud," *New York Times*, May 19, 1982, 1, 24; "U.S. Releases Moon, Ending Prison Term on Tax Fraud Count," *New York Times*, August 21, 1985, 31; Sheryl Gay Stolberg, "A Crowning at the Capital Creates a Stir," *New York Times*, June 24, 2004, 17; Andrew Ferguson, "Can Buy Me Love: The Mooning of Conservative Washington," *American Spectator*, September 1987, 20–23.

21. Fred Barnes, "A World Apart," *American Spectator*, December 1987, 64–65.

22. Carla Hall, "It's Official: Reagan Chooses Bennett for NEH," *Washington Post*, November 19, 1981, https://www.washingtonpost.com/archive/lifestyle/1981/11/19/its-official-reagan-chooses-bennett-for-neh/de49270d-fd47-446e-ab13-58277c3cb063; R. Emmett Tyrrell, *The Conservative Crack-Up* (New York: Summit Books, 1992), 236.

23. Melvin E. Bradford, "On Being a Conservative in a Post-liberal Era," *Intercollegiate Review* 21 (spring 1986): 15.

24. Gregory Wolfe, "The State of Conservatism: A Symposium, Introduction," *Intercollegiate Review* 21 (spring 1986): 4.

25. Jeffrey Hart, "Gang Warfare in Chicago," *National Review*, June 6, 1986, 32–33.

26. "The Vidal Exemption," *National Review*, June 6, 1986, 20.

27. Robert H. Bork, "Neutral Principles and Some First Amendment Problems," *Indiana Law Journal* 47, no. 1 (fall 1971): 8.

28. Robert H. Bork, *The Tempting of America: The Political Seduction of the Law* (New York: Touchstone, 1991), 268.

29. Dan Himmelfarb, "Conservative Splits," *Commentary*, May 1988, 58.

30. Russell Kirk, *The Politics of Prudence* (Bryn Mawr, PA: Intercollegiate Studies Institute, 1993), 175–176.

31. Kirk, *The Politics of Prudence*, 179–180.

32. George F. Will, "How Reagan Changed America," *Newsweek*, January 9, 1989, 16; Fred Barnes, "Bush's Big Government Conservatives," *American Spectator*, April 1990, 14–15.

33. Irving Kristol, *Two Cheers for Capitalism* (New York: Basic Books, 1978), 119; Irwin M. Stelzer, *The Neocon Reader* (New York: Grove Press, 2004), 147–148.

34. George F. Will, *Statecraft as Soulcraft: What Government Does* (New York: Simon & Schuster, 1983), 128–130.

35. Richard Brookhiser, *Right Time, Right Place: Coming of Age with William F. Buckley Jr. and the Conservative Movement* (New York: Basic Books, 2009), 147.

36. Allan Bloom, *Closing of the American Mind: How Higher Education Has Failed Democracy and Impoverished the Souls of Today's Students* (New York: Simon & Schuster, 2012), 335.

37. Dinesh D'Souza, *Letters to a Young Conservative* (New York: Basic Books, 2002), 16.

38. D'Souza, *Letters to a Young Conservative*, 27.

39. Edwards, *Power of Ideas*, 87–88.

CHAPTER ELEVEN: NEW WORLD ORDER

1. Rick Perlstein, *Nixonland: The Rise of a President and the Fracturing of America* (New York: Scribner, 2008), 533.

2. Patrick J. Buchanan, *Right from the Beginning* (Washington, DC: Regnery Gateway, 1990), 5; Morton Kondracke and Fred Barnes, *Jack*

Kemp: The Bleeding-Heart Conservative Who Changed America (New York: Penguin, 2015), 198.

3. Jon Meacham, *Destiny and Power: The American Odyssey of George Herbert Walker Bush* (New York: Random House, 2015), 362; George F. Will, "He Moved His Lips and Said Nothing," *Washington Post,* June 29, 1990; "Mr. Bush's Leadership," *Wall Street Journal,* July 2, 1990; "Read My Lips?," *National Review,* November 5, 1990, 18.

4. Francis Fukuyama, *The End of History and the Last Man* (New York: Free Press, 1992), 328.

5. Samuel P. Huntington, "No Exit: The Errors of Endism," *National Interest* 17 (fall 1989): 3–11; for more, see Samuel P. Huntington, *The Clash of Civilizations and the Remaking of World Order* (New York: Simon & Schuster, 1996).

6. Owen Harries, ed., *America's Purpose: New Visions of U.S. Foreign Policy* (New York: Macmillan, 1993), 11, 13.

7. Paul M. Weyrich and Connaught Coyne Marshner, eds., *Future 21: Directions for America in the 21st Century* (Greenwich, CT: Devin-Adair, 1984), 38; Harries, *America's Purpose,* 31.

8. Charles Krauthammer, *Things That Matter: Three Decades of Passions, Pastimes and Politics* (New York: Crown Publishing, 2013), 323.

9. "Goals in the Gulf," *Wall Street Journal,* August 29, 1990.

10. George H. W. Bush, "State of the Union Address," Miller Center, January 29, 1991, https://millercenter.org/the-presidency/presidential-speeches/january-29-1991-state-union-address.

11. David Frum, "The Conservative Bully Boy," *American Spectator* 24, no. 7 (July 1991): 12–14; Timothy Stanley, *The Crusader: The Life and Tumultuous Times of Pat Buchanan* (New York: Macmillan, 2012), 142.

12. Meacham, *Destiny and Power,* 480.

13. Robin Toner, "Buchanan, Urging New Nationalism, Joins '92 Race," *New York Times,* December 11, 1991, 1, 40.

14. Murray N. Rothbard, "A Strategy for the Right," *Rothbard-Rockwell Report,* March 1992, http://rothbard.altervista.org/articles/a-strategy-for-the-right.pdf.

15. Patrick J. Buchanan, "1992 Republican National Convention Speech," Patrick J. Buchanan—Official Website, August 17, 1992, https://buchanan.org/blog/1992-republican-national-convention-speech-148.

16. Meacham, *Destiny and Power,* 511; Stanley, *Crusader,* 210; Robert Alan Goldberg, *Barry Goldwater* (New Haven, CT: Yale University Press, 1997), 332.

17. James Bowman, "The Leader of the Opposition," *National Review*, September 6, 1993, 44–52.

18. David Brooks, ed., *Backward and Upward: The New Conservative Writing* (New York: Vintage Books, 1996), 295.

19. Richard Brookhiser, *Right Time, Right Place: Coming of Age with William F. Buckley Jr. and the Conservative Movement* (New York: Basic Books, 2009), 179.

20. "No Guardrails," *Wall Street Journal*, March 18, 1993, https://www.wsj.com/articles/SB122521124435776541.

21. William J. Bennett, ed., *The Book of Virtues: A Treasury of Great Moral Stories* (New York: Simon & Schuster, 1993); Mark Gerson, ed., *The Essential Neoconservative Reader* (New York: Basic Books, 1996), 434–443; Irving Kristol, *Neoconservatism: The Autobiography of an Idea* (New York: Free Press, 1995), 486.

22. Charles A. Murray, "The Coming White Underclass," *Wall Street Journal*, October 29, 1993.

23. Richard J. Herrnstein and Charles Murray, *The Bell Curve: Intelligence and Class Structure in American Life* (New York: Simon & Schuster, 1996), 311.

24. Matthew Continetti, "The Sage of Burkittsville," *Weekly Standard*, January 14, 2018, https://www.washingtonexaminer.com/weekly-standard/the-sage-of-burkittsville; Charles Lane, "The Tainted Sources of the Bell Curve," *New York Review of Books*, December 1, 1994.

25. Thomas Sowell, "Ethnicity and IQ," *American Spectator*, February 1995, 30–37.

26. Glenn C. Loury, "Dispirited," *National Review*, December 5, 1994.

27. Dinesh D'Souza, *The End of Racism: Principles for a Multiracial Society* (New York: Free Press, 1995), 100.

28. Interview with Vin Weber, "The Long March of Newt Gingrich," *Frontline*, PBS, https://www.pbs.org/wgbh/pages/frontline/newt/newtintwshtml/weber.html.

29. Irving Kristol, "The People's Revolution," *Washington Post*, February 17, 1995, https://www.washingtonpost.com/archive/opinions/1995/02/17/the-peoples-revolution/8f5de754-2dd9-4f0f-b9dc-b1e9a97744de.

30. William F. Buckley Jr., "Irving's Whodunit," *Weekly Standard*, October 9, 1995, 40–42; Irving Kristol, "American Conservatism, 1945–1995," *Public Interest* 121 (fall 1995): 80–91; Norman Podhoretz, "Neoconservatism: A Eulogy," *Commentary*, March 1996,

https://www.commentarymagazine.com/articles/norman-podhoretz
/neoconservatism-a-eulogy.

31. William Kristol and Robert Kagan, "Toward a Neo-Reaganite Foreign Policy," *Foreign Affairs* 75, no. 4 (July/August 1996): 18–32; Robert Kagan and William Kristol, eds., *Present Dangers: Crisis and Opportunity in American Foreign and Defense Policy* (San Francisco, CA: Encounter Books, 2000), 19.

32. William Kristol, "Time for an Insurrection," *Weekly Standard*, March 10, 1997, 16–18; William Kristol and David Brooks, "What Ails Conservatism," *Wall Street Journal*, September 15, 1997, https://www.wsj.com/articles/SB874276753849168000.

33. Robert Bork, "Good Reasons for Despair on the Right," *Wall Street Journal*, October 9, 1997.

34. David Tell, "Clinton Must Go," *Weekly Standard*, August 31, 1998, 7–8.

35. Christopher Caldwell, "The Southern Captivity of the GOP," *The Atlantic*, June 1998, https://www.theatlantic.com/magazine/archive /1998/06/the-southern-captivity-of-the-gop/377123; Christopher Caldwell, "Newt's Last Stand," *Atlantic Online*, November 11, 1998, https:// www.theatlantic.com/past/docs/unbound/polipro/pp9811.htm.

36. Paul M. Weyrich, "An Open Letter to Conservatives," Free Congress Foundation, Columbia Law School, Arthur W. Diamond Law Library, February 16, 1999, http://library.law.columbia.edu/urlmirror/11 /FreeCongressFoundationOnline.htm.

37. William Kristol, "Pat the Bunny," *Weekly Standard*, September 27, 1999, 9–10.

CHAPTER TWELVE: THE FREEDOM AGENDA

1. George W. Bush, "Acceptance Speech at the Republican National Convention," *New York Times*, August 4, 2000, http://movies2.nytimes .com/library/politics/camp/080400wh-bush-speech.html.

2. David Brooks and William Kristol, "The High Road to the High Office," *Weekly Standard*, September 25, 2000, 11–12; Robert Kagan, "Vive What Difference?," *Washington Post*, September 24, 2000, https:// www.washingtonpost.com/archive/opinions/2000/09/24/vive-what -difference/362a9534-6f76-436a-a7a5-8cdc37455069; William Kristol, "Gore's Last Stand?," *Weekly Standard*, October 23, 2000, 9–10; William

Kristol, interview on *Special Report with Brit Hume*, Fox News Network, November 6, 2000.

3. David Tell, "Gore's Spoiled Ballot," *Weekly Standard*, November 20, 2000, 9–10.

4. William Kristol and Jeffrey Bell, "Against Judicial Supremacy," *Weekly Standard*, December 4, 2000, 10–11.

5. Michael J. Gerson, *Heroic Conservatism: Why Republicans Need to Embrace America's Ideals (and Why They Deserve to Fail if They Don't)* (New York: HarperOne, 2007), 36.

6. Dan Balz, "'Armies of Compassion' in Bush's Plans," *Washington Post*, April 25, 1999, A1, https://www.washingtonpost.com/wp-srv /politics/campaigns/wh2000/stories/bush042599.htm.

7. George W. Bush, "Labor Day Address," C-SPAN, September 1, 2003, https://www.c-span.org/video/?177971-1/labor-day-address.

8. Robert Kagan and William Kristol, "No Defense," *Weekly Standard*, July 23, 2001, 11–13.

9. George W. Bush, *Decision Points* (New York: Crown, 2010), 127.

10. Charles Krauthammer, "This Is Not Crime, This Is War," *Washington Post*, September 12, 2001, www.jewishworldreview.com/cols /krauthammer091201.asp; George F. Will, "The End of Our Holiday from History," *Washington Post*, September 12, 2001, www.jewishworld review.com/cols/will091201.asp.

11. George W. Bush, "Graduation Speech at West Point," The White House: President George W. Bush, June 1, 2002, https://georgewbush -whitehouse.archives.gov/news/releases/2002/06/20020601-3.html; George W. Bush, "Remarks at the United Nations General Assembly," The White House: President George W. Bush, September 12, 2002, https://georgewbush-whitehouse.archives.gov/news/releases/2002/09 /20020912-1.html; Irwin M. Stelzer, *The Neocon Reader* (New York: Grove Press, 2004), 86.

12. James Webb, "Heading for Trouble," *Washington Post*, September 4, 2002, www.washingtonpost.com/archive/opinions/2002/09/04 /heading-for-trouble/a31061c0-dad0-44c7-8625-4da164a889f0.

13. Kevin P. Phillips, "Why I Am No Longer a Conservative," *American Conservative*, October 7, 2002, 14–17, www.unz.com/print /AmConservative-2002oct07-00014; Patrick J. Buchanan, "Whose War?," *American Conservative*, March 24, 2003, 7–14, www.unz.com /print/AmConservative-2003mar24-00007.

14. David Frum, "Unpatriotic Conservatives: A War Against America," *National Review*, April 7, 2003, 32–40.

15. Elliott Abrams et al., Letter to President Bill Clinton, Nation of Islam, January 26, 1998, www.noi.org/wp-content/uploads/2016/01 /iraqclintonletter1998-01-26-Copy.pdf; Charles Krauthammer, *Things That Matter: Three Decades of Passions, Pastimes and Politics* (New York: Crown Publishing, 2013), 333–351.

16. Francis Fukuyama, "The Neoconservative Moment," *National Interest* 76 (summer 2004): 57–68; Francis Fukuyama, "After Neoconservatism," *New York Times*, February 19, 2006, www.nytimes.com/2006 /02/19/magazine/after-neoconservatism.html; Francis Fukuyama, *America at the Crossroads: Democracy, Power, and the Neoconservative Legacy* (New Haven, CT: Yale University Press, 2006).

17. David Brooks, "A More Humble Hawk," *New York Times*, April 17, 2004, www.nytimes.com/2004/04/17/opinion/a-more-humble-hawk .html; George F. Will, "Time for Bush to See the Realities of Iraq," *Washington Post*, May 4, 2004; David D. Kirkpatrick, "National Review Founder Says It's Time to Leave Stage," *New York Times*, June 29, 2004, www.nytimes.com/2004/06/29/us/national-review-founder-says-it-s -time-to-leave-stage.html.

18. Peggy Noonan, "Way Too Much God," *Wall Street Journal*, January 21, 2005, www.wsj.com/articles/SB110627259043832254.

19. "Presidential Approval Ratings—George W. Bush," Gallup, https://news.gallup.com/poll/116500/presidential-approval-ratings -george-bush.aspx (accessed August 18, 2020); Elliott Abrams, *Realism and Democracy: American Foreign Policy After the Arab Spring* (New York: Cambridge University Press, 2017), 80.

20. Samuel P. Huntington, *Who Are We? The Challenges to America's National Identity* (New York: Simon & Schuster, 2004).

21. Roger Scruton, *The West and the Rest* (Wilmington, DE: ISI Books, 2002), 159.

22. Fred Barnes, "Cantankerous Conservatism," *Weekly Standard*, March 20, 2006, 13–14.

23. Mark Silva, "Bush: 'It Was a Thumpin,'" *Chicago Tribune*, November 8, 2006, www.chicagotribune.com/chinews-mtblog-2006-11-bush _it_was_a_thumpin-story.html.

24. David Petraeus, "The Central Front," *Weekly Standard*, May 7, 2007, 7.

25. David Corn, "Neocon Godmother Considered Iraq War a Mistake," *The Nation*, April 10, 2007, www.thenation.com/article/archive /neocon-godmother-considered-iraq-war-mistake.

26. Jacques Steinberg, "Warring on McCain, Limbaugh Sees No Reconciliation," *New York Times*, February 15, 2008; Mike Allen and Jonathan Martin, "Rush, Right Rally to McCain," *Politico*, February 21, 2008, www.politico.com/story/2008/02/rush-right-rally-to-mccain-008617.

27. Christopher Caldwell, "The Anti-war, Anti-abortion, Anti-Drug-Enforcement-Administration, Anti-Medicare Candidacy of Dr. Ron Paul," *New York Times Magazine*, July 22, 2007, www.nytimes.com/2007 /07/22/magazine/22Paul-t.html.

28. James Kirchick, "Angry White Man," *New Republic*, January 8, 2008, https://newrepublic.com/article/61771/angry-white-man; Anthony Wile, "Pat Buchanan on Ron Paul, the Internet, and Ethnic Politics in the 21st Century," Patrick J. Buchanan—Official Website, March 5, 2012, https://buchanan.org/blog/pat-buchanan-on-ron-paul -the-internet-and-ethnic-politics-in-the-21st-century-2-5025.

CHAPTER THIRTEEN: THE CRISIS OF THE TWENTY-FIRST CENTURY

1. "Rush Upstages Obama's Dinner with Washingtonian Republicans," *The Rush Limbaugh Show*, January 14, 2009, www.rushlimbaugh .com/daily/2009/01/14/rush_upstages_obama_s_dinner_with _washingtonian_republicans.

2. Charles Krauthammer, *Things That Matter: Three Decades of Passions, Pastimes and Politics* (New York: Crown Publishing, 2013), 353.

3. Robert Kagan, *The World America Made* (New York: Alfred A. Knopf, 2012), 97.

4. George F. Will, "Tea Party Would Defeat Obama by Supporting McConnell Plan on Debt," *Jewish World Review*, July 21, 2011, www .jewishworldreview.com/cols/will072211.php3#.XpSItlNKg0o; Charles Krauthammer, "Constitutionalism," *Jewish World Review*, January 7, 2011, http://jewishworldreview.com/cols/krauthammer010611.php3#.Xz7UB NNKhE9; David Brooks, "The Tea Party Teens," *New York Times*, January 5, 2010, www.nytimes.com/2010/01/05/opinion/05brooks.html.

5. Angelo Codevilla, *The Ruling Class: How They Corrupted America and What We Can Do About It* (New York: Beaufort Books, 2010), 75.

6. Charles Krauthammer, "The Way Forward: Republicans Do Not Need to Radically Change," *Jewish World Review*, November 9, 2012, www.jewishworldreview.com/cols/krauthammer110912.php3#.XpYXylNKg0o; Michael Gerson and Peter Wehner, "How to Save the Republican Party," *Commentary*, March 2013, www.commentary.org/articles/michael-gerson-2/how-to-save-the-republican-party; George F. Will, "A Better GOP: The Party Has a Lot of Thinking to Do," *Jewish World Review*, November 10, 2012, www.jewishworldreview.com/cols/will111012.php3#.XpYYbVNKg0o.

7. Sean Trende, "The Case of the Missing White Voters," *RealClearPolitics*, November 8, 2012, www.realclearpolitics.com/articles/2012/11/08/the_case_of_the_missing_white_voters_116106.html.

8. Dinesh D'Souza, *The Roots of Obama's Rage* (Washington, DC: Regnery Publishing, 2010).

9. Joshua Green, *Devil's Bargain: Steve Bannon, Donald Trump, and the Storming of the Presidency* (New York: Penguin, 2017); William Strauss and Neil Howe, *The Fourth Turning: An American Prophecy: What the Cycles of History Tell Us About America's Next Rendezvous with Destiny* (New York: Broadway Books, 1997).

10. Sarah Posner, "How Donald Trump's New Campaign Chief Created an Online Haven for White Nationalists," *Mother Jones*, August 22, 2016, www.motherjones.com/politics/2016/08/stephen-bannon-donald-trump-alt-right-breitbart-news.

11. Randy Barnett, *Our Republican Constitution: Securing the Liberty and Sovereignty of We the People* (New York: Broadside Books, 2016), 17.

12. Julie Moreau, "States Across U.S. Still Cling to Outdated Gay Marriage Bans," NBC News, February 18, 2020, www.nbcnews.com/feature/nbc-out/states-across-u-s-still-cling-outdated-gay-marriage-bans-n1137936.

13. Andrew Sullivan, "Here Comes the Groom," *New Republic*, August 28, 1989, https://newrepublic.com/article/79054/here-comes-the-groom; Jonathan Rauch, *Gay Marriage: Why It Is Good for Gays, Good for Straights, and Good for America* (New York: Times Books, 2004); David Brooks, "The Power of Marriage," *New York Times*, November 22, 2003, www.nytimes.com/2003/11/22/opinion/the-power-of-marriage.html; John B. Judis, *William F. Buckley, Jr., Patron Saint of the Conservatives* (New York: Simon & Schuster, 1988), 422.

14. William F. Buckley Jr., "Crucial Steps in Combating the AIDS Epidemic; Identify All the Carriers," *New York Times*, March 18, 1986,

https://archive.nytimes.com/www.nytimes.com/books/00/07/16/special s/buckley-aids.html.

15. Andrew Sullivan, *The Conservative Soul: How We Lost It, How to Get It Back* (New York: Harper Collins, 2006), 269.

16. Caitlin Emma, "Obama Administration Releases Directive on Transgender Rights to School Bathrooms," *Politico*, May 12, 2016, www .politico.com/story/2016/05/obama-administration-title-ix-transgender -student-rights-223149.

17. Laura Ingraham, *Billionaire at the Barricades: The Populist Revolution from Reagan to Trump* (New York: All Points Books, 2017), 164.

18. Charles Murray, *Coming Apart: The State of White America, 1960–2010* (New York: Crown Forum, 2012).

19. Nicholas Eberstadt, *Men Without Work: America's Invisible Crisis* (Philadelphia: Templeton Press, 2016); Christopher Caldwell, "American Carnage," *First Things*, April 2017, www.firstthings.com/article/2017 /04/american-carnage; Anne Case and Angus Deaton, "Rising Morbidity and Mortality in Midlife Among White Non-Hispanic Americans in the 21st Century," *Proceedings of the National Academy of Sciences* 112, no. 49 (December 8, 2015): 15078–15083, https://doi.org/10.1073/pnas .1518393112.

20. Jonathan Martin, "Conservatives Draft Manifesto to Help Republicans Attract Middle-Class Voters," *New York Times*, May 21, 2014, www .nytimes.com/2014/05/22/us/politics/conservatives-draft-manifesto-to -help-republicans-attract-middle-class-voters.html; "Opioid Abuse News," *Washington Examiner*, www.washingtonexaminer.com/tag/opioid-abuse.

21. Michael Gerson, "The Self-Refuting Idea That America Needs Donald Trump as a Savior," *Washington Post*, September 12, 2016, www .washingtonpost.com/opinions/the-self-refuting-idea-that-america -needs-donald-trump-as-a-savior/2016/09/12/d89a26ae-790b-11e6 -beac-57a4a412e93a_story.html; George F. Will, "If Trump Is Nominated, the GOP Must Keep Him Out of the White House," *Washington Post*, April 29, 2016, www.washingtonpost.com/opinions/if-trump-is -nominated-the-gop-must-keep-him-out-of-the-white-house/2016 /04/29/293f7f94-0d9d-11e6-8ab8-9ad050f76d7d_story.html; Ian Schwartz, "Krauthammer on Trump: We Have the Best Republican Field in 35 Years and We're Talking About This 'Rodeo Clown,'" *RealClearPolitics*, July 6, 2015, www.realclearpolitics.com/video/2015/07/06 /krauthammer_on_trump_we_have_the_best_republican_field_in_35 _years_and_were_talking_about_this_rodeo_clown.html.

22. Rush Limbaugh, "Trump's Message Will Resonate," *The Rush Limbaugh Show*, June 16, 2015, www.rushlimbaugh.com/daily/2015/06 /16/trump_s_message_will_resonate.

23. Rush Limbaugh, "Understanding Trump's Appeal," *Rush Limbaugh Show*, January 20, 2016, www.rushlimbaugh.com/daily/2016/01/20 /understanding_trump_s_appeal-2.

24. "Against Trump," *National Review*, February 15, 2016, 14–16; "Conservatives Against Trump," *National Review Online*, January 22, 2016, www.nationalreview.com/2016/01/donald-trump-conservatives -oppose-nomination.

25. Mark Swanson, "Richard Viguerie: Trump Campaign as Exciting Now as Reagan's in 1980," *Newsmax*, August 18, 2016, www.newsmax .com/Newsmax-Tv/Richard-Viguerie-Trump-Campaign-Shakeup -Exciting/2016/08/18/id/744135; Michael Halney, "Clint and Scott Eastwood: No Holds Barred in Their First Interview Together," *Esquire*, August 3, 2016, www.esquire.com/entertainment/a46893/double -trouble-clint-and-scott-eastwood.

26. John Marini, "Trump and the American Crisis," *Claremont Review of Books Online*, July 22, 2016, https://claremontreviewofbooks .com/digital/donald-trump-and-the-american-crisis; Angelo M. Codevilla, "After the Republic," *Claremont Review of Books Online*, September 27, 2016, https://claremontreviewofbooks.com/digital/after-the -republic; Publius Decius Mus, "The Flight 93 Election," *Claremont Review of Books Online*, September 5, 2016, https://claremontreviewof books.com/digital/the-flight-93-election.

27. Jesse Byrnes, "Bill Kristol on 'Renegade Jew' Label: 'That's Something New,'" *The Hill*, May 17, 2016, https://thehill.com/blogs/blog -briefing-room/news/280130-bill-kristol-on-renegade-jew-label-thats -something-new.

28. Lydia Saad, "Trump and Clinton Finish with Historically Poor Images," Gallup, November 8, 2016, https://news.gallup.com/poll /197231/trump-clinton-finish-historically-poor-images.aspx.

CHAPTER FOURTEEN: THE VIRAL PRESIDENT

1. Yashar Ali, "What George W. Bush Really Thought of Donald Trump's Inauguration," *New York*, March 29, 2017, https://nymag.com /intelligencer/2017/03/what-george-w-bush-really-thought-of-trumps -inauguration.html.

2. Charlie Warzel, "I Talked to the Cassandra of the Internet Age," *New York Times*, February 4, 2021, www.nytimes.com/2021/02/04 /opinion/michael-goldhaber-internet.html; Martin Gurri, *The Revolt of the Public and the Crisis of Authority in the New Millennium* (San Francisco, CA: Stripe Press, 2018).

3. Tim Alberta, "'The Ideas Made It, but I Didn't,'" *Politico*, May/ June 2017, www.politico.com/magazine/story/2017/04/22/pat-buchanan -trump-president-history-profile-215042.

4. Gladden Pappin and Maria Molla, "Affirming the American Family," *American Affairs* 3, no. 3 (fall 2019), https://americanaffairs journal.org/2019/08/affirming-the-american-family; Gladden Pappin and Maria Molla, "The Macroeconomic Impact of FamilyPay," *Harvard Law Review Blog*, January 13, 2020, https://blog.harvardlawreview.org /the-macroeconomic-impact-of-familypay.

5. Peter Thiel, "The Education of a Libertarian," *Cato Unbound*, April 13, 2009, www.cato-unbound.org/2009/04/13/peter-thiel/education -libertarian.

6. Julius Krein, "Traitor to His Class," *Weekly Standard*, September 7, 2015, www.washingtonexaminer.com/weekly-standard/traitor-to-his -class; Julius Krein, "I Voted for Trump. And I Sorely Regret It," *New York Times*, August 17, 2017, www.nytimes.com/2017/08/17/opinion /sunday/i-voted-for-trump-and-i-sorely-regret-it.html.

7. R. R. Reno, "How Both Parties Lost the White Middle Class," *New York Times*, February 1, 2016, www.nytimes.com/2016/02/02 /opinion/campaign-stops/how-both-parties-lost-the-white-middle-class .html.

8. R. R. Reno, "Republicans Are Now the 'America First' Party," *New York Times*, April 28, 2017, www.nytimes.com/2017/04/28/opinion /sunday/republicans-are-now-the-america-first-party.html; R. R. Reno, "The Spirit of Democratic Capitalism," *First Things*, October 2017, www .firstthings.com/article/2017/10/the-spirit-of-democratic-capitalism; R. R. Reno, "Building Bridges, Not Walls" *First Things*, November 2017, www.firstthings.com/article/2017/11/building-bridges-not-walls.

9. Patrick J. Deneen, *Why Liberalism Failed* (New Haven, CT: Yale University Press, 2018).

10. Adrian Vermeule, "Beyond Originalism," *The Atlantic*, March 31, 2020, www.theatlantic.com/ideas/archive/2020/03/common-good -constitutionalism/609037.

11. William Kristol, "A Populist-Nationalist Right? No Thanks!" *Weekly Standard*, October 28, 2016, www.washingtonexaminer.com /weekly-standard/a-populist-nationalist-right-no-thanks; Jonah Goldberg, *Suicide of the West: How the Rebirth of Tribalism, Populism, Nationalism, and Socialism Is Destroying American Democracy* (New York: Crown Forum, 2018); David Frum, *Trumpocracy: The Corruption of the American Republic* (New York: Harper, 2018); Charles Krauthammer, *The Point of It All: A Lifetime of Great Loves and Endeavors* (New York: Crown Forum, 2018), 299–313.

12. Kristen Bialik, "Putin Remains Overwhelmingly Unpopular in the United States," Pew Research Center, March 26, 2018, www.pewresearch .org/fact-tank/2018/03/26/putin-remains-overwhelmingly-unpopular-in -the-united-states; "An Interview with Norman Podhoretz," *Claremont Review of Books*, April 16, 2019, https://claremontreviewof books.com /digital/an-interview-with-norman-podhoretz.

13. Gabrielle Levy, "Conway to CPAC: 'Tomorrow This Will Be 'TPAC,'" *U.S. News & World Report*, February 23, 2017, www.usnews .com/news/politics/articles/2017-02-23/kellyanne-conway-to-cpac -tomorrow-this-will-be-tpac.

14. R. R. Reno, "Liberal Tradition, Yes; Liberal Ideology, No," *First Things*, December 2017, www.firstthings.com/article/2017/12/liberal -tradition-yes-liberal-ideology-no?.

15. Sohrab Ahmari, "Against David French-ism," *First Things*, May 29, 2019, www.firstthings.com/web-exclusives/2019/05/against -david-french-ism.

16. David French, "What Sohrab Ahmari Gets Wrong," *National Review Online*, May 30, 2019, www.nationalreview.com/2019/05/david -french-response-sohrab-ahmari.

17. Sohrab Ahmari, "The New American Right," *First Things*, October 2019, www.firstthings.com/article/2019/10/the-new-american -right.

18. Tucker Carlson, *Ship of Fools: How a Selfish Ruling Class Is Bringing America to the Brink of Revolution* (New York: Free Press, 2018), 18–19.

19. Charles R. Kesler, "The Republican Trump," *Claremont Review of Books*, winter 2016/2017, https://claremontreviewofbooks.com/the -republican-trump.

20. "Full Transcript: Trump's 2020 State of the Union Address," *New York Times*, February 5, 2020, www.nytimes.com/2020/02/05/us/politics /state-of-union-transcript.html.

21. "President Trump Job Approval," *RealClearPolitics*, www.real clearpolitics.com/epolls/other/president_trump_job_approval-617 9.html; Henry Olsen, "Trump Is Down, but Far from Out," *Washington Post*, November 6, 2019, www.washingtonpost.com/opinions/2019/11 /06/trump-is-down-far-out.

22. Echelon Insights (@EchelonInsights), "In a 2024 primary, Trump leads the pack of potential nominees at 52%. Other challengers are not far behind though: 45% say they'd consider Mike Pence, and 32% Ted Cruz. Trump Jr., Nikki Haley, and Marco Rubio round out the top tier," Twitter, November 23, 2020, 6:06 p.m., https://twitter.com/i/web /status/1331011254887063553.

23. Dan Barry and Sheera Frankel, "'Be There. Will Be Wild!': Trump All but Circled the Date," *New York Times*, January 6, 2021, www.ny times.com/2021/01/06/us/politics/capitol-mob-trump-supporters.html.

24. Bill Chappell, "Architect of the Capitol Outlines $30 Million in Damages from Pro-Trump Riot," NPR, February 24, 2021, www.npr.org /sections/insurrection-at-the-capitol/2021/02/24/970977612/architect -of-the-capitol-outlines-30-million-in-damages-from-pro-trump-riot; Rachel Axon et al., "Capitol Riot Arrests: See Who's Been Charged Across the U.S.," *USA Today*, March 10, 2021, www.usatoday.com/story telling/capitol-riot-mob-arrests.

25. George Archibald, *Journalism Is War: Stories of Power Politics, Sexual Dalliance, and Corruption in the Nation's Capital* (Crane, MO: Anomalos Publishing House, 2009), 273–286; Howard Kurtz, "Washington Times Clips Its Right Wing," *Washington Post*, October 19, 1995, www .washingtonpost.com/archive/lifestyle/1995/10/19/washington-times -clips-its-right-wing/dd009c93-883b-446c-bbbf-94c0a0570a1a; Alana Goodman, "Rebel Yell," *Washington Free Beacon*, July 9, 2013, https:// freebeacon.com/national-security/rebel-yell.

26. Rosie Gray, "A Daily Caller Editor Wrote for an Alt-Right Website Using a Pseudonym," *The Atlantic*, September 5, 2018, www.the atlantic.com/politics/archive/2018/09/a-daily-caller-editor-wrote-for -an-alt-right-website-using-a-pseudonym/569335; Hannah Gais, "Leaked Emails Show How White Nationalists Have Infiltrated Conservative Media," *Splinter News*, August 29, 2019, https://splinternews.com/leaked -emails-show-how-white-nationalists-have-infiltra-1837681245; Oliver Darcy, "Tucker Carlson's Top Writer Resigns After Secretly Posting Racist and Sexist Remarks in Online Forum," CNN, July 11, 2020, www.cnn .com/2020/07/10/media/tucker-carlson-writer-blake-neff/index.html.

27. "Donald Trump's Final Days," *Wall Street Journal*, January 7, 2017, www.wsj.com/articles/donald-trumps-final-days-11610062773; "An Impeachable Offense," *National Review Online*, January 13, 2021, www.nationalreview.com/2021/01/an-impeachable-offense; Tim Hains, "George Will: 'I'd Like to See January 6 Burned into the American Mind as Firmly as 9/11," *RealClearPolitics*, May 23, 2021, www.realclearpolitics.com/video/2021/05/23/george_will_id_like_to_see_january_6_burned_into_the_american_mind_as_firmly_as_911.html.

28. "Conservatives Call on State Legislators to Appoint New Electors, in Accordance with the Constitution," Conservative Action Project, http://conservativeactionproject.com/conservatives-call-on-state-legislators-to-appoint-new-electors-in-accordance-with-the-constitution.

CONCLUSION: AN AMERICAN CONSERVATISM

1. Glenn Thrush and Alan Feuer, "L. Brent Bozell IV, Son of a Prominent Conservative, Is Charged in Capitol Riot," *New York Times*, February 16, 2021, www.nytimes.com/2021/02/16/us/politics/brent-bozell-son-capitol-riot.html.

2. Timothy Noah, "The Rise and Fall of the L. Brent Bozells," *New Republic*, February 19, 2021, https://newrepublic.com/article/161431/brent-bozell-trump-capitol-riot.

3. Irving Kristol, "The Coming 'Conservative Century,'" *Wall Street Journal*, February 1, 1993.

4. Irving Kristol, *Neoconservatism: The Autobiography of an Idea* (New York: Free Press, 1995), 363.

5. Joseph Bottum, "The New Fusionism," *First Things*, June 2005, www.firstthings.com/article/2005/06/004-the-new-fusionism; Dan Balz and Mike Allen, "Four More Years Attributed to Rove's Strategy," *Washington Post*, November 7, 2004, www.washingtonpost.com/archive/politics/2004/11/07/four-more-years-attributed-to-roves-strategy/031304d7-ac7b-433b-94e2-f86590f8de3b.

6. "An Interview with Harvey Mansfield," *The Point*, January 15, 2012, https://thepointmag.com/politics/an-interview-with-harvey-mansfield.

7. Jonah Goldberg, "Back to Mencken's America," *Los Angeles Times*, June 28, 2016, www.latimes.com/opinion/op-ed/la-oe-goldberg-mencken-nock-20160628-snap-story.html.

8. George F. Will, *The Conservative Sensibility* (New York: Hachette Books, 2019), xvii; William F. Buckley Jr., "In the Beginning . . . ," *National Review*, December 1, 1970, 1265.

9. Friedrich A. von Hayek, *The Constitution of Liberty* (Abingdon, UK: Routledge, 2006), 159.

10. Charles W. Dunn, ed., *The Future of Conservatism: Conflict and Consensus in the Post-Reagan Era* (Wilmington, DE: ISI Books, 2007), 55.

AFTERWORD: THE TRUMP ERA

1. "W. E. Gladstone, 1809–1898," *Oxford Essential Quotations* (5th ed.), https://www.oxfordreference.com/view/10.1093/acref /9780191843730.001.0001/q-oro-ed5-00004876S. Portions of this afterword have been drawn from the author's articles in the following publications: "Biden's Day One Actions Haunt Him Still," *Washington Free Beacon*, October 7, 2022; "Who's Transformative Now?," *Commentary*, June 2021; "The Working-Class GOP: A Muddled Concept," *Washington Free Beacon*, April 2, 2021; "The Reddening," *Commentary*, December 2021; "Is There a Right Left?," *Commentary*, May 2022; "The GOP Summer Swoon," *Washington Free Beacon*, August 5, 2022; "The New Politics of Bifurcation," *Washington Free Beacon*, August 26, 2022; "The GOP Cavalry Arrives," *Washington Free Beacon*, September 30, 2022; "Crime Starters USA," *Washington Free Beacon*, November 4, 2022; "Understanding the Underwhelming GOP Performance," *Washington Free Beacon*, November 9, 2022; "Trump Is the Chief Obstacle to a Republican Revival," *New York Times*, November 11, 2022.

2. Eric Bradner and Sarah Mucha, "Biden Says He Is a 'Bridge' to New 'Generation of Leaders' While Campaigning with Harris, Booker, Witmer," CNN, March 9, 2020, https://www.cnn.com/2020/03/09 /politics/joe-biden-bridge-new-generation-of-leaders/index.html; Ryan Lizza, "Biden Signals to Aides That He Would Serve Only a Single Term," *Politico*, December 11, 2019, https://www.politico.com/news /2019/12/11/biden-single-term-082129.

3. Sarah D. Wire, "Slim Majorities in the New Congress Will Make Big Legislation Difficult," *Los Angeles Times*, January 3, 2021, https://www .latimes.com/politics/story/2021-01-03/house-democrats-small-majority -nancy-pelosi-challenges.

4. "Joe Biden's Unity Address," *Wall Street Journal*, January 20, 2021, https://www.wsj.com/articles/joe-bidens-unity-address-11611184535.

5. "Biden's Fossil-Fuel Freeze," *Wall Street Journal*, January 22, 2021, https://www.wsj.com/articles/bidens-fossil-fuel-freeze-11611359257.

6. Morgan Chalfant, "Biden Economic Adviser Calls Summers 'Flat-Out Wrong' with Inflation Remarks," *The Hill*, February 5, 2021, https://thehill.com/policy/finance/537563-biden-economic-adviser-calls-summers-flat-out-wrong-with-inflation-remarks.

7. Franklin Foer, "Joe Biden Has Changed," *The Atlantic*, October 16, 2020, https://www.theatlantic.com/ideas/archive/2020/10/biden-wants-transform-america-really/616748.

8. David Brooks, "Joe Biden Is a Transformative President," *New York Times*, March 11, 2021, https://www.nytimes.com/2021/03/11/opinion/biden-covid-relief-bill.html; Mike Allen, "Scoop: Inside Biden's Private Chat with Historians," *Axios*, March 25, 2021, https://www.axios.com/2021/03/25/biden-historians-meeting-filibuster; Jeffrey D. Sachs, "Biden Could Be the Most Transformative President in 75 Years," CNN, March 4, 2021, https://www.cnn.com/2021/03/04/opinions/joe-bidens-big-chance-sachs/index.html.

9. Doina Chiacu, "U.S. Facing Biggest Migrant Surge in 20 Years: Homeland Security," Reuters, March 16, 2021, https://www.reuters.com/article/us-usa-immigration-border/u-s-facing-biggest-migrant-surge-in-20-years-homeland-security-idUSKBN2B81M5; Julia Ainsley, "Migrant Border Crossings in Fiscal Year 2022 Topped 2.76 Million, Breaking Previous Record," NBC News, October 22, 2022, https://www.nbcnews.com/politics/immigration/migrant-border-crossings-fiscal-year-2022-topped-276-million-breaking-rcna53517; "Drug Overdose Deaths in the U.S. Top 100,000 Annually," CDC, National Center for Health Statistics, November 17, 2021, https://www.cdc.gov/nchs/pressroom/nchs_press_releases/2021/20211117.htm.

10. "Remarks by President Biden Celebrating Independence Day and Independence from COVID-19," White House, July 4, 2021, https://www.whitehouse.gov/briefing-room/speeches-remarks/2021/07/05/remarks-by-president-biden-celebrating-independence-day-and-independence-from-covid-19.

11. "Coronavirus in the U.S.: Latest Map and Case Count," *New York Times*, November 15, 2022, https://www.nytimes.com/interactive/2021/us/covid-cases.html.

12. "How Popular Is Joe Biden?," *FiveThirtyEight*, November 15, 2022, https://projects.fivethirtyeight.com/biden-approval-rating/?cid =rrpromo.

13. "U.S. Military Withdrawal and Taliban Takeover in Afghanistan: Frequently Asked Questions," Congressional Research Service, updated September 17, 2021, https://crsreports.congress.gov/product/pdf/R /R46879.

14. Yael Halon, "Mollie Hemingway on Trump Impeachment: Congress Isn't Thinking 'Calmly or Rationally Right Now,'" Fox News, January 13, 2021, https://www.foxnews.com/media/hemingway -impeachment-trump-capitol-riot-video-message.

15. *Politico* staff, "Read Liz Cheney's Full Statement in Support of Trump's Impeachment," *Politico*, January 12, 2021, https://www.politico .com/news/2021/01/12/liz-cheney-trump-impeachment-statement -458394.

16. "Rep. Liz Cheney," CPAC Center for Legislative Accountability, http://ratings.conservative.org/people/C001109, accessed November 16, 2022; Alex Rogers, Lucy Kafanov, and Jason Kravarik, "Matt Gaetz Rails Against Liz Cheney in Wyoming," CNN, January 29, 2021, https://www.cnn.com/2021/01/28/politics/gaetz-cheney-rally-cheyenne -republican-reaction/index.html.

17. Manu Raju, Jeff Zeleny, Clare Foran, and Ryan Nobles, "House Republicans Vote to Keep Liz Cheney in Leadership After She Defends Her Impeachment Vote," CNN, February 3, 2021, https://www.cnn .com/2021/02/03/politics/liz-cheney-house-republican-meeting/index .html; Rebecca Shabad, "McCarthy, Cheney Clash over Whether Trump Should Speak at CPAC," NBC News, February 24, 2021, https://www .nbcnews.com/politics/congress/mccarthy-cheney-clash-over-whether -trump-should-speak-cpac-n1258743.

18. Eliana Johnson, "The Real Reason Republicans Want to Oust Liz Cheney," *Politico*, May 5, 2021, https://www.politico.com/news/maga-zine/2021/05/05/the-real-reason-republicans-want-to-oust-liz-cheney -485470; Alex Rogers, "Liz Cheney Loses House Republican Leader-ship Post over Feud with Trump," CNN, May 12, 2021, https://www .cnn.com/2021/05/12/politics/liz-cheney-gop-conference-vote/index .html; "Rep. Elise Stefanik," CPAC Center for Legislative Accountabil-ity, accessed November 18, 2022, http://ratings.conservative.org/people /S001196; Barbara Spunt, "New York's Elise Stefanik Replaces Cheney

in Republican Leadership Spot," NPR, May 14, 2021, https://www.npr .org/2021/05/14/996540840/new-yorks-elise-stefanik-installed-as-new -gop-conference-chair.

19. Nicholas Fandos, "House Backs Jan. 6 Commission, but Senate Path Dims," *New York Times*, May 19, 2021, https://www.nytimes .com/2021/05/19/us/politics/house-jan-6-commission.html; Marianne Levine and Burgess Everett, "McConnell Turns Senate Republicans Against Jan. 6 Commission," *Politico*, May 19, 2021, https://www .politico.com/news/2021/05/19/mcconnell-opposes-houses-bipartisan -jan-6-commission-bill-489573; Nicholas Fandos, "Senate Republicans Filibuster Jan. 6 Inquiry Bill, Blocking an Investigation," *New York Times*, May 28, 2021, https://www.nytimes.com/2021/05/28/us/politics /capitol-riot-commission-republicans.html.

20. "The Jan. 6 Narrative Commission," *Wall Street Journal*, May 18, 2021, https://www.wsj.com/articles/the-jan-6-narrative-commission -11621377134.

21. Mariam Khan, "House Approves Resolution to Create Select Committee to Probe Jan. 6 Capitol Riot," ABC News, June 30, 2021, https://abcnews.go.com/Politics/house-approves-resolution-create-select -committee-probe-jan/story?id=78562630; Jeremy Herb, Manu Raju, and Annie Grayer, "Pelosi Says Liz Cheney Will Serve on Committee That Will Investigate January 6 Insurrection," CNN, July 1, 2021, https:// www.cnn.com/2021/07/01/politics/nancy-pelosi-announces-members-of -january-6-committee/index.html.

22. Annie Grayer and Jeremy Herb, "McCarthy Pulls His 5 GOP Members from 1/6 Committee After Pelosi Rejects 2 of His Picks," CNN, July 21, 2021, https://www.cnn.com/2021/07/21/politics/nancy -pelosi-rejects-republicans-from-committee/index.html.

23. "Pelosi's Jan. 6 Commission," *Wall Street Journal*, June 29, 2021, https://www.wsj.com/articles/pelosis-jan-6-commission-11625005856.

24. Josh Hawley (@HawleyMO), Twitter, November 3, 2020, 9:53 p.m., https://twitter.com/hawleymo/status/1323835709753593858?lang=en; Alayna Treene, "Rubio Says the GOP Needs to Reset After 2020," *Axios*, November 11, 2020, https://www.axios.com/2020/11/11/rubio-gop-reset -trump.

25. Jonathan Swan, "House GOP Memo: Embrace of Trump Agenda Is Only Option for Comeback," *Axios*, March 31, 2021, https://www .axios.com/2021/03/31/house-gop-memo-trump-embrace-only-option -for-comeback?utm_source=newsletter&utm_medium=email&utm

_campaign=newsletter_axiosam&stream=top; "Donald Trump CPAC 2021 Speech Transcript," Rev.com, February 28, 2021, https://www.rev .com/blog/transcripts/donald-trump-cpac-2021-speech-transcript.

26. Ryan Streeter, "Trumpism Is More About Culture Than Economics," *The Dispatch*, November 23, 2020, https://thedispatch.com/article /trumpism-is-more-about-culture-than.

27. Christopher F. Rufo, "Critical Race Theory: What It Is and How to Fight It," *Imprimis* 50, no. 3 (March 2021), https://imprimis.hillsdale .edu/critical-race-theory-fight.

28. Christopher F. Rufo (@realchrisrufo), Twitter, November 2, 2021, 7:41 p.m., https://twitter.com/realchrisrufo/status/145569670557639065 8?lang=en.

29. James W. Ceaser, "Four Heads and One Heart: The Modern Conservative Movement" (paper presented at APSA 2010 Annual Meeting, July 19, 2010), https://papers.ssrn.com/sol3/papers.cfm ?abstract_id =1643418.

30. Various, "Against the Dead Consensus," *First Things*, March 21, 2019, https://www.firstthings.com/web-exclusives/2019/03/against-the -dead-consensus.

31. Philip Jaffa comment on Larry Arnhart, "Appeasing Putin: The Claremont Institute's 'America First' Foreign Policy and Its Betrayal of Harry Jaffa," *Darwinian Conservative*, March 9, 2022, https://darwin ianconservatism.blogspot.com/2022/03/appeasing-putin-claremont -institutes.html.

32. "2017 Lincoln Fellows," Claremont Institute, accessed November 17, 2022, https://www.claremont.org/page/fellowships/2017- lincoln -fellows/; Christopher F. Rufo, "The Wokest Place on Earth," *City Journal*, May 7, 2021, https://www.city-journal.org/racial-politics-at-disney.

33. "Governor Ron DeSantis Signs Historic Bill to Protect Parental Rights in Education," March 28, 2022, https://flgov.com/2022/03/28 /governor- ron- desantis- signs- historic- bill-to-protect- parental- rights -in -education; "Statement from the Walt Disney Company on Signing of Florida Legislation," March 28, 2022, https://thewaltdisneycompany.com/state ment-from-the-walt-disney-company-on-signing-of-florida-legislation.

34. Madeleine Kearns, "Florida's Much-Smeared Parental Rights Bill Is Popular, Even Among Democrats," *National Review*, April 4, 2022, https://www.nationalreview.com/corner/floridas- much-smeared-parental -rights- bill-is-popular-even-among-democrats; Thomas Barrabi, "DeSantis Says Disney 'Crossed the Line' with Criticism of Fla. 'Don't Say

Gay' Law," *New York Post*, March 29, 2022, https://nypost.com /2022/03/29/desantis-rips-disney-for-criticizing-florida-dont-say-gay -law-calling-for-repeal; Sarah Whitten, "Florida Gov. DeSantis Signs Bill Revoking Disney's Special District Status," CNBC, April 22, 2022, https://www.cnbc.com/2022/04/22/florida-gov-desantis-signs-bill -revoking-disneys-special-district-status.html.

35. Charles C. W. Cooke, "Ron DeSantis's Misguided Attack on Disney's Legal Status," *National Review*, April 20, 2022, https://www .nationalreview.com/2022/04/ron-desantiss-misguided-attack-on -disneys-legal-status; Christopher F. Rufo, "Laying Siege to the Institutions," *Imprimis* 51, no. 4/5 (April/May 2022), https://imprimis.hillsdale .edu/laying-siege-to-the-institutions.

36. "Note from the Founders," *Compact*, accessed November 17, 2022, https://compactmag.com/about.

37. Christopher DeMuth, "The Nation Is the Heart of the Matter," *Law and Liberty*, April 7, 2002, https://lawliberty.org/the-nation-is-the -heart-of-the-matter.

38. Various, "Away from the Abyss," *Compact*, March 31, 2022, https://compactmag.com/article/away-from-the-abyss.

39. "Glory to Ukraine," *National Review*, March 21, 2022, https:// www.nationalreview.com/magazine/2022/03/21/the-week-107; Bernhard Zand, "'There Is No Good Example' for War in Ukraine: Interview with Henry Kissinger," *Spiegel International*, July 15, 2022, https://www .spiegel.de/international/world/interview-with-henry-kissinger-for-war -in-ukraine-there-is-no-good-historical-example-a-64b77d41-5b60 -497e-8d2f-9041a73b1892.

40. Loveday Morris, "Hungary's Orban Says Trump Is the 'Hope for Peace' in Ukraine," *Washington Post*, October 11, 2022, https://www .washingtonpost.com/world/2022/10/11/viktor-orban-ukraine-hungary -trump; Tyler Stone, "Tucker Carlson: 'Standing with Zelensky' Just Means More War," *RealClearPolitics*, September 23, 2022, https://www .realclearpolitics.com/video/2022/09/23/tucker_carlson_standing_with _zelensky_just_means_more_war.html; Christopher Caldwell, "Complications of the Ukraine War," *Imprimis* 51, no. 9 (September 2022), https://imprimis.hillsdale.edu/complications-of-the-ukraine-war; Catie Edmonson, "Why the Once-Hawkish Heritage Foundation Opposed Aid to Ukraine," *New York Times*, May 27, 2022, https://www.nytimes .com/2022/05/27/us/politics/ukraine-aid-heritage-foundation.html.

41. Glenn Ellmers, "'Conservatism' Is No Longer Enough," *American Mind*, March 24, 2021, https://americanmind.org/salvo/why-the -claremont-institute-is-not-conservative-and-you-shouldnt-be-either.

42. Ellmers, "'Conservatism' Is No Longer Enough"; Ahmari quoted in Niall Ferguson, "The China Model: Why Is the West Imitating Beijing?," *The Spectator* (UK), May 8, 2021, https://www.spectator.co.uk /article/the-china-model-why-is-the-west-imitating-beijing; "Panel: Cronyism and the Administrative State" [video], ISI, July 23, 2021, https://www.youtube.com/watch?v=-t0yrx1gN1M; "Can American Institutions Still Be Conserved?," Philadelphia Society, September 23–24, 2022, https://phillysoc.org/tps_meetings/fall-2022; Michael Anton, "What Does Fidelity to Our Founding Principles Require Today?," *American Greatness*, September 26, 2022, https://amgreatness. com/2022/09/26/what-does-fidelity-to-our-founding-principles-require -today.

43. "National Conservatism: A Statement of Principles," National Conservatism, accessed November 17, 2022, https://nationalconserva tism.org/national-conservatism-a-statement-of-principles; Brian Fraga, "'New Right' Academics Argue for Biblical Lawmaking at Steubenville Conference," *National Catholic Reporter*, October 17, 2022, https://www .ncronline.org/news/new-right-academics-argue-biblical-lawmaking -steubenville-conference.

44. Sean Davis, "*The Federalist* Names Mollie Hemingway as Editor in Chief," *The Federalist*, January 24, 2022, https://thefederalist .com/2022/01/24/the-federalist-names-mollie-hemingway-as-editor-in -chief; Mollie Hemingway, "What the Right Needs Now Is the Courage to Fight Even if It Costs Us," *The Federalist*, September 14, 2021, https://thefederalist.com/2021/09/14/what-the-right-needs-now-is-the -courage-to-fight-even-if-it-costs-us; Bruce Abramson, "The Conservative Temperament Is Dooming America," *RealClearPolitics*, September 16, 2021, https://www.realclearpolitics.com/articles/2021/09/16/the _conservative_temperament_is_dooming_america_146415.html; John Daniel Davidson, "We Need to Stop Calling Ourselves Conservatives," *The Federalist*, October 20, 2022, https://thefederalist.com/2022/10/20 /we-need-to-stop-calling-ourselves-conservatives.

45. Kevin Roberts, "The Second American Revolution" [video], NatCon3 Miami, September 12, 2022, https://www.youtube.com /watch?v=kbh-4q2nr4k; Kevin Roberts (@KevinRobertsTX), Twitter,

October 11, 2022, 8:01 a.m., https://twitter.com/KevinRobertsTX /status/1579819601428635649?s=20&t=mo3X0teM4tNmhYk2ZJlVlA.

46. Kristina Peterson, "10 House Republicans Voted to Impeach Trump. Just Two Are Left," *Wall Street Journal*, November 8, 2022, https://www.wsj.com/livecoverage/election- midterms- 2022/card/10 -house-republicans-voted-to-impeach-trump-just-two-are-left-4ddv2Fi ETdDJ2dKYEPzU; Barbara Spunt, "7 GOP Senators Voted to Convict Trump. Only 1 Faces Voters Next Year," NPR, February 15, 2021, https://www.npr.org/sections/trump -impeachment -trial - live-updates /2021/02/15/967878039/7-gop-senators-voted-to-convict-trump-only-1 -faces-voters-next-year.

47. Michael Warren, "Trump Endorses Harriet Hageman in GOP Primary Challenge to Liz Cheney," CNN, September 9, 2021, https:// www.cnn.com/2021/09/09/politics/trump- endorses- harriet- hageman -cheney-challenger/index.html; Ryan Nobles, Manu Raju, and Melanie Zanona, "McCarthy Endorses Cheney Foe in Wyoming GOP primary," CNN, February 18, 2022, https://www.cnn.com/2022/02/17/politics /kevin-mccarthy-harriet-hageman-endorsement/index.html; John Koblin, "At Least 20 Million Watched Jan. 6 Hearing," *New York Times*, June 10, 2022, https://www.nytimes.com/2022/06/10/business/media /jan-6-hearing-ratings.html.

48. "2022 Wyoming Primary Election Results," *PBS Newshour*, August 16, 2022, https://www.pbs.org/newshour/politics/2022-wyoming -primary-election-results.

49. Liz Cheney, "Our Constitutional Moment: The Danger to Rule of Law," 2022 Walter Berns Constitution Day Lecture, American Enterprise Institute, September 19, 2022, https://www.aei.org/wp-content /uploads /2022/11/Our-Constitutional-Moment.pdf?x91208; Leo Wolfson, "Hageman Rips Feds, Congress During Constitution Day Speech," *Cowboy State Daily*, September 20, 2022, https://cowboystate daily.com/2022/09/20/hageman- rips- feds -congress -during -constitution -day-speech.

50. Elena Moore, "Tracking Trump's Endorsements: Here's How His Picks Have Fared in Primaries," NPR, September 8, 2022, https://www .npr.org/sections/2022-live-primary-election-race-results/2022/09/06 /1120652541/donald-trump-republican-primary-endorsement-perfor mance; Karen Yourish, Danielle Ivory, Aaron Byrd, Weiyi Cai, Nick Corasaniti, Meg Felling, Rumsey Taylor, and Jonathan Weisman, "Over 370 Republican Candidates Have Cast Doubt on the 2020 Election," *New York*

Times, October 13, 2022, https://www.nytimes.com/interactive/2022/10/13/us/politics/republican-candidates-2020-election-misinformation.html.

51. Daniel McCarthy, "Republicans Are Doubling Down on Trumpism. It's Going to Work," *New York Times*, November 6, 2022, https://www.nytimes.com/2022/11/06/opinion/politics/republican-midterms.html.

52. "Do Voters Want Republicans or Democrats in Congress?," *FiveThirtyEight*, accessed November 17, 2022, https://projects.fivethirtyeight.com/polls/generic-ballot; Laura Weiss and Lindsey McPherson, "Semiconductor, Science Bill Passes Senate, Heads to House," *Roll Call*, July 27, 2022, https://rollcall.com/2022/07/27/semiconductor-science-bill-passes-senate-heads-to-house; "Joint Statement from Leader Schumer and Senator Manchin Announcing Agreement to Add the Inflation Reduction Act of 2022 to the FY2022 Budget Reconciliation Bill and Vote in Senate Next Week," Senate Democrats press release, July 27, 2022, https://www.democrats.senate.gov/newsroom/press-releases/senate-majority-leader-chuck-schumer-d-ny-and-sen-joe-manchin-d-wv-on-wednesday-announced-that-they-have-struck-a-long-awaited-deal-on-legislation-that-aims-to-reform-the-tax-code-fight-climate-change-and-cut-health-care-costs; Burgess Everett and Olivia Beavers, "Splitsville: McConnell and McCarthy Break on Big Votes," *Politico*, July 28, 2022, https://www.politico.com/news/2022/07/28/mccarthy-mcconnell-bill-votes-00048565.

53. Nate Cohn, "Kansas Result Suggests 4 out of 5 States Would Back Abortion Rights in Similar Vote," *New York Times*, August 4, 2022, https://www.nytimes.com/2022/08/04/upshot/kansas-abortion-vote-analysis.html.

54. Nathaniel Rakich, "Yes, Special Elections Really Are Signaling a Better-Than-Expected Midterm for Democrats," *FiveThirtyEight*, August 24, 2022, https://fivethirtyeight.com/features/yes-special-elections-really-are-signaling-a-better-than-expected-midterm-for-democrats; "New York Primary Election Results," *New York Times*, updated August 24, 2022, https://www.nytimes.com/interactive/2022/08/23/us/elections/results-new-york.html; "The GOP's Abortion Problem," *Wall Street Journal*, August 24, 2022, https://www.wsj.com/articles/the-gops-abortion-problem-congress-midterms-marc-molinaro-new-york-democrats-nancy-pelosi-11661371246?mod=opinion_lead_pos3.

55. "Wisconsin Senate: Johnson vs. Barnes," *RealClearPolitics*, accessed November 17, 2022, https://www.realclearpolitics.com/epolls/2022/senate/wi/wisconsin_senate_johnson_vs_barnes-7758.html;

"Pennsylvania Senate: Oz vs. Fetterman," accessed November 17, 2022, https://www.realclearpolitics.com/epolls/2022/senate/pa/pennsylvania_senate_oz_vs_fetterman-7695.html; Joseph Ax, "Analysis: Crime Is a Top Concern for Many Americans in Midterm Vote. How Bad Is It?," Reuters, November 1, 2022, https://www.reuters.com/world/us/crime-is-top-concern-many-americans-midterm-vote-how-bad-is-it-2022-11-01; "New York Governor—Zeldin vs. Hochul," *RealClearPolitics*, accessed November 17, 2022, https://www.realclearpolitics.com/epolls/2022/governor/ny/new_york_governor_zeldin_vs_hochul-7749.html; "New York Governor Debate Live Updates: Kathy Hochul vs. Lee Zeldin," *New York Post*, October 25, 2022, https://nypost.com/2022/10/25/ny-governor-debate-live-updates-kathy-hochul-vs-lee-zeldin.

56. Brendan Rascius, "'Not a Republican Wave.' GOP Commentators React to Midterms, with Many Blaming Trump," *McClatchy DC*, November 9, 2022, https://mcclatchydc.com/news/politics-government/election/article268513212.html.

57. Philip Wallach, "We Can Now Quantify Trump's Sabotage of the GOP's House Dreams," *Washington Post*, November 15, 2022, https://www.washingtonpost.com/opinions/2022/11/15/data-trump-weighed-down-republican-candidates.

58. Quotes from *The Federalist No. 1*, the preamble to the Constitution of the United States of America, and Abraham Lincoln's speech on the *Dred Scott* decision, June 26, 1857.

INDEX

Matthew Continetti is a senior fellow and the Patrick and Charlene Neal Chair in American Prosperity at the American Enterprise Institute. He is also the founding editor of the *Washington Free Beacon* and a columnist for *Commentary* magazine. The author of *The Persecution of Sarah Palin* and *The K Street Gang*, he lives in Virginia.